Bibliographies for Biblical Research

New Testament Series
in Twenty-One Volumes

General Editor
Watson E. Mills

Bibliographies for Biblical Research

New Testament Series
in Twenty-One Volumes

Volume V

The Acts of the Apostles

Compiled by

Watson E. Mills

MELLEN BIBLICAL PRESS
Lewiston/Queenston/Lampeter

Library of Congress Cataloging-in-Publication Data
(Revised for vol. 4)

Bibliographies for biblical research.

Includes index.
Contents: v. 1. The Gospel of Matthew / compiled by
Watson E. Mills --   -- v. 4. The Gospel of John.
1. Bible. N.T.--Criticism, interpretation, etc.--
Bibliography. I. Mills, Watson E.
Z7772.L1B4 1993 [BS2341.2]   016.2262'06   93-30864
ISBN 0-7734-2347-8 (v. 1) Matthew ISBN 0-7734-2349-4 (v. 2) Mark
ISBN 0-7734-2385-0 (v. 3) Luke   ISBN 0-7734-2357-5 (v. 4) John
ISBN 0-7734-2432-6 (v. 5) Acts

This is volume 5 in the continuing series
Bibliographies for Biblical Research
New Testament Series
Volume 5 ISBN 0-7734-2432-6
Series ISBN 0-7734-9345-X

A CIP catalog record for this book is available from the British Library.

The Edwin Mellen Press   The Edwin Mellen Press
Box 450   Box 67
Lewiston, New York   Queenston, Ontario
USA 14092   CANADA L0S 1L0

Edwin Mellen Press, Ltd.
Lampeter, Dyfed, Wales
UNITED KINGDOM SA48 7DY

Printed in the United States of America

Contents

Introduction to the Series

This volume is the fifth in a series of bibliographies on the books of the Hebrew and Christian Bibles as well as the deutero-canonicals. This ambitious series calls for some 35-40 volumes over the next 4-6 years complied by practicing scholars from various traditions.

Each author (compiler) of these volumes is working within the general framework adopted for the series, i.e., citations are to works published within the twentieth century that make important contributions to the understanding of the text and backgrounds of the various books.

Obviously the former criterion is more easily quantifiable than the latter, and it is precisely at this point that an individual compiler makes her/his specific contribution. We are not intending to be comprehensive in the sense of definitive, but where resources are available, as many listings as possible have been included.

The arrangement for the entries, in most volumes in the series, consists of three divisions: scriptural citations; subject citations; commentaries. In some cases the first two categories may duplicate each other to some degree. Multiple citations by scriptural citation are also included where relevant.

Those who utilize these volumes are invited to assist the compilers by noting textual errors as well as obvious omissions that ought to be taken into account in subsequent printings. Perfection is nowhere more elusive than in the citation of bibliographic materials. We would welcome your assistance at this point.

When the series is completed, the entire contents of all volumes (updated) will be available on CD-ROM. This option will be available, without charge, to those who have subscribed to the casebound volumes.

We hope that these bibliographies will contribute to the discussions and research going on in the field among faculty as well as students. They should serve a significant role as reference works in both research and public libraries.

I wish to thank the staff and editors of the Edwin Mellen Press, and especially Professor Herbert Richardson, for the gracious support of this series.

Watson E. Mills, Series Editor
Mercer University
Macon GA 31211
December 1994

Preface

This Bibliography on the Acts of the Apostles provides an index to the journal articles, essays in collected works, books and monographs, dissertations, commentaries, and various encyclopedia and dictionary articles published in the twentieth century through 1994 (a few titles for the early months of 1995 are included when these were available for verification). Technical works of scholarship, from many differing traditions constitute the bulk of the citations though I have included some selected works that intend to reinterpret this research to a wider audience.

Three extant bibliographies on Acts proved most helpful in the preparation of this text: Bruce M. Metzger, *An Index to Periodical Literature on the Apostle Paul.* Rev. ed. NTTS #1. Leiden: Brill, 1970; Watson E. Mills, *An Index to Periodical Literature on the Apostle Paul.* NTTS #16. Leiden: Brill, 1993; Paul-Émile Langevin, *Bibliographie biblique* (Les Presses de l'Université Laval, /1972, 1978, 1985). I had the privlede of updating Metzger's massive work (1970) during 1992-1993, though my update, like the original work, is limited to periodical materials. The third is heavily slanted toward Catholic publications but particularly the third volume begins to move toward a more balanced perspective. Langevin's work is very heavy in citations to French literature, but is meticulously indexed by scriptural citation as well as subject and contains detailed indexes.

Building the database necessary for a work of this magnitude was a tedious and time-consuming task. I acknowledge the administration of Mercer University for granting me a sabbatical leave during the 1992 academic year. Also, I acknowledge with gratitude the Education Commission of the Southern Baptist Convention which provided funds for travel to overseas libraries during the summers of 1994 and 1995.

I want to express my gratitude to the staff librarians at the following institutions: Baptist Theological Seminary (Rüschlikon, Switzerland); Oxford University (Oxford, UK); Emory University (Atlanta, GA); Duke University (Durham, NC); University of Zürich (Zürich, Switzerland); Southern Baptist Theological Seminary (Louisville, KY).

Watson E. Mills
Mercer University
Macon GA 31211
December 1995

Abbreviations

ABR	Australian Biblical Review (Melbourne)
ACR	Australian Catholic Record (Sydney)
AfER	African Ecclesial Review (Masaka, Uganda)
AfTJ	African Theological Journal (Tanzania)
AJT	The Asia Journal of Theology (Bangalore)
AmCl	L'Ami du Clerge (Languorous)
An Bib	Analecta Biblica (Rome)
Ang	Angelicum (Rome)
ANQ	Andover Newton Quarterly (New Centre, MA)
ANRW	Aufstieg und Medergang der römischen Welt (Berlin)
Ant	Antonianum (Rome)
Apuntes	Apuntes: Reflexiones Teológicas desde el Margen Hispano (Dallas, TX)
AQR	American Church Quarterly (New York)
ASB	Auxiliary Studies in the Bible (Nashville)
AsSeign	Assemblées du Seigneur (Paris)
ASTI	Annual of the Swedish Theological Institute (Leiden)
ATB	Ashland Theological Bulletin (Ashland, OH)
ATR	Anglican Theological Review (New York)
Aug	Augustinianum (Rome)
AUSS	Andrews University Seminary Studies (Berrien Springs, MI)
BA	Biblical Archaeologist (New Haven, CN)
BAR	Biblical Archaeology Review (Washington, DC)
BASP	Bulletin of the American Society of Papyrologists (New Haven, CN)
BB	Bible Bhashyam: An Indian Biblical Quarterly (Vadavathoor)

BBB	Bonner Biblische Beiträge (Bonn)
BC	Biblischer Commentar über das Alte Testament (Leipzig)
BCPE	Bulletin du Centre Protestant d'Études (Geneva)
BETL	Bibliotheca Ephemeridum theologicarum Lovaniensium (Louvain)
BETS	Bulletin of the Evangelical Theological Society (Wheaton, IL)
BEvT	Beiträge zur evangelization Theologie (Munich)
BI	Biblical Illustrator (Nashville, TN)
Bib	Biblica (Rome)
BiBe	Biblische Beiträge (Einsiedeln)
BibL	Bibel und Leben (Düsseldorf)
BibN	Biblische Notizen: Beiträge zur exegetischen Diskussion (Bamberg)
BibO	Bibbia e Oriente (Milan)
BibR	Biblia Revuo (Revenue)
BibTo	Bible Today (Colegeville, MN)
BibView	Biblical Viewpoint (Greenville, SC)
BIFAO	Bulletin de l'Institut Français d'Archéologie Orientale (Cario)
Bij	Bijdragen (Nijmegen)
BJRL	Bulletin of the John Rylands University Library (Manchester)
BK	Bibel und Kirche (Stuttgart)
BL	Bibel und Liturgie (Vienna)
BogS	Bogoslovska Smotra (Zagreb)
BR	Biblical Research (Chicago)
BSac	Bibliotheca Sacra (Dallas, TX)
BSS	Bulletin of Saint Sulpice (Paris)
BT	Bible Translator (London)
BTB	Biblical Theology Bulletin (Jamaica NY)
BTF	Bangalore Theological Forum (Bangalore)
BTS	Bible et Terre Sainte (Paris)
BVC	Bible et Vie Chretienne (Paris)
BW	Biblical World (Chicago)
BZ	Biblische Zeitschrift (Paderborn)
Cath	Catholica: Vierteljahresschrift für ökumenische Theologie (Münster)
CBQ	Catholic Biblical Quarterly (Washington, DC)
CBTJ	Calvary Baptist Theological Journal (Lansdale, PA)
CC	Christian Century (Chicago)

Ch	Churchman: A Journal of Anglican Theology (London)
ChH	Church History (Berne, IN)
ChJR	Christian-Jewish Relations (London)
Chr	Christus (Paris)
ChrM	Christian Ministry (Chicago, IL)
CICR	Communio: International Catholic Review (Spokane, WA)
CJ	Concordia Journal (St. Louis, MO)
CJT	Canadian Journal of Theology (Toronto)
ClerR	Clergy Review (London)
CM	Clergy Monthly (Ranchi)
CollT	Collectanea Theologica (Warsaw)
Communio	Communio: Commentarii internationales de ecclesia et theology (Seville)
CQR	Church Quarterly Review (London)
CrNSt	Cristianesimo nella Storia (Bologna)
Crux	Crux (Vancouver)
CS	Chicago Studies (Chicago)
CT	Christianity Today (Washington, DC)
CThM	Currents in Theology and Mission (St. Louis, MO)
CTJ	Calvin Theological Journal (Grand Rapids, MI)
CTM	Concordia Theological Monthly (St. Louis, MO)
CTQ	Concordia Theological Quarterly (Fort Wayne, IN)
CTR	Criswell Theological Review (Dallas, TX)
CuBí	Cultura Bíblica (Madrid)
CuT	Cuadernos de teologia (Burgos)
CVia	Communio Viatorum (Prague)
DBM	Deltío Biblikôn Meletôn (Athens)
Dia	Dialog (Minneapolis, MN)
Did	Didascalia (Rosario)
Direction	Direction (Fresno, CA)
DR	Downside Review (Bath)
DTD	Disciples Theological Digest (St. Louis, MO)
DTT	Dansk Teologisk Tidsskrift (Cophenhagen)
DunR	Dunwoodie Review (Yonkers, NY)
EAJT	East Asia Journal of Theology (Singapore)

EB	Estudios Bíblicos (Madrid)
EcumRev	Ecumenical Review (Geneva)
EE	Estudios Eclesiásticos (Madrid)
EGLMBS	Eastern Great Lakes and Midwest Biblical Society (Chicago)
EgT	Église et théologie (Ottawa)
Emmanuel	Emmanuel (New York)
EMQ	Evangelical Missions Quarterly (Washington, DC)
Enc	Encounter (Indianapolis, IN)
EP	Ekklesiastikos Pharos (Addis Ababa, Ethiopia)
EpRev	The Epworth Review (London)
EQ	Evangelical Quarterly (London)
ErAu	Erbe und Auftrag (Beuron)
ERev	Ecclesiastical Review (Philadelphia)
ERT	Evangelical Review of Theology (Exeter)
EstAg	Estudios agustiniano (Valladolid)
EstFr	Estudios franciscanos (Barcelona)
ET	Expository Times (Edinburgh)
ETL	Ephemerides Theologicae Lovanienses (Louvain)
ÉTR	Études Théologiques et Religieuses (Montpellier)
EV	Esprit et Vie (Langres)
EvT	Evangelische Theologie (Munich)
Exp	The Expositor (London)
FF	Forschungen und Fortschritte (Berlin)
FilN	Filologia Neotestamentaria (Cordoba)
FM	Faith and Mission (Wake Forest, NC)
Forum	Forum (Sonoma, CA)
Found	Foundations (Rochester, NY)
FT	La foi et le temps (Tournai)
FundJ	Fundamentalist Journal (Lynchburg, VA)
FV	Foi et Vie (Paris)
GeistL	Geist und Leben (Würzburg)
GGA	Göttingische gelehrte Anzeigen (Göttingen)
GNT	Grundrisse zum Neuen Testament (Göttingen)
GOTR	Greek Orthodox Theological Review (Brookline, MA)
Greg	Gregorianum (Rome)

GTJ	Grace Theological Journal (Winona Lake, IN)
GTT	Gereformeered Theologisch Tijdschrift (Aalten)
HBT	Horizons in Biblical Theology (Pittsburg, PA)
HD	Heiliger Dienst (Salzburg)
HJ	Hibbert Journal (London)
HTR	Harvard Theological Review (Cambridge, MA)
HTS	Hervormde Teologiese Studies (Pretoria)
IBS	Irish Biblical Studies (London)
IEJ	Israel Exploration Journal (Jerusalem)
IJT	Indian Journal of Theology (Serampore)
IKaZ	Internationale Katholische Zeitschrift (Communio: Rodenkirchen)
IKZ	Internationale Kirchliche Zeitschrift (Bern)
Impact	Impact: A Journal of Thought of the Disciples of Christ on the Pacific Slope (Dallas, TX)
Int	Interpretation (Richmond, VA)
Irén	Irénikon (Chevetogne)
IRM	International Review of Mission (London)
ITQ	Irish Theological Quarterly (Maynooth)
ITS	Indian Theological Studies (Bangalore)
JAAR	Journal of the American Academy of Religion (Atlanta)
JBL	Journal of Biblical Literature (Atlanta, GA)
Je	Jeevadhara (Kerala, India)
JES	Journal of Ecumenical Studies (Philadelphia, PA)
JETS	Journal of the Evangelical Theological Society (Wheaton, IL)
JianD	Jian Dao (Hong Kong)
JITC	Journal of the Interdenominational Theological Center (Atlanta)
JJRS	Japanese Journal of Religious Studies (Tokyo)
JJS	Journal of Jewish Studies (Oxford, UK)
JMP	The Journal of the Moscow Patriarchate (Moscow)
JNSL	Journal of Northwest Semitic Languages (Stellenbosch, South Africa)
JPTh	Journal of Pentecostal Theology (Sheffield, UK)
JQR	Jewish Quarterly Review (Philadelphia PA)
JR	Journal of Religion (Chicago, IL)
JRH	Journal of Religious History (Sydney, Australia)

JRPR	Journal of Religion and Psychical Research (Bloomfield, CN)
JSNT	Journal for the Study of the New Testament (Sheffield)
JSS	Journal of Semitic Studies (Manchester, UK)
JTS	Journal of Theological Studies (Oxford, UK)
JTSA	Journal of Theology for Southern Africa (Rondebosch)
Jud	Judaica (Zürich)
Judaism	Judaism (New York)
K	Kairos: Zeitschrift für Religionswissenschaft und Theologie (Salzburg)
KatB	Katechetische Blätter (Münich)
KD	Kerygma and Dogma (Göttingen)
KS	Kator Shin (Tokyo)
Laur	Laurentianum (Rome)
LB	Linguistica Biblica (Bonn)
LexTQ	Lexington Theological Quarterly (Lexington, KY)
LivL	The Living Light (Huntington, IN)
LouvS	Louvain Studies (Louvain)
LQ	Lutheran Quarterly (Gettysburg, PA)
LQHR	London Quarterly and Holbon Review (London)
LS	Life of Spirit (London)
LTJ	Lutheran Theological Journal (Adelaide)
LV	Lumen Vitae (Washington, DC)
LVie	Lumière et Vie (Lyon)
MeliT	Melita Theologia (La Valetta)
MillSt	Milltown Studies (Dublin)
MisCom	Miscelanea Comillas: Revista de Estudios Históricos (Madrid)
Miss	Missiology: An International Review (Scottsdale, PA)
MQR	Mennonite Quarterly Review (Goshen, IN)
Mus	Museon (Louvain)
NBlack	New Blackfriars (London)
Neo	Neotestamentica (Pretoria)
NGTT	Nederduiste Gereformeerde Teologiese Tijdskrif (Kaapstad)
NovT	Novum Testamentum (Leiden)
NRT	La Nouvelle revue théologique (Louvain)
NTS	New Testament Studies (Cambridge)

NTT	Norsk teologisk tidsskrift (Oslo)
OC	One in Christ (Turvey, Bedfordshire)
OCP	Orientalia christiana periodica (Rome)
Or	Orientalia (Rome)
OrChr	Oriens Christianus (Wiesbaden)
OS	Ostkirchliche Studien (Würzburg)
Para	Paraclete (Springfield, MO))
ParSpirV	Parola, spirito e vita: Quaderni di lettura biblica (Bologna)
Persp	Perspective (Pittsburgh, PA)
PerT	Perspectiva Teológica (Belo Horizonte, Brazil)
PIBA	Proceedings of the Irish Biblical Association (Dublin)
PL	Paroisse et Liturgie (Brabant, Belgium)
Pneuma	Pneuma: The Journal of the Society for Pentecostal Studies (Chicago, IL)
POC	Proche Orient Chrétien (Jerusalem)
Point	Point (Papua, New Guinea)
Pres	Presbyterion (St. Louis)
Protest	Protestantesimo (Rome)
PRS	Perspectives in Religious Studies (Macon, GA)
PSB	Princeton Seminary Bulletin (Princeton, NJ)
PV	Parole di vita (Torino)
QR	Quarterly Review (Nashville)
RÉG	Revue des Études Grecques (Paris)
RB	Revue biblique (Paris)
RBén	Revue Bénédictine (Maredsous)
RBib	Rivista Biblica (Bologna)
RCT	Revista Catalana de Teología (Barcelona)
REA	Revue des Études Augustiniennes (Paris)
REB	Revista eclesiástica brasileira (Petrópolis)
RechSR	Recherches de science religieuse (Paris)
RevAug	Revista Augustiniana (Madrid)
RevB	Revista Biblica (Buenos Aires)
RevExp	Review and Expositor (Louisville, KY)
RevQ	Revue de Qumran (Paris)
RevRel	Review for Religious (St. Louis, MO)

RevSR	Revue des Sciences religieuses (Strasbourg)
RHPR	Revue d'historie et de philosophie religieuses (Strasbourg)
RHR	Revue de l'historie des Religions (Paris)
Risk	Risk (Geneva)
RivAC	Rivista di archeologia cristiana (Rome)
RJ	Reformed Journal (Grand Rapids, MI)
RL	Religion in Life (New York)
RoczTK	Roczniki Teologiczno-Kanoniczne (Lublin)
RQ	Restoration Quarterly (Austin, TX)
RR	Reformed Review (Holland, MI)
RS	Religion and Society: Bulletin of the Christian Institute for the Study of Religion and Society (Bangalore, India)
RSB	Religious Studies Bulletin (Calgary)
RSPT	Revue des Sciences Philosophiques et Thélogiques (Paris)
RSR	Religious Studies Review (Valapariso, IN)
RT	Revue Thomiste (Paris)
RTL	Revue théologique de Louvain (Louvain)
RTP	Revue de Théologie et de Philosophie (Geneva)
RTR	Reformed Theological Review (Melbourne)
RuchB	Ruch biblijny i liturgiczny (Krakow)
RUO	Revue de l'université d'Ottawa (Ottawa)
RW	Reformed World (Geneva)
SémBib	Sémiotique et Bible (Lyon)
SacD	Sacra Doctrina (Bologna)
Sale	Salesianum (Rome)
Salm	Salmanticensis (Salamanca)
SalT	Sal terrae (Santander)
SB	Studi Biblici (Brescia)
SBFLA	Studii Biblici Franciscani Liber Annuus (Jerusalem)
SBLSP	Society of Biblical Literature Seminar Papers (Atlanta)
SBT	Studia Biblica et Theologica (Pasadena, CA)
ScC	Scuola cattolica: Rivista di scienze religiose (Milan)
ScE	Science et Esprit (Montreal)
Scr	Scripture: Quarterly of the Catholic Biblical Association (Edinburgh)

ScrB	Scripture Bulletin (Strawberry Hill, UK)
ScrSA	Scriptura: Journal of Bible and Theology in South Africa (Stellenbosch, South Africa)
SE	Sciences Ecclésiastiques (Bruges)
SEÅ	Svensk Exegetisk Årsbok (Lund)
SEAJT	South East Asia Journal of Theology (Singapore))
Semeia	Semeia (Atlanta, GA)
SJT	Scottish Journal of Theology (Edinburgh)
SkrifK	Skrif en Kerk (Pretoria)
SM	Studia Missionalia (Rome)
SMR	Saint Mark's Review (Canberra)
SNTU-A	Studien zum Neuen Testament und seiner Umwelt (Linz)
Soj	Sojourners (Washington DC)
SouJT	Southwestern Journal of Theology (Fort Worth TX)
SpirTo	Spirituality Today (Chicago)
SR	Studies in Religion/Sciences religieuses (Toronto)
ST	Studies in Theology (London)
StJudLAnt	Studies in Judaism in Late Antiquity (Leiden)
STK	Svensk teologisk kvartalskrift (Lund)
StTh	Studia theologica: Scandinavian Journal of Theology (Lund)
StTheol	Studia Theologica (Copenhagen)
Stud	Studium (Madrid)
StudE	Studia evangelica (Berlin)
SVTQ	St. Vladimir's Theological Quarterly (Crestwood, NY)
TB	Theologische Berichte (Zürich)
TBe	Theologische Beiträge (Wuppertal)
TD	Theology Digest (Deluth, MN)
TexteK	Texte und Kontexte: Exegetische Zeitschrift (Berlin)
TGeg	Theologie der Gegenwart (Münster)
TGl	Theologie und Glaube (Paderborn, Germany)
Themelios	Themelios (Leicetser, UK)
Theology	Theology (London)
TheoP	Theologie und Philosophie (Freiburg)
TJT	Toronto Journal of Theology (Toronto)
TLZ	Theologische Literaturzeitung (Leipzig)

TPQ	Theologische-praktische Quartalschrift (Linz)
TQ	Theologische Quartalschift (Tübingen)
TR	Theologische Rundschau (Tübingen)
TriJ	Trinity Journal (Deerfield, IL)
TSK	Theologische Studien und Kritiken (Hamburg)
TT	Theology Today (Princeton, NJ)
TTK	Tidsskrift for teologi og kirke (Oslo)
TTZ	Trierer Theologische Zeitschrift (Trier)
TU	Texte und Untersuchungen (Berlin)
TynB	Tyndale Bulletin (Cambridge, MA)
TZ	Theologische Zeitschrift (Basel)
Unitas	Unitas (Rome)
USQR	Union Seminary Quarterly Review (New York)
VC	Vigiliae Christianae (Leiden)
VD	Verbum Domine (Rome)
VerkF	Verkündigung und Forschung (Munich)
VoxE	Vox evangelica (London)
VS	La vie spirituelle (Paris)
WD	Wort und Dienst: Jahrbuch der theologischen Schule Bethel (Bielefeld)
WesTJ	Wesleyan Theological Journal (Lakeville, IN)
Worship	Worship (Collegeville, MN)
WTJ	Westminster Theology Journal (Philadelphia)
WW	Word and World (St. Paul, MN)
ZAW	Zeitschrift für die alttestamentliche Wissenschaft (Berlin)
ZKT	Zeitschrift für Katholische Theologie (Innsbruck)
ZNW	Zeitschrift für die neutestamentliche Wissenschaft (Berlin)
ZRGG	Zeitschrift für Religions- und Geistesgeschichte (Erlangen)
ZST	Zeitschrift für systematische Theologie (Berlin)
ZTK	Zeitschrift für Theologie und Kirche (Tübingen)
ZZ	Zwischen den Zeiten (München)

PART ONE

Citations by Chapter and Verse

1-15

0001   R. J. Knowling, "Notes and Comments on Some Earlier Portions of Acts," *BW* 19 (1902): 410-25.

0002   C. T. Norman, "The Transitional Nature of the Theology of Acts 1-15," master's thesis, Southwestern Baptist Theological Seminary, Fort Worth TX, 1962.

0003   R. A. Martin, "Syntactical Evidence of Aramaic Sources in Acts I-XV," *NTS* 11/1 (1964): 38-59.

1:1-15:35

0004   R. A. Martin, "Semitic Traditions in Some Synoptic Accounts," *SBLSP* 26 (1987): 295-335.

1:1-15:3

0005   H.-M. Schenke, ed., *Apostelgeschichte 1:1-15:3 im mittel-ägyptischen Dialekt des Koptischen.* Texte und Untersuchungen zur Geschichte der altchristlichen Literatur #137. Berlin: Akademie Verlag, 1991.

1-12

0006   Heinrich Steege, *Wie auf Erden Kirche wurde* [Apg. 1-12]. Berlin: Kranz, 1935.

0007   H. E. Dana, *Jewish Christianity. An Expository Survey of Acts 1-12, James, 1 and 2 Peter, Jude and Hebrews.* New Orleans: Bible Institute Memorial Press, 1937.

0008   Werner Kaschel, "The Holy Spirit in the Palestinian Churches: Acts I-XII; XV; XXI-XXIII," master's thesis, Southwestern Baptist Theological Seminary, Fort Worth TX, 1949.

0009   J. Rius-Camps, "El seguimiento de Jesús, 'el Señor', y de su Espíritu en los prolegómenos de la misión," *EB* 51 (1993): 73-116.

1-7

0010   William O. McClung, "The Christological Implications of Acts Chapters One through Seven as Seen in the Names Used for Jesus Christ," doctoral dissertation, Southern Baptist Theological Seminary, Louisville KY, 1953.

0011   L. O'Reilly, "Chiastic Structures in Acts 1-7," *PIBA* 7 (1983): 87-103.

__1-6__

0012 Francis Lenssen, "Biblical Communities: Christian Communities in the New Testament," *Point* 1 (1972): 24-34.

0013 J. H. Petzer, "The Textual Relationships of the Vulgate and Acts," *NTS* 39/2 (1993): 227-45.

__1-5__

0014 S. J. Case, "The First Christian Community," *BW* 33 (1909): 54-64.

0015 U. Holzmeister, "Die Urkirche von Jerusalem" in *Die zweiten Salzburger Hochschulwochen.* Salzburg: Pustet, 1933. Pp. 51-64.

0016 W. L. Blevins, "The Early Church: Acts 1-5," *RevExp* 71/4 (1974): 463-74.

0017 Mikeal C. Parsons, "Christian Origins and Narrative Openings: The Sense of a Beginning in Acts 1-5," *RevExp* 87 (1990): 403-22.

__1:1-4:44__

0018 F. Ó'Fearghail, *The Introduction to Luke-Acts: A Study in the Role of Lk. 1:1-4:44 in the Composition of Luke's Two-Volume Work.* Analecta Biblica #126. Rome: Pontifical Institute Press, 1991.

__1-2__

0019 Everett Ferguson, "Apologetics in the New Testament," *RQ* 6 (1962): 180-95.

0020 C. H. Talbert, "Redaction Critical Quest for Luke the Theologian," *Persp* 11/1-2 (1970): 171-222.

0021 Veselin Kesich, "Resurrection, Ascension, and the Giving of the Spirit," *GOTR* 25/3 (1980): 249-60.

0022 P. M. J. Stravinskas, "The Role of the Spirit in Acts 1 and 2," *BibTo* 18/4 (1980): 263-68.

0023 A. Godin, "Geschichte einer Trauer und eines neuen Pneumas (eines neuen Atems): Gedanken eines Psychoanalytikers über drei Texte der Apostelgeschichte. trans. by Kurt Gins," in Kurt Krenn, et al., eds., *Archiv für Religionspsychologie*, Bd. 18. Göttingen: Vandenhoeck & Ruprecht, 1988. Pp. 19-37.

0024 J. T. A. Marlow, "A Narrative Analysis of Acts 1-2," doctoral dissertation, Golden Gate Baptist Theological Seminary, Mill Vallley CA, 1988.

0025 H. S. Ponguta, *Para que seais mis testigos. Una presentación de los Hechos de los Apostoles. Una luxury de Act 1-2.* Caracas, Asociación Bíblica Salesiana, 1991.

0026 C. W. Wibb, "The Characterization of God in the Opening Scenes of Luke and Acts," *EGLMBS* 13 (1993): 275-92.

0027 J. Kremer, "Biblische Grundlagen zur Feier der Fünfzig Tage," *HD* 48 (1994): 3-15.

<u>1</u>

0028 R. J. Fuller, "The Choice of Matthias," *StudE* 5 (1973): 140-46.

0029 David Wenham, "The Paulinism of Acts Again: Two Historical Clues in 1 Thessalonians," *Themelios* 13/2 (1988): 53-55.

0030 J. Taylor, "The Making of Acts: A New Account," *RB* 97 (1990): 504-24.

0031 G. Mussies, "Variation in the Book of Acts," *FilN* 4 (1991): 165-82.

0032 G. O'Collins, "Luke and the Closing of the Easter Appearences" in Gerald O'Collins and G. Marconi, eds., *Luke and Acts* (festschrift in honor of Emilio Rasco). Mahwah NJ: Paulist Press, 1993. Pp. 161-66.

<u>1:1-26</u>

0033 P. W. van der Horst, "Hellenistic Parallels to the Acts of the Apostles: 1:1-26," *ZNW* 74/1-2 (1983): 17-26.

0034 Mikeal C. Parsons, "Christian Origins and Narrative Openings: The Sense of a Beginning in Acts 1-5," *RevExp* 87 (1990): 403-22.

<u>1:1-18</u>

0035 J. Murphy-O'Connor, "Paul and Gallio," *JBL* 112/2 (1990): 315-17.

1:1-14

0036 Otto Merk, "Die Apostelgeschichte im Frühwerk Rudolf Bultmanns," in Bernd Jaspert, ed., *Rudolf Bultmanns Werk und Wirkung*. Darmstadt, West Germany: Wissenschaftliche Buchgesellschaft, 1984. Pp. 303-15.

0037 Phillippe Rolland, "L'organisation du Livre des Actes et de l'ensemble de l'œuvre de Luc," *Bib* 65/1 (1984): 81-86.

0038 D. W. Palmer, "The Literary Background of Acts 1:1-14," *NTS* 33/3 (1987): 427-38.

1:1-12

0039 C. Frey, "Die Himmelfahrtsbericht des Lukas nach Apg 1:1-12. Exegetische und didaktische Problematik," *KatB* 95 (1970): 10-21.

0040 Manuel Benéitez, "Un Capítulo de Narrativa Bíblica: Los 'Encargos' de Hch 1,1-12," *MisCom* 43/83 (1985): 329-82.

0041 Raymond E. Brown, *A Risen Christ in Eastertime: Essays on the Gospel Narratives of the Resurrection*. Collegeville MN: Liturgical Press, 1991.

1:1-11

0042 Wayne E. Weissenbuehler, "Acts 1:1-11," *Int* 46 (1992): 61-65.

1:1-5

0043 Gijs Bouwman, "Der Anfang der Apostelgeschichte und der 'westliche' Text," in Tjitze J. Baarda, ed., *Text and Testimony: Essays on New Testament and Apocryphal Literatue* (festschrift for A. F. J. Klijn). Kampen: Hok, 1988. Pp. 46-55.

1:1-3

0044 J. Rius-Camps, "Las variantes de la recensión occidental de los Hechos de los Apóstoles," *FilN* 6 (1993): 59-68.

0045 S. Grzybek, "Wprowadzenie w Dzieje Apostolskie," *RuchB* 19/1 (1966): 51-56.

0046 G. Menestrina, "L'incipit dell'espitola 'Ad Diognetum,' Luca 1:1-4 et Atti 1:1-2," *BibO* 19 (1977): 215-18.

0047 A. Feuillet, "Le 'Commencement' de l'Économie Chrétienne d'après He II. 3-4; Mc I.1 et Ac 1. 1-2," *NTS* 24/2 (1978): 163-74.

1:1

0048 Pierson Parker, "The 'Former Treatise' and the Date of Acts," *JBL* 84/1 (1965): 52-58.

0049 Paul S. Minear, "Dear Theo: The Kerygmatic Intention and Claim of the Book of Acts," *Int* 27/2 (1973): 131-50.

0050 Schuyler Brown, "The Prologues of Luke-Acts in Their Relation to the Purpose of the Author," *SBLSP* 5 (1975): 1-14.

0051 L. C. A. Alexander, "Luke-Acts in its Contemporary Setting with Special Reference to the Prefaces," doctoral dissertation, Oxford University UK, 1977.

0052 Schuyler Brown, "The Role of the Prologues in Determining the Purpose of Luke-Acts," in Charles H. Talbert, ed., *Perspectives on Luke-Acts*. Macon GA: Mercer University Press, 1978. Pp. 99-111.

0053 V. K. Robbins, "Prefaces in Greco-Roman Biography and Luke-Acts," *SBLSP* 8/2 (1978): 193-208.

0054 Terrance Callan, "The Preface of Luke-Acts and Historiography," *NTS* 31 (1985): 576-81.

0055 F. Ó'Fearghail, "The Introduction to Luke-Acts: A Study of the Role of Lk 1,1-4,44 in the Composition of Luke's Two-Volume Work," doctoral dissertation, Pontifical Biblical Institute, Rome, 1987. 2 vols.

0056 L. Alexander, *The Preface to Luke's Gospel: Literary Convention and Social Context in Luke 1:1-4 and Acts 1:1*. SNTSMS #78. Cambridge: University Press, 1993.

0057 C. W. Wibb, "The Characterization of God in the Opening Scenes of Luke and Acts," *EGLMBS* 13 (1993): 275-92.

1:2-3

0058 P. Palatty, "The Ascension of Christ in Luke-Acts: An Exegetical Critical Study of Luke 24,50-53 and Acts 1,2-3.9-11," *BB* 12 (1986): 100-17, 166-81.

1:2

0059 Jacques Dupont, "'Ανελήμφθη (Acts 1:2)," *NTS* 8 (1962): 154-57.

0060 Elmer L. Towns, "The Ascension," *FundJ* 3/6 (1984): 12-14.

0061 Kevin N. Giles, "Apostles before and after Paul," *Ch* 99/3 (1985): 241-56.

0062 Mikeal C. Parsons, "The Text of Acts 1:2 Reconsidered," *CBQ* 50/1 (1988): 58-71.

1:3-11

0063 R. F. O'Toole, "Activity of the Risen Jesus in Luke-Acts," *Bib* 62/4 (1981): 471-98.

1:3-8

0064 E. J. Christiansen, "Taufe als Initiation in der Apostelgeschichte," *StTh* 40/1 (1986): 55-79.

1:3

0065 John H. Hayes, "The Resurrection as Enthronement and the Earliest Church Christology," *Int* 22/3 (1968): 333-45.

0066 David L. Mealand, "The Phrase 'Many Proofs' in Acts 1:3 and in Hellenistic Writers," *ZNW* 80/1-2 (1989): 134-35.

1:4

0067 J. Dasiewicz, "Jeruzalem—miejscem zeslania Ducha Swietego," *RoczTK* 23 (1976): 85-96.

0068 D. L. McConaughy, "An Old Syriac Reading of Acts 1:4 and More Light on Jesus' Last Meal before His Ascension," in Julius Assfalg and Hubert Kaufhold, eds., *Oriens Christianus* Bd 72: *Hefte für die Kunde des christlichen Orients*. Wiesbaden: Otto Harrassowitz, 1988. Pp. 63-67.

0069 J. Rius-Camps, "Las variantes de la recensión occidental de los Hechos de los Apóstoles," *FilN* 6 (1993): 59-68.

1:4-14

0070 J. Rius-Camps, "Las variantes de la recensión occidental de los Hechos de los Apóstoles," *FilN* 6 (1993): 59-68.

1:4-12

0071 Johannes M. Nützel, "Vom Hören zum Glauben: Der Weg zum Osterglauben in der Sicht des Lukas," in Lothar Lies, ed., *Praesentia Christi* (festschrift for Johannes Betz). Düsseldorf: Patmos, 1984. Pp. 37-49.

1:4-8

0072 John R. Donahue, "The 'Parable' of the Sheep and the Goats: A Challenge to Christian Ethics," *JTS* 47/1 (1986): 3-31.

1:4-5

0073 J. Rius-Camps, "Las variantes de la recensión occidental de los Hechos de los Apóstoles," *FilN* 6 (1993): 59-68.

0074 Marion L. Soards, "The Words of the Risen Jesus and the Angels to the Apostles," in *The Speeches in Acts: Their Content, Context, and Concerns*. Louisville: John Knox/Westminster Press, 1994. Pp. 22-26.

1:5

0075 David L. Mealand, " 'After not Many Days' in Acts 1:5 and Its Hellenistic Context," *JSNT* 42 (1991): 69-77.

1:6-11

0076 Joseph G. Kelly, "Lucan Christology and the Jewish-Christian Dialogue," *JES* 21 (1984): 688-708.

0077 D. L. Tiede, "The Exaltation of Jesus and the Restoration of Israel in Acts 1," *SBLSP* 24 (1985): 367-75.

1:6-8

0078 D. L. Tiede, "Acts 1:6-8 and the Theo-Political Claims of Christian Witness," *WW* 1/1 (1981): 41-51.

0079 L. Legrand, "The Spirit, the Mission and the Church: Acts 1:6-8," *BB*8/4 (1982): 204-15.

0080 David Hill, "The Spirit and the Church's Witness: Observations on Acts 1:6-8," *IBS* 6/1 (1984): 16-26.

0081 C. Di Sante, "The Missionizing of the East and the Meaning of Mission in the New Testament," in Frank K. Flinn and Tyler Hendricks, eds., *Religion in the Pacific Era*. New York NY: Paragon House Publishers, 1985. Pp. 3-13.

0082 V. Fusco, "Point of View and 'Implicit Reader' in Two Eschatological Texts in Frans van Sebroeck, et al., eds., *The Four Gospels 1992* (festschrift for Frans Neirynck). BETL #100. 2 vols. Louvain: Peeters, 1992. 2:1677-96.

0083 J. A. McLean, "Did Jesus Correct the Disciples' View of the Kingdom?" *BSac* 151 (1994): 215-27.

1:6

0084 Lesslie Newbigin, "The Church as Witness: A Meditation," *RW* 35/1 (1978): 5-9.

0085 Erich Grässer, "Ta peri tès basileias," in Françios Refoulé, ed., *À cause de l'Évangile: Études sur les synoptiques et les Actes* (festschrift for Jacques Dupont). Paris: Cerf, 1985. Pp. 709-25.

0086 D. L. Tiede, "The Exaltation of Jesus and the Restoration of Israel in Acts 1," *HTR* 79/1 (1986): 278-86.

0087 J. Rius-Camps, "Las variantes de la recensión occidental de los Hechos de los Apóstoles," *FilN* 6 (1993): 59-68.

0088 A. Buzard, "Acts 1:6 and the Eclipse of the Biblical Kingdom," *EQ* 66 (1994): 197-215.

1:7-8

0089 Marion L. Soards, "The Words of the Risen Jesus and the Angels to the Apostles," in *The Speeches in Acts: Their Content, Context, and Concerns*. Louisville: John Knox/Westminster Press, 1994. Pp. 22-26.

1:7

0090 R. Y. K. Fung, "Charismatic Versus Organized Ministry? An Examination of an Alleged Antithesis," *EQ* 52/4 (1980): 195-214.

0091 Luis F. Ladaria, "Dispensatio en S. Hilario de Poitiers [De Trinitate]," *Greg* 66/3 (1985): 429-55.

1:8-11

0092 J. Rius-Camps, "Las variantes de la recensión occidental de los Hechos de los Apóstoles," *FilN* 6 (1993): 59-68.

1:8

0093 H. A. Hoyt, "The Frantic Future and the Christian Directive: Acts 1:8," *GTJ* 10/1 (1969): 36-41.

0094 A. Moretti, "Mi sarete testimoni (Atti 1,8)" *PV* 15 (1970): 421-36.

0095 T. C. G. Thornton, "To the End of the Earth: Acts 1:8," *ET* 89 (1978): 374-75.

0096 Jacques Dupont, "La mission de Paul d'après Actes 26,16-23 et la mission des apôtres d'après Luc 24,44-49 et Actes 1,8," in M. D. Hooker and S. G. Wilson, eds., *Paul and Paulinism* (festschrift for C. K. Barrett). London: SPCK, 1982. Pp. 290-301.

0097 C. H. H. Scobie, "Jesus or Paul: The Origin of the Universal Mission of the Christian Church," in Peter Richardson and John C. Hurd, eds., *From Jesus to Paul* (festschrift for Francis Wright Beare). Waterloo, Ontario: Wilfrid Laurier University Press, 1984. Pp. 47-60.

0098 Gordon D. Fee, "Baptism in the Holy Spirit: The Issue of Separability and Subsequence," *Pneuma* 7/2 (1985): 87-99.

0099 Jaroslav J. Pelikan, "The Man Who Belongs to the World," *CC* 102 (1985): 827-31.

0100 J. A. Jáuregui, "Israel y la iglesia en la teologia de Lucas," *EE* 61 (1986): 129-49.

0101 Andreas Lindemann, "Erwägungen zum Problem einer 'Theologie der synoptischen Evangelien'," *ZNW* 77/1-2 (1986): 1-33.

0102 Warren McWilliams, "The Uttermost Part of the Earth: First-Century Views," *BI* 12/3 (1986): 66-69.

0103 Daniel R. Schwartz, "The End of the Genesis: Beginning or End of the Christian Vision?" *JBL* 105/4 (1986): 669-76.

0104 LaMoine DeVries, "Samaria," *BI* 14/2 (1989): 10-15.

1:9-11

0105   C. H. J. van Kempen, "Masters of the Text: is Every Age the Same," *RR* 40/1 (1986): 21-26.

0106   P. Palatty, "The Ascension of Christ in Luke-Acts: An Exegetical Critical Study of Luke 24,50-53 and Acts 1,2-3.9-11," *BB* 12 (1986): 100-17, 166-81.

0107   C. L. Stockhausen, "Luke's Stories of the Ascension: The Background and Function of a Dual Narrative," *EGLMBS* 10 (1990): 251-63.

0108   G. C. Fuller, "The Life of Jesus after the Ascension," *WTJ* 56/2 (1994): 391-98.

1:9

0109   Elmer L. Towns, "The Ascension," *FundJ* 3/6 (1984): 12-14.

1:11

0110   Gerhard Lohfink, " 'Was steht ihr da und schauet' (Apg 1.11). Die 'Himmelfahrt Jesu' in lukanischen Geschichtswerk," *BK* 20/2 (1965): 43-48.

0111   Guriy Kuzmin, "On The Feast of the Ascension," *JMP* 6 (1983): 52-53.

0112   Anthony Hoekema, "Heaven: Not Just an Eternal Day Off," *CT* 29 (1985): 18-19.

0113   Marion L. Soards, "The Words of the Risen Jesus and the Angels to the Apostles," in *The Speeches in Acts: Their Content, Context, and Concerns.* Louisville: John Knox/Westminster Press, 1994. Pp. 22-26.

1:12-8:4

0114   G. Betori, *Persiguitati a causa del nome. Strutture dei racconti di persecuzione in Atti 1,12-8,4.* Analecta Biblica #97. Rome: Biblical Institute Press, 1981.

1:12-14

0115   G. Betori, "La strutturazione del libro degli Atti: una proposta," *RBib* 42 (1994): 3-34.

1:12

0116 A. Strobel, "Der Berg der Offenbarung," in O. Böcher and K. Haacker, eds., *Verborum Veritas* (festschrift for Gustav Stählin). Wuppertal: Brockhaus, 1970. Pp. 133-46.

1:13-14

0117 B. Prete, "Il somario di Atti 1:13-14 e suo aporto per la conoscenza della Chiesa delle origini," *SacD* 18/69-70 (1973): 65-125.

0118 R. Mahoney, "Die Mutter Jesu im Neuen Testament," in Gerhard Dautzenberg, et al., eds., *Die Frau im Urchristentum*. Freiburg, Germany: Herder, 1983. Pp. 92-116.

0119 J. Rius-Camps, "Las variantes de la recensión occidental de los Hechos de los Apóstoles," *FilN* 6 (1993): 59-68.

1:13

0120 B. B. Thurston, "τὸ ὑπερῷον in Acts 1,13," *ET* 81/1 (1968): 21-22.

0121 Roger L. Omanson, "Lazarus and Simon," *BT* 40 (1989): 416-19.

0122 Günther Schwarz, "Philippon kai Bartholomaion?" *BibN* 56 (1991): 26-30.

1:14

0123 Walter Thiele, "Eine Bemerkung zu Act 1:14," *ZNW* 53 (1962): 110-11.

0124 B. Buby, "Mary, a Model of Ecclesia Orans, in Acts 1:14," in Theodore A. Koehler, ed., *Marian Studies*. Vol. 35. Dayton OH: Mariological Society of America, 1984. Pp. 87-99.

0125 M. P. W. Lewela, "Mary's Faith—Model of Our Own: A Reflection," *AFER* 27 (1985): 92-98.

0126 Richard I. Pervo, "Social and Religious Aspects of the Western Text," in Dennis E. Groh and Robert Jewett, eds., *The Living Text* (festschrift for Ernest W. Saunders). Lanham MD: University Press of America, 1985. Pp. 229-41.

0127 J. Zmijewski, "Maria im Neuen Testament," in Wolfgang Haase, ed., *Principat 26/1: Religion.* Berlin: de Gruyter, 1992. Pp. 596-716.

0128 C. Niccum, "A Note on Acts 1:14," *NovT* 36 (1994): 196-99.

1:15-2:47
   0129 L. Panier, "Comprenez pourquoi vous comprenez! Actes 1,15-2,47," *SémBib* 23 (1981): 20-43.

1:15-26
   0130 J. M. Bover, "Un fragmento de la 'Vetus Latina' en un epistolario del siglo XIII," *EE* 6 (1927): 331-34.

0131 K. H. Rengstorf, "Die Zuwahl des Matthias," *ST* 15/1 (1961): 35-67.

0132 Otto Betz, "The Dichotomized Servant and the End of Judas Iscariot," *RevQ* 5 (1964): 43-58.

0133 R. A. Martin, "Syntactical Evidence of Aramaic Sources in Acts I-XV," *NTS* 11/1 (1964): 38-59.

0134 Everett Ferguson, "Qumran and Codex D," *RevQ* 8/29 (1972): 75-80.

0135 W. Dietrich, "Das Petrusbild der Judas—Tradition in Acts i. 15-26," *NTS* 19/4 (1973): 438-52.

0136 Max Wilcox, "The Judas-Tradition in Acts 1. 15-26," *NTS* 19/4 (1973): 438-52.

0137 E. Nellessen, "Tradition und Schrift in der Perikope von der Erwahlung des Mattias," *BZ* 19/2 (1975): 205-18.

0138 Otto Merk, "Die Apostelgeschichte im Frühwerk Rudolf Bultmanns," in Bernd Jaspert, ed., *Rudolf Bultmanns Werk und Wirkung.* Darmstadt, West Germany: Wissenschaftliche Buchgesellschaft, 1984. Pp. 303-15.

0139 Kevin N. Niles, "Apostles before and after Paul," *Ch* 99/3 (1985): 241-256.

0140 L. Desautels, "La mort de Judas," *ScE* 38 (1986): 221-39.

0141 J. Capmany Casamitjana, "El perfil del obispo en la eleccón de Matías," *RCT* 14 (1989): 309-22

0142 J. Rius-Camps, "Las variantes de la recensión occidental de los Hechos de los Apóstoles," *FilN* 6 (1993): 59-68.

1:15-22
0143 Roger L. Omanson, "How Does It All Fit Together? Thoughts On Translating Acts 1:15-22 and 15:19-21," *BT* 41 (1990): 416-21.

1:16-22
0144 Marion L. Soards, "Peter's Speech and the Disciples' Prayer Prior to the Enrollment of Matthias," in *The Speeches in Acts: Their Content, Context, and Concerns*. Louisville: John Knox/Westminster Press, 1994. Pp. 26-31.

1:16-20
0145 Jacques Dupont, "La Destinée de Judas Prophetisée par David," *CBQ* 23 (1961): 41-51.

1:18-20
0146 A. Dauer, "Ergänzungen und 'Variationen' in den Reden der Apostelgeschichte gegenüber vorausgegangenen Erzählungen Beobachtungen zur literarischen Arbeitsweise des Lukas," in Hubert Frankemölle and Karl Kertelge, eds., *Vom Urchristentum zu Jesus* (festschrift for Joachim Gnilka). Freiburg: Herder, 1989. Pp. 307-24.

1:18
0147 C. M. Horne, "Toward a Biblical Apologetic," *GTJ* 2 (1961): 14-18.

0148 A. B. Gordon, "The Fate of Judas According to Acts 1:18," *EQ* 43/2 (1971): 97-100.

0149 J. Duncan M. Derrett, "Miscellanea: A Pauline Pun and Judas' Punishment," *ZNW* 72 (1981): 132-33.

1:21-22
0150 J. E. Young, "That Some Should Be Apostles," *EQ* 48 (1976): 96-104.

1:23

0151   Richard I. Pervo, "Social and Religious Aspects of the Western Text," in Dennis Groh and Robert Jewett, eds., *The Living Text* (festschrift for Ernest Saunders). Lanham MD: University Press of America, 1985. Pp. 229-41.

1:23-26

0152   A. Jaubert, "L'election de Mattheas et le tirage au sort," *TU* 112 (1973): 267-80.

1:24

0153   Bruno Kleinbeyer, "Apg 1:24 im Kontext der Weiheliturgie: zum Aufbau des Kapitels De ordinatione in Gegenwart und Geschichte," *ZKT* 107/1-2 (1985): 31-38.

0154   Johannes B. Bauer, "Kardiognostes, ein unbeachteter Aspekt," *BibN* 32/1 (1988): 114-17.

1:24-25

0155   Marion L. Soards, "Peter's Speech and the Disciples' Prayer Prior to the Enrollment of Matthias," in *The Speeches in Acts: Their Content, Context, and Concerns.* Louisville: John Knox/Westminster Press, 1994. Pp. 26-31.

2-4

0156   David L. Mealand, "Community of Goods and Utopian Allusions in Acts II-IV," *JTS* 28/1 (1977): 96-99.

2

0157   P. G. S. Hopwood, *The Religious Experience of the Primitive Church. The Period Prior to the Influence of Paul.* Edinburgh: T. & T. Clark, 1936. New York: Scribner, 1937.

0158   P.-H. Menoud, "La Pentecôte lucanienne et l'histoire," *RHPR* 42/2-3 (1962): 141-47.

0159   R. J. Fuller, "Tongues in the New Testament," *ACQ* 3 (1963): 162-68.

0160   J. A. Downes, "The Feast of Pentecost: Some Meanings of the Festival in the Bible and the Liturgy," *RUO* 34/1 (1964): 62-69.

0161 W. G. MacDonald, "Glossolalia in the New Testament," *BETS* 20 (1964): 59-68.

0162 J. Abri, "The Theological Meaning of Pentecost, " *KS* 4/1 (1965): 133-51.

0163 C. F. Sleeper, "Pentecost and Resurrection," *JBL* 84 (1965): 389-99.

0164 M. F. Unger, "The Significance of Pentecost," *BS* 122/486 (1965): 169-77.

0165 S. Svéda, "Ich gieße meinen Geist auf alles Fleisch (Joel 3,1). Alttestamentliche Geistverheißung in lukanischer Deutung," *BiKi* 21/2 (1966): 37-41.

0166 Joseph D. Collins, "Discovering the Meaning of Pentecost," *Scr* 20 (1968): 73-79.

0167 J. R. Fowler, "Holiness, the Spirit's Infilling, and Speaking with Tongues," *Para* 2 (1968): 7-9.

0168 Howard M. Ervin, "As the Spirit Gives Utterance," *CT* 13/14 (1969): 623-26.

0169 A. S. Wood, "Social Involvement in the Apostolic Church," *EQ* 42/4 (1970): 194-212.

0170 Roy A. Harrisville, "Speaking in Tongues—Proof of Tanscendence?" *Dia* 13/1 (1974): 11-18.

0171 George S. Bebis, "The Influence of Jewish Worship on Orthodox Christian Worship," *JES* 13/4 (1976): 652-58.

0172 G. Mangatt, "The Pentecostal Gift of the Spirit," *BiBe* 2 (1976): 227-39, 300-14.

0173 P. Matta-El-Meskin, "La Pentecôte," *Irén* 50/1 (1977): 5-45.

0174 A. Étienne, "Étude du récit de l'événement de Pentecôte dans Actes 2," *FV* 80/1 (1981): 47-67.

0175 Donald H. Juel, "Social Dimensions of Exegesis: The Use of Psalm 16 in Acts 2," *CBQ* 43/4 (1981): 543-56.

0176 F. M. Pierce, "Glossolalia," *JRPR* 4 (1981): 168-78.

0177 L. Legrand, "The Structure of Acts 2: The Integral Dimensions of the Charismatic Movement According to Luke," *ITS* 19/3 (1982): 193-209.

0178 Craig A. Evans, "The Prophetic Setting of the Pentecost Sermon," *ZNW* 74/1 (1983): 148-50.

0179 Gerald T. Sheppard, "Pentecostals and the Hermeneutics of Dispensationalism: The Anatomy of an Uneasy Relationship," *Pneuma* 6/2 (1984): 5-33.

0180 Daniel R. Mitchell, "Peter and the Power of Pentecost," *FundJ* 4/10 (1985): 32.

0181 R. H. Fuller, "The Passion, Death and Resurrection of Jesus According to St. John," *CS* 25/1 (1986): 51-64.

0182 M. E. Boring, "The Formation of a Tradition: Alexander Campbell and the New Testament," *DTD* 2/1 (1987): 5-62.

0183 F. R. Harm, "Structural Elements Related to the Gift of the Holy Spirit in Acts," *CJ* 14/1 (1988): 28-41.

0184 J. Rius-Camps, "Pentecostes Versus Babel Estudio Crítico de Hch 2," *FilN* 1 (1988): 35-61.

0185 Murray W. Dempster, "The Church's Moral Witness: A Study of Glossolalia in Luke's Theology of Acts," *Para* 23 (1989): 1-7.

0186 H. van de Sandt, "The Fate of the Gentiles in Joel and Acts 2: An Intertextual Study," *ETL* 66/1 (1990): 56-77.

0187 J. Taylor, "The Making of Acts: A New Account," *RB* 97 (1990): 504-24.

0188 J. A. Jáuregui, "Pentecostés, fiesta de identidad cristiana," *EE* 66 (1991): 369-96.

0189   Robert B. Sloan, "Signs and Wonders: A Rhetorical Clue to the Pentecost Discourse," *EQ* 63 (1991): 225-40.

0190   D. Cloete and D. J. Smit, "Its Name was Called Babel. . ..," *JTSA* 86 (1994): 81-87.

2:1-15

0191   Bill Kellermann, "In the Boldness of the Spirit: Pentecost," *Soj* 14/5 (1985): 28-31.

2:1-47

0192   D. L. Tiede, "Acts 2:1-47," *Int* 33/1 (1979): 62-67.

0193   P. W. van der Horst, "Hellenistic Parallels to the Acts of the Apostles," *JSNT* 25 (1985): 49-60.

0194   Mikeal C. Parsons, "Christian Origins and Narrative Openings: The Sense of a Beginning in Acts 1-5," *RevExp* 87 (1990): 403-22.

2:1-42

0195   Gerhard Krodel, "The Holy Spirit, the Holy Catholic Church: Interpretation of Acts 2:1-42," *Dia* 23/2 (1984): 97-103.

2:1-41

0196   E. J. Christiansen, "Taufe als Initiation in der Apostelgeschichte," *StTh* 40/1 (1986): 55-79.

2:1-40

0197   C. H. Giblin, "Complementarity of Symbolic Event and Discourse in Acts 2:1-40," *TU* 112 (1973): 189-96.

0198   G. Jankowski, "Was sollen wir tun? Erwägungen über Apostelgeschichte 2,1-40," *TexteK* 8 (1980): 22-44.

2:1-24

0199   S. Hauerwas, "The Church as God's New Language," in Garrett Green, *Scriptural Authority and Narrative Interpretation* (festschrift for Hans W. Frei). Philadelphia: Fortress Press, 1987. Pp. 179-98.

2:1-21

0200   Warren E. Messmann, "Pentecost Sunday: Acts 2:1-21," *CTQ* 46 (1982): 52-53.

2:1-14

0201   P. van Bergen, "L'Epître de la Pentecôte," *PL* 44 (1961): 253-62.

2:1-13

0202   E. Samain, "Le récit de la Pentecôte, Act 2:1-13," *FT* N.S. (1971):
       227-56.

0203   Ingo Broer, "Der Geist und die Gemeinde: Zur Auslegung der
       lukanischen Pfingstgeschichte," *BibL* 13/4 (1972): 261-83.

0204   A. P. O'Hagan, "The First Christian Pentecost," *SBFLA* 23 (1973):
       50-66.

0205   E. Samain, "A Igreja, uma Communidade Libertadora e Criadora?
       Uma exegese de Atos 2,1-13," *REB* 35 (1975): 326-62.

0206   H. J. Tschiedel, "Ein Pfingstwunder im Apollonhymnos *(Hymn.
       Hom. Ap.* 156-64 und Apg. 2, 1-13)" *ZRGG* 27/1 (1975): 22-39.

0207   S. Sahagian, "Tonalités de la parole. 4—Temps de l'Église—
       Actes 2:1-13," *ÉTR* 58/3 (1983): 359-67.

0208   Otto Merk, "Die Apostelgeschichte im Frühwerk Rudolf
       Bultmanns," in Bernd Jaspert, ed., *Rudolf Bultmanns Werk und
       Wirkung.* Darmstadt, West Germany: Wissenschaftliche
       Buchgesellschaft, 1984. Pp. 303-15.

0209   José Antonio Jáuregui, "Pentecostes, Fiesta de Identidad
       Cristiana," *EE* 66 (1991): 369-96.

0210   P. M. Van Buren, "Acts 2:1-13: The Truth of an Unlikely Tale,"
       in P. Ochs, ed., *The Return to Scripture in Judaism and
       Christianity.* Mahwah NJ: Paulist Press, 1993. Pp. 295-307.

0211   M. Parmentier, "Das Zungenreden bei den Kirchenvätern," *Bij*
       55/4 (1994): 376-98.

0212   A. J. M. Wedderburn, "Traditions and Redaction in Acts 2:1-13,"
       JSNT 55 (1994): 27-54.

2:1-11

0213   William D. McHardy, "The Philoxenian Text of the Acts in the
       Cambridge Syriac MS Add. 2053," *JTS* 45 (1944): 175.

0214 R. K. Levang, "The Content of an Utterance in Tongues," *Para* 23 (1989): 14.

2:1-8

0215 James E. Carter, "The Tongues of Pentecost," *BI* 13/3 (1987): 29-31.

2:1-4

0216 R. A. Martin, "Syntactical Evidence of Aramaic Sources in Acts I-XV," *NTS* 11/1 (1964): 38-59.

0217 Gennadij Nefyodov, "On the Sacraments of the Church," *JMP* 7 (1983): 69-73.

2:1

0218 R. J. Hardy, "Three Papers on the Text of Acts: 1. The Reconstruction of the Torn Leaf of Codex Bezae; 2. And When the Day of Pentecost Was Fully Come; 3. The Greek Text of Codex Laudianus," *HTR* 16 (1923): 163-86.

0219 A. Salas, "Estaban 'todos' reunidos: Precisiones críticas sobre los 'testigos' de Pentecostés," *Salma* 28/1-2 (1981): 299-314.

0220 Timothy N. Boyd, "The Feast of Pentecost," *BI* 12/3 (1986): 70-73.

2:3

0221 S. P. Brock, "The Lost Old Syriac at Luke 1:35 and the Earliest Syriac Terms for the Incarnation," in William L. Petersen, *Gospel Traditions in the Second Century: Origins, Recensions, Text, and Transmission.* Notre Dame IN: University of Notre Dame Press, 1989. Pp 117-31.

2:4

0222 P. C. Bori, "Chiesa primitiva, Atti 2:4," *RTP* 110 (1978): 306.

0223 J. Everts, "Tongues or Languages? Contextual Consistency in the Translation of Acts 2," *JPTh* 4 (1994): 71-80.

2:5-11

0224 Florentino Díez Fernandez, "Crónica arqueológica," *EB* 42/3-4 (1984): 421-28.

2:6-8
 0225 George L. Lasebikan, "Glossolalia: Its Relationship with Speech
        Disabilities and Personality Disorders," *AfTJ* 14/2 (1985): 111-20.

2:6
 0226 Ralph E. Knudsen, "Speaking in Tongues," *Found* 9 (1966):
        43-57.

2:7-11
 0227 Werner Stenger, "Beobachtungen zur sogenannten Völkerliste des
        Pfingstwunders," *K* 21/2-3 (1979): 206-14.

2:9-11
 0228 J. A. Brinkman, "The Literary Background of the 'Catalogue of
        the Nations'," *CBQ* 25/3 (1963): 418-27.

 0229 E. Güting, "Der Geographische Horizont der Sogenannten
        Volkerliste des Lukas," *ZNW* 66/3 (1975): 149-69.

 0230 George D. Kilpatrick, "A Jewish Background to Acts 2:9-11," *JJS*
        26/1-2 (1975): 48-49.

 0231 Manfred Gorg, "Apg 2:9-11 in außerbiblischer Sicht," *BibN* 1
        (1976): 15-18.

2:10
 0232 C. J. Hemer, "Phrygia: A Further Note," *JTS* 28/1 (1977): 99-101.

2:13
 0233 Harold L. Wilmington, "The Filling of the Spirit," *FundJ* 2/10
        (1983): 52.

2:14-41
 0234 Daryl D. Schmidt, "The Historiography of Acts: Deuteronomistic
        or Hellenistic," *SBLSP* 24 (1985): 417-27.

2:14-40
 0235 John J. Kilgallen, "The Unity of Peter's Pentecost Speech," *BibTo*
        82 (1976): 650-56.

 0236 Lawrence Wills, "The Form of the Sermon in Hellenistic Judaism
        and Early Christianity," *HTR* 77/3-4 (1984): 277-99.

0237 Robert B. Sloan, "Signs and Wonders: a Rhetorical Clue to the Pentecost Discourse," *EQ* 63 (1991): 225-40.

2:14-36

0238 O. J. Lafferty, "Acts 2:14-36: A Study in Christology," *DunR* 6/2 (1966): 235-53.

0239 Otto Merk, "Die Apostelgeschichte im Frühwerk Rudolf Bultmanns," in Bernd Jaspert, ed., *Rudolf Bultmanns Werk und Wirkung*. Darmstadt, West Germany: Wissenschaftliche Buchgesellschaft, 1984. Pp. 303-15.

0240 Marion L. Soards, "Peter's Speech at Pentecost," in *The Speeches in Acts: Their Content, Context, and Concerns*. Louisville: John Knox/Westminster Press, 1994. Pp. 31-38.

2:14-21

0241 Yoshiaki Hatori, "Evangelism: The Bible's Primary Message," *ERT* 12 (1988): 5-16.

2:14

0242 C. M. Horne, "Toward a Biblical Apologetic," *GTJ* 2 (1961): 14-18.

0243 E. Rasco, "La gloire de la résurrection et ses fruits," *AsSeign* 24 (1969): 6-14.

0244 Richard I. Pervo, "Social and Religious Aspects of the Western Text," in Dennis Groh and Robert Jewett, eds., *The Living Text* (festschrift for Ernest Saunders). Lanham MD: University Press of America, 1985. Pp. 229-41.

0245 Edwina Hunter, "Preaching from Acts: Homiletical Resources for Easter," *QR* 7 (1987): 76-102.

0246 R. C. Tannehill, "Mission in the 1990s: Reflections on the Easter Lections from Acts," *QR* 10/1 (1990): 84-97.

2:15

0247 C. M. Horne, "Toward a Biblical Apologetic," *GTJ* 2 (1961): 14-18.

2:16-38
> **0248** Hans Hübner, "The Holy Spirit in Holy Scripture," *EcumR* 41 (1989): 324-38.

2:16-21
> **0249** Walter Kaiser, "The Promise of God and the Outpouring of the Holy Spirit," in Morris Inch and Ronald Youngblood, eds., *The Living and Active Word of God* (festschrift for Samuel J. Schultz). Winona Lake IN: Eisenbrauns, 1983. Pp. 109-22.

> **0250** Richard J. Dillon, "The Prophecy of Christ and His Witnesses According to the Discourses of Acts," *NTS* 32/4 (1986): 544-56.

2:17-22
> **0251** J. H. Petzer, "Variation in Citations from the Old Testament in the Latin Version of Acts," *JNSL* 19 (1993): 143-57.

2:17
> **0252** F. Mußner, "In den Letzten Tagen," *BZ* 5/2 (1961): 263-65.

> **0253** David W. Miller, "The Uniqueness of New Testament Church Eldership," *GTJ* 6/2 (1985): 315-27.

> **0254** Richard I. Pervo, "Social and Religious Aspects of the Western Text," in Dennis Groh and Robert Jewett, eds., *The Living Text* (festschrift for Ernest Saunders). Lanham MD: University Press of America, 1985. Pp. 229-41.

2:18
> **0255** Shirley Stephens, "Women in the New Testament Church," *BI* 9/2 (1983): 62-66.

> **0256** Peter R. Rodgers, "Acts 2:18: καὶ προφητεύσουσιν," *JTS* 38 (1987): 95-97.

2:20
> **0257** R. L. Mayhue, "The Apostle's Watchword: Day of the Lord," in Gary T. Meadors, ed., *New Testament Essays* (festschrift for Homer A. Kent). Winona Lake IN: BMH Bks, 1991. Pp. 239-63.

2:21

0258 W. C. Van Unnik, "With All Those Who Call on the Name of the Lord," in William C. Weinrich, ed., *The New Testament Age* (festschrift for Bo Reicke). 2 vols. Macon GA: Mercer University Press, 1984. 2:533-51.

0259 Darrell L. Bock, "Jesus as Lord in Acts and in the Gospel Message," *BSac* 143 (1986): 146-54.

2:22-36

0260 John H. Hayes, "The Resurrection as Enthronement and the Earliest Church Christology," *Int* 22/3 (1968): 333-45.

0261 Burton L. Mack, "The Innocent Transgressor: Jesus in Early Christian Myth and History," *Semeia* 33 (1985): 135-65.

0262 S. Wesley Ariarajah, "The Bible and People of Other Faiths," *Risk* 26 (1985): 1-71.

2:22-32

0263 Edwina Hunter, "Preaching from Acts: Homiletical Resources for Easter," *QR* 7/1 (1987): 76-102.

2:22-28

0264 E. Rasco, "La gloire de la résurrection et ses fruits," *AsSeign* 24 (1969): 6-14.

2:22-24

0265 Eric Gans, "Christian Morality and the Pauline Revelation," *Semeia* 33 (1985): 97-108.

0266 Bill Kellermann, "In the Boldness of the Spirit: Pentecost," *Soj* 14/5 (1985): 28-31.

2:22

0267 H. K. Moulton, "Acts 2:22: Jesus—A Man Approved by God?" *BT* 30 (1979): 344-45.

0268 Eduard Schweizer, "The Testimony to Jesus in the Early Christian Community," *HBT* 7/1 (1985): 77-98.

2:23

0269 Leslie· C. Allen, "The Old Testament Background of (προ)ώρισμένη in the New Testament," *NTS* 17/1 (1970-1971): 104-108.

2:24-27

0270 A.-M. La Bonnardière, "Evodius et Augustin," in Anne-Marie La Bonnardière, ed., *Saint Augustin et la Bible*. Paris: Editions Beauchesne, 1986. Pp. 213-27.

2:24

0271 Tibor Horvath, "Who Presided at the Eucharist: A Comment on BEM," *JES* 22 (1985): 604-607.

2:25-33

0272 W. C. Kaiser, "The Promise to David in Psalm 16 and its Application in Acts 2:25-33 and 13:32-37," *JETS* 23 (1980): 219-29.

2:25-28

0273 J. H. Petzer, "Variation in Citations from the Old Testament in the Latin Version of Acts," *JNSL* 19 (1993): 143-57.

2:28

0274 W. E. Moore, "One Baptism," *NTS* 10/4 (1964): 504-16.

0275 I. de la Potterie, "L'economia fede-sacramento nel nuovo testamento," in P.-R. Tragan, ed., *Fede e sacramenti negli scritti giovannei*. Rome: Edizioni Abbazia, 1972. Pp. 27-46.

2:30-37

0276 C. Gallazzi, "P. Mil. Vogl. Inv. 1224: Novum Testamentum, Act. 2,30-37 e 2,46-3,2," *BASP* 9/1-2 (1982): 39-45.

2:30

0277 J. A. Fitzmyer, "David, 'Being Therefore a Prophet . . . '," *CBQ* 34/3 (1972): 332-39.

0278 R. F. O'Toole, "Acts 2:30 and the Davidic Covenant of Pentecost," *JBL* 102/2 (1983): 245-58.

2:32-39

0279 Darrell L. Bock, "Jesus as Lord in Acts and in the Gospel Message," *BSac* 143 (1986): 146-54.

2:32-36
> **0280** Gérard Rochais, "Jésus savait-il qu'il était Dieu: réflexions critiques à propos d'un livre récent," *SR* 14/1 (1985): 85-106.

2:32
> **0281** Joseph Plevik, " 'The Eleven and Those with Them' According to Luke," *CBQ* 40/2 (1978): 205-11.

2:33-36
> **0282** G. Dautzenberg, "Psalm 110 im Neuen Testament," in Hans Becker and Reiner Kaczynski, eds., *Liturgie und Dichtung: Ein interdisziplinäres Kompendium. 1. Historische Präsentation.* Sankt Ottilien: EOS Verlag, 1983. Pp. 141-71.

> **0283** Peter Hocken, "The Meaning and Purpose of 'Baptism in the Spirit'," *Pneuma* 7/2 (1985): 125-33.

2:33
> **0284** Michel Gourgues, "Exalté à la droite de Dieu," *SE* 27 (1975): 303-27.

> **0285** Odette Mainville, "Jésus et l'Esprit dans l'œuvre de Luc: Éclairage à Partir d'Ac 2:33," *ScE* 42 (1990): 193-208.

> **0286** R. A. Johnson, "The Narrative Function of the Quotation of Isaiah 6:9-10 and the Concomitant Hear-See Motif in the Book of Acts," doctoral dissertation, Southwestern Baptist Theological Seminary, Fort Worth TX, 1992.

2:36-47
> **0287** Edwina Hunter, "Preaching from Acts: Homiletical Resources for Easter," *QR* 7 (1987): 76-102.

2:36-40
> **0288** Otto Glombitza, "Der Schluss der Petrusrede Acta 2:36-40. Ein Beitrag zum Problem der Predigten in Acta," *ZNW* 52/1-2 (1961): 115-18.

2:36
> **0289** Gerhard Voss, " 'Zum Herrn und Messias gemacht hat Gott diesen Jesus' (Apg 2,36). Zur Christologie der lukanischen Schriften," *BK* 8/4 (1967): 236-48.

0290 D. L. Balas, "The Meaning of the 'Cross'," in Andreas Spira and Christoph Klock, eds., *The Easter Sermons of Gregory of Nyssa.* Cambridge, Massachusetts: Philadelphia Patristic Foundation, 1981. Pp. 305-18.

0291 Luis F. Landaria, "Eucaristía y escatología," *EE* 59/229 (1984): 211-16.

0292 Elmer L. Towns, "The Ascension," *FundJ* 3/6 (1984): 12-14.

0293 Donald W. McCullough, "If Jesus Is Lord, Why Does It Hurt?" *RJ* 35/7 (1985): 11-14.

0294 R. Fowler White, "The Last Adam and His Seed: An Exercise in Theological Preemption," *TriJ* 6 (1985): 60-73.

2:37

0295 Richard I. Pervo, "Social and Religious Aspects of the Western Text," in Dennis Groh and Robert Jewett, eds., *The Living Text* (festschrift for Ernest Saunders). Lanham MD: University Press of America, 1985. Pp. 229-41.

2:38-40

0296 Marion L. Soards, "Peter's Speech at Pentecost," in *The Speeches in Acts: Their Content, Context, and Concerns.* Louisville: John Knox/Westminster Press, 1994. Pp. 31-38.

2:38-39

0297 D. Mínguez, "Estructura dinámica de la conversión. Reflexión sobre Hch 2,38-39," *EE* 54/210 (1979): 383-94.

2:38

0298 R. L. Roberts, "Notes on Selected Passages," *RQ* 4 (1960): 234-58.

0299 J. C. Davis, "Another Look at the Relationship between Baptism and Forgiveness of Sins in Acts 2:38," *RQ* 24/2 (1981): 80-88.

0300 C. D. Osburn, "The Third Person Imperative in Acts 2:38," *RQ* 26/2 (1983): 81-84.

0301 Gennadij Nefyodov, "The Sacrament of Chrismation," *JMP* 7 (1984): 79-80.

0302 Lars Hartman, "La formule baptismale dans les Actes des Apôtres: quelques observations relatives au style de Luc," in François Refoulé, ed., *À cause de l'Évangile: Études sur les synoptiques et les Actes* (festschrift for Jacques Dupont). Paris: Cerf, 1985. Pp. 727-38.

0303 Gerard S. Sloyan, "Jewish Ritual of the 1st Century CE and Christian Sacramental Behavior," *BTB* 15 (1985): 98-103.

0304 L. T. Tanton, "The Gospel and Water Baptism: A Study of Acts 2:38," *JGES* 3/1 (1990): 27-52.

2:40-3:5
0305 Herbert Thompson, *Koptische Pergamente theologischen Inhalts, 1* "Mitteilungen aus der Papyrussammlung der Nationalbibliothek in Wien," N.S., 2. Folge. Vienna: Staatsdruckerei, 1934.

2:41-4:35
0306 I. Z. Herman, "Un tentativo di analisi strutturale di *Atti* 2,41-4,35 secundo il metodo di A. J. Greimas," *Ant* 56/2-3 (1981): 467-74.

2:41-47
0307 Morris Inch, "Manifestation of the Spirit," in Morris A. Inch and Ronald F. Youngblood, eds., *The Living and Active Word of God* (festschrift for Samuel J. Schultz). Winona Lake IN: Eisenbrauns, 1983. Pp. 149-55.

0308 John E. Alsup, "Prayer, Consciousness, and the Early Church: A Look at Acts 2:41-47 for Today," *ASB* 101 (1985): 31-37.

0309 J. Rius-Camps, "Els tres sumaris dels fets dels apòstols," *RCT* 14 (1989): 243-56.

0310 G. E. Sterling, " 'Athletes of Virtue': An Analysis of the Summaries in Acts," *JBL* 113/4 (1994): 679-96.

2:41-44
0311 Ralph W. Marks, "Capturing the Awesome Power of the First Church," *FundJ* 4/3 (1985): 30-31.

2:41
0312 Gennadij Nefyodov, "The Sacrament of Chrismation," *JMP* 7 (1984): 79-80.

2:42-47

0313   Heinrich Zimmermann, "Die Sammelberichte der Apostel-
       geschichte," *BZ* 5/1 (1961): 71-82.

0314   F. Schnider, "Wie wird eine Gemeinde missionarisch:
       Uberlegungen zu Apg 2,42-47," in in Walter Friedberger and Franz
       Schnider, eds., *Theologie—Gemeinde—Seelsorger.* Munich:
       Kösel-Verlag, 1979. Pp. 118-25.

0315   Edgar Haulette, "La vie en communion, phase ultime de al
       Pentecôte, Actes 2,42-47," *FV* 80/1 (1981): 69-75.

0316   J. Lach, "Katechese über die Kirche von Jerusalem in der
       Apostelgeschichte," *CollT* 52 (Supplement) (1982): 141-53.

0317   Glenn Olsen, "The Image of the First Community of Christians at
       Jerusalem in the Time of Lanfranc and Anselm," in Raymonde
       Foreville, ed., *Les mutations socio-Culturelles au tournant des
       XIue-XIIue siècles.* Paris: Centre National de la Recherche
       Scientifique, 1984. Pp. 341-53.

0318   Joseph Allen, "Renewal of the Christian Community: A Challenge
       for the Pastoral Ministry," *SVTQ* 29/4 (1985): 305-23.

0319   Clara Burini, "La 'comunione di cuori e di spirito' (Atti 2; 4) nella
       testimonianza di Cipriano," in Maria Angelini, et al., eds.,
       Testimonium Christi. Brescia: Paideia Editrice, 1985. Pp. 91-109.

0320   Agustín del Agua Perez, "El papel de la 'escuela midrásica' en la
       configuración del Nuevo Testamento," *EE* 60/234 (1985): 333-49.

0321   Robrecht Michaels, "The 'Model of Church' in the First Christian
       Community of Jerusalem: Ideal and Reality," *LouvS* 10/4 (1985):
       303-23.

0322   S. J. Joubert, "Die Gesigpunt van die Verteller en die Funksie van
       die Jerusalemgemeente Binne die: 'Opsommings' in Handelinge,"
       SkrifK 10/1 (1989): 21-35.

0323   Gary L. Carver, "Acts 2:42-47," *RevExp* 87 (1990): 475-80.

0324 M. A. Co, "The Major Summaries in Acts: Acts 2:42-47; 4:32-35; 5:12-16: Linguistic and Literary Relationships," *ETL* 68/1 (1992): 49-85.

2:42-46

0325 Bernard P. Robinson, "The Place of the Emmaus Story in Luke-Acts," *NTS* 30/4 (1984): 481-97.

2:42

0326 R. Orlett, "The Breaking of Bread in Acts," *BibTo* 1/2 (1962): 108-13.

0327 E. Glenn Hinson, "Worship in the First Century Church," *BI* 1/2 (1975): 34-41.

0328 M. Manzanera, "Koinonia en Hch 2,42. Notas sobre su interpretación y origen historico-doctrinal," *EE* 52/202 (1977): 307-29.

0329 Leopold Sabourin, "Koinonia in the New Testament," *RSB* 1/4 (1981): 109-15.

0330 B. Buby, "Mary, a Model of Ecclesia Orans, in Acts 1:14," Theodore A. Koehler, ed., *Marian Studies*. Vol. 35. Dayton OH: Mariological Society of America, 1984. Pp. 87-99.

0331 J. Timothy Coyle, "The Agape—Eucharist Relationship in 1 Corinthians 11," *GTJ* 6/2 (1985): 411-24.

0332 Donald Farmer, "The Lord's Supper Until He Comes," *GTJ* 6/2 (1985): 391-401.

0333 Paul D. Fueter, "The Therapeutic Language of the Bible," *IRM* 75 (1986): 211-21.

2:43-47

0334 D. B. McGee, "Sharing Possessions: A Study in Biblical Ethics," in Naymond Keathley, ed., *With Steadfast Purpose* (festschrift for Jack Flanders). Waco TX: Baylor University Press, 1990. Pp. 163-78.

2:44-47
> **0335** A. C. Michell, "The Social Function of Friendship in Acts 2:44-47 and 4:32-37," *JBL* 111 (1992): 255-72.

2:44-45
> **0336** S. Aalen, "Versuch einer Analyse des Diakonia-Begriffes im Neuen Testament," in William Weinrich, ed., *The New Testament Age* (festschrift for Bo Reicke). 2 vols. Macon GA: Mercer University Press, 1984. 1:1-13.

> **0337** J. L. Stotts, "By What Authority...? (Matthew 21:23): An Unscholarly Foray into Acts 2:44-45; 4:32-35," in Robert L. Stivers, ed., *Reformed Faith and Economics*. Lanham MD: University Press of America, 1989. Pp 3-13.

2:46-3:2
> **0338** C. Gallazzi, "P. Mil. Vogl. Inv. 1224: Novum Testamentum, Act. 2,30-37 e 2,46-3,2," *BASP* 9/1-2 (1982): 39-45.

2:46-47
> **0339** David Music, "The Earliest Christian Music," *BI* 9/2 (1983): 84-85.

> **0340** Tibor Horvath, "Who Presided at the Eucharist: A Comment on BEM," *JES* 22 (1985): 604-607.

2:46
> **0341** R. Orlett, "The Breaking of Bread in Acts," *BibTo* 1/2 (1962): 108-13.

> **0342** E. Dassmann, "Hausgemeinde und Bischofsamt," in Ernst Dassmann and Klaus Thraede, eds., *Vivarium* (festschrift for Theodor Klauser). Münster, West Germany: Aschendorff, 1984. Pp. 82-97.

> **0343** John T. Pless, "Implications of Recent Exegetical Studies for the Doctrine of the Lord's Supper: A Survey of the Literature," *CTQ* 48/2-3 (1984): 203-20.

> **0344** J. Timothy Coyle, "The Agape—Eucharist Relationship in 1 Corinthians 11," *GTJ* 6/2 (1985): 411-24.

> **0345** Donald Farmer, "The Lord's Supper Until He Comes," *GTJ* 6/2 (1985): 391-401.

0346David W. Miller, "The Uniqueness of New Testament Church Eldership," *GTJ* 6/2 (1985): 315-27.

2:47

0347R. L. Roberts, "Notes on Selected Passages," *RQ* 4 (1960): 234-58.

0348Frederic P. Cheetham, "Acts 2:47: ἔχοντες χάριν πρὸς ὅλον τὸν λαόν," *ET* 74 (1963-1964): 214-15.

0349É. Delebecque, "Trois simples mots, chargés d'une lumière neuve," *RT* 80/1 (1980): 75-85.

0350G. G. Gamba, "Significato letterale e portate dottrinale dell'inciso participiale di Atti 2,47b: ἔχοντες χάριν πρὸς ὅλον τὸν λαόν," Salm 43/1 (1981): 45-70.

0351T. David Anderson, "The Meaning of ἔχοντες χάριν πρὸς in Acts 2:47," *NTS* 34/4 (1988): 604-10.

3:1-4:31

0352Mikeal C. Parsons, "Christian Origins and Narrative Openings: The Sense of a Beginning in Acts 1-5," *RevExp* 87 (1990): 403-22.

3-5

0353L. Panier, "Pour lire les Actes des Apôtres. 2e partie: les chapitres 3-5," *SémBib* 29 (1983): 11-18.

3-4

0354W. R. Snell, "Jesus, the Servant of God: The Origin and Evolution of the Concept as Found in Acts 3-4," master's thesis, Southern Baptist Theological Seminary, Louisville KY, 1957.

0355Gabriel Fackre, "An Acts Theology of Evangelism," *RL* 44/1 (1975): 73-89.

0356P. W. van der Horst, "Hellenistic Parallels to Acts," *JSNT* 35 (1989): 37-46.

0357Randall C. Webber, " 'Why Were the Heathen So Arrogant?' The Socio-Rhetorical Strategy of Acts 3-4," *BTB* 22/1 (1992): 19-25.

3

0358   F. Gryglewicz, "Die Herkunft der Hymnen des Kindheits-evangeliums des Lucas," *NTS* 21/2 (1975): 265-73.

0359   C. K. Barrett, "Faith and Eschatology in Acts 3," in E. Grässer and O. Merk, eds., *Glaube und Eschatologie* (festschrift for W. G. Kümmel). Tübingen: Mohr, 1985. Pp. 1-17.

0360   M. C. Hilkert, "Naming Grace: A Theology of Proclamation," *Worship* 60/5 (1986): 434-49.

0361   J. Taylor, "The Making of Acts: A New Account," *RB* 97 (1990): 504-24.

0362   Donald H. Juel, "Hearing Peter's Speech in Acts 3: Meaning and Truth in Interpretation," *WW* 12 (1992): 43-50.

3:1-21

0363   Herbert Thompson, *Koptische Pergamente theologischen Inhalts, 1* "Mitteilungen aus der Papyrussammlung der Nationalbibliothek in Wien," N.S., 2. Folge. Vienna: Staatsdruckerei, 1934.

3:1-11

0364   Danielle Ellul, "Actes 3:1-11," *ÉTR* 64/1 (1989): 95-99.

0365   S. Sabugal, "La curación del 'cojo de nacimiento' por Pedro: Análisis histórico-tradicional," *RevAug* 32 (1991): 595-613.

3:1-10

0366   R. Filippini, "Atti 3,1-10: Proposta di analisi del racconto," *RBib* 28/3 (1980): 305-17.

0367   D. Hamm, "Acts 3:1-10: The Healing of the Temple Beggar as Lucan Theology," *Bib* 67/3 (1986): 305-19.

0368   Stanley J. Samartha, "Religion, Culture and Power—Three Bible Studies," *RS* 34 (1987): 66-79.

0369   Paul W. Walaskay, "Acts 3:1-10," *Int* 42/2 (1988): 171-75.

0370 G. Marconi, "History as a Hermeneutical Interpretation of the Difference between Acts 3:1-10 and 4:8-12," in Gerald O'Collins and G. Marconi, eds., *Luke and Acts* (festschrift in for Emilio Rasco). Mahwah NJ: Paulist Press, 1993. Pp. 167-80.

3:1

0371 Agustín del Agua Perez, "La sinagoga: origenes, ciclos de lectura y oración: estado de la cuestión," *EB* N.S. 41/3-4 (1983): 341-66.

0372 J. G. M. Willebrands, "Is Christianity Antisemitic?" *ChJR* 18/2 (1985): 8-20.

3:12-26

0373 C. H. H. Scobie, "The Use of Source Material in the Speeches of Acts III and VII," *NTS* 25/4 (1978-1979): 399-421.

0374 D. Hamm, "Acts 3:12-26: Peter's Speech and the Healing of the Man Born Lame," *PRS* 11/3 (1984): 199-217.

0375 Lawrence Wills, "The Form of the Sermon in Hellenistic Judaism and Early Christianity," *HTR* 77/3-4 (1984): 277-99.

3:12-23

0376 E. S. Buchanan, "Two Pages from the Fleury Palimpsest with Some Newly Discovered Readings," *JTS* 7 (1905-1906): 454-55.

3:12-16

0377 Marion L. Soards, "Peter's Speech in Solomon's Portico of the Temple," in *The Speeches in Acts: Their Content, Context, and Concerns*. Louisville: John Knox/Westminster Press, 1994. Pp. 38-44.

3:12

0378 H. J. Klauck, "With Paul in Paphos and Lystra: Magic and Paganism in the Acts of the Apostles," *Neo* 28 (1994): 93-108.

3:13-15

0379 E. Rasco, "La gloire de la résurrection et ses fruits," *AsSeign* 24 (1969): 6-14.

0380 P. Smulders, "Some Riddles in the Apostles Creed II. Creeds and Rules of Faith," *Bij* 32/4 (1971): 350-66.

0381 R. B. Hays, "The Righteous One as Eschatological Deliverer: A Case Study in Paul's Apocalyptic Hermeneutics," in Joel Marcus and Marion Soards, eds., *Apocalyptic and the New Testament* (festschrift for J. Louis Martyn). Sheffield: JSOT Press, 1989. Pp 191-215.

3:14

0382 George D. Kilpatrick, "Three Problems of New Testament Text," *NovT* 21/4 (1979): 289-92.

0383 Billy E. Simmons, "Christ the Holy One," *BI* 14/2 (1989): 23.

0384 Billy E. Simmons, "Christ the Just," *BI* 14/2 (1989): 39.

3:15

0385 T. Ballarini, "ARCHEGOS (Atti 3:15, 5:31; Ebr. 2:10, 12:2) autore o condottiero?" *SacD* 16/63-64 (1971): 535-51.

0386 Joseph Plevik, " 'The Eleven and Those with Them' According to Luke," *CBQ* 40/2 (1978): 205-11.

0387 I. de la Potterie, "Gesu il capo che conduce alla vita," *ParSpirV* 5 (1982): 107-26.

0388 Billy E. Simmons, "Christ the Prince of Life," *BI* 14/2 (1989): 80.

3:17-19

0389 E. Rasco, "La gloire de la résurrection et ses fruits," *AsSeign* 24 (1969): 6-14.

3:17

0390 Eldon J. Epp, "The 'Ignorance Motif' in Acts and Anti-Judaic Tendencies in Codex Bezae," *HTR* 55 (1962): 51-62.

0391 C. E. Freire, " 'Kata Agnoian' (Hch 3,17). ¿Disculpa o acusación?" *Communio* 9/2-3 (1976): 221-31.

3:18

0392 P.-R. Berger, "Kollyrium fur die Blinden Augen, Apk 3:18," *NovT* 27/2 (1985): 174-95.

0393 Erich Lubahn, "Wer ist schuld am Kreuzestode Jesu: Eine Auslegung von Apg 4,27f; 3,18," in Heinz Kremers and Erich Lubahn, eds., *Mission an Israel in heilsgeschichtlicher Sicht* Neukirchen-Vluyn: Neukirchener Verlag, 1985. Pp. 12-23.

3:19-4:17

0394 Herbert Thompson, *Koptische Pergamente theologischen Inhalts, 1* "Mitteilungen aus der Papyrussammlung der Nationalbibliothek in Wien," N.S., 2. Folge. Vienna: Staatsdruckerei, 1934.

3:19-26

0395 J. Carrón Pérez, *Jesus el Mesias manifest ado. Tradition literaria y trasfondo judio de Hch 3,19-26.* Studia Semitica Novi Testamenti #2. Madrid, Ciudad Nueva—Fundación San Justino, 1993.

3:19-21

0396 Gerhard Lohfink, "Christologie und Geschichtsbild in Apg 3:19-21," *BZ* 13/2 (1969): 223-41.

0397 Joseph G. Kelly, "Lucan Christology and the Jewish-Christian Dialogue," *JES* 21 (1984): 688-708.

0398 Klaus Haacker, "Das Bekenntnis des Paulus zur Hoffnung Israels Nach der Apostelgeschichte des Lukas," *NTS* 31 (1985): 437-51.

0399 Rudolf Schnackenburg, "Die lukanische Eschatologie im Lichte von Aussagen der Apostelgeschichte," in E. Grässer and O. Merk, eds., *Glaube und Eschatologie* (festschrift for W. G. Kümmel). Tübingen: Mohr, 1985. Pp. 249-65.

3:19

0400 P. Ternant, "Repentez-vous et convertissez-vous," *AsSeign* 21 (1963): 50-79.

0401 Beatriz Casiello, "Caminos de Conversion," *Did* 23/5 (1969): 314-24.

3:20

0402 Otto Bauernfeind, "Tradition und Komposition in dem Apokatastasisspruch Apg 3,20f," *AuV* (1963): 13-23.

0403 G. Ferraro, "*Kairoi anapsyxeōs*. Annotazioni su Atti 3:20," *RBib* 23/1 (1975): 67-78.

3:21

0404 Robert Macina, "Jean le Baptiste était-il Elie: examen de la tradition néotestamentaire," *POC* 34/3-4 (1984): 209-32.

0405 Elmer L. Towns, "The Ascension," *FundJ* 3/6 (1984): 12-14.

0406 Mark W. Karlberg, "Legitimate Discontinuities between the Testaments," *JETS* 28 (1985): 9-20.

0407 J. Carrón Pérez, "El significado de ἀποκαταστάσεως en Hch 3,21," *EB* 50 (1992): 375-94.

3:22-26

0408 Jacques Schlosser, "Moïse, Serviteur du Kérygme Apostolique d'après Ac 3:22-26," *RevSR* 61 (1987): 17-31.

3:22-23

0409 Jan de Waard, "Quotation from Deuteronomy in Acts 3:22-23 and the Palestinian Text: Additional Arguments," *Bib* 52/4 (1971): 537-40.

3:22

0410 J. M. Schubert, "The Image of Jesus as the Prophet like Moses in Luke-Acts as Advanced by Luke's Reinterpretation of Deuteronomy 18:15-18 in Acts 3:22 and 7:37," doctoral dissertation, Fordham University, New York, 1992.

3:23

0411 C. M. Martini, "L'esclusione dalla comunità del popolo di Dio e il nuovo Israele secondo Atti 3,23," *Bib* 50/1 (1969): 1-14.

3:25

0412 T. E. Brawley, "For Blessing All Families of the Earth: Covenant Traditions in Luke-Acts," *CThM* 22/1 (1995): 18-26.

4-6

0413 W.-D. Hauschild, "Die Confessio Augustana und die Altkirchliche Tradition," *KD* 26/3 (1980): 142-63.

4

0414 A. S. Wood, "Social Involvement in the Apostolic Church," *EQ* 42/4 (1970): 194-212.

0415 F. G. Downing, "Common Ground with Paganism in Luke and Josephus," *NTS* 28/4 (1982): 546-59.

0416 Kevin N. Giles, "Present-Future Eschatology in the Book of Acts (II)," *RTR* 41/1 (1982): 11-18.

4:1-31

0417 Marco Adinolfi, " 'Obbedire a Dio piuttosto che algi uomni.' La comunità cristiana e il sinedrio in Atti 4,1-31; 5,17-42," *RBib* 27/1-2 (1979): 69-93.

4:1-2

0418 R. F. O'Toole, "Christ's Resurrection in Acts 13:13-52," *Bib* 60/3 (1979): 361-72.

4:2

0419 Rudolf Schnackenburg, "Die lukanische Eschatologie im Lichte von Aussagen der Apostelgeschichte," in E. Grässer and O. Merk, eds., *Glaube und Eschatologie* (festschrift for W. G. Kümmel). Tübingen: Mohr, 1985. Pp. 249-65.

4:4

0420 J. A. Jáuregui, "Israel y la iglesia en la teologia de Lucas," *EE* 61 (1986): 129-149.

4:5-20

0421 I. W. Foulkes, "Two Semantic Problems in the Translation of Acts 4:5-20," *BT* 29/1 (1978): 121-25.

4:5-12

0422 R. A. Martin, "Syntactical Evidence of Aramaic Sources in Acts I-XV," *NTS* 11/1 (1964): 38-59.

0423 Stanley J. Samartha, "Religion, Culture and Power—Three Bible Studies," *RS* 34 (1987): 66-79.

4:5

0424 Werner Bieder, "Das Volk Gottes in Erwartung von Licht und Lobpreis," *TZ* 40/2 (1984): 137-48.

4:6

0425 E. P. Sanders, "Judaism and the Grand "Christian" Abstractions: Love, Mercy, and Grace," *Int* 39 (1985): 357-372.

0426   David Flusser, "The Ossuary of Yehohanah Granddaughter of the High Priest Theophilus," *IEJ* J 36/1 (1986): 39-44.

4:8-12

0427   M. Coune, "Sauves au nom de Jesus," *AsSeign* 12 (1964): 14-27.

0428   Irenée Fransen, "Par le nom de Jésus Christ le Nazaréen. Acts 4,8-12," *BibVie* 59 (1964): 38-44.

0429   C. K. Barrett, "Salvation Proclaimed. XII. ACTS 4:8-12," *ET* 94/3 (1982): 68-71.

0430   G. Marconi, "History as a Hermeneutical Interpretation of the Difference between Acts 3:1-10 and 4:8-12," in Gerald O'Collins and G. Marconi, eds., *Luke and Acts* (festschrift for Emilio Rasco). Mahwah NJ: Paulist Press, 1993. Pp. 167-80.

0431   Marion L. Soards, "Peter's Speech to the Jewish Authorities after His and John's Arrest," in *The Speeches in Acts: Their Content, Context, and Concerns*. Louisville: John Knox/Westminster Press, 1994. Pp. 44-47.

4:10

0432   L. Schenke, "Die Kontrast-Formel Apg 4:10b," *BZ* 26/1 (1982): 1-20.

4:11-12

0433   S. Wesley Ariarajah, "The Bible and People of Other Faiths," *Risk* 26 (1985): 1-71.

4:11

0434   U. Maiburg, "Christus der Eckstein: Ps 118:22 und Jes 28:16 im Neuen Testament und bei den lateinischen Vätern," in Ernst Dassmann and Klaus Thraede, eds., *Vivarium* (festschrift for Theodor Klauser). Münster: Aschendorff, 1984. Pp. 247-56.

0435   Wayne Grudem, "Does κεφαλη ('Head') Mean 'Source' or 'Authority Over' in Greek Literature: A Survey of 2,336 Examples," *TriJ* 6 (1985): 38-59.

4:12

0436   A. R. Gualtieri, "Confessional Theology in the Context of the History of Religions," *SR* 1/4 (1971): 347-60.

0437 Troy Organ, "A Cosmomogical Christology," *CC* 88/44 (1971): 1293-95.

0438 Magne Saebo, " 'Kein Anderer Name'," *KD* 22/3 (1976): 181-90.

0439 R. Y. K. Fung, "Charismatic Versus Organized Ministry? An Examination of an Alleged Antithesis," *EQ* 52/4 (1980): 195-214.

0440 Tokunboh Adeyemo, "The Salvation Debate and Evangelical Response: Pt. 2," *EAJT* 2/2 (1983): 4-19.

0441 Allan A. Boesak, "In the Name of Jesus: Acts 4:12," *JTSA* 52 (1985): 49-55.

0442 Julia Ching, "No Other Name," *JJRS* 12 (1985): 253-62.

0443 Malcolm J. McVeigh, "The Fate of Those Who've Never Heard: It Depends," *EMQ* 21/4 (1985): 370-379.

0444 Jaroslav J. Pelikan, "The Man Who Belongs to the World," *CC* 102 (1985): 827-31.

0445 Wolfgang Beinert, "Jesus Christus: das Ursakrament Gottes," *Catholica* 38/4 (1984): 340-351.

0446 Clark H. Pinnock, "Acts 4:12: No Other Name Under Heaven," in William Crockett, et al., eds., *Through No Fault of Their Own: The Fate of Those Who Never Heard.* Grand Rapids, MI: Baker, 1991. Pp. 107-15.

0447 Hugo H. Culpepper, "Acts 4:12: Religious Pluralism, Missions Theology," *RevExp* 89 (1992): 85-87.

4:13

0448 P. G. R. de Villiers, "The Medium is the Message: Luke and the Language of the New Testament against a Greco-Roman Background," *Neo* 24 (1990): 247-56.

4:17

0449 R. Y. K. Fung, "Charismatic Versus Organized Ministry? An Examination of an Alleged Antithesis," *EQ* 52/4 (1980): 195-214.

4:19-20

0450 Marion L. Soards, "Peter's Speech to the Jewish Authorities after His and John's Arrest," in *The Speeches in Acts: Their Content, Context, and Concerns*. Louisville: John Knox/Westminster Press, 1994. Pp. 44-47.

4:20

0451 Edwin D. Freed, "Samaritan Influence in the Gospel of John," *CBQ* 30/4 (1968): 580-87.

4:23-31

0452 R. A. Martin, "Syntactical Evidence of Aramaic Sources in Acts I-XV," *NTS* 11/1 (1964): 38-59.

0453 Raymond Schwager, "Christ's Death and the Prophetic Critique of Sacrifice," trans. P. Riordan *Semeia* 33 (1985): 109-23.

0454 Beverly R. Gaventa, "To Speak Thy Word with All Boldness Acts 4:23-31," *FM* 3/2 (1986): 76-82.

0455 A. F. Danter, "Acts 4:23-31: A Model for Enduring Persecution," doctoral dissertation, St. Louis University, St. Louis MO, 1989.

4:24-30

0456 Bruno Corsani, "Ascolto della parola e vita cristiana nell'opera di Luca," in M. Angelini, et al., eds., *Testimonium Christi* (festschrift for Jacques Dupont). Brescia: Paideia, 1985. Pp. 141-49.

0457 Marion L. Soards, "The Prayer of the Apostles and Their Friends," in *The Speeches in Acts: Their Content, Context, and Concerns*. Louisville: John Knox/Westminster Press, 1994. Pp. 47-50.

4:25-27

0458 George D. Kilpatrick, "*Laoi* at Luke ii. 31 and Acts iv. 25, 27," *JTS* 16 (1965): 127.

0459 Marion L. Soards, "Tradition, Composition, and Theology in Luke's Account of Jesus before Herod Antipas," *Bib* 66 (1985): 344-364.

4:25

0460 George D. Kilpatrick, "*Laoi* at Luke ii.31 and Acts iv.25, 27," *JTS* 16 (1965): 127.

0461 Leslie C. Allen, "The Old Testament Background of (προ)ὡρισμένη in the New Testament," *NTS* 17/1 (1970-1971): 104-108.

0462 L. V. Le Roux, "Style and the Text of Acts 4:25(a)," *Neo* 26 (1991): 29-32.

4:27-28

0463 Charles De Santo, "God and Gog," *RL* 30 (1961): 112-17.

4:27

0464 George D. Kilpatrick, "*Laoi* at Luke ii.31 and Acts iv.25, 27," *JTS* 16 (1965): 127.

0465 Erich Lubahn, "Wer ist schuld am Kreuzestode Jesu: Eine Auslegung von Apg 4,27f; 3,18," in Heinz Kremers and Erich Lubahn, eds., *Mission an Israel in heilsgeschichtlicher Sicht* Neukirchen-Vluyn: Neukirchener Verlag, 1985. Pp. 12-23.

4:28

0466 J. Kenneth Grider, "Predestination as Temporal Only," *WesTJ* 22 (1987): 56-64.

4:30

0467 James L. Travis, "Temple Personnel," *BI* 13/3 (1987): 36-39.

4:31-5:11

0468 A. Mettayer, "Ambiguïté et terrorisms du sacré: Analyse d'un texte des Actes des Apôtres," *SR* 714 (1978): 415-24.

4:31-35

0469 Johannes J. Degenhardt, "Die ersten Christen und der irdische Besitz," in Johannes J. Degenhardt, ed., *Die Freude an Gott: Unsere Kraft* (festschrift for Otto B. Knoch). Stuttgart: Verlag Katholisches Bibelwerk, 1991. Pp. 150-56.

4:32-5:42

0470 Mikeal C. Parsons, "Christian Origins and Narrative Openings: The Sense of a Beginning in Acts 1-5," *RevExp* 87 (1990): 403-22.

4:32-5:16
    0471 J. Rius-Camps, "Els tres sumaris dels fets dels apòstols," *RCT* 14 (1989): 243-56.

4:32-5:11
    0472 A.-E. Combet-Galland, "Actes 4:32-5:11," *ÉTR* 52/4 (1977): 548-53.

4:32-37
    0473 Ben Johnson, "The Question of Property in the New Testament," in Béla Harmati, ed., *Christian Ethics and the Question of Property*. Geneva: Lutheran World Federation, 1982. Pp. 50-58.

    0474 S. Aalen, "Versuch einer Analyse des Diakonia-Begriffes im Neuen Testament," in William Weinrich, ed., *The New Testament Age* (festschrift for Bo Reicke). 2 vols. Macon GA: Mercer University Press, 1984. 1:1-13.

    0475 Glenn Olsen, "The Image of the First Community of Christians at Jerusalem in the Time of Lanfranc and Anselm," in Raymonde Foreville, ed., *Les mutations socio-Culturelles au tournant des XIue-XIIue siècles*. Paris: Centre National de la Recherche Scientifique, 1984. Pp. 341-53.

    0476 Y. B. Kim, "Justice, Participation and Peace," in Chris Tremewan, ed. *Out of Control*. Singapore: Christian Conference of Asia Youth, 1985. Pp. 122-32.

    0477 John Weborg, "Giving the Soul Wings," *ChrM* 16/1 (1985): 28.

    0478 D. B. McGee, "Sharing Possessions: A Study in Biblical Ethics," in Naymond Keathley, ed., *With Steadfast Purpose* (festschrift for Jack Flanders). Waco TX: Baylor University Press, 1990. Pp. 163-78.

    0479 A. C. Michell, "The Social Function of Friendship in Acts 2:44-47 and 4:32-37," *JBL* 111 (1992): 255-72.

4:32-35
    0480 J. Lach, "Katechese über die Kirche von Jerusalem in der Apostelgeschichte," *CollT* 52 (Supplement) (1982): 141-53.

0481 Clara Burini, "La 'comunione di cuori e di spirito' (Atti 2; 4) nella testimonianza di Cipriano," in Maria Angelini, et al., eds., *Testimonium Christi*. Brescia: Paideia Editrice, 1985. Pp. 91-109.

0482 Agustín del Agua Perez, "El papel de la 'escuela midrásica' en la configuración del Nuevo Testamento," *EE* 60/234 (1985): 333-49.

0483 Richard Fraser, "Office of Deacon," *Pres* 11/1 (1985): 13-19.

0484 Robrecht Michaels, "The 'Model of Church' in the First Christian Community of Jerusalem: Ideal and Reality," *LouvS* 10/4 (1985): 303-23.

0485 Dorothee Sölle, "Church: They Had Everything In Common," *TT* 42 (1985): 215-19.

0486 Mark K. Taylor, "The Community of the Resurrected Christ," *PSB* 6/3 (1985): 228-30.

0487 J. L. Stotts, "By What Authority...? (Matthew 21:23): An Unscholarly Foray into Acts 2:44-45; 4:32-35," in Robert L. Stivers, ed., *Reformed Faith and Economics*. Lanham MD: University Press of America, 1989. Pp 3-13.

0488 M. A. Co, "The Major Summaries in Acts: Acts 2:42-47; 4:32-35; 5:12-16: Linguistic and Literary Relationships," *ETL* 68/1 (1992): 49-85.

0489 G. E. Sterling, " 'Athletes of Virtue': An Analysis of the Summaries in Acts," *JBL* 113/4 (1994): 679-96.

4:32

0490 Josef Sudbrack, "Die Schar der Gläubigen war ein Herz und eine Seele," *GeistL* 38/3 (1965): 161-68.

0491 Birger Gerhardsson, "Einige Bemerkungen zu Apg 4,32," *StTheol* 24/2 (1970): 142-49

0492 Birger Gerhardsson, "Några anmärkningar till Apg 4:32," *SEÅ* 35 (1971): 96-103.

0493 David L. Mealand, "Community of Goods at Qumran," *TZ* 31 (1975): 129-39.

0494   S. S. Bartchy, "Community of Goods in Acts: Idealization or Social Reality," in B. A. Pearson, ed., *The Future of Early Christianity* (festschrift for Helmut Koester). Minneapolis MN: Fortress Press, 1991. Pp. 309-18.

0495   Glenn W. Olsen, "One Heart and One Soul (Acts 4:32 and 34) in Dhuoda's 'Manual'," *ChH* 61 (1992): 23-33.

<u>4:33</u>

496   Joseph Plevik, " 'The Eleven and Those with Them' According to Luke," *CBQ* 40/2 (1978): 205-11.

<u>4:34</u>

0497   Glenn W. Olsen, "One Heart and One Soul (Acts 4:32 and 34) in Dhuoda's 'Manual'," *ChH* 61 (1992): 23-33.

<u>4:35</u>

0498   S. Légasse, "L' 'Homme Fort' de Luc XI 21-22," *NovT* 5 (1962): 5-9.

<u>4:36</u>

0499   S. P. Brock, "Barnabas: υἱὸς παρακλήσεως," *JTS* 25 (1974): 93-98.

0500   R. T. France, "Barnabas—Son of Encouragement," *ERT* 4/1 (1980): 91-101.

<u>5</u>

0501   J. M. Boice, "The Reliability of the Writings of Luke and Paul," *CT* 12/4 (1967): 176-78.

<u>5:1-11</u>

0502   Alfons Weiser, "Das Gottesurteil über Hananias und Saphira; Apg 5,1-11," *TGl* 69/2 (1979): 148-58.

0503   Brian J. Capper, " 'In der Hand des Ananias . . . ' Erwagungen zu IQS VI,20 und der urchristlichen Gutergemeinschaft," *RevQ* 12/2 (1986): 223-36.

0504   B. Prete, "Anania e Saffira (At 5:1-11): Componenti Letterarie e Dottrinali," *RBib* 36 (1989): 463-486.

0505 Daniel Marguerat, "Terreur dans l'Église: le drame d'Ananias et Saphira," *FV* 91 (1992): 77-88.

0506 Daniel Marguerat, "La mort d'Ananias et Saphire dans la stratégie narrative de Luc," *NTS* 39/2 (1993): 209-26.

0507 Daniel Marguerat, "Ananias et Saphira (Actes 5,1-11). Le viol du sacr," *LV* 42/215 (1993): 51-63.

5:1

0508 J. Duncan M. Derrett, "Ananias, Sapphira, and the Right of Property," *DR* 89/296 (1971): 225-32.

5:4

0509 Brian J. Capper, "The Interpretation of Acts 5:4," *JSNT* 19 (1983): 117-31.

5:12-25
0510 Agustín del Agua Perez, "El papel de la 'escuela midrásica' en la configuración del Nuevo Testamento," *EE* 60/234 (1985): 333-49.

5:12-17
0511 Robrecht Michaels, "The 'Model of Church' in the First Christian Community of Jerusalem: Ideal and Reality," *LouvS* 10/4 (1985): 303-23.

5:12-16
0512 J. Lach, "Katechese über die Kirche von Jerusalem in der Apostelgeschichte," *CollT* 52 (Supplement) (1982): 141-53.

0513 Clara Burini, "La 'comunione di cuori e di spirito' (Atti 2; 4) nella testimonianza di Cipriano," in Maria Angelini, et al., eds., *Testimonium Christi*. Brescia: Paideia Editrice, 1985. Pp. 91-109.

0514 Robrecht Michaels, "The 'Model of Church' in the First Christian Community of Jerusalem: Ideal and Reality," *LouvS* 10/4 (1985): 303-23.

0515 M. A. Co, "The Major Summaries in Acts: Acts 2:42-47; 4:32-35; 5:12-16: Linguistic and Literary Relationships," *ETL* 68/1 (1992): 49-85.

0516   G. E. Sterling, " 'Athletes of Virtue': An Analysis of the
Summaries in Acts," *JBL* 113/4 (1994): 679-96.

5:12-13
0517   David Wenham, "The Paulinism of Acts Again: Two Historical
Clues in 1 Thessalonians," *Themelios* 13/2 (1988): 53-55.

5:12
0518   R. Y. K. Fung, "Charismatic Versus Organized Ministry? An
Examination of an Alleged Antithesis," *EQ* 52/4 (1980): 195-214.

0519   René Latourelle, "Originalité et fonctions des miracles de Jésus,"
Greg 66/4 (1985): 641-653.

5:13-14
0520   Daniel R. Schwartz, "Non-Joining Sympathizers," *Bib* 64/4
(1983): 550-55.

5:14
0521   J. A. Jáuregui, "Israel y la iglesia en la teologia de Lucas," *EE* 61
(1986): 129-49.

5:15
0522   Werner Bieder, "Der Petrusschatten, Apg 5:15," *TZ* 16 (1960):
407-409.

0523   P. W. van der Horst, "Peter's Shadow: The Religio-Historical
Background of Acts V.15," *NTS* 23/2 (1977): 204-11.

5:17-42
0524   R. A. Martin, "Syntactical Evidence of Aramaic Sources in Acts
I-XV," *NTS* 11/1 (1964): 38-59.

0525   Marco Adinolfi, " 'Obbedire a Dio piuttosto che algi uomni.' La
comunità cristiana e il sinedrio in Atti 4,1-31; 5,17-42," *RBib*
27/1-2 (1979): 69-93.

5:17
0526   Morton Smith, "The Report about Peter in 1 Clement V. 4.," *NTS*
7 (1960): 86-88.

0527   E. P. Sanders, "Judaism and the Grand "Christian" Abstractions:
Love, Mercy, and Grace," *Int* 39 (1985): 357-372.

5:21-29

0528 J. A. Jáuregui, "Israel y la iglesia en la teologia de Lucas," *EE* 61 (1986): 129-149.

5:27-32

0529 E. Rasco, "La gloire de la résurrection et ses fruits," *AsSeign* 24 (1969): 6-14.

0530 Marion L. Soards, "The Speech of Peter and the Apostles to the Council," in *The Speeches in Acts: Their Content, Context, and Concerns*. Louisville: John Knox/Westminster Press, 1994. Pp. 50-53.

5:29-30

0531 Richard I. Pervo, "Social and Religious Aspects of the Western Text," in Dennis Groh and Robert Jewett, eds., *The Living Text* (festschrift for Ernest Saunders). Lanham MD: University Press of America, 1985. Pp. 229-41.

5:29

0532 Jay E. Adams, "The Church and Her Rights," *FundJ* 2/7 (1983): 16-19.

0533 Morris Inch, "Manifestation of the Spirit," in Morris A. Inch and Ronald F. Youngblood, eds., *The Living and Active Word of God* (festschrift for Samuel J. Schultz). Winona Lake IN: Eisenbrauns, 1983. Pp. 149-55.

5:30

0534 J. A. Fitzmyer, "Crucifixion in Ancient Palestine, Qumran Literature, and the New Testament," *CBQ* 40/4 (1978): 493-513.

5:31

0535 T. Ballarini, "ARCHEGOS (Atti 3:15, 5:31; Ebr. 2:10, 12:2) autore o condottiero?" *SacD* 16/63-64 (1971): 535-51.

0536 Michel Gourgues, "Exalté à la droite de Dieu," *SE* 27 (1975): 303-27.

0537 G. Dautzenberg, "Psalm 110 im Neuen Testament," in Hans Becker and Reiner Kaczynski, eds., *Liturgie und Dichtung: Ein interdisziplinäres Kompendium*. 1. *Historische Präsentation*. Sankt Ottilien: EOS Verlag, 1983. Pp. 141-71.

0538 Michael R. Austin, "Salvation and the Divinity of Jesus," *ET* 96 (1985): 271-75.

0539 Gérard Rochais, "Jésus savait-il qu'il était Dieu: réflexions critiques à propos d'un livre récent," *SR* 14/1 (1985): 85-106.

5:32

0540 Gerhard Lohfink, " 'Wir sind Zeugen dieser Ereignisse' (Apg 5,32). Die Einheit der neutestamentlichen Botschaft von Erhöhung und Himmelfahrt Jesu," *BK* 20/2 (1965): 49-52.

5:33-39

0541 Jean Delumeau, "La difficile émergence de la tolérance," in Roger Zuber and Laurent Theis, eds., *La Révocation de l'Edit de Nantes et le protestantisme français en 1685*. Paris: Société de l'Histoire du Protestantisme Français, 1986. Pp. 359-74.

5:34

0542 Klaus Haacker, "Verwendung und Vermeidung des Apostelbegriffs im Lukanischen Werk," *NovT* 30 (1988): 9-38.

0543 Fred A. Grissom, "Gamaliel," *BI* 14/2 (1989): 29-31.

5:35-16:5

0544 G. Betori, "La strutturazione del libro degli Atti: una proposta," *RBib* 42 (1994): 3-34.

5:35-39

0545 J. A. Trumbower, "The Historical Jesus and the Speech of Gamaliel," *NTS* 39/4 (1993): 500-17.

0546 Marion L. Soards, "Gamaliel's Speech to the Council," in *The Speeches in Acts: Their Content, Context, and Concerns*. Louisville: John Knox/Westminster Press, 1994. Pp. 53-55.

5:40-41

0547 E. Rasco, "La gloire de la résurrection et ses fruits," *AsSeign* 24 (1969): 6-14.

5:40

0548 S. T. Lachs, "Hebrew Elements in the Gospels and Acts," *JQR* 71/1 (1980): 31-43.

5:42

0549 E. Dassmann, "Hausgemeinde und Bischofsamt," in Ernst Dassmann and Klaus Thraede, eds., *Vivarium* (festschrift for Theodor Klauser). Münster, West Germany: Aschendorff, 1984. Pp. 82-97.

0550 Morris Inch, "Manifestation of the Spirit," in Morris A. Inch and Ronald F. Youngblood, eds., *The Living and Active Word of God* (festschrift for Samuel J. Schultz). Winona Lake IN: Eisenbrauns, 1983. Pp. 149-55.

6-12

0551 K. Beyschlag, "Zur Simon-Magua-Frage," *ZTK* 78 (1971): 395-426.

0552 John B. Polhill, "The Hellenist Breakthrough: Acts 6-12," *RevExp* 71/4 (1974): 475-86.

6:1-11:26

0553 U. Borse, "Der Rahmentext im Umkreis der Stephanusgeschichte," *BibL* 14/3 (1973): 187-204.

6-9

0554 L. Panier, "Pour lire les Actes des Apôtres. 3e série: Ac. 6-9," *SémBib* 30 (1983): 34-42.

6-8

0555 Thomas L. Brodie, "The Departure for Jerusalem as a Rhetorical Imitation of Elijah's Departure for the Jordan," *Bib* 70/1 (1989): 96-109.

0556 H. A. Brehm, "The Role of the Hellenists in Christian Origins: A Critique of Representative Models in Light of an Exegetical Study of Acts 6-8," doctoral dissertation, Southwestern Baptist Theological Seminary, Fort Worth TX, 1992.

0557 G. Jankowski, "Stephanos: Eine Auslegung von Apostelgeschichte 6-8,3," *TexteK* 15 (1992): 2-38.

6:1-8:3

0558 D. S. Dockery, "Acts 6-12: The Christian Mission beyond Jerusalem," *RevExp* 87 (1990): 423-37.

6-7

0559 Edvin Larsson, "Temple-Criticism and the Jewish Heritage: Some Reflections on Acts 6-7," *NTS* 39/3 (1993): 379-95.

0560 C. Amos, "Renewed in the Likeness of Christ: Stephen the Servant Martyr," *IrBibStud* 16 (1994): 31-37.

6

0561 Otto Glombitza, "Zur Charakterisiering des Stephanus in Act 6 und 7," *ZNW* 53 (1962): 238-44.

0562 A. S. Wood, "Social Involvement in the Apostolic Church," *EQ* 42/4 (1970): 194-212.

0563 Kevin N. Giles, "Is Luke an Exponent of 'Early Protestantism'? Church Order in the Lukan Writings. Part II," *EQ* 55/1 (1983): 3-20.

0564 S. K. Tsitsigos, "What Was the Task of the Seven Deacons?" *DBM* 21 (1992): 52-58.

6:1-15

0565 Martin Hengel, "Zwischen Jesus und Paulus. Die 'Hellenisten,' die 'Sieben' und Stephanus," *ZTK* 72/2 (1975): 151-206.

0566 F. Hahn, "Zum Problem der antiochenischen Quelle in der Apostelgeschichte," in B. Jaspert, ed., *Rudolf Bultmanns Werk und Wirkung*. Darmstadt: Wissenschaftliche Buchgesellschaft, 1984. Pp. 316-31.

6:1-8

0567 Edvin Larsson, "Die Hellenisten und die Urgemeinde," *NTS* 33/2 (1987): 205-225.

6:1-7

0568 Barbara Hall, "La communauté chrétienne dans le livre des Actes: Actes 6:1-7 et 10:1-11:18," *FV* Suppl (1971): 146-56.

0569 B. Domagalski, "Waren die 'Sieben' Diakone?" *BZ* 26/1 (1982): 21-33.

0570 Joseph B. Tyson, "Acts 6:1-7 and Dietary Regulations in Early Christianity," *PRS* 10/2 (1982): 145-61.

0571 Michel Cornillon, "De l'appel du Christ à l'appel de l'Église: trois récits du Nouveau Testament," *BSS* 10 (1984): 107-50.

0572 Carl J. Diemer, "Deacons and Other Endangered Species: A Look at the Biblical Office of Deacon," *FundJ* 3/3 (1984): 21-24.

0573 Justo L. González, "Pluralismo, justicia y misión: un estudio bíblico sobre Hechos 6:1-7," *Apuntes* 10 (1990): 3-8.

6:1-6

0574 J. D. McCaughey, "The Intention of the Author: Some Questions About the Exegesis of Acts 6:1-6," *ABR* 7 (1959): 27-36.

0575 J. T. Lienhard, "Acts 6:1-6: A Redactional View," *CBQ* 37/2 (1975): 228-36.

0576 Richard Fraser, "Office of Deacon," *Pres* 11/1 (1985): 13-19.

6:1-4

0577 Oscar Cullmann, "Dissensions within the Early Church," *USQR* 22/2 (1967): 83-92.

0578 LaVonne Neff, "Three Women Out of Four: How the Church Can Meet the Needs of Its Widows," *CT* 29/16 (1985): 30-33.

0579 C. J. Mork, "Women's Ordination and the Leadership of the Church," *WW* 7/4 (1987): 374-79.

6:1-2

0580 S. Aalen, "Versuch einer Analyse des Diakonia-Begriffes im Neuen Testament," in William Weinrich, ed., *The New Testament Age* (festschrift for Bo Reicke). 2 vols. Macon GA: Mercer University Press, 1984. 1:1-13.

6:1

0581 J. Delorme, "Les Hellénistes des Actes des Apôtres," *AmiCl* 71 (1961): 445-47.

0582 Everett Ferguson, "The Hellenists in the Book of Acts," *RQ* 12/4 (1969): 159-80.

0583 R. Pesch, E. Gerhart, and F. Schilling, " 'Hellenisten' und 'Hebräer.' Zu Apg 9:29 und 6:1," *BZ* N.S. 23/1 (1979): 87-92.

0584 Craig A. Evans, "The Citation of Isaiah 60:17 in 1 Clement," *VC* 36/2 (1982): 105-107.

0585 N. Walter, "Apostelgeschichte 6.1 und die Anfänge der Urgemeinde in Jerusalem," *NTS* 29/3 (1983): 370-93.

6:2-4

0586 Marion L. Soards, "The Speech by the Twelve Prior to the Appointment of the Seven," in *The Speeches in Acts: Their Content, Context, and Concerns*. Louisville: John Knox/Westminster Press, 1994. Pp. 55-57.

6:2

0587 E. S. Buchanan, "Some Noteworthy Readings of the Fleury Palimpsest," *JTS* 9 (1907-1908): 98-100.

6:4

0588 A. Feuillet, " 'Temoins Oculaires et Serviteurs de la Parole'," *NovT* 15/4 (1973): 241-59.

6:5

0589 Norbert Brox, "Nikolaos und Nikolaiten," *VC* 19/1 (1965): 23-30.

0590 James E. Carter, "The Chosen," *BI* 14/2 (1989): 50-52.

6:6

0591 R. Y. K. Fung, "Charismatic Versus Organized Ministry? An Examination of an Alleged Antithesis," *EQ* 52/4 (1980): 195-214.

6:7-15

0592 E. Pistelli, "Atti 6:7-9, 11-15," *Papiri greci e latini* Vol. 2, "Pubblicazioni della Società italiana per la ricerca dei papiri greci e latini in Egitto." Firenze: Tip. Ariani, 1913. Pp. 26-27.

6:7

0593 M. H. Franzmann, "The Word of the Lord Grew," *CTM* 30 (1959): 563-81.

0594 J. Kodell, " 'The Word of God Grew.' The Ecclesial Tendency of *Logos* in Acts 6:7; 12:24; 19:20," *Bib* 55/4 (1974): 505-19.

0595 M. H. Grumm, "Another Look at Acts," *ET* 96/11 (1985): 333-37.

0596   J. A. Jáuregui, "Israel y la iglesia en la teologia de Lucas," *EE* 61 (1986): 129-49.

6:8-8:2

0597   M.-É. Boismard, "Le martyre d'Étienne. Actes 6:8-8:2," *RechSR* 69/2 (1981): 181-94.

0598   P. Doble, "The Son of Man Saying in Stephen's Witnessing: Acts 6:8-8:2," *NTS* 31/1 (1985): 68-84.

6:8

0599   C. H. Giblin, "A Prophetic Vision of History and Things," *BibTo* 63 (1972): 994-1001.

6:9

0600   Jeff Cranford, "The Synagogue of the Libertines," *BI* 13/3 (1987): 40-41.

0601   B. W. W. Dombrowski, "Synagoge in Acts 6:9," in Zdzislaw Kapera, ed., *Intertestamental Essays* (festschrift for Józef Tadeusz Milik). Cracow: Enigma Press, 1992. Pp. 53-65.

6:11-15

0602   Alfons Weiser, "Zur Gesetzes- und Tempelkritik der 'Hellenisten'," in Johannes Beutler and Karl Kertelge, eds., *Das Gesetz im Neuen Testament*. Freiburg: Herder, 1986. Pp. 146-68.

6:11-14

0603   Edvin Larsson, "Temple-Criticism and the Jewish Heritage: Some Reflections on Acts 6-7," *NTS* 39/3 (1993): 379-95.

6:13-14

0604   F. D. Weinert, "Luke, Stephen, and the Temple in Luke-Acts," *BTB* 17 (1987): 88-90.

0605   A. Dauer, "Ergänzungen und 'Variationen' in den Reden der Apostelgeschichte gegenüber vorausgegangenen Erzählungen Beobachtungen zur literarischen Arbeitsweise des Lukas," in Hubert Frankemölle and Karl Kertelge, eds., *Vom Urchristentum zu Jesus* (festschrift for Joachim Gnilka). Freiburg: Herder, 1989. Pp. 307-24.

6:13

0606   Gerald L. Borchert, "Acts 6:13," *RevExp* 88 (1991): 73-78.

6:14

0607   Edwin D. Freed, "Samaritan Influence in the Gospel of John," *CBQ* 30/4 (1968): 580-87.

0608   Sasagu Arai, "Zum 'Tempelwort' Jesu in Apostelgeschichte 6:14," *NTS* 34/3 (1988): 397-410.

0609   D. L. Balch, " 'You Teach All the Jews . . . to Forsake Moses, Telling Them not to . . . Observe the Customs'," *SBLSP* 32 (1993): 369-83.

6:35

0610   F. Hahn, "Zum Problem der antiochenischen Quelle in der Apostelgeschichte," in B. Jaspert, ed., *Rudolf Bultmanns Werk und Wirkung*. Darmstadt: Wissenschaftliche Buchgesellschaft, 1984. Pp. 316-31.

7-8

0611   R. J. Coggins, "The Samaritans and Acts," *NTS* 28/3 (1981-1982): 423-34.

7:2-8:3

0612   David P. Moessner, " 'The Christ Must Suffer': New Light on the Jesus-Peter, Stephen, Paul Parallels in Luke-Acts," *NovT* 28/3 (1986): 220-56.

7

0613   Otto Glombitza, "Zur Charakterisiering des Stephanus in Act 6 und 7," *ZNW* 53 (1962): 238-44.

0614   R. Pesch, "Der Christ als Nachahmer Christi: Der Tod des Stephanus (Apg 7) im Vergleich mit dem Tode Christi," *BK* 24/1 (1969): 10-11.

0615   H. W. Mare, "Acts 7: Jewish or Samaritan in Character?" *WTJ* 34/1 (1971): 1-21.

0616   Cyril J. Barber, "Moses: A Study of Hebrews 11:23-29a," *GTJ* 14/2 (1973): 14-28.

0617 G. Stemberger, "Die Stephanusrede (Apg 7) und die judische Tradition," *SNTU-A* 1 (1976): 154-74.

0618 Rex A. Koivisto, "Stephen's Speech: A Case Study in Rhetoric and Biblical Inerrancy," *JETS* 20/4 (1977): 353-64.

0619 Earl Richard, "Acts 7: An Investigation of the Samaritan Evidence," *CBQ* 39/2 (1977): 190-208.

0620 Robert W. Thurston, "Midrash and 'Magnet' Words in the New Testament," *EQ* 51/1 (1979): 22-39.

0621 Klaus Seybold, "Die Geschichte des 29: Psalms und Ihre Theologische Bedeutung," *TZ* 36/4 (1980): 208-19.

0622 T. L. Donaldson, "Moses Typology and the Sectarian Nature of Early Christian Anti-Judaism: A Study in Acts 7," *JSNT* 12 (1981): 27-52.

0623 Jacques Dupont, "La Structure Oratoire du Discours d'Étienne," *Bib* 66/2 (1985): 153-67.

0624 Jean Lambert, "L'Echappée Belle: Rubriques en Marge du Discours d'Étienne, Actes 7," *FV* 84/6 (1985): 25-32.

0625 Unité de recherche associée, "Sur le discours d'Étienne en Actes 7," in Françios Refoulé, ed., *À cause de l'Évangile: Études sur les synoptiques et les Actes* (festschrift for Jacques Dupont). Paris: Cerf, 1985. Pp. 739-55.

0626 D. A. DeSilva, "The Stoning of Stephen: Purging and Consolidating an Endangered Institution," *SBT* 17/2 (1989): 165-85.

0627 R. F. Wolfe, "Rhetorical Elements in the Speeches of Acts 7 and 17," *JTT* 6 (1993): 274-83.

7:1-53

0628 R. A. Martin, "Syntactical Evidence of Aramaic Sources in Acts I-XV," *NTS* 11/1 (1964): 38-59.

0629 M. H. Scharlemann, "Stephen's Speech: A Lucan Creation?" *CJ* 4/2 (1978): 52-57.

0630 J. A. Jáuregui, "Israel y la iglesia en la teologia de Lucas," *EE* 61 (1986): 129-49.

0631 F. F. Bruce, "Stephen's Apologia," in Barry Thompson, ed., *Scripture: Meaning and Method* (festschrift for A. T. Hanson). Hull: University Press, 1987. Pp. 37-50.

7:2-53

0632 F. J. Foakes-Jackson, "Stephen's Speech in Acts," *JBL* 49 (1930): 283-86.

0633 John J. Kilgallen, "The Stephen Speech: A Literary and Redactional Study of Acts 7:2-53," *CBQ* 40 (1978): 639.

0634 Jacques Dupont, "La Structure Oratoire du Discours d'Étienne," *Bib* 66/2 (1985): 153-67.

0635 C. K. Barrett, "Old Testament History according to Stephen and Paul," in Wolfgang Schrage, ed., *Studien zum Text und zur Ethik des Neuen Testaments* (festschrift for Heinrich Greeven). Berlin: de Gruyter, 1986. Pp. 57-69.

0636 Rex A. Koivisto, "Stephen's Speech: a Theology of Errors?" *GTJ* 8 (1987): 101-14.

0637 S. Szymik, "The Literary Structure of Saint Stephen's Speech," *RoczTK* 35 (1988): 101-16.

0638 John J. Kilgallen, "The Function of Stephen's Speech," *Bib* 70/2 (1989): 173-93.

0639 J. P. White, "Lucan Composition of Acts 7:2-53 in Light of the Author's Use of Old Testament Texts," doctoral dissertation, Southwestern Baptist Theological Seminary, Fort Worth TX, 1992.

0640 Marion L. Soards, "Stephen's Speech," in *The Speeches in Acts: Their Content, Context, and Concerns.* Louisville: John Knox/Westminster Press, 1994. Pp. 57-70.

7:2

0641 T. E. Brawley, "For Blessing All Families of the Earth: Covenant Traditions in Luke-Acts," *CThM* 22/1 (1995): 18-26.

7:6

0642 Jack R. Riggs, "The Length of Israel's Sojourn in Egypt," *GTJ* 12/1 (1971): 18-35.

0643 James R. Battenfield, "A Consideration of the Identity of the Pharaoh of Genesis 47," *JETS* 15 (1972): 77-85.

7:8

0644 T. E. Brawley, "For Blessing All Families of the Earth: Covenant Traditions in Luke-Acts," *CThM* 22/1 (1995): 18-26.

7:9-60

0645 C. K. Barrett, "Submerged Christology in Acts," in Cilliers Breytenbach and Henning Paulsen, eds., *Anfänge der Christologie* (festschrift for Ferdinand Hahn). Göttingen: Vandenhoeck & Ruprecht, 1991. Pp. 237-44.

7:9-16

0646 Earl Richard, "The Polemical Character of the Joseph Episode in Acts 7," *JBL* 98/2 (1979): 255-67.

7:14-18

0647 T. Lefort and Honoratus Coppieters, "Fragments des Actes des Apôtres en dialecte dit 'moyen égyptien'," *Mus* 15 (1914): 49-60.

0648 Stephen Gaselee, "Two Fayoumic Fragments of the Acts," *JTS* 11 (1909-1910): 514-17.

7:17-43

0649 J. C. Atienza, "Hechos 7,17-43 y las corrientes cristológicas dentro de la primitiva comunidad cristiana," *EB* 33/1 (1974): 31-62.

0650 M. Balagué, "Hechos 7,17-43 y las corrientes cristológicas dentro de la primitiva communidad cristiana," *EB* 33 (1974): 33-67.

7:32

0651 T. E. Brawley, "For Blessing All Families of the Earth: Covenant Traditions in Luke-Acts," *CThM* 22/1 (1995): 18-26.

7:33

0652 I. Howard Marshall, "New Wine in Old Wineskins: V. The Biblical Use of the Word 'Ekklesia'," *ET* 84/12 (1973): 359-64.

7:35-37
> **0653** E. J. Via, "An Interpretation of Acts 7:35-37 from the Perspective of Major Themes in Luke-Acts," *PRS* 6/3 (1979): 190-207.

7:37
> **0654** J. M. Schubert, "The Image of Jesus as the Prophet like Moses in Luke-Acts as Advanced by Luke's Reinterpretation of Deuteronomy 18:15-18 in Acts 3:22 and 7:37," doctoral dissertation, Fordham University, New York, 1992.

7:38
> **0655** A. Vanhoye, "A Mediator of Angels in Gal 3:19-20," *Bib* 59/3 (1978): 403-11.

7:42-43
> **0656** G. L. Prato, "Idolatry Compelled to Search for Its Gods: A Peculiar Agreement between Textual Tradition and Exegesis," in Gerald O'Collins and G. Marconi, eds., *Luke and Acts* (festschrift for Emilio Rasco). Mahwah NJ: Paulist Press, 1993. Pp. 181-96.

7:42
> **0657** H. van de Sandt, "Why Is Amos 5,25-27 Quoted in Acts 7,42f?" *ZNW* 82 (1991): 67-87.

7:43
> **0658** J. Murphy-O'Connor, "The Damascus Document Revisited," *RB* 92 (1985): 223-46.

> **0659** R. Borger, "Amos 5,26, Apostelgeschichte 7,43 und urpu II, 180," *ZAW* 100/1 (1988): 70-81.

7:44-50
> **0660** Mary E. Moore, "Living in God's House," *Impact* 14 (1985): 1-7.

> **0661** Edvin Larsson, "Temple-Criticism and the Jewish Heritage: Some Reflections on Acts 6-7," *NTS* 39/3 (1993): 379-95.

7:46-50
> **0662** Dennis D. Sylva, "The Meaning and Function of Acts 7:46-50," *JBL* 106/2 (1987): 261-75.

7:48

0663 R. Le Deaut, "Actes 7,48 et Matthieu 17,4 (par.) à la lumière du targum palestinien," *RechSR* 52/1 (1964): 85-90.

0664 A. G. van Aarde, " 'The Most High God Does Live in Houses, but not Houses Built by Men': The Relativity of the Metaphor 'Temple' in Luke-Acts," *Neo* 26 (1991): 51-64.

7:51-53

0665 R. B. Hays, "The Righteous One as Eschatological Deliverer: A Case Study in Paul's Apocalyptic Hermeneutics," in Joel Marcus and Marion Soards, eds., *Apocalyptic and the New Testament* (festschrift for J. Louis Martyn). Sheffield: JSOT Press, 1989. Pp 191-215.

7:54-8:3

0666 Martin Hengel, "Zwischen Jesus und Paulus. Die 'Hellenisten,' die 'Sieben' und Stephanus," *ZTK* 72/2 (1975): 151-206.

7:54-8:1

0667 M. J. Kingston, "God Guarantees the Church," *ET* 97/10 (1986): 305-306.

7:55-60

0668 Edwina Hunter, "Preaching from Acts: Homiletical Resources for Easter," *QR* 7 (1987): 76-102.

0669 R. C. Tannehill, "Mission in the 1990s: Reflections on the Easter Lections from Acts," *QR* 10/1 (1990): 84-97.

7:55-56

0670 J. Duncan M. Derrett, "The Son of Man Standing," *BibO* 30 (1988): 71-84.

0671 S. Légasse, "Encore Hestota en Actes 7:55-56," *FilN* 3 (1990): 63-66.

7:55

0672 R. Pesch, "Die Vision des Stephanus Apg 7:55f. im Rahmen der Apostelgeschichte," *BibL* 6/2 (1965): 92-107.

0673 G. Dautzenberg, "Psalm 110 im Neuen Testament," in Hans
Becker and Reiner Kaczynski, eds., *Liturgie und Dichtung: Ein
interdisziplinäres Kompendium*. 1. *Historische Präsentation*. Sankt
Ottilien: EOS Verlag, 1983. Pp. 141-71.

0674 H. Baarlink, "Friede im Himmel. Die Lukanische Redaktion von
Lk 19,38 und Ihre Deutung," *ZNW* 76/3 (1985): 170-86.

7:56

0675 George D. Kilpatrick, "Acts 7:56: Son of Man?" *TZ* 21/3 (1965):
209.

0676 George D. Kilpatrick, "Again Acts 7:56: Son of Man?" *TZ* 34/4
(1978): 232.

0677 M. Sabbe, "The Son of Man Saying in Acts 7,56," in J. Kremer,
ed., *Les Actes des Apôtres*. BETL #48. Louvain: University Press,
1979. Pp. 241-79.

0678 Marion L. Soards, "Stephen's Speech," in *The Speeches in Acts:
Their Content, Context, and Concerns*. Louisville: John
Knox/Westminster Press, 1994. Pp. 57-70.

7:58-8:1

0679 P. Van Minnen, "Paul the Roman Citizen," *JSNT* 56 (1994):
43-52.

7:58

0680 Thomas L. Brodie, "The Accusing and Stoning of Naboth (1 Kgs
2:18-13) as One Component of the Stephen Text," *CBQ* 45/3
(1983): 417-32.

0681 Paula Fredriksen, "Paul and Augustine: Conversion Narratives,
Orthodox Traditions, and the Retrospective Self," *JTS* 37/1 (1986):
3-34.

7:59-60

0682 Marion L. Soards, "Stephen's Speech," in *The Speeches in Acts:
Their Content, Context, and Concerns*. Louisville: John Knox/West-
minster Press, 1994. Pp. 57-70.

7:59
0683 W. C. Van Unnik, "With All Those Who Call on the Name of the Lord," in William C. Weinrich, ed., *The New Testament Age* (festschrift for Bo Reicke). 2 vols. Macon GA: Mercer University Press, 1984. 2:533-51.

8:1-12:25
0684 A. Smith, " 'Do You Understand What You are Reading?': A Literary Critical Reading Reading of the Ethiopian (Cachet) Episode," *JITC* 22/1 (1994): 48-70.

8:1-11:18
0685 R. F. O'Toole, "Philip and the Ethiopian Eunuch," *JSNT* 17 (1983): 25-34.

8
0686 Joseph Hanimann, " 'Nous Avons ete Abreuves d'un Seul Esprit': Note sur 1 Co 12, 13b," *NRT* 94/4 (1972): 400-405.

0687 C. H. H. Scobie, "The Origins and Development of Samaritan Christianity," *NTS* 19/4 (1973): 390-414.

0688 B. E. Thiering, "Qumran Initiation and New Testament Baptism," *NTS* 27/5 (1981): 615-31.

0689 Roland Bergmeier, "Die Gestalt des Simon Magus in Apg 8 und in der Simonianischen Gnosis—Aporiae einer Gesamtdeutung," *ZNW* 77/3 (1986): 267-75.

0690 Gerd Lüdemann, "The Acts of the Apostles and the Beginnings of Simonian Gnosis," *NTS* 33/3 (1987): 420-26.

0691 F. R. Harm, "Structural Elements Related to the Gift of the Holy Spirit in Acts," *CJ* 14/1 (1988): 28-41.

0692 Mikeal C. Parsons, " 'Making Sense of What We Read': The Place of Biblical Hermeneutics," *SouJT* 35/3 (1993): 12-20.

8:1-4
0693 G. Betori, "La strutturazione del libro degli Atti: una proposta," *RBib* 42 (1994): 3-34.

8:1

0694   Morris Inch, "Manifestation of the Spirit," in Morris A. Inch and Ronald F. Youngblood, eds., *The Living and Active Word of God* (festschrift for Samuel J. Schultz). Winona Lake IN: Eisenbrauns, 1983. Pp. 149-55.

0695   F. F. Bruce, "The Church of Jerusalem in the Acts of the Apostles," *BJRL* 67/2 (1985): 641-61.

8:2-25

0696   Dietrich-Alex Koch, "Geistbesitz, Geistverleihung und Wundermacht. Erwgungen zur Tradition und zur Lukanischen Redaktion in Act 8:5-25," *ZNW* 77/1 (1986): 64-82.

8:4-40

0697   D. S. Dockery, "Acts 6-12: The Christian Mission beyond Jerusalem," *RevExp* 87 (1990): 423-37.

8:4-25

0698   O. C. Edwards, "The Exegesis of Acts 8:4-25 and Its Implications for Confirmation and Glossolalia: A Review Article of E. Haenchen's Acts Commentary," *ATR* 55 (1973): 100-12.

0699   Kevin N. Giles, "Is Luke an Exponent of 'Early Protestantism'? Church Order in the Lukan Writings. Part I," *EQ* 54/4 (1982): 193-205.

0700   E. J. Christiansen, "Taufe als Initiation in der Apostelgeschichte," *StTh* 40/1 (1986): 55-79.

8:4-24

0701   F. Garcá Bazán, "En torno a Hechos 8,4-24. Milagro y magia entre los gnósticos," *RevB* 40/1 (1978): 27-38.

0702   H. J. Klauck, "With Paul in Paphos and Lystra: Magic and Paganism in the Acts of the Apostles," *Neo* 28 (1994): 93-108.

8:4

0703   Paul Muench, "The New Testament Scope of Ministry," *Point* 5/1 (1976): 77-84.

0704   Morris Inch, "Manifestation of the Spirit," in Morris A. Inch and
Ronald F. Youngblood, eds., *The Living and Active Word of God*
(festschrift for Samuel J. Schultz). Winona Lake IN: Eisenbrauns,
1983. Pp. 149-55.

0705   Eduard Schweizer, "The Testimony to Jesus in the Early Christian
Community," *HBT* 7/1 (1985): 77-98.

0706   Fred A. Grissom, "The Church Scattered," *BI* 13/3 (1987): 55-58.

8:5-25

0707   Michel Gourgues, "Esprit des Commencements et Esprit des
Prolongements dans les Actes: Note sur la 'Pentecôte des
Samaritains'," *RB* 93/3 (1986): 376-85.

0708   Dietrich-Alex Koch, "Geistbesitz, Geistverleihung und Wundermacht: Erwägungen zur Tradition und zur Lukanischen Redaktion
in Apg 8:5-25," *ZNW* 77/1-2 (1986): 64-82.

8:5-8

0709   R. Massó, "La promesa del Espíritu," *CuBí* 29 (1972): 342-48.

8:9-40

0710   Thomas L. Brodie, "Towards Unraveling the Rhetorical Imitation
of Sources in Acts: 2 Kgs 5 as One Component of Acts 8:9-40,"
Bib 67/1 (1986): 41-67.

8:9-24

0711   J. Duncan M. Derrett, "Simon Magus," *ZNW* 73/1-2 (1982):
52-68.

8:9-11

0712   S. Haar, "Lens or Mirror: The Image of Simon and Magic in Early
Christian Literature," *LTJ* 27 (1993): 113-21.

8:9

0713   E. Haenchen, "Simon Magus in der Apostelgeschichte," *GNT* 3
(1973): 267-79.

0714   W. A. Meeks, "Simon Magus in Recent Research," *RSR* 3/3
(1977): 137-42.

0715   K. Rudolph, "Simon—Magus oder Gnosticus? Zur Stand der
Debatte," *TR* 42/4 (1977): 279-359.

8:12

0716 I. de la Potterie, "L'economia fede-sacramento nel nuovo testamento," in P.-R. Tragan, ed., *Fede e sacramenti negli scritti giovannei*. Rome: Edizioni Abbazia, 1972. Pp. 27-46.

0717 E. A. Russell, "They Believed Philip Preaching," *IBS* 1 (1979): 169-76.

8:13

0718 E. Haenchen, "Simon Magus in der Apostelgeschichte," *GNT* 3 (1973): 267-79.

8:14-25

0719 F. Hahn, "Zum Problem der antiochenischen Quelle in der Apostelgeschichte," in B. Jaspert, ed., *Rudolf Bultmanns Werk und Wirkung*. Darmstadt: Wissenschaftliche Buchgesellschaft, 1984. Pp. 316-31.

0720 David A. Handy, "Acts 8:14-25," *Int* 47 (1993): 289-94.

8:14-17

0721 R. Massó, "La promesa del Espíritu," *CuBí* 29 (1972): 342-48.

0722 Heribert Schützeichel, "Calvins Stellungnahme zu den Trienter Canones über die Sakramente im Allgemeinen," *Cath* 38/4 (1984): 317-39.

8:16

0723 W. E. Moore, "One Baptism," *NTS* 10/4 (1964): 504-16.

8:18

· **0724** Klaus Haacker, "Einige Falle von 'Erlebter Rede' im Neuen Testament," *NovT* 12/1 (1970): 70-77.

8:24

0725 E. Haenchen, "Simon Magus in der Apostelgeschichte," *GNT* 3 (1973): 267-79.

8:25-40

0726 D. Mínguez, "Hechos 8,25-40. Análisis estructural del relato," *Bib* 57/2 (1976): 168-91.

0727 R. F. O'Toole, "Philip and the Ethiopian Eunuch," *JSNT* 17 (1983): 25-34.

8:26-40

0728 J. M. Grassi, "Emmaus Revisited," *CBQ* 26 (1964): 463-67.

0729 M. Corbin, "Connais-tu ce que tu lis? Une lecture d'Actes 8,v.26 à 40," *Chr* 24 (1977): 73-85.

0730 Paul de Meester, " 'Philippe et l'Eunuque éthiopien' ou 'le baptême d'un pèlerin de Nubie'?" *NRT* 103/3 (1981): 360-74.

0731 Lawrence Mitchell, "1st Sunday after Easter," *CTQ* 46 (1982): 329-30.

0732 Bernard P. Robinson, "The Place of the Emmaus Story in Luke-Acts," *NTS* 30/4 (1984): 481-97.

0733 F. F. Bruce, "Philip and the Ethiopian," *JSS* 34 (1989): 377-86.

0734 Clarice J. Martin, "A Chamberlain's Journey and the Challenge of Interpretation for Liberation," *Semeia* 47 (1989): 105-35.

0735 Yehudah Rapuano, "Did Philip Baptize the Eunuch at Ein Yael?" *BAR* 16/6 (1990): 44-49.

0736 F. Scott Spencer, "The Ethiopian Eunuch and His Bible: A Social-Science Analysis," *BTB* 22 (1992): 155-65.

0737 Mikeal C. Parsons, " 'Making Sense of What We Read': The Place of Biblical Hermeneutics," *SouJT* 35 (1993): 12-20.

0738 T. M. Rosica, "Two Journeys of Faith," *BibTo* 31 (1993): 177-80.

0739 W. A. Gage and J. R. Beck, "The Gospel, Zion's Barren Woman and the Ethipian Eunuch," *Crux* 30 (1994): 35-43.

0740 A. Smith, " 'Do You Understand What You are Reading?': A Literary Critical Reading Reading of the Ethiopian (Cachet) Episode," *JITC* 22/1 (1994): 48-70.

8:26-39
0741   John M. Gibbs, "Luke 24:13-33 and Acts 8:26-39: The Emmaus Incident and the Eunuch's Baptism as Parallel Stories," *BTF* 7 (1975): 17-30.

0742   Bo Reicke, "Der Gottesknecht im Alten und Neuen Testament," *TZ* 35/6 (1979): 342-50.

0743   John M. Gibbs, "Luke 24:13-33 and Acts 8:26-39," *NRT* 103 (1981): 360-74.

8:26-38
0744   Holsten Fagerberg, "Har exegetiken nagon betydelse för homiletiken," *STK* 60/3 (1984): 97-106.

8:26-32
0745   Carl H. Kraeling, "P^{50}. Two Selections from Acts," *Quantulacumque. Studies Presented to Kirsopp Lake.* Edited by Robert P. Casey, Silva Lake, and Agnes K. Lake. London: Christophers, 1937. Pp. 163-72.

0746   Bruce M. Metzger, "Recently Published Greek Papyri of the New Testament," *BA* 10 (1947): 25-44.

8:26
0747   Robert Coleman, "Gaza," *BI* 16/1 (1989): 35-37.

8:27
0748   Irenée Fransen, "Le baptême de l'eunuque: Philippe baptise un Ethopien," *BTS* 72 (1965): 18-19.

0749   Klaus Haacker, "Einige Falle von 'Erlebter Rede' im Neuen Testament," *NovT* 12/1 (1970): 70-77.

0750   Rice A. Pierce, "Candance, Queen of Ethiopia," *BI* 9/2 (1983): 68-73.

0751   Mike Fuhrman, "North African Jews," *BI* 13/3 (1987): 52-54.

8:29
0752   R. Wayne Jones, "Chariots," *BI* 14/2 (1989): 52-55.

8:30-38

0753 R. F. O'Toole, "Philip and the Ethiopian Eunuch," *JSNT* 17 (1983): 25-34.

8:30

0754 P. Trummer, "Verstehst du auch, was du liest?" *K* 22 (1980): 103-13.

0755 K. Kertelge, " 'Verstehst du auch, was du liest'?" in A. T. Khoury and L. Muth, eds., *Glauben durch Lesen? Für eine christliche Lesekultur.* Frieburg: Herder, 1990. Pp. 14-22.

8:37

0756 Antonio Orbe, "Cristo, sacrificio y manjar," *Greg* 66/2 (1985): 185-239.

0757 Richard I. Pervo, "Social and Religious Aspects of the Western Text," in Dennis Groh and Robert Jewett, eds., *The Living Text* (festschrift for Ernest Saunders). Lanham MD: University Press of America, 1985. Pp. 229-41.

0758 Jenny Heimerdinger, "La Foi de l'eunuquee Éthiopien: le Problème Textuel d'Actes 8:37," *ÉTR* 63/4 (1988): 521-28.

0759 R. J. Porter, "What Did Philip Say to the Eunuch?" *ET* 100 (1988): 54-55.

8:39

0760 J. H. Crehan, "The Confirmation of the Ethiopian Eunuch," *OCP* 195 (1974): 187-95.

0761 Richard I. Pervo, "Social and Religious Aspects of the Western Text," in Dennis Groh and Robert Jewett, eds., *The Living Text* (festschrift for Ernest Saunders). Lanham MD: University Press of America, 1985. Pp. 229-41.

8:40

0762 Sherman E. Johnson, "Caesarea Maritima," *LTQ* 20 (1985): 28-32.

0763 Eduard Schweizer, "The Testimony to Jesus in the Early Christian Community," *HBT* 7/1 (1985): 77-98.

9-15

0764 F. W. Beare, "The Sequence of Events in Acts 9-15," *JBL* 62 (1943): 295-306.

9

0765 D. M. Stanley, "Paul's Conversion in Acts: Why the Three Accounts?" *CBQ*, 15 (1953): 315-38.

0766 Gerhard Lohfink, "Eine alttestamentliche Darstellungsform für Gotteserscheinungen in den Damaskusberichten," *BZ* N.S. 9/2 (1965): 246-57.

0767 D. Gill, "The Structure of Acts 9," *Bib* 55/4 (1974): 546-48.

0768 O. H. Steck, "Formgeschichtliche Bemerkungen zur Darstellung des Damaskusgeschens in der Apostelgeschichte," *ZNW* 67/1 (1976): 20-28.

0769 R. F. Collins, "Paul's Damascus Experience: Reflections on the Lukan Account," *LouvS* 11/2 (1986): 99-118.

0770 Marvin W. Meyer, "The Light and Voice on the Damascus Road," *Forum* 2 (1986): 27-35.

0771 S. R. Bechtler, "The Meaning of Paul's Call and Commissioning in Luke's Story: An Exegetical Study of Acts 9, 22, and 26," *SBT* 15 (1987): 53-77.

0772 Olubayo Obijole, "The Influence of the Conversion of St. Paul on His Theology of the Cross," *EAJT* 6/2 (1987): 27-36.

0773 Ronald D. Witherup, "Functional Redundancy in the Acts of the Apostles: A Case Study," *JSNT* 48 (1992): 67-86.

9:1-31

0774 Beverly R. Gaventa, "The Overthrown Enemy: Luke's Portrait of Paul," *SBLSP* 24 (1985): 439-49.

0775 C. H. Talbert, "Discipleship in Luke-Acts," in Fernando F. Segovia, ed., *Displeship in the New Testament.* Philadelphia: Fortress Press, 1985. Pp. 62-75.

0776 D. S. Dockery, "Acts 6-12: The Christian Mission beyond Jerusalem," *RevExp* 87 (1990): 423-37.

9:1-30

0777 David P. Moessner, "The Christ Must Suffer: New Light on the Jesus—Peter, Stephen, Paul Parallels in Luke-Acts," *NovT* 28/3 (1986): 220-56.

9:1-29

0778 John T. Townsend, "Acts 9:1-29 and Early Church Tradition," *SBLSP* 27 (1988): 119-31.

9:1-28

0779 Jaroslav B. Stanek, "Lukas: Theologie der Heilgeschichte," *CVia* 28/1-2 (1985): 9-31.

9:1-20

0780 M. Trotter, "Acts in Esther," *QR* 14/4 (1994-1995): 435-47.

9:1-19

0781 C. W. Hedrick, "Paul's Conversion-Call: A Comparative Analysis of the Three Reports in Acts," *JBL* 100/3 (1981): 415-32

0782 Karl H. Schelkle, "Im Leib oder Ausser des Leibes: Paulus als Mystiker," in William C. Weinrich, ed., *The New Testament Age* (festschrift for Bo Reicke). 2 vols. Macon GA: Mercer University Press, 1984. 2:455-65.

0783 D. Hamm, "Paul's Blindness and Its Healing: Clues to Symbolic Intent," *Bib* 71/1 (1990): 63-72.

9:1-10

0784 Robert V. Thompson, "Eyesight and Insight," *ChrM* 17/1 (1986): 29-31.

9:1-9

0785 O. F. A. Meinardus, "The Site of the Apostle Paul's Conversion at Kaukab," *BA* 44/1 (1981): 57-59.

9:1-5

0786 Raymond Schwager, "Christ's Death and the Prophetic Critique of Sacrifice," trans. P. Riordan *Semeia* 33 (1985): 109-23.

9:1-2

0787 C. S. Mann, "Saul and Damascus," *ET* 99 (1988): 331-34.

9:1

0788 P. W. van der Horst, "Drohung und Hord schnaubend," *NovT* 12/3 (1970): 257-69.

9:2-3

0789 S. Sabugal, "La Mencion neotestamentaria de Damasco ¿ciudad de Siria o region de Qumran?" *BETL* 45 (1978): 403-13.

9:2

0790 A. Zón, "Eklezjologiczny sens terminus 'Droga' w Dz 9, 2," *RuchB* 17/4 (1964): 207-15.

0791 Eduard Schweizer, "The Testimony to Jesus in the Early Christian Community," *HBT* 7/1 (1985): 77-98.

9:3-9

0792 Kakichi Kadowaki, "Mit dem Körper lesen: Paulus und Dogen," in Hans Waldenfels and Thomas Immoos, eds., *Fernöstliche Weisheit* (festschrift for Heinrich Dumoulin). Mainz: Matthias Grünewald Verlag, 1985. Pp. 68-78.

9:3-4

0793 R. A. Johnson, "The Narrative Function of the Quotation of Isaiah 6:9-10 and the Concomitant Hear-See Motif in the Book of Acts," doctoral dissertation, Southwestern Baptist Theological Seminary, Fort Worth TX, 1992.

9:4-6

0794 J. Doignon, "Le dialogue de Jesus et de Paul: Sa'pointe' dans l'exegese latine la plus ancienne," *RSPT 64/4* (1980): 477-89.

9:4

0795 Elmar Salmann, "Trinität und Kirche: eine dogmatische Studie," *Cath* 38/4 (1984): 352-74.

9:5

0796 P.-W. Scheele, "Wer bist du Herr: Vom rechten Fragen nach dem Christus praesens," in Lothar Lies, ed., *Praesentia Christi* (festschrift for Johannes Betz). Düsseldorf: Patmos Verlag, 1984. Pp. 19-24.

9:7

0797 Robert G. Bratcher, "*Akouo* in Acts 9:7 and 22:9," *ET* 71 (1960): 243-45.

0798 Gert Steuernagel, "Ἀκούοντες μὲν τῆς φωνῆς: Ein Genitiv in der Apostelgeschichte," *NTS* 35/4 (1988-1989): 619-24.

9:8-10

0799 S. Sabugal, "La Mencion neotestamentaria de Damasco ¿ciudad de Siria o region de Qumran?" *BETL* 45 (1978): 403-13.

9:10-20

0800 R. A. Martin, "Syntactical Evidence of Aramaic Sources in Acts I-XV," *NTS* 11/1 (1964): 38-59.

9:15

0801 Gerhard Lohfink, " 'Meinen Namen zu Tragen . . . ,'' *BZ* 10/1 (1966): 108-15.

0802 C. H. H. Scobie, "Jesus or Paul: The Origin of the Universal Mission of the Christian Church," in Peter Richardson and John C. Hurd, eds., *From Jesus to Paul* (festschrift for Francis Wright Beare). Waterloo, Ontario: Wilfrid Laurier University Press, 1984. Pp. 47-60.

0803 C. Di Sante, "The Missionizing of the East and the Meaning of Mission in the New Testament," in Frank K. Flinn and Tyler Hendricks, eds., *Religion in the Pacific Era*. New York NY: Paragon House Publishers, 1985. Pp. 3-13.

9:16

0804 L. Legrand, "How Much He Must Suffer for My Name," *CM* 31/3 (1967): 109-11.

0805 Robert Culver, "Authority for a Going and Sending Ministry in the Christian Mission of World Evangelism," in Morris Inch and Ronald Youngblood, eds., *The Living and Active Word of God* (festschrift for Samuel J. Schultz). Winona Lake IN: Eisenbrauns, 1983. Pp. 157-70.

9:17-19

0806 Robert V. Thompson, "Eyesight and Insight," *ChrM* 17/1 (1986): 29-31.

9:18
> **0807** E. S. Buchanan, "Some Noteworthy Readings of the Fleury Palimpsest," *JTS* 9 (1907-1908): 98-100.

9:19-30
> **0808** A. Wainwright, "The Historical Value of Acts 9:19b-30," *TU* 112/6 (1973): 589-94.

9:19-25
> **0809** Charles Masson, "A Propos de Act 9:19b-25," *TZ* 18 (1962): 161-66.

9:19-22
> **0810** David L. Jones, "Luke's Unique Interest in Historical Chronology," *SBLSP* 28 (1989): 378-87.

9:20
> **0811** Donald L. Jones, "The Title huios theou in Acts," *SBLSP* 24 (1985): 451-63.

9:20
> **0812** J. Kremer, " 'Dieser ist der Sohn Gottes: Bibeltheologische Erwägungen zur Bedeutung von 'Sohn Gottes' in lukanischen Doppelwerk," in C. Bussmann and W. Radl, eds., *Der Treue Gottes trauem: Beiträge zum Wekre des Lukas* (festschrift for Gerhard Schneider). Freiburg: Herder, 1991. Pp. 137-58.

9:22
> **0813** Norbert Lohfink, "Eine alttestamentliche Darstellungsform für Gotteserscheinungen in den Damaskusberichten," *BZ* N.S. 9 (1965): 246-57.

> **0814** Robert L. Reymond, "The Justification of Theology with a Special Application to Contemporary Christology," *Pres* 12/1 (1986): 1-16.

9:23-25
> **0815** Mark Harding, "On the Historicity of Acts: Comparing Acts 9:23-25 with 2 Corinthians 11:32-33," *NTS* 39/4 (1993): 518-38.

9:25
> **0816** Jos Janssens, "Il cristiano di fronte al martirio imminente: testimonianze e dottrina nella chiesa antica," *Greg* 66/3 (1985): 405-27.

9:26-30
- **0817** F. F. Bruce, "Galatian Problems: 1. Autobiographical Data," *BJRL* 11/2 (1969): 292-309.

0818 C. J. Hemer, "Acts and Galatians Reconsidered," *Themelios* 20/3 (1977): 81-88.

0819 J. Morgado, "Paul in Jerusalem: A Comparison of His Visits in Acts and Galatians," *JETS* 37 (1994): 55-68.

9:26

0820 Jules Cambier, "Le Voyage de Saint Paul à Jérusalem en Act 9:26ss et le Schéma Missionaire Théologique de Saint Luc," *NTS* 8 (1961-1962): 249-57.

0821 Norbert Lohfink, "Eine alttestamentliche Darstellungsform für Gotteserscheinungen in den Damaskusberichten," *BZ* N.S. 9 (1965): 246-57.

0822 C. J. Hemer, "Acts and Galatians Reconsidered," *Themelios* 2/3 (1977): 81-88.

0823 John Weborg, "Giving the Soul Wings," *ChrM* 16/1 (1985): 28.

9:27

0824 R. T. France, "Barnabas—Son of Encouragement," *ERT* 4/1 (1980): 91-101.

9:28-39

0825 Stephen Gaselee, "Two Fayoumic Fragments of the Acts," *JTS* 11 (1909-10): 514-17.

9:29

0826 Everett Ferguson, "The Hellenists in the Book of Acts," *RQ* 12/4 (1969): 159-80.

0827 R. Pesch, E. Gerhart, and F. Schilling, " 'Hellenisten' und 'Hebräer.' Zu Apg 9:29 und 6:1," *BZ* N.S. 23/1 (1979): 87-92.

9:30

0828 Sherman E. Johnson, "Caesarea Maritima," *LTQ* 20 (1985): 28-32.

9:31-43
> **0829** R. A. Martin, "Syntactical Evidence of Aramaic Sources in Acts I-XV," *NTS* 11/1 (1964): 38-59.

9:31
> **0830** Kevin N. Giles, "Luke's Use of the Term 'Ekklesia' with Special Reference to Acts 20.28 and 9.31," *NTS* 31/1 (1985): 135-42.

> **0831** Eduard Schweizer, "The Testimony to Jesus in the Early Christian Community," *HBT* 7/1 (1985): 77-98.

9:32-11:18
> **0832** D. S. Dockery, "Acts 6-12: The Christian Mission beyond Jerusalem," *RevExp* 87 (1990): 423-37.

9:32-43
> **0833** F. Hahn, "Zum Problem der antiochenischen Quelle in der Apostelgeschichte," in B. Jaspert, ed., *Rudolf Bultmanns Werk und Wirkung*. Darmstadt: Wissenschaftliche Buchgesellschaft, 1984. Pp. 316-31.

9:32-35
> **0834** M. Zovkic, "Krscani kao obraceni gospodinu: Christiani tamquan conversi ad Cominum in Acts 9,32-35; 11,19-21," *BogS* 44 (1974): 507-23.

9:34-38
> **0835** H. A. Sanders, "A Third Century Papyrus of Matthew and Acts," in R. P. Casey, et aL., eds., *Quantulacumque: Studies Presented to Kirsopp Lake*. London: Christophers, 1937. Pp. 151-61.

9:34-10:1
> **0836** Bruce M. Metzger, "Recently Published Greek Papyri of the New Testament," *BA* 10 (1947): 25-44.

9:36-11:18
> **0837** Raimundo Panikkar, "The Crux of Christian Ecumenism: Can Universality and Chosenness Be Held Simultaneously?" *JES* 26 (1989): 82-99.

9:36-43
> **0838** M. Trotter, "Acts in Esther," *QR* 14/4 (1994-1995): 435-47.

9:37

0839 J. Smit Sibinga, "Acts 9,37 and Other Cases of Ellipsis Obiecti," in Tjitze J. Baarda, ed., *Text and Testimony: Essays on New Testament and Apocryphal Literatue* (festschrift for A. F. J. Klijn). Kampen: Hok, 1988. Pp. 242-46.

9:40-10:1

0840 H. A. Sanders, "A Third Century Papyrus of Matthew and Acts," in R. P. Casey, et aL., eds., *Quantulacumque: Studies Presented to Kirsopp Lake*. London: Christophers, 1937. Pp. 151-61.

10:1-11:18

0841 François Bovon, "Tradition et rédaction en Actes 10,1-11,18," *TZ* 26 (1970): 22-45.

0842 Edgar Haulette, "Fondation d'une communauté de type universel: Actes 10,1-11,18. Étude critique sur la rédaction, la 'structure' et la 'tradition' du récit," *RSR* 58/1 (1970): 63-100.

0843 Louis Marin, "Essai d'analyse structurale d'Actes 10,1-11,18," *RSR* 58/1 (1970): 39-61.

0844 Barbara Hall, "La communauté chrétienne dans le livre des Actes: Actes 6:1-7 et 10:1-11:18," *FV* Suppl (1971): 146-56.

0845 Mark A. Plunkett, "Ethnocentricity and Salvation History in the Cornelius Episode," *SBLSP* 24 (1985): 465-79.

0846 A. Dauer, "Ergänzungen und 'Variationen' in den Reden der Apostelgeschichte gegenüber vorausgegangenen Erzählungen Beobachtungen zur literarischen Arbeitsweise des Lukas," in Hubert Frankemölle and Karl Kertelge, eds., *Vom Urchristentum zu Jesus* (festschrift for Joachim Gnilka). Freiburg: Herder, 1989. Pp. 307-24.

0847 John H. Elliott, "Household and Meals vs. Temple Purity: Replication Patterns in Luke-Acts," *BTB* 21 (1991): 102-108.

0848 J. Julius Scott, "The Cornelius Incident in the Light of its Jewish Setting," *JETS* 34 (1991): 475-84.

0849 J. C. Congo, "Etapas do nascimento duma Igreja Segundo o episódio de Cornélio," doctoral dissertation, Rome, Pontificial University, Rome, 1992.

0850 J. I. H. McDonald, "Rhetorical Issue and Rhetorical Strategy in Luke 10:25-37 and Acts 10:1-11:18," in S. E. Porter and T. H. Olbricht, eds., *Rhetoric in the New Testament*. Sheffield: JSOT, 1993. Pp. 59-73.

0851 Ronald D. Witherup, "Cornelius Over and Over and Over Agian: 'Functional Redundancy' in the Acts of the Apostles," *JSNT* 49 (1993): 45-66.

10:1-11:8
0852 C. Lukasz, *Evangelization e conflitto. Indagine sulla coerenza letteraria e tematica della pericope di Cornelio (Acts 10:1-11:8)*. Franfurt am Main: Lang, 1993.

10
0853 Edward Hanahoe, "St. Paul, Apostle of the Nations," *Unitas* 12 (1960): 248-55.

0854 Klaus Haacker, "Einige Falle von 'Erlebter Rede' im Neuen Testament," *NovT* 12/1 (1970): 70-77.

0855 B. E. Thiering, "Qumran Initiation and New Testament Baptism," *NTS* 27/5 (1981): 615-31.

0856 C. House, "Defilement by Association: Some Insights from the Usage of Koino/Doino in Acts 10 and 11," *AUSS* 21/2 (1983): 143-53.

0857 Jouette M. Bassler, "Luke and Paul On Impartiality," *Bib* 66/4 (1985): 546-52.

0858 Willy Beppler, "Die ökumenische Bekehrung des Petrus," *OR* 34/3 (1985): 373-79.

0859 Glenn N. Davis, "When Was Cornelius Saved?" *RTR* 46/2 (1987): 43-49.

0860 Robert W. Wall, "Peter, 'Son' of Jonah: the Conversion of Cornelius in the Context of Canon," *JSNT* 29 (1987): 79-90.

0861 F. R. Harm, "Structural Elements Related to the Gift of the Holy Spirit in Acts," *CJ* 14/1 (1988): 28-41.

0862 Abraham Friesen, "Acts 10: The Baptism of Cornelius as Interpreted by Thomas Muntzer and Felix Manz," *MQR* 64/1 (1990): 5-22.

0863 H. E. Dollar, "The Conversion of the Messenger," *Miss* 21/1 (1993): 13-19.

0864 Roland Barthes, "L'Analyse Structurale du Récit. À propos d'Actes 10-11," *RechSR* 58/1 (1970): 17-37.

0865 Sherman E. Johnson, "Caesarea Maritima," *LTQ* 20 (1985): 28-32.

10:1-33

0866 J. Julius Scott, "The Cornelius Incident in the Light of Its Jewish Setting," *JETS* 34 (1991): 475-84.

10:2

0867 Gerhard Delling, "Zur Taufe von 'Hausern' im Urchristentum," *NovT* 7 (1965): 285-311.

10:4

0868 George L. Lasebikan, "Glossolalia: Its Relationship with Speech Disabilities and Personality Disorders," *AfTJ* 14/2 (1985): 111-20.

10:23-48

0869 J. O'Callaghan, "Nuevo pergamino de la Vulgate latina," *Bib* 56/3 (1975): 410-15.

10:24-48

0870 Sherman E. Johnson, "Caesarea Maritima," *LTQ* 20 (1985): 28-32.

10:24-25

0871 Richard I. Pervo, "Social and Religious Aspects of the Western Text," in Dennis Groh and Robert Jewett, eds., *The Living Text* (festschrift for Ernest Saunders). Lanham MD: University Press of America, 1985. Pp. 229-41.

10:25-26

0872 H. J. Klauck, "With Paul in Paphos and Lystra: Magic and Paganism in the Acts of the Apostles," *Neo* 28 (1994): 93-108.

10:26-43
>   **0873** R. A. Martin, "Syntactical Evidence of Aramaic Sources in Acts
>   I-XV," *NTS* 11/1 (1964): 38-59.

10:26-31
>   **0874** Carl H. Kraeling, "P⁵⁰. Two Selections from Acts,"
>   *Quantulacumque. Studies Presented to Kirsopp Lake.* Edited by
>   Robert P. Casey, Silva Lake, and Agnes K. Lake. London:
>   Christophers, 1937. Pp. 163-72.

>   **0875** Bruce M. Metzger, "Recently Published Greek Papyri of the New
>   Testament," *BA* 10 (1947): 25-44.

10:28-29
>   **0876** Charles Perrot, "Un Fragment Christo-palestinien Découvert à
>   Khirbet Mird: Actes des Apôtres," *RB* 70 (1963): 506-55.

>   **0877** Marion L. Soards, "Peter's Speech at Cornelius's House," in *The
>   Speeches in Acts: Their Content, Context, and Concerns.*
>   Louisville: John Knox/Westminster Press, 1994. Pp. 70-77.

10:30
>   **0878** Eduard Schweizer, "The Testimony to Jesus in the Early Christian
>   Community," *HBT* 7/1 (1985): 77-98.

10:32-41
>   **0879** Charles Perrot, "Un Fragment Christo-palestinien Découvert à
>   Khirbet Mird: Actes des Apôtres," *RB* 70 (1963): 506-55.

10:33
>   **0880** Richard I. Pervo, "Social and Religious Aspects of the Western
>   Text," in Dennis Groh and Robert Jewett, eds., *The Living Text*
>   (festschrift for Ernest Saunders). Lanham MD: University Press of
>   America, 1985. Pp. 229-41.

10:34-48
>   **0881** Denton Lotz, "Peter's Wider Understanding of God's Will: Acts
>   10:34-48," *IRM* 77 (1988): 201-207.

10:34-44
>   **0882** N. Alldrit, "La Kristologia de la Parolado de Sankta Petro en Agoj
>   10:34-44," *BibR* 7 (1966): 28-31.

10:34-43

0883 E. Plümacher, "Die Missionsreden der Apostelgeschichte und Dionys von Halikarnass," *NTS* 39/2 (1993): 161-77.

0884 R. S. MacKenzie, "The Western Text of Acts: Some Lucanisms in Selected Sermons," *JBL* 104/4 (1985): 637-50.

0885 F. J. Matera, "Acts 10:34-43," *Int* 41/1 (1987): 62-66.

0886 R. C. Tannehill, "Mission in the 1990s: Reflections on the Easter Lections from Acts," *QR* 10/1 (1990): 84-97.

0887 S. Sabugal, " ¡'Dios lo constituy juez de vivos y muertos!' An lisis histrico-tradicional," *EstAg* 27 (1992): 253-71.

0888 E. Plümacher, "Die Missionsreden der Apostelgeschichte und Dionys von Halikarnass," *NTS* 39 (1993): 161-77.

0889 J. Rius-Camps, "El discurs de Pere deviant Corneli, interromput per l'Esperit Sant pel seu cire judaïtzant," in F. Rauell, et al., eds., *Tradició i Traducció de la Paraula* (festschrift for Guiu Camps). Montserrat: Associación Bíblica de Catalunya, 1993. Pp. 169-88.

0890 Marion L. Soards, "Peter's Speech at Cornelius's House," in *The Speeches in Acts: Their Content, Context, and Concerns.* Louisville: John Knox/Westminster Press, 1994. Pp. 70-77.

10:34-40

0891 Pieter de Villiers, "God Raised Him on the Third Day and Made Him Manifest . . and He Commanded Us to Preach to the People," *JTSA* 70 (1990): 55-63.

10:34-35

0892 John B. Polhill, "No Respecter of Persons: God's View of Race Relations," *BI* 12/4 (1986): 66-71.

10:34

0893 Troy Organ, "A Cosmomogical Christology," *CC* 88/44 (1971): 1293-95.

10:36-43

0894 F. Neirynck, "Le Livre des Actes (6): Ac 10, 36-43 et L'Évangile," *ETL* 60/1 (1984): 109-17.

0895   Alfons Weiser, "Tradition und lukanische Komposition in Apg
        10:36-43," in Françios Refoulé, ed., À cause de l'Évangile: Études
        sur les synoptiques et les Actes (festschrift for Jacques Dupont).
        Paris: Cerf, 1985. Pp. 757-67.

10:36
        0896   Giovanni Rinaldi, "Lógos in Atti 10:36," BibO 12/4-5 (1970):
                223-25.

        0897   J. Corell, "Actos 10:36," EstFr 76/1 (1975): 101-13.

        0898   F. Neirynck, "Acts 10:36a: τὸν λόγον ὅν," ETL 60/1 (1984):
                118-23.

        0899   Jacques Dupont, "Le Seigneur de tous," in Gerald F. Hawthorne
                and Otto Betz, eds., Tradition & Interpretation in the New
                Testament (festschrift for E. Earle Ellis). Grand Rapids MI:
                Eerdmans, 1987. Pp. 229-36.

10:37-43
        0900   Wilhelm Wilkens, "Die Theologische Struktur der Komposition
                des Lukas-Evangelium," TZ 34/1 (1978): 1-13.

10:37
        0901   O. Knoch, "Jesus, der 'Wohltäter' und 'Befreier' des Menschen.
                Das Christuszeugnis der Predigt des Petrus vor Kornelius," GeistL
                46/1 (1973): 1-7.

10:39
        0902   J. A. Fitzmyer, "Crucifixion in Ancient Palestine, Qumran
                Literature, and the New Testament," CBQ 40/4 (1978): 493-513.

10:41
        0903   Juan J. Bartolome, "Synesthiein en la Obra Lucana: Lc 15,2; Hch
                10,41; 11,3," Sale 46/2 (1984): 269-88.

10:42
        0904   Leslie C. Allen, "The Old Testament Background of
                (προ)ὡρισμένη in the New Testament," NTS 17/1 (1970-1971):
                104-108.

        0905   A. J. Mattill, "Naherwartung, Fernerwartung, and the Purpose of
                Luke-Acts: Weymouth Reconsidered," CBQ 34/3 (1972): 276-93.

0906 Rudolf Schnackenburg, "Die lukanische Eschatologie im Lichte von Aussagen der Apostelgeschichte," in E. Grässer and O. Merk, eds., *Glaube und Eschatologie* (festschrift for W. G. Kümmel). Tübingen: Mohr, 1985. Pp. 249-65.

10:43

0907 I. de la Potterie, "L'economia fede-sacramento nel nuovo testamento," in P.-R. Tragan, ed., *Fede e sacramenti negli scritti giovannei.* Rome: Edizioni Abbazia, 1972. Pp. 27-46.

10:44-48

0908 R. K. Levang, "The Content of an Utterance in Tongues," *Para* 23/1 (1989): 14-20.

10:46

0909 Ralph E. Knudsen, "Speaking in Tongues," *Found* 9 (1966): 43-57.

0910 Robert W. Graves, "Use of γάρ in Acts 10:46," *Para* 22 (1988): 15-18.

0911 J. Everts, "Tongues or Languages? Contextual Consistency in the Translation of Acts 2," *JPTh* 4 (1994) 71-80.

10:47

0912 Marion L. Soards, "Peter's Speech at Cornelius's House," in *The Speeches in Acts: Their Content, Context, and Concerns.* Louisville: John Knox/Westminster Press, 1994. Pp. 70-77.

11

0913 B. P. Grenfell and A. S. Hunt, "Acts, Chap. 11," in *The Amherst Papyri.* Part 1. London: Henry Frowde, 1900. Pp. 41-43.

0914 A. S. Wood, "Social Involvement in the Apostolic Church," *EQ* 42/4 (1970): 194-212.

0915 Francis Lenssen, "Biblical Communities: Christian Communities in the New Testament," *Point* 1 (1972): 24-34.

0916 É. Delebecque, "La montée de Pierre de Césarée à Jerusalem selon le Codex Bezae au chapitre 11 des Actes des Apôtres," *ETL* 58/1 (1982): 106-10.

0917 C. House, "Defilement by Association: Some Insights from the Usage of Koino/Doino in Acts 10 and 11," *AUSS* 21/2 (1983): 143-53.

<u>11:1-18</u>
0918 R. A. Martin, "Syntactical Evidence of Aramaic Sources in Acts I-XV," *NTS* 11/1 (1964): 38-59.

0919 D. L. Tiede, "Acts 11:1-18," *Int* 42/2 (1988): 175-80.

0920 M. Trotter, "Acts in Esther," *QR* 14/4 (1994-1995): 435-47.

<u>11:2</u>
0921 Richard I. Pervo, "Social and Religious Aspects of the Western Text," in Dennis Groh and Robert Jewett, eds., *The Living Text* (festschrift for Ernest Saunders). Lanham MD: University Press of America, 1985. Pp. 229-41.

<u>11:3</u>
0922 Juan J. Bartolome, "Synesthiein en la Obra Lucana: Lc 15,2; Hch 10,41; 11,3," *Sale* 46/2 (1984): 269-88.

<u>11:4</u>
0923 E. Dassmann, "Hausgemeinde und Bischofsamt," in Ernst Dassmann and Klaus Thraede, eds., *Vivarium* (festschrift for Theodor Klauser). Münster, West Germany: Aschendorff, 1984. Pp. 82-97.

<u>11:5-17</u>
0924 Marion L. Soards, "Peter's Speech to the Circumcision Party," in *The Speeches in Acts: Their Content, Context, and Concerns.* Louisville: John Knox/Westminster Press, 1994. Pp. 77-79.

<u>11:5</u>
0925 Timothy Trammel, "Joppa," *BI* 13/2 (1987): 55-59.

<u>11:14</u>
0926 Gerhard Delling, "Zur Taufe von 'Hausern' im Urchristentum," *NovT* 7 (1965): 285-311.

<u>11:15</u>
0927 John J. Kilgallen, "Did Peter Actually Fail to Get a Word in?" *Bib* 71/3 (1990): 405-10.

11:17

0928 Richard I. Pervo, "Social and Religious Aspects of the Western Text," in Dennis Groh and Robert Jewett, eds., *The Living Text* (festschrift for Ernest Saunders). Lanham MD: University Press of America, 1985. Pp. 229-41.

0929 J. A. Jáuregui, "Israel y la iglesia en la teologia de Lucas," *EE* 61 (1986): 129-49.

11:18

0930 Troy Organ, "A Cosmomogical Christology," *CC* 88/44 (1971): 1293-95.

11:19-30

0931 David P. Moessner, "The Christ Must Suffer: New Light on the Jesus—Peter, Stephen, Paul Parallels in Luke-Acts," *NovT* 28/3 (1986): 220-56.

0932 D. S. Dockery, "Acts 6-12: The Christian Mission beyond Jerusalem," *RevExp* 87 (1990): 423-37.

0933 D. Z. Niringiye, "Jerusalem to Antioch to the World: A Biblical Missions Strategy," *EMQ* 26/1 (1990): 56-61.

11:19-26

0934 Otto Merk, "Die Apostelgeschichte im Frühwerk Rudolf Bultmanns," in Bernd Jaspert, ed., *Rudolf Bultmanns Werk und Wirkung*. Darmstadt, West Germany: Wissenschaftliche Buchgesellschaft, 1984. Pp. 303-15.

11:19-21

0935 M. Zovkic, "Krscani kao obraceni gospodinu: Christiani tamquan conversi ad Cominum in Acts 9,32-35; 11,19-21," *BogS* 44 (1974): 507-23.

11:19-20

0936 Wayne Dehoney, "Cyprus," *BI* 13/3 (1987): 67-69.

11:19

0937 Fred A. Grissom, "The Church Scattered," *BI* 13/3 (1987): 55-58.

11:20

0938 Pierson Parker, "Three Variant Readings in Luke-Acts," *JBL* 83 (1964): 165-70.

0939 Everett Ferguson, "The Hellenists in the Book of Acts," *RQ* 12/4 (1969): 159-80.

0940 C. H. H. Scobie, "Jesus or Paul: The Origin of the Universal Mission of the Christian Church," in Peter Richardson and John C. Hurd, eds., *From Jesus to Paul* (festschrift for Francis Wright Beare). Waterloo, Ontario: Wilfrid Laurier University Press, 1984. Pp. 47-60.

11:22

0941 R. T. France, "Barnabas—Son of Encouragement," *ERT* 4/1 (1980): 91-101.

0942 F. F. Bruce, "The Church of Jerusalem in the Acts of the Apostles," *BJRL* 67/2 (1985): 641-61.

11:25

0943 R. T. France, "Barnabas—Son of Encouragement," *ERT* 4/1 (1980): 91-101.

11:26-28

0944 É. Delebecque, "Saul et Luc avant le premier voyage missionaire: Comparaison des deux versions des Actes 11:26-28," *RSPT* 66/4 (1982): 551-59.

11:26

0945 Harold B. Mattingly, "The Origin of the Name 'Christiani'," *JTS* N.S. 9 (1958): 26-37.

0946 Ian Macleod, "Chance Names Which Stuck," *ET* 96 (1985): 242.

0947 C. Schuppan, "Bewegung in Antiochia. Eine narrative Exegese zu Apg 11,26," in A. Meinhold and R. Lux (ed.), *Gottesvolk: Beiträge zu einem Thema biblischer Theologie* (festschrift for Günter Wagner). Berlin: Evangelische Verlagsanstalt, 1991. Pp. 125-35.

0948 J. Taylor, "Why Were the Disciples First Called 'Christians' at Antioch?" *RB* 101 (1994): 75-94.

11:27-12:25
0949 Suzanne Poque, "Une lecture d'Actes: 11,27-12,25," *ÉTR* 55/2 (1980): 265-78.

11:27-30
0950 D. F. Robinson, "A Note on Acts 11:27-30," *JBL* 63 (1944): 169-72.

0951 Georg Strecker, "Die sogenannte zweite Jerusalemreise des Paulus," *ZNW* 53 (1962): 67-77.

0952 David R. Catchpole, "Paul, James and the Apostolic Decree," *NTS* 23/4 (1976-1977): 428-44.

0953 R. P. Martin, "The Setting of 2 Corinthians," *TynB* 37 (1986): 3-19.

11:27
0954 Georg Strecker, "Die sogenannte zweite Jerusalemreise des Paulus," *ZNW* 53 (1962): 67-77.

11:28
0955 H. Patsch, "Die Prophetie des Agabus," *TZ* 28 (1972): 228-32.

0956 Scott Andrew, "Claudius Caesar," *BI* 14 (1989): 62-65.

11:29
0957 S. Aalen, "Versuch einer Analyse des Diakonia-Begriffes im Neuen Testament," in William Weinrich, ed., *The New Testament Age* (festschrift for Bo Reicke). 2 vols. Macon GA: Mercer University Press, 1984. 1:1-13.

11:30
0958 F. F. Bruce, "Galatian Problems: 1. Autobiographical Data," *BJRL* 11/2 (1969): 292-309.

0959 R. H. Stein, "The Relationship of Galatians 2:1-10 and Acts 15:1-35; Two Neglected Arguments," *JETS* 17/4 (1974): 239-42.

0960 C. J. Hemer, "Acts and Galatians Reconsidered," *Themelios* 20/3 (1977): 81-88.

0961 R. T. France, "Barnabas—Son of Encouragement," *ERT* 4/1 (1980): 91-101.

0962 J. Morgado, "Paul in Jerusalem: A Comparison of His Visits in Acts and Galatians," *JETS* 37 (1994): 55-68.

12-28
0963 T. C. Geer, "The Two Faces of Codex 33 in Acts," *NovT* 31/1 (1989): 39-47.

12-21
0964 George D. Kilpatrick, "Jesus, His Family and His Disciples," *JSNT* 15 (1982): 3-19.

12
0965 W. Radl, "Befreiung aus dem Gefängnis-die Darstellung Eines Biblischen Grundthemas in Apg 12," *BZ* 27/1 (1983): 81-96.

12:1-25
0966 R. A. Martin, "Syntactical Evidence of Aramaic Sources in Acts I-XV," *NTS* 11/1 (1964): 38-59.

12:1-24
0967 D. S. Dockery, "Acts 6-12: The Christian Mission beyond Jerusalem," *RevExp* 87 (1990): 123-37.

0968 Susan R. Garrett, "Exodus from Bondage: Luke 9:31 and Acts 12:1-24," *CBQ* 52 (1990): 656-80.

0969 W. Rakocy, "Trionfo del piano salvifico di Dio," doctoral dissertation, Pontifical University Gregorium, Rome, 1991.

12:1-23
0970 Rolf Eulenstein, "Die wundersame Befreiung des Petrus aus Todesgefahr, Acta 12,1-23," *WD* 12 (1973): 43-69.

12:1-23
0971 F. Hahn, "Zum Problem der antiochenischen Quelle in der Apostelgeschichte," in B. Jaspert, ed., *Rudolf Bultmanns Werk und Wirkung*. Darmstadt: Wissenschaftliche Buchgesellschaft, 1984. Pp. 316-31.

12:1-17
0972 Robert W. Wall, "Successors to 'The Twelve' According to Acts 12:1-17," *CBQ* 53 (1991): 628-43.

12:2
0973 Josef Blinzler, "Rechtsgeschichtliches zur Hinrichtung des Zebedäiden Jakobus," *NovT* 5 (1962): 191-206.

0974 Günther Zunts, "Wann wurde das Evangelium Marci geschrieben," in Hubert Cancik, ed., *Markus-Philologie*. Tübingen: Mohr, 1984. Pp. 47-71.

12:6-7
0975 Jerome D. Quinn, "Seven Times He Wore Chains," *JBL* 97 (1978): 574-76.

12:6
0976 S. T. Lachs, "Hebrew Elements in the Gospels and Acts," *JQR* 71/1 (1980): 31-43.

12:12
0977 Norbert Brox, "Zur Pseudepigraphischen Rahmung des Ersten Petrusbriefes," *BZ* 19/1 (1975): 78-96.

0978 C. C. Black, "The Presentation of John Mark in the Acts of the Apostles," *PRS* 20 (1993): 235-54.

12:17
0979 Morton Smith, "The Report about Peter in 1 Clement V. 4.," *NTS* 7 (1960): 86-88.

0980 E. Dassmann, "Hausgemeinde und Bischofsamt," in Ernst Dassmann and Klaus Thraede, eds., *Vivarium* (festschrift for Theodor Klauser). Münster, West Germany: Aschendorff, 1984. Pp. 82-97.

0981 C. P. Thiede, "Babylon, der andere Ort: Anmerkungen zu 1 Petr 5,13 und Apg 12,17," *Bib* 67/4 (1986): 532-38.

12:19
0982 Sherman E. Johnson, "Caesarea Maritima," *LTQ* 20 (1985): 28-32.

12:20-23
    0983 Mark R. Strom, "An Old Testament Background to Acts 12:20-23," *NTS* 32/2 (1986): 289-92.

12:21-23
    0984 H. J. Klauck, "With Paul in Paphos and Lystra: Magic and Paganism in the Acts of the Apostles," *Neo* 28 (1994): 93-108.

12:23
    0985 F. C. Conybeare, "Two Notes on Acts," *ZNW* 20 (1921): 136-42.

    0986 Josef Blinzler, "Rechtsgeschichtliches zur Hinrichtung des Zebedäiden Jakobus," *NovT* 5 (1962): 191-206.

12:24
    0987 M. H. Franzmann, "The Word of the Lord Grew," *CTM* 30 (1959): 563-81.

    0988 J. Kodell, " 'The Word of God Grew.' The Ecclesial Tendency of *Logos* in Acts 6:7; 12:24; 19:20," *Bib* 55/4 (1974): 505-19.

    0989 M. H. Grumm, "Another Look at Acts," *ET* 96/11 (1985): 333-37.

12:25
    0990 Jacques Dupont, "La mission de Paul à Jérusalem," *NovT* 1 (1956): 275-303.

    0991 R. H. Stein, "The Relationship of Galatians 2:1-10 and Acts 15:1-35; Two Neglected Arguments," *JETS* 17/4 (1974): 239-42.

    0992 E. G. Edwards, "On Using the Textual Apparatus of the UBS Greek New Testament," *BT* 28/1 (1977): 121-42.

    0993 R. T. France, "Barnabas—Son of Encouragement," *ERT* 4/1 (1980): 91-101.

    0994 S. Aalen, "Versuch einer Analyse des Diakonia-Begriffes im Neuen Testament," in William Weinrich, ed., *The New Testament Age* (festschrift for Bo Reicke). 2 vols. Macon GA: Mercer University Press, 1984. 1:1-13.

    0995 J. Morgado, "Paul in Jerusalem: A Comparison of His Visits in Acts and Galatians," *JETS* 37 (1994): 55-68.

13-25

0996 H. Dixon Slingerland, " 'The Jews' in the Pauline Portion of Acts," *JAAR* 54/2 (1986): 305-21.

13-19

0997 R. Alan Culpepper, "Paul's Mission to the Gentile World: Acts 13-19," *RevExp* 71/4 (1974): 487-97.

0998 J. L. Blevins, "Acts 13-19: The Tale of Three Cites," *RevExp* 87 (1990): 439-50.

13-14

0999 R. L. Roberts, "Notes on Selected Passages," *RQ* 4 (1960): 234-58.

1000 David R. Catchpole, "Paul, James and the Apostolic Decree," *NTS* 23/4 (1976-1977): 428-44.

1001 Ken Kilinski, "How Churches Can Follow Antioch's Model," *EMQ* 15/1 (1979): 19-23.

1002 J. Rius-Camps, "La misión hacia el paganismo avalada por el Señor Jesús y el Espíritu Santo," *EB* 52 (1994): 341-60.

13

1003 Francis Lenssen, "Biblical Communities: Christian Communities in the New Testament," *Point* 1 (1972): 24-34.

1004 F. F. Bruce, "Was Paul a Mystic?" *RTR* 34/3 (1975): 66-75.

1005 Harold R. Cook, "Who Really Sent the First Missionaries?" *EMQ* 11/4 (1975): 233-39.

1006 A. W. Swamidoss, "The Speeches of Paul in Acts 13, 17 and 20," doctoral dissertation, Fuller Theological Seminary, Pasadena CA, 1979.

1007 Glenn N. Davis, "When Was Cornelius Saved?" *RTR* 46/2 (1987): 43-49.

13:1-5

1008 Carl H. Morgan, "Vision and Action at Antioch," *Found* 3 (1960): 362-64; 4 (1961): 77-80.

13:1-4

1009 Robert Culver, "Authority for a Going and Sending Ministry in the Christian Mission of World Evangelism," in Morris Inch and Ronald Youngblood, eds., *The Living and Active Word of God* (festschrift for Samuel J. Schultz). Winona Lake IN: Eisenbrauns, 1983. Pp. 157-70.

1010 Alvaro Huerga, "La Implantation de la Iglesia en el nuevo Mundo," *Ang* 63/2 (1986): 227-56.

1011 J. Fain, "Church-Mission Relationships: What We Can Learn from Acts 13:1-4," *SouJT* 2 (1994): 19-39.

13:1-3

1012 Ernest Best, "Acts 13:1-3," *JTS* 11 (1960): 344-48.

1013 S. Dockx, "L'ordination de Barnabé et de Saul d'après Actes 13:1-3," *NRT* 98/3 (1976): 238-58.

1014 D. Z. Niringiye, "Jerusalem to Antioch to the World: A Biblical Missions Strategy," *EMQ* 26/1 (1990): 56-61.

13:1-2

1015 R. T. France, "Barnabas—Son of Encouragement," *ERT* 4/1 (1980): 91-101.

13:1

1016 Richard Glover, " 'Luke the Antiochene' and Acts," *NTS* 11/1 (1964): 97-106.

1017 Agustín del Agua Perez, "El papel de la 'escuela midrásica' en la configuración del Nuevo Testamento," *EE* 60/234 (1985): 333-49.

1018 John Wenham, "The Identification of Luke," *EQ* 63/1 (1991): 3-44.

13:3

1019 R. L. Roberts, "Notes on Selected Passages," *RQ* 4 (1960): 234-58.

1020 Timothy N. Boyd, "The Laying on of Hands," *BI* (1989): 9-10.

13:4-12
1021   H. J. Klauck, "With Paul in Paphos and Lystra: Magic and Paganism in the Acts of the Apostles," *Neo* 28 (1994): 93-108.

13:5
1022   C. C. Black, "The Presentation of John Mark in the Acts of the Apostles," *PRS* 20 (1993): 235-54.

13:6-12
1023   L. Yaure, "Elymas—Nehelamite—Pethor," *JBL* 79 (1960): 297-314.

13:6
1024   Constantin Daniel, "Un Essénien mentionné dans les Actes des Apôtres: Barjésu," *Mus* 84/3-4 (1971): 455-76.

13:7-2
1025   R. T. France, "Barnabas—Son of Encouragement," *ERT* 4/1 (1980): 91-101.

13:8
1026   J. M. Fenasse, "Paul recontre le magicien Elymas," *BTS* 136 (1971): 14.

13:9
1027   F. C. Synge, "Acts 13:9: Saul, Who is Also Paul," *Theology* 63 (1960): 199-200.

13:13-52
1028   R. F. O'Toole, "Christ's Resurrection in Acts 13:13-52," *Bib* 60/3 (1979): 361-72.

1029   Otto Merk, "Die Apostelgeschichte im Frühwerk Rudolf Bultmanns," in Bernd Jaspert, ed., *Rudolf Bultmanns Werk und Wirkung*. Darmstadt, West Germany: Wissenschaftliche Buchgesellschaft, 1984. Pp. 303-15.

1030   Joseph B. Tyson, "Jews and Judaism in Luke-Acts: Reading as a Godfearer," *NTS* 41 (1995): 19-38.

13:13-43
1031   Danielle Ellul, "Antoiche de Pisidie: Une predication . . . trois credos?" *FilN* 5 (1992): 3-14.

13:13-41
1032 Clifton Black, "The Rhetorical Form of the Hellenistic Jewish and Early Christian Sermon," *HTR* 81 (1988): 1-18.

13:13
1033 C. C. Black, "The Presentation of John Mark in the Acts of the Apostles," *PRS* 20 (1993): 235-54.

13:14-52
1034 E. Plümacher, "Die Missionsreden der Apostelgeschichte und Dionys von Halikarnass," *NTS* 39 (1993): 161-77.

13:14-41
1035 Lawrence Wills, "The Form of the Sermon in Hellenistic Judaism and Early Christianity," *HTR* 77/3-4 (1984): 277-99.

13:14
1036 J. W. Bowker, "Speeches in Acts: A Study in Proem and Yelammedenu Form," *NTS* 14/1 (1967-1968): 96-111.

13:15
1037 Joseph Plevik, " 'The Eleven and Those with Them' According to Luke," *CBQ* 40/2 (1978): 205-11.

13:16-41
1038 Lars Hartman, "Davids Son. Apropa Acta 13,16-41," *SEÅ* 28-29 (1963-1964): 117-34.

1039 R. A. Martin, "Syntactical Evidence of Aramaic Sources in Acts I-XV," *NTS* 11/1 (1964): 38-59.

1040 Oscar J. F. Seitz, "Gospel Prologues: A Common Pattern?" *JBL* 83 (1964): 262-68.

1041 F. F. Bruce, "Is the Paul of Acts the Real Paul?" *BJRL* 58/2 (1976): 282-305.

1042 M. Dumais, "Le langage de l'Évangélisation: L'annonce missionnaire en milieu juif," *JTS* 29 (1978): 198.

1043 Agustín del Agua Perez, "El papel de la 'escuela midrásica' en la configuración del Nuevo Testamento," *EE* 60/234 (1985): 333-49.

1044 R. S. MacKenzie, "The Western Text of Acts: Some Lucanisms in Selected Sermons," *JBL* 104/4 (1985): 637-50.

1045 F. F. Bruce, "Paul's Use of the Old Testament in Acts," in Gerald F. Hawthorne and Otto Betz, eds., *Tradition & Interpretation in the New Testament* (festschrift for E. Earle Ellis). Grand Rapids MI: Eerdmans, 1987. Pp. 71-79.

1046 Adriana Bottino, "Il Discorso Missionario di Paolo," *RechSR* 2 (1990): 81-97.

1047 D. A. DeSilva, "Paul's Sermon in Antioch of Pisidia," *BSac* 151 (1994): 32-49.

1048 Marion L. Soards, "Paul's Speech at Antioch of Pisidia," in *The Speeches in Acts: Their Content, Context, and Concerns.* Louisville: John Knox/Westminster Press, 1994. Pp. 79-88.

13:18

1049 Robert P. Gordon, "Targumic Parallels to Acts XIII 18 and Didache XIV 3," *NovT* 16/4 (1974): 285-89.

13:20

1050 Eugene H. Merrill, "Paul's Use of 'About 450 Years' in Acts 13:20," *BSac* 138 (1981): 246-57.

13:26

1051 T. E. Brawley, "For Blessing All Families of the Earth: Covenant Traditions in Luke-Acts," *CThM* 22/1 (1995): 18-26.

13:29

1052 J. A. Fitzmyer, "Crucifixion in Ancient Palestine, Qumran Literature, and the New Testament," *CBQ* 40/4 (1978): 493-513.

13:31

1053 Edvin Larsson, "Paul: Law and Salvation," *NTS* 31 (1985): 425-36.

13:32-52

1054 H. van de Sandt, "The Quotations in Acts 13:32-52 as a Reflection of Luke's LXX: Interpretation," *Bib* 75 (1994): 26-58.

13:32-37
1055 Evald Lövestam, "Son and Saviour: A Study of Acts
      13:32-37—With an Appendix: 'Son of God' in the Synoptic
      Gospels," *CNeo* 18 (1961): 5-134.

1056 W. C. Kaiser, "The Promise to David in Psalm 16 and its
      Application in Acts 2:25-33 and 13:32-37," *JETS* 23 (1980): 219-
      29.

13:33-37
1057 Dale Goldsmith, "Acts 13:33-37: A *Pesher* on 2 Samuel 7," *JBL*
      87/3 (1968): 321-24.

13:33-35
1058 C. Ghidelli, "Un saggio di lettura dell'AT nel libro degli Atti," *PV*
      9 (1964): 83-91.

13:33
1059 George D. Kilpatrick, "Acts 13:33 and Tertullian, Adv Marc
      IV:xxii.8," *JTS* 11 (1960): 53.

1060 John H. Hayes, "The Resurrection as Enthronement and the
      Earliest Church Christology," *Int* 22/3 (1968): 333-45.

1061 Donald L. Jones, "The Title huios theou in Acts," *SBLSP* 24
      (1985): 451-63.

1062 Gérard Rochais, "Jésus savait-il qu'il était Dieu: réflexions
      critiques à propos d'un livre récent," *SR* 14/1 (1985): 85-106.

13:38-39
1063 Edvin Larsson, "Paul: Law and Salvation," *NTS* 31 (1985):
      425-36.

1064 John J. Kilgallen, "Acts 13:38-39: Culmination of Paul's Speech
      in Pisidia," *Bib* 69/4 (1988): 480-506.

13:38
1065 P. Ellingworth, "Acts 13:38—A Query," *BT* 45 (1994): 242-43.

13:39
1066 W. H. Bates, "A Note on Acts 13:39," *TU* 112 (1973): 8-10.

13:44-48
1067 Charles E. McLain, "Israel During the Church Age," *CBTJ* 2/1 (1986): 39-55.

13:44
1068 Balmer H. Kelly, "Revelation 7:9-17," *Int* 40/3 (1986): 288-95.

13:45
1069 Slayden A. Yarbrough, "The Judaizers," *BI* (1989): 16-19.

13:46-47
1070 Marion L. Soards, "Paul's Speech at Antioch of Pisidia," in *The Speeches in Acts: Their Content, Context, and Concerns.* Louisville: John Knox/Westminster Press, 1994. Pp. 79-88.

13:46
1071 R. T. France, "Barnabas—Son of Encouragement," *ERT* 4/1 (1980): 91-101.

1072 R. C. Tannehill, "Rejection by Jews and Turning to Gentiles: the Pattern of Paul's Mission in Acts," *SBLSP* 25 (1986): 130-41.

13:47
1073 P. Grelot, "Note sur Actes 13:47," *RB* 88/3 (1981): 368-72.

1074 John R. Donahue, "The 'Parable' of the Sheep and the Goats: A Challenge to Christian Ethics," *JTS* 47/1 (1986): 3-31.

13:50
1075 R. T. France, "Barnabas—Son of Encouragement," *ERT* 4/1 (1980): 91-101.

14-22
1076 Henning Paulsen, "Erwangugen zu Acta Apollonii 14-22," *ZNW* 66/1 (1975): 117-26.

14
1077 H. C. Shank, "Qoheleth's World and Life View as Seen in His Recurring Phrases," *WTJ* 37/1 (1974): 57-73.

14:1-20

1078 Johannes Beutler, "Die paulinische Heidenmission am Vorabend des Apostelkonzils: Zur Redaktionsgeschichte von Apg 14:1-20," *TheoP* 43 (1968): 360-83.

14:2

1079 Slayden A. Yarbrough, "The Judaizers," *BI* (1989): 16-19.

14:4

1080 S. Dockx, "L'ordination de Barnabé et de Saul d'après Actes 13:1-3," *NRT* 98/3 (1976): 238-58.

14:5-14

1081 E. S. Buchanan, "Two Pages from the Fleury Palimpsest with Some Newly Discovered Readings," *JTS* 7 (1905-1906): 454-55.

14:6

1082 G. Ogg, "Derbe," *NTS* 9/4 (1963): 367-70.

14:8-18

1083 D. Wiens, "Luke on Pluralism: Flex with History," *Direction* 23 (1994): 44-53.

14:8-15

1084 B. Gaertner, "Paulus und Barnabas in Lystra. Zu Apg. 14.8-15," *SEÅ* 27 (1962): 83-88.

14:11-17

1085 Cilliers Breytenbach, "Zeus und der lebendige Gott: Anmerkungen zu Apostelgeschichte 14:11-17," *NTS* 39/3 (1993): 369-413.

14:11-13

1086 F. G. Downing, "Common Ground with Paganism in Luke and Josephus," *NTS* 28/4 (1982): 546-59.

14:12

1087 R. T. France, "Barnabas—Son of Encouragement," *ERT* 4/1 (1980): 91-101.

1088 L. H. Martin, "Gods or Ambassadors of God? Barnabas and Paul in Lystra," *NTS* 41/1 (1995): 152-56.

14:14

1089 E. S. Buchanan, "Some Noteworthy Readings of the Fleury Palimpsest," *JTS* 9 (1907-1908): 98-100.

1090 W. M. Green, "Apostels—Actes 14:14," *RQ* 4 (1960): 245-47.

1091 R. L. Roberts, "Notes on Selected Passages," *RQ* 4 (1960): 234-58.

1092 S. Dockx, "L'ordination de Barnabé et de Saul d'après Actes 13:1-3," *NRT* 98/3 (1976): 238-58.

1093 R. T. France, "Barnabas—Son of Encouragement," *ERT* 4/1 (1980): 91-101.

1094 George D. Kilpatrick, "Epithuein and Epikrinein in the Greek Bible," *ZNW* 74/1 (1983): 151-53.

14:15-23

1095 E. S. Buchanan, "More Pages from the Fleury Palimpsest," *JTS* 8 (1906-07): 96-100.

14:15-18

1096 Ernst Lerle, "Die Predigt in Lystra," *NTS* 7 (1960): 46-55.

14:15-17

1097 S. Légasse, "Le discours de Paul à Lystres," in J. Doré, ed., *Penser la foi: Recherches en théologie aujour-d'nui* (festschrift for J. Moingt). Paris: Cerf, 1993. Pp. 127-36.

1098 Marion L. Soards, "The Speech of Barnabas and Paul at Lystra" in *The Speeches in Acts: Their Content, Context, and Concerns.* Louisville: John Knox/Westminster Press, 1994. Pp. 88-90.

14:15

1099 C. M. Horne, "Toward a Biblical Apologetic," *GTJ* 2 (1961): 14-18.

14:16

1100 Klaus Haacker, "Gott und die Wege der Völker," *TBe* 21 (1990): 281-84.

<u>14:17</u>
1101 W. M. Pickard, "Biblical Perspective for Dialogue," *Enc* 31/1 (1970): 42-55.

1102 Troy Organ, "A Cosmomogical Christology," *CC* 88/44 (1971): 1293-95.

1103 Jacques Dupuis, "The Practice of Agape Is the Reality of Salvation," *IRM* 74 (1985): 472-77.

1104 Ernst Lerle, "Kardia als Bezeichnung fur den Mageneingang," *ZNW* 76/3 (1985): 292-94.

1105 Malcolm J. McVeigh, "The Fate of Those Who've Never Heard: It Depends," *EMQ* 21/4 (1985): 370-79.

<u>14:20</u>
1106 G. Ogg, "Derbe," *NTS* 9/4 (1963): 367-70.

1107 R. T. France, "Barnabas—Son of Encouragement," *ERT* 4/1 (1980): 91-101.

1108 Jimmy Albright, "Derbe," *BI* 15/1 (1988): 69-72.

<u>14:21-23</u>
1109 D. F. Detweiler "Paul's Approach to the Great Commission in Acts 14:21-23," *BSac* 152/605 (1995): 33-41.

<u>14:22</u>
1110 A. J. Mattill, " 'The Way of Tribulation'," *JBL* 98/4 (1979): 531-46.

<u>14:23</u>
1111 A. Feuillet, " 'Temoins Oculaires et Serviteurs de la Parole'," *NovT* 15/4 (1973): 241-59.

1112 S. Dockx, "L'ordination de Barnabé et de Saul d'après Actes 13:1-3," *NRT* 98/3 (1976): 238-58.

1113 R. Y. K. Fung, "Charismatic Versus Organized Ministry? An Examination of an Alleged Antithesis," *EQ* 52/4 (1980): 195-214.

1114 E. Nellessen, "Die Einsetzung von Presbytern durch Barnabas und Paulus," *BBB* 53 (1980): 175-93.

14:27-15:35
1115 A. T. M. Cheung, "A Narrative Analysis of Acts 14:27-15:35: Literary Shaping in Luke's Account of the Jerusalem Council," *WTJ* 55/1 (1993): 137-54.

14:27-28
1116 G. Betori, "La strutturazione del libro degli Atti: una proposta," *RBib* 42 (1994): 3-34.

15

1117 Werner Kaschel, "The Holy Spirit in the Palestinian Churches: Acts I-XII; XV; XXI-XXIII," master's thesis, Southwestern Baptist Theological Seminary, Fort Worth TX, 1949.

1118 E. Ravarotto, "De Hierosolymitano Concilio," *Ant* 37/2 (1962): 185-218.

1119 Stanley D. Toussaint, "The Chronological Problem of Galatians 2:1-10," *BSac* 120 (1963): 334-40.

1120 E. S. English, "Was St. Peter Ever in Rome?" *BSac* 124 (1967): 314-20.

1121 Pierson Parker, "Once More, Acts and Galatians," *JBL* 86/2 (1967): 175-82.

1122 Francis Lenssen, "Biblical Communities: Christian Communities in the New Testament," *Point* 1 (1972): 24-34.

1123 T. Holtz, "Die Bedeutung des Apostelkonzils für Paulus," *NovT* 16 (1974): 110-33.

1124 A. Strobel, "Das Aposteldedret in Galatien: Zur Situation von Gal I und II," *NTS* 20/2 (1974): 177-90.

1125 John J. Kilgallen, "Acts: Literary and Theological Turning Points," *BTB* 7/4 (1977): 177-80.

1126 E. W. Johnson, "Extra-Biblical Ecclesiastical Systems," *BRR* 7/2 (1978): 13-17.

1127 I. M. Ellis, "Codex Bezae at Acts 15," *IBS* 2 (1980): 134-40.

1128 A. Wainwright, "Where Did Silas Go? And What Was His Connection with Galatians?" *JSNT* 8 (1980): 66-70.

1129 John Wenham, "The Theology of Unclean Food," *EQ* 53/1 (1981): 6-15.

1130 C. K. Barrett, "Quomodo Historia Conscribenda Sit," *NTS* 28/3 (1982): 303-20.

1131 Charles Perrot, "The Decrees of the Council of Jerusalem," *TD* 30/1 (1982): 21-24.

1132 C. K. Barrett, "Apostles in Council and in Conflict," *ABR* 31 (1983): 14-32.

1133 D. H. King, "Paul and the Tannaim: A Study in Galatians," *WTJ* 45/2 (1983): 340-70.

1134 J. Julius Scott, "Textual Variants of the 'Apostolic Decree' and Their Setting in the Early Church," in Morris A. Inch and Ronald F. Youngblood, eds., *The Living and Active Word of God* (festschrift for Samuel J. Schultz). Winona Lake IN: Eisenbrauns, 1983. Pp. 171-83.

1135 Marvin R. Wilson, "Hebrew Thought in the Life of the Church," in Morris A. Inch and Ronald F. Youngblood, eds., *The Living and Active Word of God* (festschrift for Samuel J. Schultz). Winona Lake IN: Eisenbrauns, 1983. Pp. 123-35.

1136 Earl Richard, "The Divine Purpose: The Jews and the Gentile Mission," in Charles H. Talbert, ed., *Luke-Acts: New Perspectives from the Society of Biblical Literature.* New York: Crossroad, 1984. Pp. 188-211.

1137 Darrell L. Whiteman, "Communicating Across Cultures," *Point* 5 (1984): 56-83.

1138 W. Radl, "Das Gesetz in Apg 15," in Johannes Beutler and Karl Kertelge, eds., *Das Gesetz im Neuen Testament.* Freiburg: Herder, 1986. Pp. 169-74.

1139 M. A. Seifrid, "Jesus and the Law in Acts," *JSNT* 30 (1987): 39-57.

1140 Edward A. Synan, "Some Medieval Perceptions of the Controversy on Jewish Law," in Clemens Thoma and Michael Wyschogrod, eds., *Understanding Scripture: Explorations of Jewish and Christian Tradition of Interpretation.* New York: Paulist Press, 1987. Pp. 102-24.

1141 Michael Wyschogrod, "A Jewish Reading of St. Thomas Aquinas on the Old Law," in Clemens Thoma and Michael Wyschogrod, eds., *Understanding Scripture: Explorations of Jewish and Christian Tradition of Interpretation.* New York: Paulist Press, 1987. Pp. 125-38.

1142 Donald Hohensee, "To Eat or Not to Eat? Christians and Food Laws," *EMQ* 25/1 (1989): 74-81.

1143 J. L. Nolland, "Acts 15: Discerning the Will of God in Changing Circumstances," *Crux* 27 (1991): 30-34.

1144 C. N. Jefford, "Tradition and Witness in Antioch: Acts 15 and Didache 6," *PRS* 19 (1992): 409-19.

1145 J. Morgado, "Paul in Jerusalem: A Comparison of His Visits in Acts and Galatians," *JETS* 37 (1994): 55-68.

1146 J. Rius-Camps, "La misión hacia el paganismo avalada por el Señor Jesús y el Espíritu Santo," *EB* 52 (1994): 341-60.

15:1-35

1147 Veselin Kesich, "The Apostolic Council at Jerusalem," *SVTQ* 6/3 (1962): 108-17.

1148 R. H. Stein, "The Relationship of Galatians 2:1-10 and Acts 15:1-35; Two Neglected Arguments," *JETS* 17/4 (1974): 239-42.

1149 R. G. Hoerber, "A Review of the Apostolic Council After 1925 Years," *CJ* 214 (1976): 155-59.

1150 F. Hahn, "Zum Problem der antiochenischen Quelle in der
Apostelgeschichte," in B. Jaspert, ed., *Rudolf Bultmanns Werk und
Wirkung*. Darmstadt: Wissenschaftliche Buchgesellschaft, 1984. Pp.
316-31.

1151 Otto Merk, "Die Apostelgeschichte im Frühwerk Rudolf
Bultmanns," in Bernd Jaspert, ed., *Rudolf Bultmanns Werk und
Wirkung*. Darmstadt, West Germany: Wissenschaftliche
Buchgesellschaft, 1984. Pp. 303-15.

1152 Alfons Weiser, "Dad 'Apostel-Konzil' (Apg 15,1-35)-Ereignis,
uberlieferung, Lukanische Deutung," *BZ* 28/2 (1984): 145-67.

1153 Royce Dickinson, "The Theology of the Jerusalem Conference:
Acts 15:1-35," *RQ* 32/2 (1990): 65-83.

1154 S. M. Donegan, "Acts 15:1-35: Tradition and Composition within
a Dramatic Episode," doctoral dissertation, Fordham University,
New York, 1993.

1155 P. Nepper-Christensen, "Apostelmødet i Jerusalem," *DTT* 56
(1993): 169-88.

1156 P. Refoulé, "Le discours de Pierre a l'Assemblée de Jerusalem,"
RB 100 (1993): 239-51.

1157 A. J. M. Wedderburn, "The 'Apostolic Decree': Tradition and
Redaction," *NovT* 35 (1993): 362-89.

15:1-34
1158 J. Taylor, "Ancient Texts and Modern Critics: Acts 15:1-34," *RB*
99 (1992): 373-78.

15:1-33
1159 M.-É. Boismard, "Le 'Concile' de Jérusalem (Act 15:1-33): Essai
de Critique Littéraire," *ETL* 64/4 (1988): 433-40.

15:1-29
1160 Lewis Sperry, "An Introduction to the Study of Prophecy," *BSac*
100 (1943): 98-133.

1161 Brian Schwarz, "Contextualization and the Church in Melanesia,"
Point 7 (1985): 104-20.

1162 Robert P. Lightner, "Theological Perspectives on Theonomy; Pt 3: a Dispensational Response to Theonomy," *BSac* 143 (1986): 228-45.

1163 Joseph B. Tyson, "Jews and Judaism in Luke-Acts: Reading as a Godfearer," *NTS* 41 (1995): 19-38.

15:1

1164 David R. Catchpole, "Paul, James and the Apostolic Decree," *NTS* 23/4 (1976-1977): 428-44.

15:2

1165 R. T. France, "Barnabas—Son of Encouragement," *ERT* 4/1 (1980): 91-101.

15:6-21

1166 H. van de Sandt, "An Explanation of Acts 15:6-21 in the Light of Deuteronomy 4:29-35," *JSNT* 46 (1992): 73-97.

15:6-11

1167 Barbara Hall, "La communauté chrétienne dans le livre des Actes: Actes 6:1-7 et 10:1-11:18," *FV* Suppl (1971): 146-56.

15:6

1168 J. L. North, "Is ἰδεῖν περί a Latinsim?" *NTS* 29/2 (1983): 265-66.

15:7-11

1169 F. Refoulé, "Le discours de Pierre à l'assemblée de Jérusalem," *RB* 64 (1957): 35-47.

1170 Troy Organ, "A Cosmomogical Christology," *CC* 88/44 (1971): 1293-95.

1171 Marion L. Soards, "Peter's Speech at the Jerusalem Conference," in *The Speeches in Acts: Their Content, Context, and Concerns.* Louisville: John Knox/Westminster Press, 1994. Pp. 90-92.

15:8

1172 Johannes B. Bauer, "Kardiognostes, ein unbeachteter Aspekt," *BibN* 32/1 (1988): 114-17.

15:10-29
    1173 J. A. Jáuregui, "Israel y la iglesia en la teologia de Lucas," *EE* 61 (1986): 129-49.

15:10
    1174 J. L. Nolland, "A Fresh Look at Acts 15:10," *NTS* 27/1 (1980): 105-15.

15:12
    1175 R. T. France, "Barnabas—Son of Encouragement," *ERT* 4/1 (1980): 91-101.

15:13-21
    1176 Marion L. Soards, "James's Speech at the Jerusalem Conference," in *The Speeches in Acts: Their Content, Context, and Concerns.* Louisville: John Knox/Westminster Press, 1994. Pp. 92-95.

15:13-18
    1177 W. M. Aldrich, "The Interpretation of Acts 15:13-18," *BSac* 111 (1954): 317-23.

    1178 W. C. Kaiser, "The Davidic Promise and the Inclusion of the Gentiles: A Test Passage for Theological Systems," *JETS* 20/2 (1977): 97-111.

15:14-17
    1179 Charles Zimmerman, " 'To This Agree the Words of the Prophets'," *GTJ* 4 (1963): 28-40.

15:14
    1180 Jacques Dupont, "Un Peuple d'entre les Nations," *NTS* 31/3 (1985): 321-35.

15:19-21
    1181 Daniel R. Schwartz, "The Futility of Preaching Moses," *Bib* 67/2 (1986): 276-81.

    1182 Roger L. Omanson, "How Does It All Fit Together? Thoughts On Translating Acts 1:15-22 and 15:19-21," *BT* 41 (1990): 416-21.

    1183 Roger L. Omanson, "Acts 15:19-21: Some Further Discussion," *BT* 42 (1991): 234-41.

15:20-29
> **1184** F. Manns, "Remarques sur Actes 15,20.29," *Ant* 53/3 (1978): 443-51.

15:20
> **1185** Thorleif Boman, "Das textkritische Problem des sogenannten Aposteldekrets," *NovT* 7/1 (1964): 26-36.

> **1186** A. F. J. Klijn, "The Pseudo Clementines and the Apostolic Decree," *NovT* 10/4 (1968): 305-12.

> **1187** H. W. Bartsch, "Traditionsgeschichtliches zur 'Goldenen Regel' und zum Aposteldekret," *ZNW* 75/1 (1984): 128-32.

> **1188** Terrance Callan, "The Background of the Apostolic Decree," *CBQ* 55 (1993): 284-97.

15:21
> **1189** Daniel R. Schwartz, "The Futility of Preaching Moses," *Bib* 67/2 (1986): 276-81.

15:22-40
> **1190** B. N. Kaye, "Acts' Portrait of Silas," *NTS* 21/1 (1979): 13-26.

15:22-29
> **1191** Torstein Jorgensen, "Acta 15:22-29: Historiske Og Eksegetiske Problemer," *NTT* 90/1 (1989): 31-45.

15:22
> **1192** R. T. France, "Barnabas—Son of Encouragement," *ERT* 4/1 (1980): 91-101.

15:23-29
> **1193** M. Simon, "The Apostolic Decree and Its Setting in the Ancient Church," *BJRL* 52/2 (1970): 437-60.

> **1194** F. F. Bruce, "The Apostolic Decree of Acts 15," in Wolfgang Schrage, ed., *Studien zum Text und zur Ethik des Neuen Testaments* (festschrift for Heinrich Greeven). Berlin: de Gruyter, 1986. Pp. 115-24.

15:25

1195 R. T. France, "Barnabas—Son of Encouragement," *ERT* 4/1 (1980): 91-101.

15:26

1196 Morris Inch, "Manifestation of the Spirit," in Morris A. Inch and Ronald F. Youngblood, eds., *The Living and Active Word of God* (festschrift for Samuel J. Schultz). Winona Lake IN: Eisenbrauns, 1983. Pp. 149-55.

15:28-29

1197 R. L. Roberts, "Notes on Selected Passages," *RQ* 4 (1960): 234-58.

1198 H. W. Bartsch, "Traditionsgeschichtliches zur 'Goldenen Regel' und zum Aposteldekret," *ZNW* 75/1 (1984): 128-32.

1199 V. M. Fernández, "Santiago, la plenificación cristiana de la espiritualidad postexilica," *RevB* 53 (1991): 29-33.

15:28

1200 John N. Suggit, "The Holy Spirit and We Resolved. . .," *JTSA* 79 (1992): 38-48.

15:29

1201 Thorleif Boman, "Das textkritische Problem des sogenannten Aposteldekrets," *NovT* 7/1 (1964): 26-36.

1202 A. F. J. Klijn, "The Pseudo Clementines and the Apostolic Decree," *NovT* 10/4 (1968): 305-12.

1203 C. K. Barrett, "The Apostolic Decree of Acts 15:29," *ABR* 35 (1987): 50-59.

1204 Terrance Callan, "The Background of the Apostolic Decree," *CBQ* 55 (1993): 284-97.

15:34

1205 É. Delebecque, "Silas, Paul et Barnabe a Antioche Selon le Texte 'Occidental' d'Actes, 15, 34 et 38," *RHPR* 64/1 (1984): 47-52.

15:35-37
1206   R. T. France, "Barnabas—Son of Encouragement," *ERT* 4/1
        (1980): 91-101.

15:36-16:5
1207   Jacques Dupont, "La Question du Plan des Actes des Apôtres à la
        lumière d'un Texte de Lucien de Samosate," *NovT* 21/3 (1979):
        220-31.

15:36-40
1208   C. C. Black, "The Presentation of John Mark in the Acts of the
        Apostles," *PRS* 20 (1993): 235-54.

15:38
1209   É. Delebecque, "Silas, Paul et Barnabe a Antioche Selon le Texte
        'Occidental' d'Actes, 15, 34 et 38," *RHPR* 64/1 (1984): 47-52.

15:39
1210   G. B. Bruzzone, "Il dissenso tra Paolo e Barnaba in Atti 15,39,"
        EB 35 (1976): 121.

1211   R. T. France, "Barnabas—Son of Encouragement," *ERT* 4/1
        (1980): 91-101.

15:41
1212   Y. Tissot, "Les prescriptions des presbytres (Actes 15,41). Exégèse
        et origine du décret dans le texte syro-occidental des *Actes*," *RB*
        77/3 (1970): 321-46.

16:1-18:22
1213   J. Rius-Camps, "Jesús y el Espíritu Santo conducen la misión
        hacia Europa," *EB* 52/4 (1994): 517-34.

16
1214   Paul E. Davies, "The Macedonian Scene of Paul's Journeys," *BA*
        26 (1963): 91-106.

1215   É. Delebecque, "De Lystres a Philippes (Ac 16) avec le Codex
        Bezae," *Bib* 63/3 (1982): 395-405.

1216   J. K. Howard, "New Testament Exorcism and Its Significance
        Today," *ET* 96/4 (1985): 105-09.

1217   I. Richter-Reimer, "Die Geschichte der Frauen rekonstruieren. Betrachtungen über den Arbeit und den Status von Lydia in Apg 16," *TexteK* 14 (1991): 16-29.

1218   J. Gillman, "Hospitality in Acts 16," *LouvS* 17 (1992): 181-96.

16:1-3

1219   W. O. Walker, "The Timothy-Titus Problem Reconsidered," *ET* 92/8 (1981): 231-35.

1220   S. J. D. Cohen, "Was Timothy Jewish? Patristic Exegesis, Rabbinic Law, and Matrilineal Descent," *JBL* 105/2 (1986): 251-68.

1221   Christopher Bryan, "A Further Look at Acts 16:1-3," *JBL* 107/2 (1988): 292-94.

16:1

1222   G. Ogg, "Derbe," *NTS* 9/4 (1963): 367-70.

1223   R. Y. K. Fung, "Charismatic Versus Organized Ministry? An Examination of an Alleged Antithesis," *EQ* 52/4 (1980): 195-214.

16:6-40

1224   F. Martin, "Ke geôlier et la marchande de pourpre: Actes des Apôtres 16:6-40," *SémBib* 59 (1990): 9-29.

16:6-9

1225   W. Till, "Ein fayyumisches Acta-Fragment," *Mus* 42 (1929): 193-96.

16:6

1226   F. F. Bruce, "Galatian Problems: 2. North or South Galatians?" *BJRL* 52/2 (1970): 243-66.

1227   G. M. Lee, "The Past Participle of Subsequent Action," *NovT* 17/3 (1975): 199.

1228   C. J. Hemer, "Phrygia: A Further Note," *JTS* 28/1 (1977): 99-101.

16:7

1229   Romano Penna, "Lo 'Spirito di Gesù' in Atti 16,7. Analisi letteraria e Teologica," *RBib* 20/3 (1972): 241-61.

16:8

1230 W. P. Bowers, "Paul's Route Through Mysia: A Note on Acts XVI.8," *JTS* 30/2 (1979): 507-11.

16:9-17:5

1231 B. Schwank, " 'Setz über nach Mazedonien und hilf uns!' Reisenotizen zu Apg 16,9-17,5," *ErAu* 39/5 (1963): 399-416.

16:9-15

1232 Otto Glombitza, "Der Schritt nach Europa: Erwagungen zu Act 16:9-15," *ZNW* 53 (1962): 77-82.

1233 M. Trotter, "Acts in Esther," *QR* 14/4 (1994-1995): 435-47.

16:9-10

1234 E. Farahian, "Paul's Vision at Troas," in Gerald O'Collins and G. Marconi, eds., *Luke and Acts* (festschrift for Emilio Rasco). Mahwah NJ: Paulist Press, 1993. Pp. 197-207.

16:10-17

1235 Susan Marie Praeder, "The Problem of First Person Narration in Acts," *NovT* 29 (1987): 193-218.

16:10

1236 Richard Glover, " 'Luke the Antiochene' and Acts," *NTS* 11/1 (1964): 97-106.

16:11-40

1237 Y. Redalie, "Conversion ou liberation? Notes sur Actes 16,11-40," *BCPE* 26/7 (1974): 7-17.

16:12

1238 M. F. Unger, "Archaeology and Paul's Campaign at Philippi," *BSac* 119 (1962): 150-60.

16:13-40

1239 H. Boterman, "Der Heidenapostel und sein Historiker: Zur historischen Kritik der Apostelgeschichte," *TBe* 24 (1993): 62-84.

16:13-14

1240 W. Till, "Ein fayyumisches Acta-Fragment," *Mus* 42 (1929): 193-96.

16:14-15
1241   Charles L. Cohen, "Two Biblical Models of Conversion: An Example of Puritan Hermeneutics," *ChH* 58 (1989): 182-96.

16:14
1242   R. Stephen Cherry, "Acts 16:14f.," *ET* 75 (1964-1965): 114.

1243   A. J. Conyers, "Lydia of Thyatira," *BI* 13/3 (1987): 81-83.

16:15
1244   Gerhard Delling, "Zur Taufe von 'Hausern' im Urchristentum," *NovT* 7 (1965): 285-311.

1245   E. Dassmann, "Hausgemeinde und Bischofsamt," in Ernst Dassmann and Klaus Thraede, eds., *Vivarium* (festschrift for Theodor Klauser). Münster, West Germany: Aschendorff, 1984. Pp. 82-97.

16:16-34
1246   M. Trotter, "Acts in Esther," *QR* 14/4 (1994-1995): 435-47.

16:16-24
1247   Monique Veillé, "Écriture et prédication: Actes 16,16-24," *ÉTR* 54/2 (1979): 271-78.

16:16-18
1248   Paul R. Trebilco, "Paul and Silas—'Servants of the Most High God'," *JSNT* 36 (1989): 51-73.

1249   H. J. Klauck, "With Paul in Paphos and Lystra: Magic and Paganism in the Acts of the Apostles," *Neo* 28 (1994): 93-108.

16:16
1250   C. J. Hemer, "The Adjective 'Phrygia'," *JTS* 27/1 (1976): 122-26.

16:19
1251   B. N. Kaye, "Acts' Portrait of Silas," *NTS* 21/1 (1979): 13-26.

16:20-21
1252   Daniel R. Schwartz, "The Accusation and the Accusers at Philippi," *Bib* 65/3 (1984): 357-63.

16:22

1253 F. F. Bruce, "St. Paul in Macedonia," *BJRL* 61/2 (1979): 337-54.

16:25-34

1254 Jack Boyd, "The Jailkeeper: The Story of a Prisoner's Witness," *FundJ* 7 (1988): 14-17.

1255 E. A. LaVerdiere, "The Eucharist in the New Testament and the Early Church—VI: The Breaking of the Bread. The Eucharist in the Acts of the Apostles," *Emmanuel* 100 (1994): 324-35.

16:25

1256 B. N. Kaye, "Acts' Portrait of Silas," *NTS* 21/1 (1979): 13-26.

16:27-36

1257 C. S. de Vos, "The Significance of the Change from οἶκος to οἰκία in Luke's Account of the Philippian Gaoler," *NTS* 41/2 (1995): 292-96.

16:29

1258 B. N. Kaye, "Acts' Portrait of Silas," *NTS* 21/1 (1979): 13-26.

16:30-34

1259 J. Ramsey Michaels, "Apostolic Hardships and Righteous Gentiles," *JBL* 84 (1965): 27-37.

16:31

1260 Gerhard Delling, "Zur Taufe von 'Hausern' im Urchristentum," *NovT* 7 (1965): 285-311.

16:35-39

1261 P. Van Minnen, "Paul the Roman Citizen," *JSNT* 56 (1994): 43-52.

16:37-38

1262 Mark Black, "Paul and Roman Law in Acts," *RQ* 24/4 (1981): 209-18.

1263 W. Stegemann, "War der Apostel Paulus ein Römischer Bürger?" *ZNW* 78/3-4 (1987): 200-29.

<u>17</u>

1264   Everett Ferguson, "Apologetics in the New Testament," *RQ* 6
       (1962): 180-95.

1265   Paul E. Davies, "The Macedonian Scene of Paul's Journeys," *BA*
       26 (1963): 91-106.

1266   A. W. Swamidoss, "The Speeches of Paul in Acts 13, 17 and 20,"
       doctoral dissertation, Fuller Theological Seminary, Pasadena CA,
       1979.

1267   L. Legrand, "The Unknown God of Athens: Acts 17 and the
       Religion of the Gentiles," *IJT* 30/3 (1981): 158-67.

1268   Dean W. Zweck, "The Areopagus Speech of Acts 17," *LTJ* 21
       (1987): 111-22.

1269   T. F. Torrance, "*Phusikos kai Theologikos Logos:* St. Paul and
       Athenagoras at Athens," *SJT* 41/1 (1988): 11-26.

1270   David Wenham, "The Paulinism of Acts Again: Two Historical
       Clues in 1 Thessalonians," *Themelios* 13/2 (1988): 53-55.

1271   J. H. Neyrey, "Acts 17, Epicureans, and Theodicy: A Study in
       Stereotypes," in David L. Balch, et al., eds., *Greeks, Romans, and
       Christians* (festschrift for Abraham J. Malherbe) Minneapolis:
       Fortress, 1990. Pp. 118-34.

1272   Darrell L. Bock, "Athenians Who Have Never Heard," in William
       Crockett, et al., eds., *Through No Fault of Their Own: The Fate of
       Those Who Never Heard*. Grand Rapids MI: Baker, 1991. Pp.
       117-24.

1273   G. Betori, "Luke 24:47: Jerusalem and the Beginning of the
       Preaching to the Pagans in the Acts of the Apostles," in Gerald
       O'Collins and G. Marconi, eds., *Luke and Acts* (festschrift for
       Emilio Rasco). Mahwah NJ: Paulist Press, 1993. Pp. 103-20.

1274   R. F. Wolfe, "Rhetorical Elements in the Speeches of Acts 7 and
       17," *JT* 6 (1993): 274-83.

17:1

1275　M. D. Roberts, "Images of Paul and the Thessalonians," doctoral dissertation, Harvard University, Cambridge MA, 1992.

17:1-10

1276　Néstor O. Míguez, "Lectura Socio-Politica de Hechos 17:1-10," *RevB* 50/2-3 (1988): 183-206.

17:1-9

1277　C. U. Manus, "Luke's Account of Paul in Thessalonica," in Raymond F. Collins, ed., *The Thessalonian Correspondence.* Louvain: Peeters, 1990. Pp. 27-38.

1278　H. Boterman, "Der Heidenapostel und sein Historiker: Zur historischen Kritik der Apostelgeschichte," *TBe* 24 (1993): 62-84.

17:2-3

1279　Robert L. Reymond, "The Justification of Theology with a Special Application to Contemporary Christology," *Pres* 12/1 (1986): 1-16.

17:4-15

1280　É. Delebecque, "Paul à Thessalonique et à Bérée selon le texte occidental des Actes," *RT* 82/4 (1982): 605-15.

17:4

1281　B. N. Kaye, "Acts' Portrait of Silas," *NTS* 21/1 (1979): 13-26.

1282　Richard I. Pervo, "Social and Religious Aspects of the Western Text," in Dennis E. Groh and Robert Jewett, eds., *The Living Text* (festschrift for Ernest W. Saunders). Lanham MD: University Press of America, 1985. Pp. 229-41.

17:5-9

1283　Florence Morgan Gillman, "Jason of Thessalonica," in Raymond F. Collins, ed., *The Thessalonian Correspondence.* Louvain: Peeters, 1990. Pp. 39-49.

17:5-7

1284　E. A. Judge, "The Decrees of Caesar at Thessalonica," *RTR* 39/1 (1971): 1-7.

17:10-13
1285 J. Kremer, "Einfuhrung in die Problematik heutiger Acta-Forschung an hand von Apg 17,10-13," *ETL* 48 (1978): 11-20.

17:10
1286 B. N. Kaye, "Acts' Portrait of Silas," *NTS* 21/1 (1979): 13-26.

17:11
1287 E. Nestle, "Act 17:11," *ZNW* 15 (1914): 91-92.

1288 F. W. Danker, "Menander and the New Testament," *NTS* 10 (1963-1964): 365-68.

17:12
1289 Richard I. Pervo, "Social and Religious Aspects of the Western Text," in Dennis Groh and Robert Jewett, eds., *The Living Text* (festschrift for Ernest Saunders). Lanham MD: University Press of America, 1985. Pp. 229-41.

17:14-15
1290 B. N. Kaye, "Acts' Portrait of Silas," *NTS* 21/1 (1979): 13-26.

17:14
1291 W. A. Meeks, "Who Went Where and How? A Consideration of Acts 17:14," *BT* 44/2 (1993): 201-206.

17:15-21
1292 Henri Munier, "Recueil de manuscrits coptes de l'Ancien et du Nouveau Testament," *BIFAO* 12 (1916): 245-57.

17:15-16
1293 R. E. Wycherley, "St. Paul at Athens," *JTS* 9/2 (1968): 619-21.

1294 C. J. Hemer, "Paul at Athens: A Topographical Note," *NTS* 20/3 (1974): 341-50.

1295 Gil Lain, "Ancient Athens," *BI* (1989): 24-29.

17:16-34
1296 Kenneth Grayston, "Theology as Exploration," *LQHR* 191 (1966): 183-95.

1297 J. Calloud, "Paul devant l'Aréopage d'Athènes: Actes 17:16-34," *RechSR* 69/2 (1981): 209-48.

1298 C. U. Manus, "The Areopagus Speech (Acts 17:16-34): a Study of Luke's Approach to Evangelism and its Significance in the African Context," *AThJ* 14/1 (1985): 3-18.

1299 Larry R. Thornton, "Paul's Apologetic at Athens and Ours," *CBTJ* 2/2 (1986): 121.

1300 Joel Marcus, "Paul at the Areopagus: Window on the Hellenistic World," *BTB* 18 (1988): 143-48.

1301 Raymond H. Bailey, "Acts 17:16-34," *RevExp* 87 (1990): 481-85.

1302 M. Me. Adam, "Philosophy and the Bible: The Areopagus Speech," *Faith and Philos* 9 (1992): 135-50.

1303 P. Sciberras, "The Figure of Paul in the Acts of the Apostles: The Areopagus Speech," *MeliT* 43 (1992): 1-15.

1304 Heinz Külling, *Eine Auslegung von Apostelgeschiche 17:16-34.* AZTANT #79. Zurich: Theologischer Verlag, 1993.

1305 K. O. Sandnes, "Paul and Socrates: The Aim of Paul's Areopagus Speech," *JSNT* 50 (1993): 13-26.

1306 H. J. Klauck, "With Paul in Paphos and Lystra: Magic and Paganism in the Acts of the Apostles," *Neo* 28 (1994): 93-108.

1307 D. Wiens, "Luke on Pluralism: Flex with History," *Direction* 23 (1994): 44-53.

1308 P. Bossuyt and J. Radermakers, "Rencontre de l'incroyant et inculturation. Paul à Athènes," *NRT* 117/1 (1995): 19-43.

17:16-31

1309 Mark R. Shaw, "Is There Salvation Outside the Christian Faith," *EAJT* 2/2 (1983): 42-62.

1310 Sherman E. Johnson, "Paul in Athens," *LexTQ* 17/3 (1982): 37-43.

17:18-25
1311   C. K. Barrett, "Submerged Christology in Acts," in Cilliers
Breytenbach and Henning Paulsen, eds., *Anfänge der Christologie*
(festschrift for Ferdinand Hahn). Göttingen: Vandenhoeck &
Ruprecht, 1991. Pp. 237-44.

17:18
1312   C. Di Sante, "The Missionizing of the East and the Meaning of
Mission in the New Testament," in Frank K. Flinn and Tyler
Hendricks, eds., *Religion in the Pacific Era*. New York NY:
Paragon House Publishers, 1985. Pp. 3-13.

1313   George D. Kilpatrick, "The Acts of the Apostles, 17:18," *TZ* 42/5
(1986): 431-32.

1314   K. L. McKay, "Foreign Gods Identified in Acts 17:18?" *TynB* 45
(1994): 411-12.

17:19-31
1315   D. L. Balch, "The Areopagus Speech: An Appeal to the Stoic
Historian Posidonius against Later Stoics and the Epicureans," in
David L. Balch, et al., eds., *Greeks, Romans, and Christians*
(festschrift for Abraham J. Malherbe) Minneapolis MN: Fortress,
1990. Pp. 52-79.

17:22-34
1316   F. F. Bruce, "Paul and the Athenians," *ET* 88/11 (1976): 8-12.

17:22-33
1317   Heinz Külling, "Zur Bedeutung des Agnostos Thoes," *TZ* 36/2
(1980): 22-23.

17:22-32
1318   J.-C. Lebram, "Der Aufbau der Areopagrede," *ZNW* 55/3-4
(1964): 221-43.

17:22-31
1319   Wolfgang Nauck, "Die Tradition und Komposition der
Aeropagrede," *ZTK* 53 (1956): 11-52.

1320   K. O. Gangel, "Paul's Areopagus Speech," *BSac* 127 (1970):
308-12.

1321 A.-M. Dubarle, "Le discours à l'Aréopage (Actes 17:22-31) et son arrièreplan biblique," *RSPT* 57/4 (1973): 576-610.

1322 Jacques Dupont, "Le discours à l'Aréopage: Lieu de Reconntre entre Christianisme et Hellenisme," *Bib* 60/4 (1979): 530-46.

1323 F. G. Downing, "Common Ground with Paganism in Luke and Josephus," *NTS* 28/4 (1982): 546-59.

1324 R. S. MacKenzie, "The Western Text of Acts: Some Lucanisms in Selected Sermons," *JBL* 104/4 (1985): 637-50.

1325 S. J. Samuel, "Paul on the Areopagus: a Mission Perspective," *BTF* 18/1 (1986): 17-32.

1326 Stephen R. Spencer, "Is Natural Theology Biblical?" *GTJ* 9 (1988): 59-72.

1327 S. Sabugal, "El kerygma de Pablo en el Areópago ateniense: Análisis hisórico-tradicional," *RevAug* 31 (1990): 505-34.

1328 R. C. Tannehill, "Mission in the 1990s: Reflections on the Easter Lections from Acts," *QR* 10/1 (1990): 84-97.

1329 Marion L. Soards, "Paul's Speech in the Middle of the Areopagus," in *The Speeches in Acts: Their Content, Context, and Concerns*. Louisville: John Knox/Westminster Press, 1994. Pp. 95-100.

1330 K.-K. Yeo, "A Rhetorical Study of Acts 17:22-31," *JianD* 1 (1994): 75-107.

17:22-23
1331 Dean W. Zweck, "The Exordium of the Areopagus Speech, Acts 17:22,23," *NTS* 35/1 (1989): 94-103.

17:22
1332 C. M. Horne, "Toward a Biblical Apologetic," *GTJ* 2 (1961): 14-18.

1333 H. A. Moellering, "Deisidaimonia: A Footnote to Acts 17:22," *CTM* 34 (1963): 466-71.

1334 É. des Places, "Quasi superstitiosiores," *AnBib* 17-18/2 (1963): 183-91.

1335 R. E. Wycherley, "St. Paul at Athens," *JTS* 9/2 (1968): 619-21.

1336 C. J. Hemer, "Paul at Athens: A Topographical Note," *NTS* 20/3 (1974): 341-50.

1337 Gil Lain, "Ancient Athens," *BI* (1989): 24-29.

17:23-31
1338 Pierre Auffret, "Essai sur la Structure Litteraire du Discours d'Athenes," *NovT* 20/3 (1978): 185-202.

17:23
1339 Hans Kosmala, "Agnostos Theos," *ASTI* 2 (1963): 106-108.

17:24-30
1340 B. E. Shields, "The Areopagus Sermon and Romans 1:18ff.: A Study in Creation Theology," *RQ* 20/1 (1977): 23-40.

17:24-27
1341 Lawrence Wills, "The Form of the Sermon in Hellenistic Judaism and Early Christianity," *HTR* 77/3-4 (1984): 277-99.

17:24
1342 É. des Places, "Des temples faits de main d'homme" *Bib* 42/2 (1961): 217-23.

17:25
1343 É. des Places, "Actes 17:25," *Bib* 46 (1965): 219-22.

17:26
1344 Roger Lapointe, "Que Sont les Kaiaoi d'Act 17,26? Étude Semantique et Stylistique," *EgT* 3/3 (1972): 323-38.

17:27-29
1345 H. U. von Balthasar, "Toward a Theology of Christian Prayer," *CICR* 12 (1985): 245-57.

17:27
1346 É. des Places, "Actes 17:27," *Bib* 48/1 (1967): 1-6.

17:28

1347 É. des Places, "Ipsius enim et genus sumus," *Bib* 43/3 (1962): 388-95.

1348 G. Folliet, "Les citations de *Actes* 17,28 et *Tite* 1,12 chez Augustin," *REA* 11/3-4 (1965): 293-95.

1349 Peter Colaclides, "Acts 17:28a and Bacchae 506," *VC* 27/3 (1973): 161-64.

1350 Walter Magass, "Theologie und Wetterregel: Semiotische Variationen über Arats 'Phainomena'," *LB* 49 (1981): 7-26.

1351 Gary M. Poulton, "The Poets of Ancient Greece," *BI* 13/4 (1987): 13-16.

1352 M. J. Edwards, "Quoting Aratus: Acts 17,28," *ZNW* 83 (1992): 26-29.

17:29

1353 Michael R. Austin, "Salvation and the Divinity of Jesus," *ET* 96 (1985): 271-75.

17:30-31

1354 É. des Places, "Actes 17:30-31," *Bib* 52/4 (1971): 526-34.

1355 R. F. O'Toole, "Christ's Resurrection in Acts 13:13-52," *Bib* 60/3 (1979): 361-72.

17:31

1356 G. Schneider, "Urchristliche Gottesver-Kindigung in Hellenistischer Umwelt," *BZ* 13/1 (1969): 59-75.

1357 Leslie C. Allen, "The Old Testament Background of (προ)ώρισμένη in the New Testament," *NTS* 17/1 (1970-1971): 104-108.

1358 Rudolf Schnackenburg, "Die lukanische Eschatologie im Lichte von Aussagen der Apostelgeschichte," in E. Grässer and O. Merk, eds., *Glaube und Eschatologie* (festschrift for W. G. Kümmel). Tübingen: Mohr, 1985. Pp. 249-65.

17:34

1359 J. G. Griffiths, "Was Damaris an Egyptian?" *BZ* 8/2 (1964): 293-95.

1360 Richard I. Pervo, "Social and Religious Aspects of the Western Text," in Dennis Groh and Robert Jewett, eds., *The Living Text* (festschrift for Ernest Saunders). Lanham MD: University Press of America, 1985. Pp. 229-41.

18

1361 L. E. Keck, "Listening to and Listening for: From Text to Sermon," *Int* 27/2 (1973): 184-202.

1362 F. R. Harm, "Structural Elements Related to the Gift of the Holy Spirit in Acts," *CJ* 14/1 (1988): 28-41.

18:1-18

1363 W. Dixon Slingerland, "Acts 18:1-18: The Gallio Inscription, and Absolute Pauline Chronology," *JBL* 110 (1991): 439-49.

18:1-17

1364 H. Dixon Slingerland, "Acts 18:1-17 and Lüdemann's Pauline Chronology," *JBL* 109 (1990): 686-90.

1365 H. Boterman, "Der Heidenapostel und sein Historiker: Zur historischen Kritik der Apostelgeschichte," *TBe* 24 (1993): 62-84.

18:1

1366 R. E. Wycherley, "St. Paul at Athens," *JTS* 9/2 (1968): 619-21.

1367 C. J. Hemer, "Paul at Athens: A Topographical Note," *NTS* 20/3 (1974): 341-50.

1368 Gil Lain, "Ancient Athens," *BI* (1989): 24-29.

18:2

1369 R. G. Hoerber, "The Decree of Claudius in Acts 18:2," *CTM* 31 (1960): 690-94.

1370 F. F. Bruce, "Christianity Under Claudius," *BJRL* 44 (1962): 309-26.

18:3

    1371 H. Szesnat, "What Did the σκηνοποιός Paul Produce?" *Neo* 27 (1993): 391-402.

18:5

    1372 B. N. Kaye, "Acts' Portrait of Silas," *NTS* 21/1 (1979): 13-26.

18:6

    1373 Marion L. Soards, "Paul's Speech to the Corinthian Jews," in *The Speeches in Acts: Their Content, Context, and Concerns.* Louisville: John Knox/Westminster Press, 1994. Pp. 100-101.

18:7-8

    1374 K. C. Hartmann, "Did Paul Turn His Back on the Jew Forever?" *LQ* 11 (1959): 57-59.

18:8

    1375 Gerhard Delling, "Zur Taufe von 'Hausern' im Urchristentum," *NovT* 7 (1965): 285-311.

    1376 E. Dassmann, "Hausgemeinde und Bischofsamt," in Ernst Dassmann and Klaus Thraede, eds., *Vivarium* (festschrift for Theodor Klauser). Münster, West Germany: Aschendorff, 1984. Pp. 82-97.

18:11-17

    1377 Klaus Haacker, "Die Gallio-Episode und die paulinische Chronologie," *BZ* 16/2 (1972): 252-55.

18:12-17

    1378 A. Plassart, "L'inscription de Delphes mentionnant le procounsul Gallion," *RÉG* 80 (1967): 165-72.

18:14-15

    1379 Marion L. Soards, "Gallio's Speech to the Corinthian Jews," in *The Speeches in Acts: Their Content, Context, and Concerns.* Louisville: John Knox/Westminster Press, 1994. Pp. 101-102.

18:15

    1380 J. L. North, "Is ἰδεῖν περί a Latinsim?" *NTS* 29/2 (1983): 265-66.

18:21-23
1381 Sherman E. Johnson, "Caesarea Maritima," *LTQ* 20 (1985): 28-32.

18:21
1382 J. M. Ross, "The Extra Words in Acts 18:21," *NovT* 34 (1992): 247-49.

18:22
1383 J. Morgado, "Paul in Jerusalem: A Comparison of His Visits in Acts and Galatians," *JETS* 37 (1994): 55-68.

18:23
1384 F. F. Bruce, "Galatian Problems: 2. North or South Galatians?" *BJRL* 52/2 (1970): 243-66.

1385 C. J. Hemer, "Phrygia: A Further Note," *JTS* 28/1 (1977): 99-101.

18:24-19:10
1386 Kevin N. Giles, "Is Luke an Exponent of 'Early Protestantism'? Church Order in the Lukan Writings. Part I," *EQ* 54/4 (1982): 193-205.

18:24-19:7
1387 Michael Wolter, "Apollos und die Ephesinischen Johannesjünger," *ZNW* 78/1-2 (1987): 49-73.

18:24
1388 George D. Kilpatrick, "Apollos—Apelles," *JBL* 89/1 (1970): 77.

1389 J. Schwartz, "Vestiges Alexandrins dans quelques Acta Martyrum," *BASP* 21/1-4 (1984): 207-209.

1390 Mikeal C. Parsons, "Ancient Alexandria," *BI* (1989): 30-34.

18:25
1391 J. Giblet, "Baptism in the Spirit in the Acts of the Apostles," *OC* 10 (1974): 162-71.

1392 J. D. G. Dunn, "The Birth of a Metaphor: Baptized in the Spirit (I)," *ET* 89/5 (1978-1979): 134-38.

18:26

1393 G. G. Blum, "Das Amt der Frau im Neuen Testament," *NovT* 7 (1964): 142-61.

18:27-19:6

1394 L. G. Fonseca, "Novum Fragmentum papyraceum Actuum Apostolorum," *VD* 7 (1927): 157-59.

1395 M.-J. Lagrange, "Un nouveau papyrus contenant un fragment des Actes," *RB* 36 (1927): 549-60.

1396 H. A. Sanders, "A Papyrus Fragment of Acts in the Michigan Collection," *HTR* 20 (1927): 1-20.

1397 A. C. Clark, "The Michigan Fragment of the Acts," *JTS* 29 (1927-1928): 18-28.

1398 D. Plooij, "Prof. Sanders' Bezan Papyrus of Acts," *BBC* 5 (1928): 22-25.

18:27

1399 Werner Bieder, "Das Volk Gottes in Erwartung von Licht und Lobpreis," *TZ* 40/2 (1984): 137-48.

18:28

1400 Robert L. Reymond, "The Justification of Theology with a Special Application to Contemporary Christology," *Pres* 12/1 (1986): 1-16.

19-20

1401 T. Y. Mullins, "A Comparison between 2 Timothy and the Book of Acts," *AUSS* 31 (1993): 199-203.

19

1402 Donald K. Campbell, "Paul's Ministry at Ephesus," *BSac* 118 (1961): 304-10.

1403 Joseph Hanimann, " 'Nous Avons ete Abreuves d'un Seul Esprit': Note sur 1 Co 12, 13b," *NRT* 94/4 (1972): 400-405.

1404 Sherman E. Johnson, "The Apostle Paul and the Riot in Ephesus," *LexTQ* 14/4 (1979): 79-88.

1405 B. E. Thiering, "Qumran Initiation and New Testament Baptism," *NTS* 27/5 (1981): 615-31.

1406 Richard B. Cunningham, "Wide Open Doors and Many Adversaries," *RevExp* 89 (1992): 89-98.

1407 P. Lampe, "Acta 19 im Spiegel der ephesischen Inschriften," *BZ* 36/1 (1992): 59-76.

19:1-7

1408 J. K. Parratt, "The Rebaptism of the Ephesian Disciples," *ET* 79/6 (1968): 182-83.

1409 C. B. Kaiser, "The 'Rebaptism' of the Ephesian Twelve: Exegetical Study on Acts 19:1-7," *RR* 31/1 (1977): 57-61.

1410 F. W. Norris, " 'Christians Only, But Not the Only Christians'," *RQ* 28/2 (1985): 97-105.

1411 Hermann Lichtenberger, "Täufergemeinden und Frühchristliche Täuferpolemik im Letzten Drittel," *ZTK* 84/1 (1987): 36-57.

19:1-6

1412 R. K. Levang, "The Content of an Utterance in Tongues," *Para* 23/1 (1989): 14-20.

19:1

1413 Klaus Haacker, "Einige Falle von 'Erlebter Rede' im Neuen Testament," *NovT* 12/1 (1970): 70-77.

1414 George D. Kilpatrick, "Apollos—Apelles," *JBL* 89/1 (1970): 77.

1415 W. A. Strange, "The Text of Acts 19:1," *NTS* 38 (1992): 145-48.

19:2

1416 C. Burchard, "Ei nach einem Ausdruck des Wissins oder Nichtwissens Joh 9:25, Act 19:2, 1 Cor 1:16, 7:16," *ZNW* 52/1-2 (1961): 73-82.

19:4

1417 John J. Kilgallen, "Paul's Speech to the Ephesian Elders: Its Structure," *ETL* 70 (1994): 112-21.

19:5-6

1418 I. de la Potterie, "L'economia fede-sacramento nel nuovo testamento," in P.-R. Tragan, ed., *Fede e sacramenti negli scritti giovannei*. Rome: Edizioni Abbazia, 1972. Pp. 27-46.

1419 Richard I. Pervo, "Social and Religious Aspects of the Western Text," in Dennis Groh and Robert Jewett, eds., *The Living Text* (festschrift for Ernest Saunders). Lanham MD: University Press of America, 1985. Pp. 229-41.

19:5

1420 W. E. Moore, "One Baptism," *NTS* 10/4 (1964): 504-16.

1421 Gerard S. Sloyan, "Jewish Ritual of the 1st Century CE and Christian Sacramental Behavior," *BTB* 15 (1985): 98-103.

19:6

1422 Ralph E. Knudsen, "Speaking in Tongues," *Found* 9 (1966): 43-57.

1423 Timothy N. Boyd, "The Laying on of Hands," *BI* (1989): 9-10.

1424 J. Everts, "Tongues or Languages? Contextual Consistency in the Translation of Acts 2," *JPTh* 4 (1994): 71-80.

19:8

1425 Erich Grässer, "Ta peri tès basileias," in François Refoulé, ed., *À cause de l'Évangile: Études sur les synoptiques et les Actes* (festschrift for Jacques Dupont). Paris: Cerf, 1985. Pp. 709-25.

19:11-20

1426 H. J. Klauck, "With Paul in Paphos and Lystra: Magic and Paganism in the Acts of the Apostles," *Neo* 28 (1994): 93-108.

19:11-19

1427 J. Rius-Camps, "Els tres sumaris dels fets dels apòstols," *RCT* 14 (1989): 243-56.

19:12-16

1428 L. G. Fonseca, "Novum Fragmentum papyraceum Actuum Apostolorum," *VD* 7 (1927): 157-59.

1429   Rendel Harris, "The Western Greek Text of Acts: A Surprising
           Discovery," *BBC* 4 (1927): 15-16.

1430   M.-J. Lagrange, "Un nouveau papyrus contenant un fragment des
           Actes," *RB* 36 (1927): 549-60.

1431   H. A. Sanders, "A Papyrus Fragment of Acts in the Michigan
           Collection," *HTR* 20 (1927): 1-20.

1432   A. C. Clark, "The Michigan Fragment of the Acts," *JTS* 29
           (1927-1928): 18-28.

1433   D. Plooij, "Prof. Sanders' Bezan Papyrus of Acts," *BBC* 5 (1928):
           22-25.

19:12
1434   T. J. Leary, "The 'Aprons' of St. Paul—Acts 19:12," *JTS* 41
           (1990): 527-29.

19:13-20
1435   É. Delebecque, "La mésaventure des fils de Scévas selon ses deux
           versions," *RSPT* 66/2 (1982): 225-32.

19:14
1436   B. A. Mastin, "A Note on Acts 19:14," *Bib* 59/1 (1978): 97-99.

1437   W. C. Van Unnik, "With All Those Who Call on the Name of the
           Lord," in William C. Weinrich, ed., *The New Testament Age*
           (festschrift for Bo Reicke). 2 vols. Macon GA: Mercer University
           Press, 1984. 2:533-51.

1438   W. A. Strange, "The Sons of Sceva and the Text of Acts 19:14,"
           JTS 38 (1987): 97-106.

19:15-17
1439   Chrys C. Caragounis, "Divine Revelation," *ERT* 12 (1988):
           226-39.

19:18
1440   Robert L. Reymond, "The Justification of Theology with a Special
           Application to Contemporary Christology," *Pres* 12/1 (1986): 1-16.

19:20-22
1441 G. Betori, "La strutturazione del libro degli Atti: una proposta," *RBib* 42 (1994): 3-34.

19:20
1442 M. H. Franzmann, "The Word of the Lord Grew," *CTM* 30 (1959): 563-81.

1443 A. W. Argyle, "Acts 19:20," *ET* 75 (1964): 151.

1444 J. Kodell, " 'The Word of God Grew.' The Ecclesial Tendency of *Logos* in Acts 6:7; 12:24; 19:20," *Bib* 55/4 (1974): 505-19.

1445 M. H. Grumm, "Another Look at Acts," *ET* 96/11 (1985): 333-37.

19:21-23
1446 Maurice Carrez, "Notes sur les événements d'Ephèse et l'appel de Paul à sa citoyenneté romaine," in Françios Refoulé, ed., *À cause de l'Évangile: Études sur les synoptiques et les Actes* (festschrift for Jacques Dupont). Paris: Cerf, 1985. Pp. 769-77.

19:22-27
1447 S. Sabugal, "La Mencion neotestamentaria de Damasco ¿ciudad de Siria o region de Qumran?" *BETL* 45 (1978): 403-13.

19:23-41
1448 R. E. Oster, "Acts 19:23-41 and an Ephesian Inscription," *HTR* 77/2 (1984): 233-37.

1449 Larry J. Kreitzer, "A Numismatic Clue to Acts 19.23-41: The Ephesian Cistophori of Claudius and Agrippina," *JSNT* 30 (1987): 59-70.

1450 Robert F. Stoops, "Riot and Assembly: the Social Context of Acts 19:23-41," *JBL* 108 (1989): 73-91.

19:24-40
1451 É. Delebecque, "La révolte des orfèvres à Éphèse et deux versions," *RT* 83/3 (1983): 419-29.

19:24
1452 F. Sokolowski, "A New Testimony on the Cult of Artemis of Ephesus," *HTR* 58/4 (1965): 427-31.

1453 E. Heinzel, "Zum Kult der Artemis en Ephesos," *JOAI* 50 (1972): 243-51.

19:25-27
1454 Marion L. Soards, "Demetrius's Speech," in *The Speeches in Acts: Their Content, Context, and Concerns.* Louisville: John Knox/Westminster Press, 1994. Pp. 102-103.

19:26
1455 R. A. Johnson, "The Narrative Function of the Quotation of Isaiah 6:9-10 and the Concomitant Hear-See Motif in the Book of Acts," doctoral dissertation, Southwestern Baptist Theological Seminary, Fort Worth TX, 1992.

19:27-28
1456 E. Heinzel, "Zum Kult der Artemis en Ephesos," *JOAI* 50 (1972): 243-51.

19:27
1457 Steven M. Baugh, "Phraseology and the Reliability of Acts," *NTS* 36/2 (1990): 290-94.

19:34-35
1458 E. Heinzel, "Zum Kult der Artemis en Ephesos," *JOAI* 50 (1972): 243-51.

19:35-40
1459 Lawrence Wills, "The Form of the Sermon in Hellenistic Judaism and Early Christianity," *HTR* 77/3-4 (1984): 277-99.

1460 Marion L. Soards, "The Speech of the Ephesian Town Clerk," in *The Speeches in Acts: Their Content, Context, and Concerns.* Louisville: John Knox/Westminster Press, 1994. Pp. 103-104.

19:37
1461 T. C. G. Thornton, "The Destruction of Idols: Sinful or Meritorius?" *JTS* 37/1 (1986): 121-29.

1462 Steven M. Baugh, "Phraseology and the Reliability of Acts," *NTS* 36/2 (1990): 290-94.

20-28

1463 H. S. Songer, "Paul's Mission to Jerusalem: Acts 20-28," *RevExp* 71/4 (1974): 499-510.

1464 H. S. Songer, "Acts 20-28: From Ephesus to Rome," *RevExp* 87 (1990): 451-63.

20

1465 Paul E. Davies, "The Macedonian Scene of Paul's Journeys," *BA* 26 (1963): 91-106.

1466 Thomas L. Budesheim, "Paul's *Abschiedsrede* in the Acts of the Apostles," *HTR* 69/1 (1976): 9-30.

1467 A. W. Swamidoss, "The Speeches of Paul in Acts 13, 17 and 20," doctoral dissertation, Fuller Theological Seminary, Pasadena CA, 1979.

1468 W.-D. Hauschild, "Die Confessio Augustana und die Altkirchliche Tradition," *KD* 26/3 (1980): 142-63.

20:1-21:14

1469 A. Moda, "Paolo prigioniero e martire. Gli avvenimenti gerosolimitiani," *BibO* 34 (1992): 193-252.

20:3-6

1470 É. Delebecque, "Les deux Versions du Voyage de Saint Paul de Corinthe à Troas," *Bib* 64/4 (1983): 556-64.

20:4

1471 G. Ogg, "Derbe," *NTS* 9/4 (1963): 367-70.

20:7-12

1472 Bernard Morel, "Eutychus et les Fondements Bibliques du Culte," *ÉTR* 37/1 (1962): 41-47.

1473 Bernard Trémel, "A propos d'Actes 20,7-12: puissance du thaumaturge ou du témoin?" *RTP* 30/4 (1980): 359-69.

1474 David H. C. Read, "Eutychus—Or the Perils of Preaching," *PSB* 6/3 (1985): 168-78.

1475 A. D. Bulley, "Hanging in the Balance: A Semiotic Study of Acts 20:7-12," *EgT* 25 (1994): 171-88.

1476 E. A. LaVerdiere, "The Eucharist in the New Testament and the Early Church—VI: The Breaking of the Bread. The Eucharist in the Acts of the Apostles," *Emmanuel* 100 (1994): 324-35.

20:7

1477 C. H. Dodd, "New Testament Translation Problems I," *BT* 27/3 (1976): 301-11.

1478 Bernard P. Robinson, "The Place of the Emmaus Story in Luke-Acts," *NTS* 30/4 (1984): 481-97.

1479 J. Timothy Coyle, "The Agape—Eucharist Relationship in 1 Corinthians 11," *GTJ* 6/2 (1985): 411-24.

20:9

1480 Donald F. Deer, "Getting the 'Story' Straight in Acts 20:9," *BT* 39 (1988): 246-47.

1481 T. Naden, "Another Stor(e)y," *BT* 41/2 (1990): 243.

20:11

1482 Bernard P. Robinson, "The Place of the Emmaus Story in Luke-Acts," *NTS* 30/4 (1984): 481-97.

1483 J. Timothy Coyle, "The Agape—Eucharist Relationship in 1 Corinthians 11," *GTJ* 6/2 (1985): 411-24.

20:13-37
1484 D. Wiens, "Luke on Pluralism: Flex with History," *Direction* 23 (1994): 44-53.

20:14
1485 Werner Bieder, "Das Volk Gottes in Erwartung von Licht und Lobpreis," *TZ* 40/2 (1984): 137-48.

20:17-38
1486 Alberto Casalegno, "Il discorso di Miletoi," *RBib* 25/1 (1977): 29-58.

1487 J. S. Petofi, "La struttura della comunicazione in Atti 20:17-38," *RBib* 29/3-4 (1981): 359-78.

1488 Lewis R. Donelson, "Cult Histories and the Sources of Acts," *Bib* 68/1 (1987): 1-21.

1489 C. J. Hemer, "The Speeches of Acts: 1. The Ephesian Elders at Miletus," *TybB* 40 (1989): 77-85.

1490 C. J. Hemer, "The Speeches of Acts. 2. The Areopagus Address," *TynB* 40/2 (1989): 239-59.

1491 T. C. Alexander, "Paul's Final Exhortation to the Elders from Ephesus: The Rhetoric of Acts 20:17-38," doctoral dissertation, Emory University, Atlanta GA, 1990.

1492 Duane F. Watson, "Paul's Speech to the Ephesian Elders (Acts 20.17-38): Epideictic Rhetoric of Farewell," in Duane F. Watson, *Persuasive Artistry: Studies in New Testament Rhetoric* (festschrift for George A. Kennedy). Sheffield: JSOT Press, 1991. Pp. 184-208.

20:17-35
1493 Lawrence Wills, "The Form of the Sermon in Hellenistic Judaism and Early Christianity," *HTR* 77/3-4 (1984): 277-99.

1494 Robert L. Reymond, "The Justification of Theology with a Special Application to Contemporary Christology," *Pres* 12/1 (1986): 1-16.

20:17-30
1495 Phillip Sigal, "Aspects of Dual Covenant Theology: Salvation," *HBT* 5/2 (1983): 1-48.

20:18-35
1496 C. Exum and C. Talbert, "The Structure of Paul's Speech to the Ephesian Elders," *CBQ* 29/2 (1967): 233-36.

1497 F. F. Bruce, "Is the Paul of Acts the Real Paul?" *BJRL* 58/2 (1976): 282-305.

1498 F. Zeilinger, "Lukas, Anwalt des Paulus. überlegungen zur Abschiedsrede von Milet Apg 20,18-35," *BL* 54/3 (1981): 167-72.

1499 P.-R. Tragan, "Les 'destinataires' du Discours de Milet: une approche du cadre communautaire d'Ac 20:18-35," in Françios Refoulé, ed., *À cause de l'Évangile: Études sur les synoptiques et les Actes* (festschrift for Jacques Dupont). Paris: Cerf, 1985. Pp. 779-98.

1500 Evald Lövestam, "En gammaltestamentlig nyckel till Paulus-talet I Miletos," *SEÅ* 51 (1986): 137-47.

1501 L. Aejmelaeus, *Die Rexeption der Paulusbriefe in der Miletrede.* Helsinki: Suomalainen Tiedeakatemia, 1987.

1502 Evald Lövestam, "Paul's Address at Miletus," *ST* 41/1 (1987): 1-10.

1503 A. Dauer, "Ergänzungen und 'Variationen' in den Reden der Apostelgeschichte gegenüber vorausgegangenen Erzählungen Beobachtungen zur literarischen Arbeitsweise des Lukas," in Hubert Frankemölle and Karl Kertelge, eds., *Vom Urchristentum zu Jesus* (festschrift for Joachim Gnilka). Freiburg: Herder, 1989. Pp. 307-24.

1504 John J. Kilgallen, "Paul's Speech to the Ephesian Elders: Its Structure," *ETL* 70 (1994): 112-21.

1505 Marion L. Soards, "Paul's Speech to the Ephesian Elders," in *The Speeches in Acts: Their Content, Context, and Concerns.* Louisville: John Knox/Westminster Press, 1994. Pp. 104-108.

20:23-31

1506 Herbert Thompson, *Koptische Pergamente theologischen Inhalts, 1* "Mitteilungen aus der Papyrussammlung der Nationalbibliothek in Wien," N.S., 2. Folge. Vienna: Staatsdruckerei, 1934.

20:28

1507 I. Howard Marshall, "New Wine in Old Wineskins: V. The Biblical Use of the Word 'Ekklesia'," *ET* 84/12 (1973): 359-64.

1508 Kevin N. Giles, "Luke's Use of the Term ecclesia (ἐκκλησία) with Special Reference to Acts 20:28 and 9:31," *NTS* 31 (1985): 135-42.

1509 K. G. Dolfe, "The Greek Word of 'Blood' and the Interpretation of Acts 20:28," *SEÅ* 55 (1990): 64-70.

20:29

1510 K. A. D. Smelik, "John Chrysostom's Homilies Against the Jews: Some Comments," *NTT* 39 (1985): 194-200.

20:32

1511 A. Feuillet, " 'Temoins Oculaires et Serviteurs de la Parole'," *NovT* 15/4 (1973): 241-59.

20:35

1512 Eduard Schweizer, "The Testimony to Jesus in the Early Christian Community," *HBT* 7/1 (1985): 77-98.

1513 John J. Kilgallen, "Acts 20:35 and Thucydides," *JBL* 112 (1993): 312-14.

1514 R. F. O'Toole, "What Role Does Jesus' Sayings in Acts 20:35 Play in Paul's Address to the Ephesian Elders?" *Bib* 75 (1994): 329-49.

21-28

1515 G. Jasper, "Der Rat des Jakobus: Das Ringen des Paulus, der Urgemeinde, die Möglichkeit der Mission unter Israel zu erhalten, Apg Kap 21-28," *Jud* 19/3 (1963): 147-62.

21-28

1516 S.-H. Yoo, "Une étude sur le procès de Paul," doctoral dissertation, University of Strasbourg, Strasbourg, 1991.

21-23

1517 Werner Kaschel, "The Holy Spirit in the Palestinian Churches: Acts I-XII; XV; XXI-XXIII," master's thesis, Southwestern Baptist Theological Seminary, Fort Worth TX, 1949.

21

1518 R. J. Hardy, "Three Papers on the Text of Acts: 1. The Reconstruction of the Torn Leaf of Codex Bezae; 2. And When the Day of Pentecost Was Fully Come; 3. The Greek Text of Codex Laudianus," *HTR* 16 (1923): 163-86.

21:8

1519   Richard Glover, " 'Luke the Antiochene' and Acts," *NTS* 11/1 (1964): 97-106.

1520   Carl J. Diemer, "Deacons and Other Endangered Species: A Look at the Biblical Office of Deacon," *FundJ* 3/3 (1984): 21-24.

1521   Timothy Trammel, "Caesarea Maritima," *BI* (1989): 38-48.

21:10

1522   H. Patsch, "Die Prophetie des Agabus," *TZ* 28 (1972): 228-32.

21:11

1523   Marion L. Soards, "Agabus's Speech in Caesarea," in *The Speeches in Acts: Their Content, Context, and Concerns.* Louisville: John Knox/Westminster Press, 1994. Pp. 108-109.

21:14-26

1524   F. Blass, "Zu den zwei Texten der Apostelgeschichte," *TSK* 73 (1900): 5-28.

21:14-26

1525   Matthew Black, "A Palestinian Syriac Palimpsest Leaf of Acts 21:14-26," *BJRL* 23 (1939): 201-14.

21:15-26

1526   A. Moda, "Paolo prigioniero e martire. Gli avvenimenti gerosolimitiani," *BibO* 34 (1992): 193-252.

21:16-17

1527   É. Delebecque, "La dernière étape du troisième voyage missionnaire de saint Paul selon les deux versions des Actes des Apôtres," *RTL* 14/4 (1983): 446-55.

21:17-26

1528   Giovanni Rinaldi, "Giacomo, Paolo e i Giudei," *RBib* 14/4 (1966): 407-23.

21:17

1529   J. Morgado, "Paul in Jerusalem: A Comparison of His Visits in Acts and Galatians," *JETS* 37 (1994): 55-68.

21:20-25
> **1530** Marion L. Soards, "The Speech of James and the Jerusalem Elders," in *The Speeches in Acts: Their Content, Context, and Concerns*. Louisville: John Knox/Westminster Press, 1994. Pp. 109-10.

21:21
> **1531** D. L. Balch, " 'You Teach All the Jews . . . to Forsake Moses, Telling Them not to . . . Observe the Customs'," *SBLSP* 32 (1993): 369-83.

21:23-30
> **1532** John Fischer, "Paul in His Jewish Context," *EQ* 57 (1985): 211-36.

21:25
> **1533** Thorleif Boman, "Das textkritische Problem des sogenannten Aposteldekrets," *NovT* 7/1 (1964): 26-36.

> **1534** A. F. J. Klijn, "The Pseudo Clementines and the Apostolic Decree," *NovT* 10/4 (1968): 305-12.

> **1535** Terrance Callan, "The Background of the Apostolic Decree," *CBQ* 55 (1993): 284-97.

21:26
> **1536** E. P. Sanders, "Judaism and the Grand "Christian" Abstractions: Love, Mercy, and Grace," *Int* 39 (1985): 357-72.

> **1537** J. G. M. Willebrands, "Is Christianity Antisemitic?" *ChJR* 18/2 (1985): 8-20.

21:27-23:22
> **1538** A. Moda, "Paolo prigioniero e martire. Gli avvenimenti gerosolimitiani," *BibO* 34 (1992): 193-252.

21:27-26:32
> **1539** S. Légasse, "L'apologétique à l'égard de Rome dans le procès de Paul," *RechSR* 69/2 (1981): 249-55.

21:37
> **1540** Larry V. Crutchfield, "The Fortress Antonia," *BI* (1989): 2-3, 7-8.

21:39

1541 Harvie M. Conn, "Lucan Perspectives and the City," *Miss* 13 (1985): 409-28.

22-28

1542 Jacob Jervell, "Paulus—der Lehrer Israels," *NovT* 10/2 (1968): 164-90.

22-26

1543 J. H. Neyrey, "The Forensic Defense Speech and Paul's Trial Speeches in Acts 22-26: Form and Function," in Charles H. Talbert, ed., *Luke-Acts: New Perspectives from the Society of Biblical Literature*. New York: Crossroad, 1984. Pp. 210-24.

22

1544 D. M. Stanley, "Paul's Conversion in Acts: Why the Three Accounts?" *CBQ*, 15 (1953): 315-38.

1545 Gerhard Lohfink, "Eine alttestamentliche Darstellungsform für Gotteserscheinungen in den Damaskusberichten," *BZ* N.s. 9/2 (1965): 246-57.

1546 Boyd Reese, "The Apostle Paul's Exercise of His Rights as a Roman Citizen as Recorded in the Book of Acts," *EQ* 47/3 (1975): 138-45.

1547 Thomas L. Budesheim, "Paul's *Abschiedsrede* in the Acts of the Apostles," *HTR* 69/1 (1976): 9-30.

1548 O. H. Steck, "Formgeschichtliche Bemerkungen zur Darstellung des Damaskusgeschens in der Apostelgeschichte," *ZNW* 67/1 (1976): 20-28.

1549 S. R. Bechtler, "The Meaning of Paul's Call and Commissioning in Luke's Story: An Exegetical Study of Acts 9, 22, and 26," *SBT* 15 (1987): 53-77.

1550 Gert Steuernagel, "Ἀκούοντες μὲν τῆς φωνῆς: Ein Genitiv in der Apostelgeschichte," *NTS* 35/4 (1988-1989): 619-24.

1551 Ronald D. Witherup, "Functional Redundancy in the Acts of the Apostles: A Case Study," *JSNT* 48 (1992): 67-86.

22:1

1552 Marion L. Soards, "Paul's Speech to the Jerusalem Jews," in *The Speeches in Acts: Their Content, Context, and Concerns.* Louisville: John Knox/Westminster Press, 1994. Pp. 111-14.

1553 Marion L. Soards, "The Speech to the Jews from Asia," in *The Speeches in Acts: Their Content, Context, and Concerns.* Louisville: John Knox/Westminster Press, 1994. Pp. 110-11.

22:1-20

1554 Jaroslav B. Stanek, "Lukas: Theologie der Heilgeschichte," *CVia* 28/1-2 (1985): 9-31.

22:3-21

1555 Marion L. Soards, "Paul's Speech to the Jerusalem Jews," in *The Speeches in Acts: Their Content, Context, and Concerns.* Louisville: John Knox/Westminster Press, 1994. Pp. 111-14.

1556 Marion L. Soards, "The Speech to the Jews from Asia," in *The Speeches in Acts: Their Content, Context, and Concerns.* Louisville: John Knox/Westminster Press, 1994. Pp. 110-11.

22:3

1557 A. I. Baumgarten, "The Name of the Pharisees," *JBL* 102/3 (1983): 411-28.

1558 E. P. Sanders, "Judaism and the Grand "Christian" Abstractions: Love, Mercy, and Grace," *Int* 39 (1985): 357-72.

22:4-16

1559 C. W. Hedrick, "Paul's Conversion-Call: A Comparative Analysis of the Three Reports in Acts," *JBL* 100/3 (1981): 415-32.

1560 Karl H. Schelkle, "Im Leib oder Ausser des Leibes: Paulus als Mystiker," in William C. Weinrich, ed., *The New Testament Age* (festschrift for Bo Reicke). 2 vols. Macon GA: Mercer University Press, 1984. 2:455-65.

22:6-21

1561 Roy A. Harrisville, "Acts 22:6-21," *Int* 42 (1988): 181-85.

22:6-16
> **1562** D. Hamm, "Paul's Blindness and Its Healing: Clues to Symbolic Intent," *Bib* 71/1 (1990): 63-72.

22:8
> **1563** C. J. Hemer, "The Name of Paul," *TynB* 36 (1985): 179-83.

22:9
> **1564** Robert G. Bratcher, "*Akouo* in Acts 9:7 and 22:9," *ET* 71 (1960): 243-45.

22:10-21
> **1565** Robert Culver, "Authority for a Going and Sending Ministry in the Christian Mission of World Evangelism," in Morris Inch and Ronald Youngblood, eds., *The Living and Active Word of God* (festschrift for Samuel J. Schultz). Winona Lake IN: Eisenbrauns, 1983. Pp. 157-70.

22:13
> **1566** L. Legrand, "Faith and the Church; 'Ananias Came to Me'," *CM* 32/2 (1968): 91-92.

22:14-21
> **1567** David P. Moessner, "The Christ Must Suffer: New Light on the Jesus—Peter, Stephen, Paul Parallels in Luke-Acts," *NovT* 28/3 (1986): 220-56.

22:14-15
> **1568** R. B. Hays, "The Righteous One as Eschatological Deliverer: A Case Study in Paul's Apocalyptic Hermeneutics," in Joel Marcus and Marion Soards, eds., *Apocalyptic and the New Testament* (festschrift for J. Louis Martyn). Sheffield: JSOT Press, 1989. Pp 191-215.

22:17-22
> **1569** C. R. A. Morray-Jones, "Paradise Revisited: The Jewish Mystical Background of Paul's Apostolate," *HTR* 86 (1993): 265-92.

22:17
> **1570** L. Legrand, "The Prayer of the Apostle 'When I Was at Prayer'," *CM* 32/4 (1968): 184-86.

22:21

1571 Kevin N. Giles, "Apostles before and after Paul," *Ch* 99/3 (1985): 241-56.

22:22-29

1572 P. Van Minnen, "Paul the Roman Citizen," *JSNT* 56 (1994): 43-52.

22:25-29

1573 Mark Black, "Paul and Roman Law in Acts," *RQ* 24/4 (1981): 209-18.

22:29

1574 R. A. Johnson, "The Narrative Function of the Quotation of Isaiah 6:9-10 and the Concomitant Hear-See Motif in the Book of Acts," doctoral dissertation, Southwestern Baptist Theological Seminary, Fort Worth TX, 1992.

22:30-23:11

1575 D. Cox, "Paul Before the Sanhedrin: Acts 22:30-23:11," *SBFLA* 21 (1971): 54-75.

23:1

1576 Marion L. Soards, "Paul's Speech before the Council," in *The Speeches in Acts: Their Content, Context, and Concerns.* Louisville: John Knox/Westminster Press, 1994. Pp. 114-16.

23:3-6

1577 E. P. Sanders, "Judaism and the Grand "Christian" Abstractions: Love, Mercy, and Grace," *Int* 39 (1985): 357-72.

23:6-8

1578 Rudolf Schnackenburg, "Die lukanische Eschatologie im Lichte von Aussagen der Apostelgeschichte," in E. Grässer and O. Merk, eds., *Glaube und Eschatologie* (festschrift for W. G. Kümmel). Tübingen: Mohr, 1985. Pp. 249-65.

23:8-9

1579 B. T. Viviano, "Sadducees, Angels, and Resurrection," *JBL* 111 (1992): 496-98.

23:9
>   **1580**   Marion L. Soards, "The Pharisees' Speech in the Council," in *The Speeches in Acts: Their Content, Context, and Concerns.* Louisville: John Knox/Westminster Press, 1994. Pp. 116-17.

23:10
>   **1581**   Larry V. Crutchfield, "The Fortress Antonia," *BI* (1989): 2-3, 7-8.

23:12-16
>   **1582**   W. H. P. Hatch, "Six Coptic Fragments of the New Testament from Nitria," *HTR* 26 (1933): 99-108.

23:23-26:32
>   **1583**   A. Moda, "Paolo prigioniero e martire. Gli avvenimenti di Cesarea," *BibO* 35 (1993): 21-59.

23:23
>   **1584**   George D. Kilpatrick, "Acts 23:23 Dexiolbous," *JTS* 14 (1963): 393-94.

>   **1585**   Sherman E. Johnson, "Caesarea Maritima," *LTQ* 20 (1985): 28-32.

23:24-26
>   **1586**   F. F. Bruce, "The Full Name of the Procurator Felix," *JSNT* 1 (1978): 33-36.

24
>   **1587**   Boyd Reese, "The Apostle Paul's Exercise of His Rights as a Roman Citizen as Recorded in the Book of Acts," *EQ* 47/3 (1975): 138-45.

>   **1588**   Giovanni Rinaldi, "Procurator Felix: note prosopografiche in margine ad una rilettura di At 24," *RBib* 39 (1991): 423-66.

24:1-21
>   **1589**   Bruce W. Winter, "The Importance of the Captatio Benevolentiae in the Speeches of Tertullus and Paul in Acts 24:1-21," *JTS* 42 (1991): 505-31.

24:2-8

1590 Marion L. Soards, "Tertullus's Speech," in *The Speeches in Acts: Their Content, Context, and Concerns*. Louisville: John Knox/Westminster Press, 1994. Pp. 117-18.

24:6-8

1591 É. Delebecque, "Saint Paul avec ou sans le tribun Lysias en 58 à Cesarée. Texte court ou texte long?" *RT* 81/3 (1981): 426-34.

24:10-21

1592 Marion L. Soards, "Paul's Speech before Felix," in *The Speeches in Acts: Their Content, Context, and Concerns*. Louisville: John Knox/Westminster Press, 1994. Pp. 118-19.

24:14

1593 H. John McLachlan, "The Spirit of the Place," *FF* 39/116 (1986): 59-65.

24:15

1594 Rudolf Schnackenburg, "Die lukanische Eschatologie im Lichte von Aussagen der Apostelgeschichte," in E. Grässer and O. Merk, eds., *Glaube und Eschatologie* (festschrift for W. G. Kümmel). Tübingen: Mohr, 1985. Pp. 249-65.

24:17

1595 A. Dauer, "Ergänzungen und 'Variationen' in den Reden der Apostelgeschichte gegenüber vorausgegangenen Erzählungen Beobachtungen zur literarischen Arbeitsweise des Lukas," in Hubert Frankemölle and Karl Kertelge, eds., *Vom Urchristentum zu Jesus* (festschrift for Joachim Gnilka). Freiburg: Herder, 1989. Pp. 307-24.

24:22-26

1596 C. Taylor, ed., "The Acts," in *Hebrew-Greek Cairo Genizah Palimpsests from the Taylor-Schechter Collection*. Cambridge: University Press, 1900. Pp. 93-95.

24:25-27

1597 F. F. Bruce, "The Full Name of the Procurator Felix," *JSNT* 1 (1978): 33-36.

24:25
    1598 Paul G. Kuntz, "Whitehead the Anglican and Russell the Puritan: the Traditional Origins of Muddleheadedness and Simple-mindedness," *PS* 17 (1988): 40-44.

24:27
    1599 C. Taylor, ed., "The Acts," in *Hebrew-Greek Cairo Genizah Palimpsests from the Taylor-Schechter Collection.* Cambridge: University Press, 1900. Pp. 93-95.

    1600 Sherman E. Johnson, "Caesarea Maritima," *LTQ* 20 (1985): 28-32.

25:1-26:32
    1601 R. F. O'Toole, "Luke's Notion of 'Be Imitators of Me as I Am of Christ' in Acts 25-26," *BTB* 8/4 (1978): 155-61.

25:6-12
    1602 P. Van Minnen, "Paul the Roman Citizen," *JSNT* 56 (1994): 43-52.

25:8
    1603 A. Moda, "Paolo prigioniero e martire. Gli avvenimenti di Cesarea," *BibO* 35 (1993): 21-59.

25:8
    1604 Marion L. Soards, "Paul's Speech before Fetus," in *The Speeches in Acts: Their Content, Context, and Concerns.* Louisville: John Knox/Westminster Press, 1994. Pp. 119-20.

25:9
    1605 A. Schalit, "Zu AG 25:9," *ASTI* 6 (1968): 106-13.

25:10-11
    1606 Marion L. Soards, "Paul's Speech before Fetus," in *The Speeches in Acts: Their Content, Context, and Concerns.* Louisville: John Knox/Westminster Press, 1994. Pp. 119-20.

25:11
    1607 H. W. Tajra, "L'appel à César: séparation d'avec le Christianisme?" *ÉTR* 56/4 (1981): 593-98.

25:14-21
   1608   Marion L. Soards, "Festus's Speech," in *The Speeches in Acts:
            Their Content, Context, and Concerns.* Louisville: John
            Knox/Westminster Press, 1994. Pp. 120-22.

25:21
   1609   Giuseppe Scarpat, "Ancora Sulla Data di Composizione Della
            Sapientia Salomonis. Il Termine Diagnosis," *RBib* 36 (1988):
            363-75.

25:24-27
   1610   Marion L. Soards, "Festus's Speech," in *The Speeches in Acts:
            Their Content, Context, and Concerns.* Louisville: John
            Knox/Westminster Press, 1994. Pp. 120-22.

26
   1611   D. M. Stanley, "Paul's Conversion in Acts: Why the Three
            Accounts?" *CBQ*, 15 (1953): 315-38.

   1612   Gerhard Lohfink, "Eine alttestamentliche Darstellungsform für
            Gotteserscheinungen in den Damaskusberichten," *BZ* N.S. 9/2
            (1965): 246-57.

   1613   Boyd Reese, "The Apostle Paul's Exercise of His Rights as a
            Roman Citizen as Recorded in the Book of Acts," *EQ* 47/3 (1975):
            138-45.

   1614   O. H. Steck, "Formgeschichtliche Bemerkungen zur Darstellung
            des Damaskusgeschens in der Apostelgeschichte," *ZNW* 67/1
            (1976): 20-28.

   1615   R. F. O'Toole, "Acts 26: The Christological Climax of Paul's
            Defense," *TLZ* 104 (1979): 825.

   1616   W. G. Marx, "A New Theophilus," *EQ* 52/1 (1980): 17-26.

   1617   S. R. Bechtler, "The Meaning of Paul's Call and Commissioning
            in Luke's Story: An Exegetical Study of Acts 9, 22, and 26," *SBT*
            15 (1987): 53-77.

   1618   Ronald D. Witherup, "Functional Redundancy in the Acts of the
            Apostles: A Case Study," *JSNT* 48 (1992): 67-86.

26:1-23
> **1619**   Jaroslav B. Stanek, "Lukas: Theologie der Heilgeschichte," *CVia* 28/1-2 (1985): 9-31.

26:2-23
> **1620**   John J. Kilgallen, "Paul before Agrippa: Some Considerations," *Bib* 69/2 (1988): 170-95.

> **1621**   Marion L. Soards, "Paul's Speech before King Agrippa," in *The Speeches in Acts: Their Content, Context, and Concerns.* Louisville: John Knox/Westminster Press, 1994. Pp. 122-27.

26:2-22
> **1622**   Robert J. Kepple, "The Hope of Israel: The Resurrection of the Dead, and Jesus: A Study of Their Relationship in Acts with Particular Regard to the Understanding of Paul's Trial Defense," *JETS* 20/3 (1977): 231-41.

26:2
> **1623**   A. O. Collins, "Herod Agrippa II," *BI* (1989): 68-71.

26:5
> **1624**   Dick Avi, "Church: Mission and Development," *Point* 8/1 (1979): 29-38.

> **1625**   A. I. Baumgarten, "The Name of the Pharisees," *JBL* 102/3 (1983): 411-28.

26:6-8
> **1626**   R. F. O'Toole, "Christ's Resurrection in Acts 13:13-52," *Bib* 60/3 (1979): 361-72.

26:7
> **1627**   I. Peri, "Gelangen zur Vollkommenheit: Zur Lateinischen Interpretation von Katantao in Eph 4:13," *BZ* 23/2 (1979): 269-78.

26:9-18
> **1628**   Karl H. Schelkle, "Im Leib oder Ausser des Leibes: Paulus als Mystiker," in William C. Weinrich, ed., *The New Testament Age* (festschrift for Bo Reicke). 2 vols. Macon GA: Mercer University Press, 1984. 2:455-65.

26:10

1629   S. Légasse, "Paul sanhédrite: à propos d'Ac 26:10," in Françios Refoulé, ed., *À cause de l'Évangile: Études sur les synoptiques et les Actes* (festschrift for Jacques Dupont). Paris: Cerf, 1985. Pp. 799-807.

26:12-23

1630   D. Hamm, "Paul's Blindness and Its Healing: Clues to Symbolic Intent," *Bib* 71/1 (1990): 63-72.

26:12-18

1631   C. W. Hedrick, "Paul's Conversion-Call: A Comparative Analysis of the Three Reports in Acts," *JBL* 100/3 (1981): 415-32.

26:12

1632   Bobby D. Box, "Damascus," *BI* 13/4 (1987): 23-27.

26:14

1633   S. Reyero, " 'Durum est tibi contra stimulum calcitrare.' Hechos de los Apóstoles, 26:14," *Stud* 10/2 (1970): 367-78.

26:16-23

1634   Jacques Dupont, "La mission de Paul d'après Actes 26,16-23 et la mission des apotres d'après Luc 24,44-49 et Actes 1,8," in M. D. Hooker and S. G. Wilson, eds., *Paul and Paulinism* (festschrift for C. K. Barrett). London: SPCK, 1982. Pp. 290-301.

1635   David P. Moessner, "The Christ Must Suffer: New Light on the Jesus—Peter, Stephen, Paul Parallels in Luke-Acts," *NovT* 28/3 (1986): 220-56.

26:16-18

1636   Edward Fudge, "Paul's Apostolic Self-Consciousness at Athens," *JETS* 14/3 (1971): 193-98.

26:18

1637   B. Prete, "Il contenuto ecclesiologico del termine 'eredità' (κλῆρος) in Atti 26,18," *SacD* 38 (1993): 625-53.

26:22-23

1638   R. F. O'Toole, "Christ's Resurrection in Acts 13:13-52," *Bib* 60/3 (1979): 361-72.

26:25-27
  1639 Marion L. Soards, "Paul's Speech before King Agrippa," in *The Speeches in Acts: Their Content, Context, and Concerns.* Louisville: John Knox/Westminster Press, 1994. Pp. 122-27.

26:28-29
  1640 Paul Harlé, "Un 'Private-Joke' de Paul dans le livre des Actes," *NTS* 24/4 (1978): 527-33.

26:29
  1641 Marion L. Soards, "Paul's Speech before King Agrippa," in *The Speeches in Acts: Their Content, Context, and Concerns.* Louisville: John Knox/Westminster Press, 1994. Pp. 122-27.

26:33
  1642 Bent Noack, "Si passibilis Christus," *SEÅ* 37/38 (1972-1973): 211-21.

27-28
  1643 A. Acworth, "Where Was St. Paul Shipwrecked? A Re-examination of the Evidence," *JTS* 24/1 (1973): 190-93.

  1644 O. F. A. Meinardus, "Melita Illyrica or Africana: An Examination of the Site of St. Paul's Shipwreck," *OS* 23/1 (1974): 21-36.

  1645 G. B. Miles and G. W. Trompf, "Luke and Antiphon: The Theology of Acts 27-28 in the Light of Pagan Beliefs about Divine Retribution, Pollution, and Shipwreck," *HTR* 69/3 (1976): 259-67.

  1646 D. Ladouceur, "Hellenistic Preconceptions of Shipwreck and Pollution, as a Context for Acts 27-28," *HTR* 73 (1980): 435-49.

  1647 Susan Marie Praeder, "The Narrative Voyage: An Analysis and Interpretation of Acts 27-28," doctoral dissertation, Graduate Theological Union, Berkeley, 1982.

  1648 G. W. Trompf, "On Why Luke Declined to Recount the Death of Paul: Acts 27-28 and Beyond," in Charles H. Talbert, ed., *Luke-Acts: New Perspectives from the Society of Biblical Literature.* New York: Crossroad, 1984. Pp. 225-39.

  1649 C. J. Hemer, "First Person Narrative in Acts 27-28," *TynB* 36 (1985): 79-109.

1650 J. Wehnert, "Gestrandet: Zu einer neuen These über den Schiff-bruch des Apostels Paulus auf dem Wege nach Rom," *ZTK* 87 (1990): 67-99.

1651 J. Wehnert, " . . . und da erfuhren wir, daß die Insel Kephallenia heißt. Zur neuesten Auslegung von Apg 27-28 und ihrer Methode," *ZTK* 88 (1991): 169-80.

1652 Daniel Marguerat, " 'Et quand nous sommes entrés dans Rome': L'énigme de la fin du livre des Actes," *RHPR* 73/1 (1993): 1-21.

1653 A. Moda, "Paolo prigioniero e martire. Gli avvenimenti di Cesarea," *BibO* 35 (1993): 21-59.

27:1-28:16

1654 Susan Marie Praeder, "Acts 27:1-28:16: Sea Voyages in Ancient Literature and the Theology of Luke-Acts," *CBQ* 46/4 (1984): 683-706.

1655 Alfred Suhl, "Gestrandet! Bemerkungen zum Streit über die Romfahrt des Paulus," *ZTK* 88/1 (1991): 1-28.

27:1-28:13

1656 W. Leonard, "From Caesarea to Malta: St. Paul's Voyage and Shipwreck," *ACR* 37 (1960): 274-84.

27

1657 R. W. Orr, "Paul's Voyage and Shipwreck," *EQ* 35/2 (1963): 103-104.

1658 P. Pokorn·, "Die Romfahrt des Paulus und der antike Roman," - *ZNW* 64/3-4 (1973): 233-44.

1659 C. K. Barrett, "Paul Shipwrecked," in Barry Thompson, ed., *Scripture: Meaning and Method* (festschrift for A. T. Hanson). Hull: University Press, 1987. Pp. 51-64.

1660 Michael Oberweis, "Ps. 33 als Interpretationsmodell für Act 27," *NovT* 30/2 (1988): 169-83.

1661 C. Sant and J. Sammut, "Paulus war doch auf Malta!" *TGl* 80 (1990): 327-32.

1662   G. Girardet, "Il primo evangelo scritto. Marco 4:1-9; Atti 27,"
           Protestantesimo 49 (1993): 154-61.

27:1-44
1663   T. A. Hawthorne, "Discourse Analysis of Paul's Shipwreck: Acts
           27:1-44," *JTT* 6 (1993): 253-73.

27:1-13
1664   E. S. Buchanan, "More Pages from the Fleury Palimpsest," *JTS* 8
           (1906-1907): 96-100.

1665   M.-É. Boismard and A. Lamouille, "Le Texte Occidental des Actes
           des Apôtres: à propos de Actes 27:1-13," *ETL* 63/1 (1987): 48-58.

27:1-10
1666   J. Rouge, "Actes 27:1-10," *VC* 14/4 (1960): 193-203.

27:1-5
1667   A. Moda, "Paolo prigioniero e martire. Gli avvenimenti romani,"
           BibO 35 (1993): 89-118.

27:4-13
1668   James M. Robinson and Robert A. Kraft, "A Sahidic Parchment
           Fragment of Acts 27:4-13 at the University Museum, Philadelphia
           (E 16690 Coptic 1)," *JBL* 94/2 (1975): 256-65.

27:6-13
1669   A. Moda, "Paolo prigioniero e martire: Gli avvenimenti romani,"
           BibO 35 (1993): 89-118.

27:7-12
1670   B. Schwank, " 'Wir umsegelten Kreta bei Salmone.' Reisebericht
           zu Apg 27,7-12," *ErAu* 48/1 (1972): 16-25.

27:10
1671   A. Moda, "Paolo prigioniero e martire: Gli avvenimenti romani,"
           BibO 35 (1993): 89-118.

1672   Marion L. Soards, "Paul's Speech(es) during the Sea Voyage to
           Rome," in *The Speeches in Acts: Their Content, Context, and
           Concerns*. Louisville: John Knox/Westminster Press, 1994. Pp.
           122-27.

27:13
1673 R. Alan Culpepper, "Crete," *BI* (1989): 72-75.

27:14-26
1674 A. Moda, "Paolo prigioniero e martire: Gli avvenimenti romani," *BibO* 35 (1993): 89-118.

27:18-19
1675 David J. Clark, "What Went Overboard First?" *BT* 26/1 (1975): 144-46.

27:21-26
1676 Marion L. Soards, "Paul's Speech(es) during the Sea Voyage to Rome," in *The Speeches in Acts: Their Content, Context, and Concerns*. Louisville: John Knox/Westminster Press, 1994. Pp. 122-27.

27:27
1677 B. Schwank, " 'Als wir schon die vierzehnte Nacht auf der Adria trieben'," *ErAu* 66 (1990): 44-49.

27:27-44
1678 A. Moda, "Paolo prigioniero e martire: Gli avvenimenti romani," *BibO* 35 (1993): 89-118.

27:31
1679 A. Moda, "Paolo prigioniero e martire: Gli avvenimenti romani," *BibO* 35 (1993): 89-118.

1680 Marion L. Soards, "Paul's Speech(es) during the Sea Voyage to Rome," in *The Speeches in Acts: Their Content, Context, and Concerns*. Louisville: John Knox/Westminster Press, 1994. Pp. 122-27.

27:33-38
1681 A. Moda, "Paolo prigioniero e martire: Gli avvenimenti romani," *BibO* 35 (1993): 89-118.

1682 E. A. LaVerdiere, "The Eucharist in the New Testament and the Early Church—VI: The Breaking of the Bread. The Eucharist in the Acts of the Apostles," *Emmanuel* 100 (1994): 324-35.

27:33-34
1683 Marion L. Soards, "Paul's Speech(es) during the Sea Voyage to Rome," in *The Speeches in Acts: Their Content, Context, and Concerns*. Louisville: John Knox/Westminster Press, 1994. Pp. 122-27.

28
1684 D. S. Tam, "The Literary and Theological Unity Between Luke 1-2 and Luke 3-Acts 28," doctoral dissertation, Duke University, Durham NC, 1978.

1685 N. Heutger, " 'Paulus auf Malta' im Lichte der maltesischen Topographie," *BZ* 28/1 (1984): 86-88.

1686 S. Uhlig, "Ein pseudepigraphischer Actaschluss in der äthiopischen Version," *OrChr* 73 (1989): 129-36.

28:1-10
1687 B. Schwank, "Also doch Malta? Spurensuche auf Kefalonia," *BK* 45 (1990): 43-46.

28:1-6
1688 H. J. Klauck, "With Paul in Paphos and Lystra: Magic and Paganism in the Acts of the Apostles," *Neo* 28 (1994): 93-108.

28:1
1689 W. Jürgen, "Und da Erfuhren Wir, Dass die Insel Kephallenia Heisst: Zur Neuesten Auslegung von Apg 27-28 und Ihrer Methode," *ZTK* 88/2 (1991): 169-80.

28:4
1690 Giovanni Rinaldi, "Nota: Dike in Atti 28:4," *BibO* 24/133 (1982): 186.

28:7
1691 A. Suhl, "Zum Titel πρώτῳ τῆς νήσου," *BZ* 36 (1992): 220-26.

28:13-14
1692 Marco Adinolfi, "San Paolo á Pozzuoli," *RBib* 8/3 (1960): 206-24.

1693 R. Calvino, "Cristiani a Puteoli nell'anno 61. Riflessioni zu sull'importanza della notizia concisa degli 'Atti' (28,13b-14a) e risposta all'interrogativo sulle testimonianze monumentali coeve," *RivAC* 56/3-4 (1980): 323-30.

28:14-16

1694 G. Betori, "La strutturazione del libro degli Atti: una proposta," *RBib* 42 (1994): 3-34.

28:14

1695 B. Schwank, " 'Und so kamen wir nach Rom (Apg 28,14).' Reisenotizen zu den letzten beiden Kapiteln der Apostelgeschichte," *ErAu* 36/3 (1960): 169-93.

28:16-31

1696 C. B. Ouskas, "The Conclusion of Luke-Acts: An Investigation of the Literary Function and Theological Significance of Acts 28:16-31," doctoral dissertation, St. Louis University, St. Louis MO, 1979.

1697 B. Prete, "L'arrivo di Paolo a Roma e il suo significato secondo Atti 28:16-31," *RBib* 31/2 (1983): 147-87.

1698 Bar Jan Koet, "Paul in Rome (Acts 28:16-31): A Farewell to Judaism?" *Bij* 48 (1987): 397-415.

1699 Daniel Marguerat, " 'Et quand nous sommes entres dans Rome': L'enigme de la fin du livre des Actes," *RHPR* 73 (1993): 1-21.

28:17-31

1700 R. H. Smith, "The Theology of Acts," *CTM* 42/8 (1971): 527-35.

28:17-28

1701 A. Moda, "Paolo prigioniero e martire. Gli avvenimenti di Cesarea," *BibO* 35 (1993): 21-59.

1702 Joseph B. Tyson, "Jews and Judaism in Luke-Acts: Reading as a Godfearer," *NTS* 41 (1995): 19-38.

28:17-20

1703 Marion L. Soards, "Paul's Speech to the Roman Jewish Leaders," in *The Speeches in Acts: Their Content, Context, and Concerns.* Louisville: John Knox/Westminster Press, 1994. Pp. 130-33.

28:25-28
   1704   Marion L. Soards, "Paul's Speech to the Roman Jewish Leaders,"
            in *The Speeches in Acts: Their Content, Context, and Concerns.*
            Louisville: John Knox/Westminster Press, 1994. Pp. 130-33.

   1705   H. van de Sandt, "Acts 28,28: No Salvation for the People of
            Israel? An Answer in the Perspective of the LXX," *ETL* 70/4
            (1994): 341-58.

28:25
   1706   François Bovon, " 'Schön Hat der Heilige Geist durch den
            Propheten Jesaja zu Euren Vatern Gesprochen'," *ZNW* 75/3 (1984):
            226-32.

28:26
   1707   H. Baarlink, "Friede im Himmel. Die Lukanische Redaktion von
            Lk 19,38 und Ihre Deutung," *ZNW* 76/3 (1985): 170-86.

28:27
   1708   R. A. Johnson, "The Narrative Function of the Quotation of Isaiah
            6:9-10 and the Concomitant Hear-See Motif in the Book of Acts,"
            doctoral dissertation, Southwestern Baptist Theological Seminary,
            Fort Worth TX, 1992.

28:28
   1709   J. Riedl, "Sabed que Dios envía su salud a los gentiles," *RevB* 27
            (1965): 153-55, 162.

   1710   R. C. Tannehill, "Israel In Luke-Acts: A Tragic Story," *JBL* 104/1
            (1985): 69-85.

28:30-31
   1711   Adolf Deissmann, "Pergament Act Ap 28 und Jac 1," in *Die
            Septuaginta-Papyri und andere altchristliche Texte der
            Heidelberger Papyrus-Sammlung.* Veröffentlichungen aus der
            Heidelberger Papyrus-Sammlung 1. Heidelberg: Winter, 1905. P.
            85.

   1712   David Garland, "Rome," *BI* 13/4 (1987): 41-49.

   1713   David L. Mealand, "The Close of Acts and Its Hellenistic Greek
            Vocabulary," *NTS* 36 (1990): 583-97.

1714   A. Moda, "Paolo prigioniero e martire. Gli avvenimenti di Cesarea," *BibO* 35 (1993): 21-59.

28:30

1715   E. Hansack, "Er lebte . . . von seinem eigenen Einkommen," *BZ* 19/2 (1975): 249-53.

1716   Franz Saum, " 'Er Lebte . . . von seinem eigenen Einkommon'," *BZ* 20/2 (1976): 226-29.

1717   E. Hansack, "Nochmals zu Apostelgeschichte 28,30. Erwiderung auf F. Saums kritische Anmerkungen," *BZ* 21/1 (1977): 118-21.

28:31

1718   Gerhard Delling, "Das Letzte Wort der Apostelgeschichte," *NovT* 15/3 (1973): 193-204.

1719   Frank Stagg, "The Unhindered Gospel," *RevExp* 71/4 (1974): 451-62.

PART TWO

Citations by Subjects

Aprippa
1720   M. F. Unger, "Archaeology and Paul's Visit to Iconium, Lystra, and Derbe," *BSac* 118/470 (1961): 107-12.

1721   Larry J. Kreitzer, "A Numismatic Clue to Acts 19.23-41: The Ephesian Cistophori of Claudius and Agrippina," *JSNT* 30 (1987): 59-70.

1722   Günther Schwarz, "Philippon kai Bartholomaion?" *BibN* 56 (1991): 26-30.

Ananias and Sapphira
1723   M. Del Verme, "La comunione dei beni nella comunità primitiva di Gerusalemme," *RivB* (1975): 353-82.

1724   Alfons Weiser, "Das Gottesurteil über Hananias und Saphira," *TGl* 69 (1979): 148-58.

1725   G. Geiger, "Sünde und Tod. Versuch der Neuerzählung der Perikope von Hananias and Saphira," *BiLit* 53 (1980): 160-64.

1726   Daniel Marguerat, "Ananias et Saphira (Actes 5,1-11). Le viol du sacré," *LV* 42/215 (1993): 51-63.

1727   Daniel Marguerat, "La mort d'Ananias et Saphira (Ac 5,1-11) dans la stratégie narrative de Luk," *NTS* 39 (1993): 209-26.

Antioch
1728   J. H. Stovall, "The Significance of the Church at Antioch of Syria in Its Formative Period," master's thesis, New Orleans Baptist Theological Seminary, New Orleans LA, 1954.

1729   Georg Strecker, "Die sogenannte zweite Jerusalemreise des Paulus," *ZNW* 53 (1962): 67-77.

1730   Sherman E. Johnson, "Antioch, the Base of Operations," *LexTQ* 18/2 (1983): 64-73.

1731   J. L. Blevins, "Acts 13-19: The Tale of Three Cites," *RevExp* 87 (1990): 439-50.

1732   C. N. Jefford, "Tradition and Witness in Antioch: Acts 15 and Didache 6," *PRS* 19 (1992): 409-19.

1733   D. A. DeSilva, "Paul's Sermon in Antioch of Pisidia," *BSac* 151 (1994): 32-49.

1734 J. Taylor, "Why Were the Disciples First Called 'Christians' at Antioch?" *RB* 101 (1994): 75-94.

Antisemitism
1735 Erich Lubahn, "Wer ist schuld am Kreuzestode Jesu: Eine Auslegung von Apg 4,27f; 3,18," in Heinz Kremers and Erich Lubahn, eds., *Mission an Israel in heilsgeschichtlicher Sicht* Neukirchen-Vluyn: Neukirchener Verlag, 1985. Pp. 12-23.

1736 J. G. M. Willebrands, "Is Christianity Antisemitic?" *ChJR* 18/2 (1985): 8-20.

1737 Lloyd Gaston, "Anti-Judaism and the Passion Narrative in Luke and Acts," in P. Richardson and D. Granskou, eds., *Anti-Judaism in Early Christianity: 1. Paul and the Gospels*. Waterloo: Wilfrid Laurier University Press, 1986. Pp. 127-53.

apostles
1738 H. M. Luckock, *Footprints of the Apostles as Traced by St. Luke in the Acts*. 2 vols. London; New York; Bombay: Longmans, Green, & Co., 1897. New edition (1 vol.): 1905.

1739 J. Kruszynski, *Ewangelie i Dzieje Apostolskie*. Wloclawek, 1908.

1740 A. J. A. Klinkenberg, "De Handelingen der Apostelen," *NTS* 10 (1927): 193-205.

1741 R. Cunill Puig, *El Apostolado de los seglares en los primeros tiempos de la Iglesia*. Barcelona: Seminario Conciliar. Imp. Altés, 1946.

1742 François Bovon, "L'origine des recits concernant les apôtres," *RTP* 17/5 (1967): 345-50.

1743 Jacob Jervell, "Die Zeichen des Apostels. Die Wunder beim lukansichcn und paulinischen Paulus," *SNTU-A* 4 (1979): 54-75.

1744 J. A. Pierce, "The Twelve as Apostolic Overseers," *BibTo* 18 (1980): 72-76.

1745 R. F. O'Toole, "Parallels between Jesus and His Disciples in Luke-Acts: A Further Study," *BZ* 27 (1983): 195-212.

1746 Kevin N. Giles, "Apostles before and after Paul," *Ch* 99/3 (1985): 241-56.

1747 Günther Schwarz, "Philippon kai Bartholomaion?" *BibN* 56 (1991): 26-30.

1748 A. Campbell, "The Elders of the Jerusalem Church," *JTS* 44 (1993): 511-28.

Aramaic in

1749 James A. Montgomery, "Some Aramaisms in the Gospels and Acts," *JBL* 46 (1927): 69-73.

1750 George A. Barton, "Professor Torrey's Theory of the Aramaic Origin of the Gospels and the First Half of the Acts of the Apostles," *JTS* 36 (1935): 357-73.

1751 R. A. Martin, "Syntactical Evidence of Aramaic Sources in Acts I-XV," *NTS* 11/1 (1964): 38-59.

1752 R. A. Martin, "Semitic Traditions in Some Synoptic Accounts," *SBLSP* 26 (1987): 295-335.

Archaeology

1753 M. F. Unger, "Archaeology and Paul's Tour of Cyprus," *BSac* 117/467 (1960): 229-33.

1754 Florentino Díez Fernandez, "Crónica arqueológica," *EB* 42/3-4 (1984): 421-28.

1755 R. E. Oster, "Acts 19:23-41 and an Ephesian Inscription," *HTR* 77/2 (1984): 233-37.

1756 J. McRay, "Archaeology and the Book of Acts," *CTR* 5 (1990-1991): 69-82.

Areopagus

1757 W. G. Morrice, "Where Did Paul Speak in Athens—On Mars' Hill or Before the Court of the Areopagus?" *ET* 83/12 (1972): 377-78.

1758 L. Legrand, "The Areopagus Speech, its Theological Kerygma and its Missionary Significance," *BETL* 41 (1976): 337-50.

1759 K. Plötz, "Die Areopagrede des Apostels Paulus: Ein Beispiel urkirchlicher Verkündigung," *IKaZ* 17 (1988): 111-17.

1760 M. Me. Adam, "Philosophy and the Bible: The Areopagus Speech," *Faith and Philos* 9 (1992): 135-50.

1761 P. Sciberras, "The Figure of Paul in the Acts of the Apostles: The Areopagus Speech," *MeliT* 43 (1992): 1-15.

1762 K. O. Sandnes, "Paul and Socrates: The Aim of Paul's Areopagus Speech," *JSNT* 50 (1993): 13-26.

1763 K.-K. Yeo, "A Rhetorical Study of Acts 17:22-31," *JianD* 1 (1994): 75-107.

ascension
1764 J. L. Gondal, *Au temps des apôtres: De l'ascension du Sauveur à la mort de Saint Jean*. Paris: Roger & Chernoviz, 1904.

1765 P. A. van Stempvoort, "The Interpretation of the Ascension in Luke and Acts," *NTS* 5 (1958-1959): 30-42.

1766 Pierre Miquel, "Christ's Ascension and Our Glorification," *TD* 9 (1961): 67-73.

1767 J. A. T. Robinson, "Ascendancy," *ANQ* 5/2 (1964): 5-9.

1768 John F. Walvoord, "The Ascension of Christ," *BS* 121 (1964): 3-12.

1769 J. Blenkinsopp, "The Bible and the People: The Ascension as Mystery of Salvation," *ClerR* 50/5 (1965): 369-74.

1770 Bruce M. Metzger, "The Meaning of Christ's Ascension," *CT* 10 (1966): 863-64.

1771 G. Schille, "Die Himmelfahrt," *ZNW* 57/3-4 (1966): 183-99.

1772 W. Kern, "Das Fortgehen Jesu und das Kommen des Geistes oder Christi Himmelfahrt," *GeistL* 41/2 (1968): 85-90.

1773 Stephen G. Wilson, "The Ascension: A Critique and an Interpretation," *ZNW* 59 (1968): 269-81.

1774 E. Franklin, "The Ascension and the Eschatology of Luke-Acts,"
SJT 23/2 (1970): 191-200.

1775 R. C. Devor, "The Ascension of Christ and the Dissension of the
Church," *Enc* 33/4 (1972): 340-58.

1776 F. Hahn, "Die Himmelfahrt Jesu. Ein Gespräch Lohfink," *Bib* 55
(1974): 418-26.

1777 E. A. LaVerdiere, "The Ascension of the Risen Lord," *BibTo* 95
(1978): 1553-59.

1778 D. W. Gooding, "Demythologizing Old and New, and Luke's
Description of the Ascension: A Layman's Appraisal," *IBS* 2
(1980): 95-119.

1779 Veselin Kesich, "Resurrection, Ascension, and the Giving of the
Spirit," *GOTR* 25/3 (1980): 249-60.

1780 Eldon J. Epp, "The Ascension in the Textual Tradition of
Luke-Acts," in Elton J. Epps and Gordon D. Fee, eds., *New
Testament Textual Criticism* (festschrift for Bruce M. Metzger).
Oxford: Clarendon Press, 1981. Pp. 131-45.

1781 É. Delebecque, "Ascension et Pentecôte dans les Actes des Apôtres
selon le codex Bezae," *RT* 82/2 (1982): 79-89.

1782 Walter Kasper, "Christi Himmelfahrt—Geschichte und
theologische Bedeutung," *IKaZ* 12/3 (1983): 205-13.

1783 Guriy Kuzmin, "On The Feast of the Ascension," *JMP* 6 (1983):
52-53.

1784 Elmer L. Towns, "The Ascension," *FundJ* 3/6 (1984): 12-14.

1785 Mikeal C. Parsons, "The Ascension Narratives in Luke-Acts,"
doctoral dissertation, Southern Baptist Theological Seminary,
Louisville KY, 1985.

1786 John F. Maile, "The Ascension in Luke-Acts," *TynB* 37 (1986):
29-59.

1787 P. Palatty, "The Ascension of Christ in Luke-Acts: An Exegetical Critical Study of Luke 24,50-53 and Acts 1,2-3.9-11," *BB* 12 (1986): 100-17, 166-81.

1788 Mikeal C. Parsons, *The Departure of Jesus in Luke-Acts: The Ascension Narratives in Context.* Sheffield: JSOT Press, 1987.

1789 C. L. Stockhausen, "Luke's Stories of the Ascension: The Background and Function of a Dual Narrative," *EGLMBS* 10 (1990): 251-63.

1790 G. C. Fuller, "The Life of Jesus after the Ascension," *WTJ* 56/2 (1994): 391-98.

1791 J. Kremer, "Biblische Grundlagen zur Feier der Fünfzig Tage," *HD* 48 (1994): 3-15.

Athens

1792 R. E. Wycherley, "St. Paul at Athens," *JTS* 9/2 (1968): 619-21.

1793 George T. Montague, "Paul and Athens," *BibTo* 49 (1970): 14-23.

1794 C. J. Hemer, "Paul at Athens: A Topographical Note," *NTS* 20/3 (1974): 341-50.

1795 F. F. Bruce, "Paul and the Athenians," *ET* 88/11 (1976): 8-12.

1796 G. L. Bahnsen, "The Encounter of Jerusalem with Athens," *ATB* 13/1 (1980): 4-40.

1797 R. F. O'Toole, "Paul at Athens and Luke's Notion of Worship," *RBib* 89/2 (1982): 185-97.

1798 Gil Lain, "Ancient Athens," *BI* (1989): 24-29.

1799 J. L. Blevins, "Acts 13-19: The Tale of Three Cites," *RevExp* 87 (1990): 439-50.

audience criticism

1800   R. J. Cassidy, "Luke's Audience, the Chief Priests, and the Motives for Jesus' Death," in R. J. Cassidy and P. J. Scharper, eds., *Political Issues in Luke-Acts*. Maryknoll NY: Orbis, 1983. Pp. 146-67.

1801   C. Cook, "The Sense of Audience in Luke: A Literary Examination," *NBlack* 72 (1991): 19-30.

1802   P. Meierding, "Jews and Gentiles: A Narrative and Rhetorical Analysis of the Implied Audience in Acts," doctoral dissertation, Luther Northwestern Seminary, St. Paul MN, 1992.

Authorship

1803   Servaas H. Rossouw, "The Authorship of the Book of Acts," doctoral dissertation, Southern Baptist Theological Seminary, Louisville KY, 1919.

1804   B. E. Beck, "The Common Authorship of Luke and Acts," *NTS* 23 (1976-1977): 346-52.

baptism

1805   Gerhard Delling, "Zur Taufe von 'Hausern' im Urchristentum," *NovT* 7 (1965): 285-311.

1806   J. K. Parratt, "The Holy Spirit and Baptism. Part 1. The Gospels and the Acts of the Apostles," *ET* 82/8 (1971): 231-35.

1807   I. de la Potterie, "L'economia fede-sacramento nel nuovo testamento," in P.-R. Tragan, ed., *Fede e sacramenti negli scritti giovannei*. Rome: Edizioni Abbazia, 1972. Pp. 27-46.

1808   J. Giblet, "Baptism in the Spirit in the Acts of the Apostles," *OC* 10 (1974): 162-71.

1809   Schuyler Brown, " 'Water-Baptism' and 'Spirit-Baptism' in Luke-Acts," *ATR* 59/2 (1977): 135-51.

1810   Bruce Terry, "Baptized in One Spirit," *RQ* 21/4 (1978): 193-299.

1811   P. Korby, "Christologie et Baptême à l'Époque du Christianisme Primitif," *NTS* 27 (1981): 270.

1812   B. E. Thiering, "Qumran Initiation and New Testament Baptism,"
           NTS 27/5 (1981): 615-31.

1813   Jan P. Versteeg, "De doop volgens het Nieuwe Testament," in
           Willem van't Spijker, et al., eds., *Rondom de doopvont: leer en
           gebruik van de heilige doop in het NT en in de geschiedenis van de
           westerse kerk*. Kampen: De Groot Goudriaan, 1983. Pp. 9-133.

1814   Lars Hartman, "La formule baptismale dans les Actes des Apôtres:
           quelques observations relatives au style de Luc," in Françios
           Refoulé, ed., *À cause de l'Évangile: Études sur les synoptiques et
           les Actes* (festschrift for Jacques Dupont). Paris: Cerf, 1985. Pp.
           727-38.

1815   R. Fowler White, "The Last Adam and His Seed: An Exercise in
           Theological Preemption," *TriJ* 6 (1985): 60-73.

1816   E. J. Christiansen, "Taufe als Initiation in der Apostelgeschichte,"
           StTh 40/1 (1986): 55-79.

1817   A.-M. La Bonnardière, "Evodius et Augustin," in Anne-Marie La
           Bonnardière, ed., *Saint Augustin et la Bible*. Paris: Editions
           Beauchesne, 1986. Pp. 213-27.

1818   Michael Wolter, "Apollos und die Ephesinischen Johannesjünger,"
           ZNW 78/1-2 (1987): 49-73.

1819   S. A. Panimolle, "Il battesimo e la Pentecoste dei samaritani," in
           Giustino Farnedi, ed., *Traditio et progressio: studi liturgici*. Rome:
           Benedictina-Edizioni, 1988. Pp. 413-36.

1820   Abraham Friesen, "Acts 10: The Baptism of Cornelius as
           Interpreted by Thomas Muntzer and Felix Manz," *MQR* 64/1
           (1990): 5-22.

1821   J. D. G. Dunn, "Baptism in the Spirit: A Response to Pentecostal
           Scholarship on Luke-Acts," *JPTh* 3 (1993): 3-27.

Barnabas
1822   V. W. Morgan, "Barnabas and His Relationship to the Primitive
           Church," master's thesis, Southern Baptist Theological Seminary,
           Louisville KY, 1952.

1823 Richard Glover, " 'Luke the Antiochene' and Acts," *NTS* 11/1 (1964): 97-106.

1824 S. Dockx, "L'ordination de Barnabé et de Saul d'après Actes 13:1-3," *NRT* 98/3 (1976): 238-58.

1825 R. T. France, "Barnabas—Son of Encouragement," *ERT* 4/1 (1980): 91-101.

1826 W. Radl, "Das 'Apostelkonzil' und seine Nachgeschichte, dargestellt am Weg des Barnabas," *TQ* 162/1 (1982): 45-61.

1827 D. S. Dockery, "Acts 6-12: The Christian Mission beyond Jerusalem," *RevExp* 87 (1990): 423-37.

1828 L. H. Martin, "Gods or Ambassadors of God? Barnabas and Paul in Lystra," *NTS* 41/1 (1995): 152-56.

bibliography
1829 H. A. A. Kennedy, "Recent Books on the Apostolic Age and the Life of Paul," *AJT* 9 (1905): 540-46.

1830 Hans Windisch, "Literature on the New Testament in Germany, Austria, Switzerland, Holland, and the Scandinavian Countries, 1914-1920," *HTR* 15 (1922): 115-216.

1831 G. W. Wade, "The Ten Best Books on the Apostolic Age," *Exp* Series 9, Vol. 3 (1925): 5-14.

1832 Joseph Freundorfer, "Bibliographischc Notizen. C. Das Neue Testament," *BZ* 19 (1931): 271-415; 20 (1932): 163-229, 383-427; 21 (1933): 189-236; 22 (1934): 153-94, 359-434; 23 (1935-1936): 194-228, 289-332; 24 (1938-1939): 199-232, 383-445.

1833 W. G. Kümmel, "Textkritik und Textgeschichte des Neuen Testaments 1914-1937," *TR* N.F. 10 (1938): 206-21, 292-327; 11 (1939): 84-107.

1834 W. N. Lyons, *New Testament Literature in 1941*. Edited by the New Testament Club of the University of Chicago, 1942.

1835 A. Theissen, "Catholic Bibliography of Acts, Catholic Epistles and Apocalypse," *Scr* 2 (1947): 53-57.

1836   W. G. Kümmel, "Das Urchristentum," *TR* N.F. 17 (1948-1949):
3-50, 103-42.

1837   E. Käsemann, "Aus der neutestamentlichen Arbeit der letzten
Jahre," *Verkündigung und Forschtung; Theologischer
Jahresbericht 1947/48.* München: Chr. Kaiser, 1949/1950. Pp.
195-223.

1838   E. Käsemann, "Ein neutestamentlicher überblick," *Verkündigung
und Forschung; Theologischer Jahresbericht 1949/50.* München:
Chr. Kaiser, 1951/1952. Pp. 191-218.

1839   W. G. Kümmel, "Das Urchristentum," *TR* N.F. 18 (1950): 1-53;
N.F. 22 (1954): 138-70, 191-211.

1840   Bruce M. Metzger, *Annotated Bibliography of the Textual Criticism
of the New Testament, 1914-1939.* "Studies and Documents," *16.*
Edited by Silva Lake and Carsten Høeg. Copenhagen: Ejnar
Munksgaard, 1955.

1841   Luis Arnaldich, *Los Estudios Bíblicos en España desde el Año
1900 al Año 1955.* Madrid: Imprenta de Aldecoa. Burgos, 1957.

1842   A. F. J. Klijn, "A Survey of the Researches into the Western Text
of the Gospels and Acts (1949-1959)," *NovT* 3 (1959): 1-27,
161-73.

1843   Donald Guthrie, "Recent Literature on the Acts of the Apostles,"
VoxE 2 (1963): 33-49.

1844   I. Howard Marshall, "Recent Study of the Acts of the Apostles,"
ET 80/10 (1969): 292-96.

1845   Bruce M. Metzger, *An Index to Periodical Literature on the
Apostle Paul.* Rev. ed. NTTS #1. Leiden: Brill, 1970.

1846   F. Neirynck, "Le Livre des Actes dans les récents commentaires,"
ETL 59/4 (1983): 338-49.

1847   E. Plümacher, "Acta-Forschung 1974-1982," *TR* 48/1 (1983):
1-56.

1848   Gérard Rochais, "Jésus savait-il qu'il était Dieu: réflexions critiques à propos d'un livre récent," *SR* 14/1 (1985): 85-106.

1849   Günter Wagner, *An Exegetical Bibliography of the New Testament*. 3. *Luke-Acts*. Macon GA: Mercer University Press, 1985.

1850   J. A. Ziesler, "Which is the Best Commentary? V. The Acts of the Apostles," *ET* 98/3 (1986): 73-77.

1851   Watson E. Mills, *An Index to Periodical Literature on the Apostle Paul*. NTTS #16. Leiden: Brill, 1993.

Chester Beatty papyri

1852   J. Lindblom, "Nya handskriftsfynd till gamla och nya testamentet," *STK* 8 (1932): 154-61.

1853   Silva New, "The New Chester Beatty Papyrus," *JBL* 51 (1932): 73-74.

1854   F. C. Burkitt, "The Chester Beatty Papyri," *JTS* 34 (1933): 363-68.

1855   Frederic G. Kenyon, *The Chester Beatty Biblical Papyri*. Fasc. 1: *General Introduction*. Fasc. 2: *The Gospels and Acts, Text, Plates*. London: Walker, 1933-1934.

1856   Augustinus Merk, "Codex Evangeliorum et Actuum ex collectione Chester Beatty," in *Miscellanea Biblica*. 2: *Scripta pontificii instituti biblici*. Romae: Schola typographica Pio X, 1934. 2:375-406.

1857   Frederic G. Kenyon, "Some Notes on the Chester Beatty Gospels and Acts," in Robert P. Casey, Silva Lake, and Agnes K. Lake, eds., *Quantulacumque: Studies Presented to Kirsopp Lake*. London: Christophers, 1937. Pp. 145-48.

1858   G. Lindeskog, "De senaste textfynden tiu Nya Testamentet," *SEÅ* 2 (1937): 169-73.

1859   C. C. Tarelli, "Omissions, Additions, and Conflations in the Chester Beatty Papyrus," *JTS* 40 (1939): 382-87.

christology

1860 A. J. Malherbe, "Christology in Luke-Acts," *RQ* 2 (1958): 62-66.

1861 S. S. Smalley, "The Christology of Acts," *ET* 73 (1962): 358-62.

1862 O. J. Lafferty, "Acts 2:14-36: A Study in Christology," *DunR* 6/2 (1966): 235-53.

1863 T. Jacobs, "De christologie van de redevoeringen der Handelingen," *Bij* 28/2 (1967): 177-96.

1864 Una Luz, "Cristo y la Iglesia, según Hechos," *RBib* 29/4 (1967): 206-23.

1865 C. M. Martini, "Riflessioni sulla cristologia degli Atti," *SacD* 16/63-64 (1971): 525-34.

1866 G. W. MacRae, " 'Whom Heaven Must Receive Until the Time.' Reflections on the Christology of Acts," *Int* 27/2 (1973): 151-65.

1867 Michel Gourgues, "Lecture christologique du Psaume CX et fête de la Pentecôte," *RB* 83/1 (1976): 5-24.

1868 R. F. O'Toole, "Acts 26: The Christological Climax of Paul's Defense," *TLZ* 104 (1979): 825.

1869 William S. Kurz, "Hellenistic Rhetoric in the Christological Proof of Luke-Acts," *CBQ* 42 (1980): 171-95.

1870 Frederick W. Danker, "Graeco-Roman Cultural Accommodation in the Christology of Luke-Acts," *SBLSP* 13 (1983): 391-414.

1871 G. Dautzenberg, "Psalm 110 im Neuen Testament," in Hans Becker and Reiner Kaczynski, eds., *Liturgie und Dichtung: Ein interdisziplinäres Kompendium. 1. Historische Präsentation.* Sankt Ottilien: EOS Verlag, 1983. Pp. 141-71.

1872 R. R. Recker, "The Lordship of Christ and Mission in the Book of Acts," *RR* 37/3 (1984): 177-86.

1873 D. L. Tiede, "The Exaltation of Jesus and the Restoration of Israel in Acts 1," *HTR* 79/1 (1986): 278-86.

1874 M. de Jonge, "The Christology of Luke-Acts," in *Christology in Context: The Earliest Christian Response to Jesus.* Philadelphia: Westminster, 1988. Pp. 97-111.

1875 R. B. Hays, "The Righteous One as Eschatological Deliverer: A Case Study in Paul's Apocalyptic Hermeneutics," in Joel Marcus and Marion Soards, eds., *Apocalyptic and the New Testament* (festschrift for J. Louis Martyn). Sheffield: JSOT Press, 1989. Pp 191-215.

1876 M. A. Seifrid, "Messiah and Mission in Acts: A Brief Response to J. B. Tyson," *JSNT* 36 (1989): 47-50.

1877 David P. Moessner, " 'The Christ Must Suffer,' The Church Must Suffer: Rethinking the Theology of Luke-Acts," *SBLSP* 29 (1990): 165-95.

1878 C. K. Barrett, "Submerged Christology in Acts," in C. Breytenbach and H. Paulsen, eds., *Anfänge der Christologie* (festschrift for Ferdinand Hahn). Göttingen: Vandenhoeck & Ruprecht, 1991. Pp. 237-44.

1879 B. D. Ehrman, "The Cup, the Bread, and the Salvific Effect of Jesus' Death in Luke-Acts," *SBLSP* 30 (1991): 576-91.

chronology
1880 L. Peretto, "Pietro e Paolo e l'anno 49 nella complessa situazione palestinese," *RBib* 15/3 (1967): 295-308.

1881 W. A. Meeks, "Who Went Where and How? A Consideration of Acts 17:14," *BT* 44 (1993): 201-206.

1882 J. Morgado, "Paul in Jerusalem: A Comparison of His Visits in Acts and Galatians," *JETS* 37 (1994): 55-68.

Codex Bezae
1883 F. C. Burkitt, "The Date of Codex Bezae," *JTS* 3 (1901-1902): 501-13.

1884 K. S. de Vogel, "Quelques observations sur le texte Latin du 'Codex Bezae'," *BJRL* 8 (1924): 398-403.

1885 R. C. Stone, "The Language of Codex Bezae," doctoral dissertation, University of Illinois, Urbana IL, 1936.

1886 Eldon J. Epp, "Theological Tendency in the Textual Variants of *Codex Bezae Cantabrigiensis:* Anti-Judaic Tendencies in Acts," doctoral dissertation, Harvard University, Cambridge MA, 1961.

community

1887 Jacques Dupont, "L'Union entre les premiers chrétiens dans les Actes des Apôtres," *NRT* 91/9 (1969): 897-915.

1888 Francis Lenssen, "Biblical Communities: Christian Communities in the New Testament," *Point* 1 (1972): 24-34.

1889 F. Schnider, "Wie wird eine Gemeinde missionarisch: Uberlegungen zu Apg 2,42-47," in Walter Friedberger and Franz Schnider, eds., *Theologie—Gemeinde—Seelsorger.* Munich: Kösel-Verlag, 1979. Pp. 118-25.

1890 E. Dassmann, "Hausgemeinde und Bischofsamt," in Ernst Dassmann and Klaus Thraede, eds., *Vivarium* (festschrift for Theodor Klauser). Münster: Aschendorff, 1984. Pp. 82-97.

1891 C. H. Talbert, "Discipleship in Luke-Acts," in Fernando F. Segovia, ed., *Discipleship in the New Testament.* Philadelphia: Fortress Press, 1985. Pp. 62-75.

1892 G. Mangatt, "Believing Community according to the Acts of the Apostles," *BB* 16 (1990): 172-81.

1893 C. Amt Zettner, *Gemeinde und kirchliche Einheit in der Apostelgeschichte des Lukas.* Paris: Lang, 1991.

1894 M. Dumais, *Communauté et mission. Une lecture des Actes des Apôtres pour aujourd'hui.* Paris: Desclee, 1992.

1895 J. Driver, "The Trouble with Inclusiveness: A Perspective on the Acts of the Apostles," *SMR* 157 (1994): 24-31.

Cornelius

1896 J. M. Fenasse, "Pierre et Corneille, Le Centurion," *BTS* 41 (1961): 4-5.

1897 P. L. Schoonheim, "De centurio Cornelius," *NTT* 18/6 (1964): 453-75.

1898 Barbara Hall, "La communauté chrétienne dans le livre des Actes: Actes 6:1-7 et 10:1-11:18," *FV* Suppl (1971): 146-156.

1899 K. Löning, "Die Korneliustradition," *BZ* 18/1 (1974): 1-19.

1900 Glenn N. Davis, "When Was Cornelius Saved?" *RTR* 46/2 (1987): 43-49.

1901 Robert W. Wall, "Peter, 'Son' of Jonah: the Conversion of Cornelius in the Context of Canon," *JSNT* 29 (1987): 79-90.

1902 D. S. Dockery, "Acts 6-12: The Christian Mission beyond Jerusalem," *RevExp* 87 (1990): 423-37.

1903 Abraham Friesen, "Acts 10: The Baptism of Cornelius as Interpreted by Thomas Muntzer and Felix Manz," *MQR* 64/1 (1990): 5-22.

1904 H. E. Dollar, "The Conversion of the Messenger," *Miss* 21/1 (1993): 13-19.

1905 Ronald D. Witherup, "Cornelius Over and Over and Over Again: 'Functional Redundancy' in the Acts of the Apostles," *JSNT* 49 (1993): 45-66.

literary criticism

1906 E. A. Belcher and C. C. Carter, *Notes on the Acts of the Apostles, 1-16. For the Use of Candidates for the Oxford and Cambridge Local Examinations.* London: Relfe, 1900.

1907 E. W. Benson, *Addresses on the Acts of the Apostles.* New York: Macmillan, 1901.

1908 Dionysius Carthusianusn, "Enarratio in Actus Apostolorum," in *Doctoris ecstatici D. Dionysii Cartusiani Opera Omnia in unum corpus digesta..* Monstrolii: Typis Cartusiae Sanctae Mariae de Pratis, 1901. 14:81-220.

1909 I. N. Johns, *The Acts of the Apostles and Reference Passages.* Sunbury PA: Alpha, 1901.

1910　D. J. Burrell, *Early Church. Studies in the Acts of the Apostles.*
London: Robinson, 1904.

1911　W. E. Beck, *The Acts of the Apostles in the Revised Version.*
London: U.T.P., 1937.

1912　D. H. Hall, "Acts as an Apologetic," doctoral dissertation,
Southern Baptist Theological Seminary, Louisville KY, 1937.

1913　Stephen L. Caiger, "The First History Book of the Christian
Church," in H. Balmforth, et al., *The Story of the Bible.* New
York: W. H. Wise, 1948. 4:1303-32.

1914　Henry G. Russell, "Which Was Written First, Luke or Acts?" *HTR*
48 (1955) 167-74.

1915　Peggy M. Brook, *Talks on the Acts of the Apostles.* London:
Foundational Book Company, 1956.

1916　Heinrich Zimmermann, "Die Sammelberichte der Apostelgeschichte," *BZ* 5/1 (1961): 71-82.

1917　T. Fahy, "A Phenomenon of Literary Style in Acts of Apostles,"
ITQ 29/4 (1962): 314-18.

1918　André Pelletier, "Une création de l'apologétique chrétienne:
moschopoiein," *RechSR* 54/3 (1966): 411-16.

1919　H. Klein, "Zur Frage nach dem Abfassungsort der Lukaschriften,"
EvT 32 (1972): 467-77.

1920　Norman Perrin, "The Evangelist as Author: Reflections on Method
in the Study and Interpretation of the Synoptic Gospels and Acts,"
BR 17 (1972): 5-18.

1921　Frank Stagg, "The Unhindered Gospel," *RevExp* 71/4 (1974):
451-62.

1922　E. Franklin, *Christ the Lord: A Study in the Purpose and Theology
of Luke-Acts.* London: SPCK, 1976.

1923 Benjamin J. Hubbard, "The Role of Commissioning Accounts in Acts," *PRS* 5 (1978): 187-98.

1924 Donald R. Miesner, "The Missionary Journeys Narrative: Patterns and Implications," *PRS 5* (1978): 199-214.

1925 U. Borse, "Kompositionsgeschichtliche Beobachtungen zum Apostelkonzil," *BBB* 53 (1980): 195-212.

1926 W. R. Long, "The Speeches in Defense of Paul in the Book of Acts: A Study in Ancient Historiography," doctoral dissertation, Brown University, Providence RI, 1981.

1927 Susan Marie Praeder, "Luke-Acts and the Ancient Novel," *SBLSP* 11 (1981): 269-92.

1928 K. P. Donfried, "Attempt at Understanding the Purpose of Luke-Acts: Christology and the Salvation of the Gentiles," in R. F. Berkey and S. A. Edwards, eds. *Christological Perspectives* (festschrift for H. K. McArthur). New York: Pilgrim Press, 1982. Pp. 112-22.

1929 Sharon H. Ringe, "The Jubilee Proclamation in the Ministry and Teaching of Jesus: A Tradition-Critical Study in the Synoptic Gospels and Acts," doctoral dissertation, Union Theological Seminary, New York, 1982.

1930 L. O'Reilly, "Chiastic Structures in Acts 1-7," *PIBA* 7 (1983): 87-103.

1931 L. Panier, "Parcours pour lire les Actes des Apôtres," *SémBib* 32 (1983): 27-32.

1932 A. J. Walworth, "The Narrator of Acts," doctoral dissertation, Southern Baptist Theological Seminary, Louisville KY, 1984.

1933 Lawrence Wills, "The Form of the Sermon in Hellenistic Judaism and Early Christianity," *HTR* 77/3-4 (1984): 277-99.

1934 John A. Darr, " 'Glorified in the Presence of Kings': A Literary-Critical Study of Herod the Tetrarch in Luke-Acts," doctoral dissertation, Vanderbilt University, Nashville TN, 1987.

1935　William S. Kurz, "Narrative Approaches to Luke-Acts," *Bib* 68 (1987): 195-220.

1936　R. A. Martin, "Semitic Traditions in Some Synoptic Accounts," *SBLSP* 26 (1987): 295-335.

1937　Richard I. Pervo, *Profit with Delight: The Literary Genre of the Acts of the Apostles.* Philadelphia: Fortress, 1987.

1938　J. T. A. Marlow, "A Narrative Analysis of Acts 1-2," doctoral dissertation, Golden Gate Baptist Theological Seminary, Mill Vallley CA, 1988.

1939　S. McA. Sheeley, "Narrative Asides and Narrative Authority in Luke-Acts," *BTB* 18 (1988): 102-107.

1940　H. Dixon Slingerland, "The Composition of Acts: Some Redaction-Critical Observations," *JAAR* 56 (1988): 99-113.

1941　J. R. Donahue, "Two Decades of Research on the Rich and the Poor in Luke-Acts," in D. A. Knight and P. J. Paris, eds., *Justice and the Holy* (festschrift for Walter Harrelson) Atlanta GA: Scholars Press, 1989. Pp. 129-44.

1942　David R. Gowler, "A Socio-Narratological Character Anaylsis of the Pharisees in Luke-Acts," doctoral dissertation, Southern Baptist Theological Seminary, Louisville KY, 1989.

1943　M. R. D'Angelo, "Women in Luke-Acts: A Redactional View," *JBL* 109 (1990): 441-61.

1944　C. House, "Suffering and the Purpose of Acts," *JETS* 33 (1990): 317-30.

1945　William S. Kurz, "Narrative Models for Imitation in Luke-Acts," in D. Balch, E. Ferguson and W. A. Meeks, eds., *Greeks, Romans, and Christians* (festschrift for Abraham J. Malherbe) Minneapolis MN: Fortress Press, 1990. Pp. 171-89.

1946　F. Ó'Fearghail, *The Introduction to Luke-Acts: A Study of the Role of Lk 1,1-4,44 in the Composition of Luke's Two-Volume Work.* Rome: Biblical Institute Press, 1991.

1947 David L. Mealand, "Hellenistic Historians and the Style of Acts," *ZNW* 82 (1991): 42-66.

1948 F. Mußner, "Die Erzählintention des Lukas in der Apostelgeschichte," in C. Bussmann and W. Radl, eds., *Der Treue Gottes trauem: Beiträge zum Wekre des Lukas* (festschrift for Gerhard Schneider). Freiburg: Herder, 1991. Pp. 29-41.

1949 K. Salo, *Luke's Treatment of the Law: A Redaction-Critical Investigation.* Helsinki: Suomalainen Tiedeakatemia, 1991.

1950 ʹM. A. Co, "The Major Summaries in Acts: Acts 2:42-47; 4:32-35; 5:12-16: Linguistic and Literary Relationship," *ETL* 68/1 (1992): 49-85.

1951 P. Meierding, "Jews and Gentiles: A Narrative and Rhetorical Analysis of the Implied Audience in Acts," doctoral dissertation, Luther Northwestern Seminary, St. Paul MN, 1992.

1952 Daniel Marguerat, "La mort d'Ananias et Saphira dans la stratégie narrative de Luc," *NTS* 39 (1993): 209-26.

1953 J. J. Murphy, "Early Christianity as a 'Persuasive Campaign': Evidence from the Acts of the Apostles and the Letters of Paul," in S. E. Porter and T. H. Olbricht, eds., *Rhetoric in the New Testament.* Sheffield: JSOT, 1993. Pp. 90-99.

1954 A. J. M. Wedderburn, "The 'Apostolic Decree': Tradition and Redaction," *NovT* 35 (1993): 362-89.

1955 A. Smith, " 'Do You Understand What You are Reading?': A Literary Critical Reading Reading of the Ethiopian (Cachet) Episode," *JITC* 22/1 (1994): 48-70.

1956 Marion L. Soards, "The Speeches in Acts in Relation to Other Pertinent Ancient Literature," *ETL* 70 (1994): 65-90.

deacon

1957 Carl J. Diemer, "Deacons and Other Endangered Species: A Look at the Biblical Office of Deacon," *FundJ* 3/3 (1984): 21-24.

1958 Richard Fraser, "Office of Deacon," *Pres* 11/1 (1985): 13-19.

1959 S. K. Tsitsigos, "What Was the Task of the Seven Deacons?" *DBM* 21 (1992): 52-58.

Discipleship

1960 Joseph Allen, "Renewal of the Christian Community: A Challenge for the Pastoral Ministry," *SVTQ* 29/4 (1985): 305-323.

1961 M. P. W. Lewela, "Mary's Faith—Model of Our Own: A Reflection," *AFER* 27 (1985): 92-98.

1962 C. H. Talbert, "Discipleship in Luke-Acts," in F. F. Segovia, ed., *Discipleship in the New Testament*. Philadelphia: Fortress Press, 1985. Pp. 62-75.

1963 John R. Donahue, "The 'Parable' of the Sheep and the Goats: A Challenge to Christian Ethics," *JTS* 47/1 (1986): 3-31.

1964 Dennis M. Sweetland, *Our Journey with Jesus: Discipleship in Luke and Acts*. Collegeville MN: Liturgical Press, 1991.

early church

1965 C. F. G. Heinrici, *Das Urchristentum*. Göttingen: Vandenhoeck & Ruprecht, 1902.

1966 F. J. Foakes-Jackson, *The History of the Christian Church: From the Earliest Times to A.D. 461*. New York: George H. Doran, 1902.

1967 Ernst von Dobschütz, *Probleme des apostolischen Zeitalters*. Leipzig: J. C. Hinrichs, 1904.

1968 George P. Fisher, *The Beginnings of Christianity with a View of the State of the Roman World at the Birth of Christ*. New York: Scribner, Armstrong & Co., 1905.

1969 C. Guignebert, *Manuel d'histoire ancienne du Christianisme: les origines*. Paris: Alphonse Picard et fils, 1906.

1970 Otto Pfleiderer, *Christian Origins*. Translated by Daniel A. Huebsch. New York: B. W. Huebsch, 1906.

1971 R. Rackham, *How the Church Began*. New York: Longmans, Green & Co., 1906.

1972 J. H. Ropes, *The Apostolic Age in the Light of Modern Criticism.* New York: Scribner, 1906.

1973 F. K. Sanders, *Historical Notes on the Apostolic Leaders.* Boston: Bible Study Publishing Co., 1907.

1974 Adolf Harnack, *The Mission and Expansion of Christianity in the First Three Centuries.* 2 vols. Translated by James Moffatt. 2d ed. "Theological Translation Library," Vols. 19-20. London: Williams & Norgate; New York: G. P. Putnam, 1908.

1975 Ernst von Dobschütz, *The Apostolic Age.* Translated by F. L. Pogson. London: Philip Green, 1909.

1976 Walter Bauer, "Apostelgeschichte und apostolisches Zeitalter," *TR* 12 (1909): 459-59; 14 (1911): 269-94; 17 (1914): 209-23; 20 (1917): 115-38.

1977 Max Maurenbrecher, *Von Jerusalem nach Rom.* Berlin: Buchverlag der Hilfe, 1910.

1978 Otto Pfleiderer, *Primitive Christianity. Its Writings and Teachings in Their Historical Connections.* 4 vols. Translated by W. Montgomery. New York: G. P. Putnam, 1911.

1979 W. M. Ramsay, *The First Christian Century: Notes on Dr. Moffatt's Introduction to the Literature of the New Testament.* London; New York; Toronto: Hodder & Stoughton, 1911.

1980 George Edmundson, *The Church in Rome in the First Century.* London: Longmans, Green & Co., 1913.

1981 E. F. Scott, *The Beginnings of the Church.* New York: Scribner, 1914.

1982 C. F. Kent, *The Work and Teachings of the Apostles.* New York; Chicago; Boston: Scribner, 1916.

1983 J. I. Still, *The Earliest Jewish Christian Church. Acts of Apostles.* Part 1. 3d ed. Edinburgh: United Free Church of Scotland, 1917.

1984 S. C. Carpenter, *Christianity according to Saint Luke.* New York: Macmillan, 1919.

1985 H. A. A. Kennedy, *Vital Forces of the Early Church.* London: S.C.M., 1920.

1986 Kirsopp Lake, *Landmarks in the History of Early Christianity.* New York: Macmillan, 1920.

1987 Otto Schmitz, *Die Vorbildlichkeit der urchristlichen Gemeinden für die kirchliche Lage der Gegenwart* Berlin: Verlag des evangelischen Bundes, 1921.

1988 W. B. Hill, *The Apostolic Age. A Study of the Early Church and Its Achievements.* New York; Chicago; London; Edinburgh: Fleming H. Revell, 1922.

1989 J. I. Still, *The Early Gentile Church. Acts of Apostles.* Part 2. 4th ed. Edinburgh: United Free Church of Scotland, 1922.

1990 Leon Bournet, *Le christianisme naissant: expansion et luttes.* Paris: Tequi, 1923.

1991 W. Grant, *Ideals of the Early Church: the Religious Ideas of Acts.* London: James Clarke, 1923.

1992 F. J. Foakes-Jackson, *Studies in the Life of the Early Church.* New York: George H. Doran, 1924.

1993 Alexander Henderson, *Sketches of Primitive Christianity.* London: Faith Press, 1925.

1994 Mary Mooyaart, *In the Days of the Apostles. The Acts Retold. Illustrated.* London: Religious Tract Society, 1925.

1995 D. I. Lanslots, *The Primitive Church or the Church in the Days of the Apostles.* St. Louis, Missouri; London: B. Herder, 1926.

1996 A. Schlatter, *Die Geschichte der ersten Christenheit.* Gütersloh: C. Bertelsmann, 1926.

1997 E. F. Scott, *The First Age of Christianity.* New York: Macmillan; London: Allen & Unwin, 1926.

1998 F. J. Foakes-Jackson, *The Rise of Gentile Christianity.* New York: George H. Doran, 1927.

1999 George L. Clark, "The Acts of the Apostles," in *Fundamentals of Early Christianity*. New York: Mathers, 1928. Pp. 509-77.

2000 Arthur C. McGiffert, *A History of Christianity in the Apostolic Age*. "International Theological Library." Rev ed. New York: Scribner, 1928.

2001 F. J. Foakes-Jackson, "The Apostolic Age of Church History. Outline of a Reading Course," *ATR* 11 (1928-1929): 251-60.

2002 H. J. Heuser, *From Tarsus to Rome. The Story of the First Christian Hierarchy*. London; New York; Toronto: Longmans, Green & Co., 1929.

2003 J. W. Hunkin, *The Earliest Christian Church*. New York: Macmillan; Cambridge, England: University Press, 1929.

2004 M. Kreuser, *Die apostolische Kirche. Apostelgescltichte in Betrachtungen*. Gladbach-Rheidt: Volksvereinsverlag, 1929.

2005 G. A. Bergh van Eysinga, et al., *Premier écrits du christianisme*. Paris: Les éditions Rieder, 1930.

2006 S. von Dunin Borkowski, *Die junge Kirche. Betrach tungen für Theologen aus der Apostelgeschichte*. Hildesheim: Franz Borgmeyer, 1932.

2007 C. C. Martindale, *The Apostolic Church*. London: Catholic Truth Society, 1934.

2008 Ludwig Albrecht, *Die ersten fünfzehn Jahre der christlichen Kirche*. 2. Aufl. Berlin: Hermann Meier, 1935.

2009 MacKinley Helm, *After Pentecost. A History of Christian Ideas and Institutions from Peter and Paul to Ignatius of Antioch*. New York; London: Harper, 1936.

2010 L. de Lacger, *Le Christianisme aux origines et à l'âge apostolique*. Rabat: Institut d'études de religions, 1936.

2011 P. H. Pedersen, *Fra Jerusalem til Rom. Aposteltidens historie*. Kolding: Konrad Jørgensen, 1936.

2012 William Scott, *A History of the Early Christian Church*. Nashville: Cokesbury, 1936.

2013 P. G. S. Hopwood, *The Religious Experience of the Primitive Church. The Period prior to the Influence of Paul*. New York: Scribner, 1937.

2014 Hans Lietzmann, *A History of the Early Church*. I: *The Beginnings of the Christian Church*. Translated by Bertram Lee Woolf. |"Meridian Books." New York: World, 1937.

2015 Arnold Ehrhardt, *Wie es begann. Bilder aus der Urgemeinde*. Leipzig: Klotz, 1938.

2016 C. H. Dodd, "The History and Doctrine of the Apostolic Age," in T. W. Manson, ed., *A Companion to the Bible*. New York: Scribner, 1939. Pp. 390-417.

2017 F. Schenke, *Das Christentum im ersten Jahrhundert völkisch gesehen*. "Studien zu deutscher Theologie und Frömmigkeit," Bd. 5. Erfurt: Verlag Deutsche Christen Weimar, 1940.

2018 E. Iglesias, *Los Cuarenta Primeros Años de la Iglesia*. 2 tomos. Mexico, D.F.: Buena Prensa, 1940-1941.

2019 Otto Dibelius, "Bilder aus der frühen Christenheit," *Gestalten und Kräfte evangelischer Kirchengeschichte* Bd. I. Herausgegeben von Manfred Müller. Stuttgart: Evang. Missionsverlag, 1941. Pp. 1-32.

2020 Jules Lebreton and Jacques Zeiller, *The History of the Primitive Church*. Vol. I: *The Church in the New Testament*. Translated from the French by Ernest C. Messenger. London: Burns, Oates & Washbourne, 1942.

2021 Joseph Klausner, *From Jesus to Paul*. Translated from the Hebrew by William F. Stinespring. New York: Macmillan, 1943.

2022 Wilfred L. Knox, *Some Hellenistic Elements in Primitive Christianity*. London: Oxford University Press, 1944.

2023 E. W. Barnes, *The Rise of Christianity*. New York: Longmans, Green & Co., 1947. 3d ed., 1948.

2024 H. Daniel-Rops, *L'Église des Apôtres et des Martyrs*. Histoire de l'Église du Christ I. Paris: Arthème Fayard, 1948.

2025 A. Loisy, *The Birth of the Christian Religion*. Translated by L. P. Jacks. London: George Allen & Unwin, 1948.

2026 Albert Peel, "From Jerusalem to Rome: The Apostles in the Wider World," in H. Balmforth et al, *The Story of the Bible*. Vol. 4. New York: Wm. H. Wise, 1948. Pp. 1275-97.

2027 Maurice Goguel, "La seconde génération chrétienne," *RHR* 136 (1949): 31-57, 180-208.

2028 Isidore O'Brien, *Peter and Paul Apostles. An Account of the Early Years of the Church*. Paterson, New Jersey: St. Anthony Guild Press, 1950.

2029 H. J. Schoeps, *Aus frühchristlicher Zeit. Religionsgeschichtliche Untersuchungen*. Tübingen: Mohr, 1950.

2030 E. F. Scott, "The History of the Early Church. 1. The Beginnings," *The Interpreter's Bible*. Vol. 7. Edited by George Arthur Buttrick. New York; Nashville: Abingdon-Cokesbury, 1951. Pp. 176-86.

2031 F. F. Bruce, *The Spreading Flame: The Rise and Progress of Christianity*. Grand Rapids MI: Eerdmans, 1953.

2032 A. T. Robertson, *The Origins of Christianity*. London: Lawrence & Wishart, 1953. New York: International Publishers, 1954.

2033 George T. Purves, *Christianity in the Apostolic Age*. "Historical Series for Bible Students," Vol. 8. New York: Scribner, 1900. Grand Rapids, Michigan: Baker, 1955.

2034 A. Schlatter, *The Church in the New Testament Period*. Translated by Paul P. Levertoff. London: S.P.C.K., 1955.

2035 Nazaire Faivre, *L'Église au siècle apostolique*. Tome I: *SaintPierre*. Tome 2: *Saint Paul*. Bourg-la-Reine (Seine): M. l'Abbé Faivre, 1957-1958.

2036 M. H. Franzmann, "The Word of the Lord Grew," *CTM* 30 (1959): 563-81.

2037 W. M. Ramsay, *Pictures of the Apostolic Church. Its Life and Thought.* Philadelphia: Sunday School Times Co., 1910. Grand Rapids, Michigan: Baker, 1959.

2038 Hans Conzelmann, "Geschichte, Geschichtsbild und Geschichtsdarstellung bei Lukas," *TLZ* 85 (1960): 241-50.

2039 E. A. Judge, "Die Frühen Christen als scholastische Gemeinschaft," *JRH* 1 (1960): 4-15.

2040 Philip Schaff, *History of the Christian Church. Vol. 1: Apostolic Christianity, A.D. 1-100.* Grand Rapids, Michigan: Wm. B. Eerdmans, 1960. Reprint.

2041 C. Spicq, "Ce que signifie le titre de chrétien," *StTheol* 15/1 (1961): 68-78.

2042 B. Lifshitz, "L'origine du nom des Chrétiens," *VC* 16/2 (1962): 65-70.

2043 E. Haenchen, "Judentum und Christentum in der Apostelgeschichte," *ZNW* 54/3-4 (1963): 155-87.

2044 Jacob Jervell, "Zur Frage der Traditionsgrundlage der Apostelgeschichte," *ST* 16/1 (1963): 25-41.

2045 T. Barrosse, "Religious Community and the Primitive Church," *RevRel* 25/6 (1966): 971-85.

2046 Karl Maly, "Apostolische Gemeindeführung," *TGl* 10 (1967): 219-22.

2047 P. Jovino, "L'Église communauté des saints dans les 'Actes des Apôtres' et dans les 'Épitres aux Thessaloniciens'," *RBib* 16/5 (1968): 495-526.

2048 I. Maisch, "Dienst am Wort und für die Tische. Vier Worte aus der Apostelgeschichte zum kirchlichen Dienst," *BibL* 10/1 (1969): 83-87.

2049 J. Salguero, "La comunità cristiana primitiva," *SacD* 14/54 (1969): 217-49.

2050 Pierson Parker, "Mark, Acts and Galilaean Christianity," *NTS* 16/3 (1969-1970): 295-304.

2051 A. S. Wood, "Social Involvement in the Apostolic Church," *EQ* 42/4 (1970): 194-212.

2052 P. Gibert, "Les premiers chrétiens d'après les Actes des Apôtres," *Chr* 18/70 (1971): 219-28.

2053 Barbara Hall, "La communauté chrétienne dans le livre des Actes: Actes 6:1-7 et 10:1-11:18," *FV* Suppl (1971): 146-56.

2054 Gerhard Delling, "Die Jesusgeschichte in der Verkündigung nach Acta," *NTS* 19/4 (1972-1973): 373-89.

2055 A. L. Conde, "¿Vida Monastica en las Acta Apostolorum?" *TU* 112/6 (1973): 321-27.

2056 J. J. Gunther, "The Fate of the Jerusalem Church," *TZ* 29 (1973): 81-94.

2057 W. L. Blevins, "The Early Church: Acts 1-5," *RevExp* 71/4 (1974): 463-74.

2058 T. Holtz, "Die Bedeutung des Apostelkonzils für Paulus," *NovT* 16 (1974): 110-33.

2059 Robert A. Evans, "The Quest for Community," *USQR* 30/2 (1975): 188-202.

2060 K. Kliesch, "Das Heilsgeschichtliche Credo in den Reden der Apostelgeschichte," *BBB* 44 (1975): n.p.

2061 J. Julius Scott, "Parties in the Church of Jerusalem as Seen in the Book of Acts," *JETS* 18/4 (1975): 217-27.

2062 M. Simon, "La prière non religieuse chez Luc," *FV* 74 (1975): 8-22.

2063 F. J. Schierse, "Geschichte und Geschichten. Hermeneutische überlegungen zur Apostelgeschichte," *BK* 31/2 (1976): 34-38.

2064 J. K. Elliott, "Jerusalem in Acts and the Gospels," *NTS* 23/4 (1976-1977): 462-69.

2065 J. Downey, "The Early Jerusalem Christians," *BibTo* 91 (1977): 1295-1303.

2066 Dieter Luhrumann, "Glaude im frühen Christentum," *TLZ* 103 (1978): 188-91.

2067 P. L. Maier, "The First Corinthians: Pentecost and the Spread of Christianity," *SB* 8 (1978): 47.

2068 A. Rayan, "The Growth of the Church in the Acts," *BB* 4/2 (1978): 98-116.

2069 Siegfried Schulz, "Die Mitte der Schrift: der Fruhkatholizismus im NT," *TZ* 34 (1978): 113.

2070 H. A. Snydere, "The Community of the King," *CTJ* 13 (1978): 246-50.

2071 Tord Fornberg, "An Early Church in a Pluralistic Society," *CBQ* 41 (1979): 333.

2072 Martin Hengel, *Acts and the History of Earliest Christianity.* London: SCM, 1979.

2073 F. Manns, "Essais sur le Judeo-Christianisme," *RBib* 27 (1979): 433-37.

2074 Antoni Mlotek, "La Vita spirituale dei primi cristiani e la lettura della Bibbia," *SacD* 24 (1979): 439-48.

2075 A. Paul, "Le Christianisme Primitif. Diaspora, Dissemination et exclusion," *LVie* 141 (1979): 5-16.

2076 A. Sand, "Überlegungen zur gegenwartigen Diskussion über den 'Frühkatholizismus'," *Cath* 33 (1979): 49-62.

2077 R. B. Williams, "Reflections on the Transmission of Tradition in the Early Church," *Enc* 40 (1979): 273-85.

2078 M. Clavel-Lévéque and R. Nouailhat, "Ouverture et compromis: Les actes de apôtres, résponse idéologique aux nouvelles réalitiés impériales," *LV* 30 (1981): 35-58.

2079 É. Delebecque, "L'hellenisme de la 'relative complexe' dans le Nouveau Testament at principalement chez saint Luc," *Bib* 62 (1981): 232-35.

2080 R. G. Hoerber, "Evangelism in Acts," *CJ* 7/3 (1981): 89-90.

2081 Antoine Lion, "Actes et utopies des apôtres et des socialistes," *LVie* 30/153 (1981): 167-73.

2082 U. B. Muller, "Zur Rezeption Gesetzeskritischer Jesusüberlieferung im frühen Christentum," *NTS* 27 (1981): 163-67.

2083 G. Baumbach, "Die Anfänge der Kirchwerdung im Urchristentum," *K* 24/1-2 (1982): 17-30.

2084 Fabien Blanquart, "Le discernement au temps de jeunes communautés," *NRT* 104/4 (1982): 577-84.

2085 A. García del Moral, "Disciplina y pastoral en el Libro de los Hechos, al narrar el itinerario paulino. La vida eclesial de San Pablo, presupuesto y contexto de sus cartas," *Communio* 15/3 (1982): 319-92.

2086 Joseph Pathrapankal, "The Hellenists and Their Missionary Dynamism in the Early Church and its Message for Our Times," *BB* 8/4 (1982): 216-26.

2087 Jacob Jerbell, "The Acts of the Apostles and the History of Early Christianity," *ST* 37/1 (1983): 17-32.

2088 Joseph Pathrapankal, "Creative Crises of Leadership in the Acts of the Apostles," *IJT* 32/1 (1983): 52-60.

2089 B. N. Kaye, "Lightfoot and Baur on Early Christianity," *NovT* 26/3 (1984): 193-224.

2090   François Bovon, "Effet de réel et flou prophétique dans l'œuvre de
       Luc," in À cause de l'Évangile: Études sur les synoptiques et les
       Actes (festschrift for Jacques Dupont). Paris: Cerf, 1985. Pp.
       349-59.

2091   Donald L. Jones, "The Title Huios Theou (υἱὸς θεοῦ) in Acts,"
       SBLSP 15 (1985): 451-63.

2092   Eduard Schweizer, "The Testimony to Jesus in the Early Christian
       Community," HBT 7/1 (1985): 77-98.

2093   A. T. Kraabel, "Greeks, Jews, and Lutherans in the Middle Half
       of Acts," HTR 79/1 (1986): 147-57.

2094   R. J. Cassidy, Society and Politics in the Acts of the Apostles.
       Maryknoll NY: Orbis, 1987.

2095   P. F. Esler, Community and Gospel in Luke-Acts: The Social and
       Political Motivations of Lucan Theology. SNTSMS #57.
       Cambridge: University Press, 1990.

2096   S. S. Bartchy, "Community of Goods in Acts: Idealization or
       Social Reality," in B. A. Pearson, ed., The Future of Early
       Christianity (festschrift for Helmut Koester). Minneapolis MN:
       Fortress Press, 1991. Pp. 309-18.

2097   E. Earle Ellis, " 'Das Ende der Erde," in C. Bussmann and W.
       Radl, eds., Der Treue Gottes trauem: Beiträge zum Wekre des
       Lukas (festschrift for Gerhard Schneider). Freiburg: Herder, 1991.
       Pp. 277-87.

2098   A. T. Kraabel, "The God-Fearers Meet the Beloved Disciples," in
       B. A. Pearson, ed., The Future of Early Christinaity (festschrift for
       Helmut Koester). Minneapolis MN: Fortress Press, 1991. Pp.
       276-84.

2099   R. F. O'Toole, "Poverty and Wealth in Luke-Acts," CS 16 (1991):
       29-41.

2100   J. Roloff, "Konflikte un Konfliktlösungen nach der
       Apostelgeschichte," in C. Bussmann and W. Radl, eds., Der Treue
       Gottes trauem: Beiträge zum Wekre des Lukas (festschrift for
       Gerhard Schneider). Freiburg: Herder, 1991. Pp. 111-26.

2101 Alfons Weiser, "Christsein und kirchliche Lebensformen nach der Apostelgeschichte," in J. Degenhardt, ed., *Die Freude an Gott—unsere Kraft* (festschrift for Otto Bernhard Knoch). Stuttgart: Katholisches Bibelwerk, 1991. Pp. 157-63.

2102 K. Löning, "Das Gottesbild der Apostelgeschichte im Spannungsfeld von Fruhjüdentum und Fremdreligion," in H.-J. Klauck, ed., *Monotheismus und Christologie*. Wien: Herder, 1992. Pp. 88-117.

ecclesiology

2103 H. von Soden, *Die Entstehung der christlichen Kirche*. Leipzig: Teubner, 1919.

2104 R. H. Crompton, *The Church of the First Century*. London: Author-Partner Press, 1937.

2105 W. F. J. Ryan, "The Church as the Servant of God in Acts," *Scr* 15/32 (1963): 110-15.

2106 H. Jenny Epp, "L'éstablissement de l'Église dans le livre des Actes," *AsSeign* 52 (1965): 29-45.

2107 Nikolaus Adler, "Die Kirche baute sich auf . . . und mehrte sich durch den Beistand nach der Apostelgeschichte," *BK* 21/2 (1966): 48-51.

2108 Una Luz, "Cristo y la Iglesia, según Hechos," *RBib* 29/4 (1967): 206-23.

2109 Francis Lenssen, "Biblical Communities: Christian Communities in the New Testament," *Point* 1 (1972): 24-34.

2110 J. H. Roberts, "Ekklēsia in Acts—Linguistic and Theology: A Venture in Methodology," *Neo* 7 (1973): 73-93.

2111 E. Luther Copeland, "Church Growth in Acts," *Miss* 4/1 (1976): 13-26.

2112 L. Legrand, "The Church in the Acts of the Apostles," *BB* 4/2 (1978): 83-97.

2113   A. Rayan, "The Growth of the Church in the Acts," *Bhash* 4/2 (1978): 98-116.

2114   W. C. Van Unnik, "With All Those Who Call on the Name of the Lord," in William C. Weinrich, ed., *The New Testament Age* (festschrift for Bo Reicke). 2 vols. Macon GA: Mercer University Press, 1984. 2:533-51.

2115   K. N. Giles, "Luke's Use of the Term ecclesia (ἐκκλήσια) with Special Reference to Acts 20:28 and 9:31," *NTS* 31 (1985): 135-42.

2116   Alvaro Huerga, "La Implantacion de la Iglesia en el nuevo Mundo," *Ang* 63/2 (1986): 227-56.

2117   J. A. Jáuregui, "Israel y la iglesia en la teologia de Lucas," *EE* 61 (1986): 129-49.

2118   S. Hauerwas, "The Church as God's New Language," in Garrett Green, *Scriptural Authority and Narrative Interpretation.* (festschrift for Hans W. Frei). Philadelphia: Fortress Press, 1987. Pp. 179-98.

2119   F. J. May, "The Book of Acts and Church Growth," doctoral dissertation, Fuller Theological Seminary, Pasadena CA, 1989.

2120   David P. Moessner, " 'The Christ Must Suffer,' The Church Must Suffer: Rethinking the Theology of Luke-Acts," *SBLSP* 29 (1990): 165-95.

2121   J. Driver, "The Trouble with Inclusiveness: A Perspective on the Acts of the Apostles," *SMR* 157 (1994): 24-31.

2122   M. Trotter, "Acts in Esther," *QR* 14/4 (1994-1995): 435-47.

Emmaus

2123   Joseph A. Grassi, "Emmaus Revisited," *CBQ* 26 (1964): 463-67.

2124   John M. Gibbs, "Luke 24:13-33 and Acts 8:26-39: The Emmaus Incident and the Eunuch's Baptism as Parallel Stories," *BTF* 7 (1975): 17-30.

2125 Bernard P. Robinson, "The Place of the Emmaus Story in Luke-Acts," *NTS* 30/4 (1984): 481-97.

Eschatology

2126 F. P. Forwood, "The Eschatology of the Church of Jerusalem as Seen in the Book of Acts," doctoral dissertation, Southern Baptist Theological Seminary, Louisville KY, 1957.

2127 C. R. Stam, *Acts Dispensationally Considered*. 4 vols. Chicago: Berean Bible Society, 1960.

2128 Gerhard Lohfink, "Aufgefahren in den Himmel," *GeistL* 35/2 (1962): 84-85.

2129 C. E. B. Cranfield, "The Parable of the Unjust Judge and the Eschatology of Luke-Acts," *SJT* 16 (1963): 297-301.

2130 Gerhard Lohfink, "Der historische Ansatz der Himmelfahrt Christi," *Cath* 17/1 (1963): 44-84.

2131 R. Haubst, "Eschatologie, 'Der Wetterwinkel'—'Theologie der Hoftnung'," *TTZ* 77 (1968): 365.

2132 E. Franklin, "The Ascension and the Eschatology of Luke-Acts," *SJT* 23/2 (1970): 191-200.

2133 C. H. Talbert, "Redaction Critical Quest for Luke the Theologian," *Persp* 11/1-2 (1970): 171-222.

2134 R. H. Hiers, "The Problem of the Delay of the Parousia in Luke-Acts," *NTS* 20 (1973-1974): 145-55.

2135 Beverly R. Gaventa, "The Eschatology of Luke-Acts Revisited," *Enc* 43 (1982): 27-42.

2136 Kevin N. Giles, "Present-Future Eschatology in the Book of Acts," *RTR* 41/1 (1982): 11-18.

2137 Luis F. Landaria, "Eucaristía y escatología," *EE* 59/229 (1984): 211-16.

2138 Robert Macina, "Jean le Baptiste était-il Elie: examen de la tradition néotestamentaire," *POC* 34/3-4 (1984): 209-32.

2139   Erich Grässer, "Ta peri tès basileias," in Françios Refoulé, ed., *À cause de l'Évangile: Études sur les synoptiques et les Actes* (festschrift for Jacques Dupont). Paris: Cerf, 1985. Pp. 709-25.

2140   Luis F. Ladaria, "Dispensatio en S. Hilario de Poitiers," *Greg* 66/3 (1985): 429-55.

2141   E. J. Christiansen, "Taufe als Initiation in der Apostelgeschichte," *StTh* 40/1 (1986): 55-79.

2142   John T. Carroll, *Response to the End of History: Eschatology and Situation in Luke-Acts*. Atlanta GA: Scholars Press, 1988.

2143   David P. Moessner, "Paul in Acts: Preacher of Eschatological Repentance to Israel," *NTS* 34/1 (1988): 96-104.

2144   R. L. Mayhue, "The Apostle's Watchword: Day of the Lord," in Gary T. Meadors, ed., *New Testament Essays* (festschrift for Homer A. Kent). Winona Lake IN: BMH Bks, 1991. Pp. 239-63.

2145   A. E. Nielsen, "The Purpose of the Lucan Writings with Particular Reference to Eschatology," in P. Luomanen, ed., *Luke-Acts: Scandinavian Perspectives*. Göttingen: Vandenhoeck & Ruprecht, 1991. Pp. 76-93.

2146   V. Fusco, "Point of View and 'Implicit Reader' in Two Eschatological Texts in Frans van Sebroeck, et al., eds., *The Four Gospels 1992* (festschrift for Frans Neirynck). BETL #100. 2 vols. Louvain: Peeters, 1992. 2:1677-96.

2147   J. Carrón Pérez, "El significado de ἀποκαταστάσεως en Hch 3,21,"*EB* 50/1-4 (1992): 375-94.

2148   J. A. Jáuregui, "En el centro del tiempo: La teología de Lucas," *EE* 68 (1993): 3-24.

ethics

2149   W. E. Pilgrim, *Good News to the Poor: Wealth and Poverty in Luke-Acts*. Minneapolis MN: Augsburg, 1981.

2150   Ben Johnson, "The Question of Property in the New Testament," in Béla Harmati, ed., *Christian Ethics and the Question of Property*. Geneva: Lutheran World Federation, 1982. Pp. 50-58.

2151 Jay E. Adams, "The Church and Her Rights," *Fundamentalist Journal* 2/7 (1983): 16-19.

2152 R. F. O'Toole, "Luke's Position on Politics and Society in Luke-Acts," in R. J. Cassidy and P. J. Scharper, eds., *Political Issues in Luke-Acts.* Maryknoll NY: Orbis Books, 1983. Pp. 1-17.

2153 W. M. Swartley, "Politics and Peace (eiréné) in Luke's Gospel," in R. J. Cassidy and P. J. Scharper, eds., *Political Issues in Luke-Acts.* Maryknoll NY: Orbis, 1983. Pp. 18-37.

2154 C. H. Talbert, "Martyrdom in Luke-Acts and the Lukan Social Ethic," in R. J. Cassidy and P. J. Scharper, eds., *Political Issues in Luke-Acts.* Maryknoll NY: Orbis, 1983. Pp. 99-110.

2155 John R. Donahue, "The 'Parable' of the Sheep and the Goats: A Challenge to Christian Ethics," *JTS* 47/1 (1986): 3-31.

2156 D. L. Balch, "The Areopagus Speech: An Appeal to the Stoic Historian Posidonius against Later Stoics and the Epicureans," in David L. Balch, et al., eds., *Greeks, Romans, and Christians* (festschrift for Abraham J. Malherbe) Minneapolis MN: Fortress, 1990. Pp. 52-79.

2157 K. Kertelge, " 'Verstehst du auch, was du liest'?" in David L. Balch, et al., eds., *Greeks, Romans, and Christians* (festschrift for Abraham J. Malherbe). Minneapolis MN: Fortress, 1990. Pp. 52-79.

2158 D. B. McGee, "Sharing Possessions: A Study in Biblical Ethics," in Naymond Keathley, ed., *With Steadfast Purpose* (festschrift for Jack Flanders). Waco TX: Baylor University Press, 1990. Pp. 163-78.

ethiopian eunuch

2159 J. H. Crehan, "The Confirmation of the Ethiopian Eunuch," *OCP* 195 (1974): 187-95.

2160 John M. Gibbs, "Luke 24:13-33 and Acts 8:26-39: The Emmaus Incident and the Eunuch's Baptism as Parallel Stories," *BTF* 7 (1975): 17-30.

2161 W. A. Gage and J. R. Beck, "The Gospel, Zion's Barren Woman and the Ethipian Eunuch," *Crux* 30 (1994): 35-43.

Gallio
2162   A. Plassart, "L'inscription de Delphes mentionnant le procounsul
       Gallion," *RÉG* 80 (1967): 165-72.

2163   J. Murphy-O'Connor, "Paul and Gallio," *JBL* 112 (1993): 315-17.

Gamaliel
2164   G. D. Schwartz, "The Pharisees and the Church," *BibTo* 31
       (1993): 301-304.

2165   J. A. Trumbower, "The Historical Jesus and the Speech of
       Gamaliel," *NTS* 39 (1993): 500-17.

gentiles
2166   J. I. Still, *The Early Gentile Church. Acts of Apostles.* Part 2. 4th
       ed. Edinburgh: United Free Church of Scotland, 1922.

2167   C. C. Warren, "Peter's Difficulty about the Conversion of the
       Gentiles," doctoral dissertation, Southern Baptist Theological
       Seminary, Louisville KY, 1928.

2168   W. E. Langford, "Contributions Made to the Ministry of Paul by
       Certain of His Gentile Companions," doctoral dissertation, Golden
       Gate Baptist Theological Seminary, Mill Valley CA, 1955.

2169   Jacques Dupont, "Le Salut des Gentils et le signification
       Theologique du Libre des Actes," *NTS* 6 (1959-1960): 132-55.

2170   Jacob Jervell, "Das gespaltene Israel und die Heidenvölker. Zur
       Motivierung der Heidenmission in der Apostelgeschichte," *ST*
       19/1-2 (1965): 68-96.

2171   Jacob Jervell, "Det splittede Israel og folkeslagene. Til
       motiveringen av hedningemisjonen i apostlenes gjerninger," *NTT*
       66/4 (1965): 232-59.

2172   J. Ramsey Michaels, "Apostolic Hardships and Righteous
       Gentiles," *JBL* 84 (1965): 27-37.

2173   L. C. Crockett, "Luke 4:25-27 and Jewish-Gentile Relations in
       Luke-Acts," *JBL* 88 (1969): 177-83.

2174 C. H. H. Scobie, "Jesus or Paul: The Origin of the Universal Mission of the Christian Church," in Peter Richardson and John C. Hurd, eds., *From Jesus to Paul* (festschrift for Francis Wright Beare). Waterloo, Ontario: Wilfrid Laurier University Press, 1984. Pp. 47-60.

2175 John G. Gager, "Jews, Gentiles, and Synagogues in the Book of Acts," *HTR* 79/1 (1986): 91-99.

2176 J. A. Sanders, "Who Is A Jew and Who Is A Gentile in the Book of Acts?" *NTS* 37 (1991): 434-55.

2177 W. Stegemann, " 'Licht der Völker' bei Lukas," in C. Bussmann and W. Radl, eds., *Der Treue Gottes trauem: Beiträge zum Wekre des Lukas* (festschrift for Gerhard Schneider). Freiburg: Herder, 1991. Pp. 81-97.

2178 D. W. Palmer, "Mission to Jews and Gentiles in the Last Episode of Acts," *RTR* 52 (1993): 62-73.

2179 H. van de Sandt, "The Quotations in Acts 13:32-52 as a Reflection of Luke's LXX: Interpretation," *Bib* 75 (1994): 26-58.

glossolalia

2180 Nat Tracy, "Speaking in Tongues," doctoral dissertation, New Orleans Baptist Theological Seminary, New Orleans LA, 1936.

2181 A. Alvarez de Linera, "Glosólalo y Intéprete," *EB* 9 (1950): 193-208.

2182 F. Amiot, "Glossolalie," *Cath* 5 (1962): 67-69.

2183 P.-H. Menoud, "La Pentecôte lucanienne et l'histoire," *RHPR* 42/2-3 (1962): 141-47.

2184 S. L. Johnson, "The Gift of Tongues and the Book of Acts," *BSac* 120 (1963): 309-11.

2185 W. G. MacDonald, "Glossolalia in the New Testament," *BETS* 20 (1964): 59-68.

2186 W. E. Moore, "One Baptism," *NTS* 10/4 (1964): 504-16.

2187 R. J. Banks and G. N. Moon, "Speaking in Tongues: A Survey of New Testament Evidence," *Ch* 80 (1966): 278-94.

2188 Ralph E. Knudsen, "Speaking in Tongues," *Found* 9 (1966): 43-57.

2189 J. R. Fowler, "Holiness, the Spirit's Infilling, and Speaking with Tongues," *Para* 2 (1968): 7-9.

2190 Carl G. Tuland, "The Confusion about Tongues," *CT* 13/5 (1968): 207-09.

2191 Watson E. Mills, *Speaking in Tongues*. Grand Rapids MI: Eerdmans, 1971.

2192 O. C. Edwards, "The Exegesis of Acts 8:4-25 and Its Implications for Confirmation and Glossolalia: A Review Article of E. Haenchen's Acts Commentary," *ATR* 55 (1973): 100-12.

2193 W. M. Green, "Glossolalia in the Second Century," *RQ* 16 (1973): 99-126.

2194 G. Mangatt, "The Pentecostal Gift of the Spirit," *BiBe* 2 (1976): 227-39, 300-14.

2195 I. Howard Marshall, "The Significance of Pentecost," *SJT* 30/4 (1977): 347-69.

2196 P. Matta-El-Meskin, "La Pentecôte," *Irén* 50/1 (1977): 5-45.

2197 D. Mínguez, "Pentecostes. Ensayo de semiotica narrativa en Hch," *CBQ* 40 (1978): 643.

2198 Gordon D. Fee, "Tongues—Least of the Gifts: Some Exegetical Observations," *Pneuma* 2/2 (1980): 3-14.

2199 A. Étienne, "Étude du récit de l'événement de Pentecôte dans Actes 2," *FV* 80/1 (1981): 47-67.

2200 L. Panier, "La mort de Judas. Éléments d'analyse sémiotique du récit de la pentecôte," *LV* 30/153-54 (1981): 111-22.

2201 F. M. Pierce, "Glossolalia," *JRPR* 4 (1981): 168-78.

2202 George L. Lasebikan, "Glossolalia: Its Relationship with Speech Disabilities and Personality Disorders," *AfTJ* 14/2 (1985): 111-120.

2203 J. Rius-Camps, "Pentecostes versus Babel. Estudio critico de Hch 2," *FilN* 1/1 (1988): 35-61.

2204 P. F. Esler, "Glossolalia and the Admission of Gentiles into the Early Christian Community," *BTB* 22 (1992): 136-42.

2205 J. Everts, "Tongues or Languages? Contextual Consistency in the Translation of Acts 2," *JPTh* 4 (1994): 71-80.

2206 M. Parmentier, "Das Zungenreden bei den Kirchenvätern," *Bij* 55/4 (1994): 376-98.

grammar

2207 W. E. Crum and H. I. Bell, *Wadi Sarga, Coptic and Greek Texts, from the Excavations Undertaken by the Byzantine Research Account*. Hauniae: Gyldendalske Boghandel-Nordisk Forlag, 1922.

2208 J. T. Luper, "Aorist Tense in the Writings of Luke," doctoral dissertation, Southwestern Baptist Theological Seminary, Fort Worth TX, 1934.

2209 James W. Carpenter, "The *Aktionsart* of the Aorist in Acts," doctoral dissertation, Southern Baptist Theological Seminary, Louisville KY, 1942.

2210 Gilbert N. Callaway, "A Study of the Greek Terms Used in Acts and the Pauline Epistles for the Oral Communication of the Christian Message," doctoral dissertation, Southwestern Baptist Theological Seminary, Fort Worth TX, 1963.

2211 A. W. Argyle, "The Greek of Luke and Acts," *NTS* 20 (1973-1974): 441-45.

2212 Nigel Turner, "The Quality of the Greek of Luke-Acts," in J. K. Elliott, ed., *Studies in New Testament Language and Text* (festschrift for G. D. Kilpatrick). Leiden: Brill, 1976. Pp. 387-400.

2213 C. D. Osburn, "The Third Person Imperative in Acts 2:38," *RQ* 26/2 (1983): 81-84.

2214   G. P. V. Du Plooy, "The Use of the Optative in Luke-Acts:
       Grammatical Classification and Implications for Translation,"
       ScrSA 19 (1986): 25-43.

2215   J. Smit Sibinga, "The Function of Verbal Forms in Luke-Acts,"
       FilN 6 (1993): 31-50.

hellenists
2216   Everett Ferguson, "The Hellenists in the Book of Acts," *RQ* 12/4
       (1969): 159-80.

2217   Joseph Pathrapankal, "The Hellenists and Their Missionary
       Dynamism in the Early Church and its Message for Our Times,"
       BB 8/4 (1982): 216-26.

2218   H. A. Brehm, "The Role of the Hellenists in Christian Origins: A
       Critique of Representative Models in Light of an Exegetical Study
       of Acts 6-8," doctoral dissertation, Southwestern Baptist
       Theological Seminary, Fort Worth, TX, 1992.

2219   É. Trocmé, " 'C'est le ciel qui est mon trône.' La polémique
       contre le Temple et la theology des Hellenistes," in *M. Philonenko,
       ed., Le Trône de Dieu.* WUNT #69. Tübingen: Mohr, 1993. Pp.
       195-203.

introduction
2220   W. M. Ramsay, "Some Recent Editions of the Acts of the
       Apostles," *Exp* Series 6, vol. 2 (1900): 321-35.

2221   Peter Corssen, "Acta Apostolorum," *GGA* 163 (1901): 1-15.

2222   William Robertson, *Studies in the Acts of the Apostles.* "The Guild
       Text Books." New York; Chicago; Toronto: Revell, 1901.

2223   Carl Clemen, "Apostelgeschichte und apostolisches Zeitalter," *TR*
       3 (1900): 50-56; 4 (1901): 66-79; 6 (1903): 79-90; 7 (1904):
       278-86.

2224   R. R. Wright, "An Introduction to the Acts of the Apostles,"
       master's thesis, University of Chicago, Chicago IL, 1904.

2225   W. Bousset, "Neueste Forschungen zur Apostelgeschichte," *TR* 11
       (1908): 185-205.

2226 A. Schlatter, *Erläuterungen zum Neuen Testament*. 1: *Die Evangelien und die Apostelgeschichte*. Stuttgart: Calwer, 1908.

2227 Arthur Wright, "A Short Introduction to the Study of the Acts of the Apostles," *Int* 5 (1908-1909): 34-45.

2228 Jospeh Felten, *Neutestanlentliclte Zeitgeschichte, oder Judentum und Heidentum zur Zeit Christi und der Apostel*. Bd. 2. München-Regensburg: G. J. Manz, 1910.

2229 Heinrich Koch, *Die Abfassungszeit des lukanischen Geschichtswerkes. Eine historisch-kritische und exegetische Untersuchung*. Leipzig: A. Deichert, 1911.

2230 A. H. Nairne, "The Acts of the Apostles," *Int* 10 (1913-1914): 237-49.

2231 A. Jülicher, "Kritische Analyse der lateinischen übersetzungen der Apostelgeschichte," *ZNW* 15 (1914): 163-88.

2232 D. Lynch, *The Story of the Acts of the Apostles*. New York; Cincinnati; Chicago: Benziger Bros., 1917.

2233 D. A. Hayes, *The Synoptic Gospels and the Book of Acts*. "Biblical Introduction Series." New York: Methodist Book Concern, 1919.

2234 G. C. Glanville, "The Aramaic Acts," *ET* 31 (1919-20): 38-41.

2235 Walter Drum, "Commentaries on Acts," *ERev* 62 (1920): 692-96.

2236 G. Mackinlay, *Recent Discoveries in St. Luke's Writings*. London; Edinburgh; New York: Marshall Bros., 1921.

2237 Konstantin Rosch, *Die Apostelgeschichte übersetzt und erklärt*. Paderborn: Schöningh, 1923.

2238 Friedrich Zundel, *Aus der Apostelzeit*. Neue Ausgabe. München: Kaiser, 1923.

2239 F. C. Burkitt, *Christian Beginnings*. London: University of London Press, 1924.

2240   U. Holzmeister, "Neuere Literatur über die Apostelgeschichte,"
       ZKT 49 (1925): 87-99.

2241   J. Vernon Bartlet, *The Apostolic Age, Its Life, Doctrine, Worship
       and Polity.* Edinburgh: T. & T. Clark, 1926.

2242   Oskar Holtzmann, "Apostelgeschichte," in *Das Neue Testament
       nach dem Stuttgarter griechischen Text übersetzt und erklärt.*
       Giessen: Alfred Töpelmann, 1926. Pp. 334-456.

2243   W. Glynne, "Psychology and the Book of Acts," *CQR* 106 (1928):
       281-300.

2244   A. Roth, *An den Quellen des Reiches Gottes. Die Apostelgeschichte
       für unsere Zeit ausgelegt.* Neumunster: G. Ihloff, 1929.

2245   A. M. Anzini, *Il Vangelo de Gesù e gli Atti degli Apostoli. Traduz.
       unificata del testo disposto in ordine cronologico. Con riassunti ed
       illustrazioni.* Torino: Società Ed. Internazionale, 1930.

2246   A. C. Clark, "Blass' Hypothesis," *BBC* 8 (1930): 16-17.

2247   H. J. Cadbury, "Lexical Notes on Luke-Acts: Luke and the Horse
       Doctors," *JBL* 52 (1933): 55-65.

2248   Kirsopp Lake and Silva Lake, "The Acts of the Apostles," *JBL* 53
       (1934): 34-45.

2249   Rendel Harris, "The Acts of the Apostles," *BBC* 11 (1936): 5-9.

2250   H. A. Sanders, "On the New Editions of the Acts of the
       Apostles," *BBC* 11 (1936): 12-15.

2251   G. Kunze, *Aus der Frühzeit der Kirche Jesu Christi. Ein Gang
       durch die Apostelgeschichte des Lucas.* Göttingen: Vandenhoeck &
       Ruprecht, 1938.

2252   Venerabilis Beda, *Expositio Actuum apostolorum et Retractatio,*
       M. L. W. Laistner, ed. The Mediaeval Academy of America, 35.
       Cambridge MA: The Mediaeval Academy of America, 1939.

2253   Frank L. Cox, *According to Luke.* Austin TX: Firm Foundation
       Publishing House, 1941.

2254 L. Laurent, *Aventures apostoliques. Les Actes des Apôtres*. Quebec: Franc. Miss., 1942.

2255 George M. Lamsa, *New Testament Commentary: from the Aramaic and the Ancient Eastern Customs*. Philadelphia: A. J. Holman, 1945.

2256 E. E. Stringfellow, *Acts and Epistles. A Translation and Annotations*. Dubuque, IA: Brown, 1945.

2257 G. R. Hall, *What Jesus Said and Did. A Study of Luke-Acts*. "Gustavus Series of Textbooks and Studies." Rock Island, Illinois: Augustana Book Concern, 1947.

2258 Pius Parsch, *Evangelien und Apostelgeschichte*. Von Jakob Schafer übersetzt und erklärt. Wien: Volksliturgischer Verlag, 1947.

2259 A. Loisy, *The Origins of the New Testament*. Translated by L. P. Jacks. London: George Allen & Unwin, 1950.

2260 Joseph M. Gettys, "The Book of Acts," *Int* 5 (1951): 216-30.

2261 Maurice Goguel, "Quelques observations sur l'œuvre de Luc," *RHPR* 33 (1953): 37-51.

2262 G. H. C. Macgregor, "The Acts of the Apostles," *The Interpreter's Bible*. Vol. 9. Edited by George Arthur Buttrick. New York; Nashville: Abingdon-Cokesbury, 1954. Pp. 3-352.

2263 C. F. D. Moule, *Christ's Messengers. Studies in the Acts of the Apostles*. "World Christian Books." Edited by Stephen Neill. New York: Association Press, 1957.

2264 A. E. Haefner, "The Bridge between Mark and Acts," *JBL* 77 (1958): 67-71.

2265 Lucien Cerfaux, "Les Actes des Apôtres," in Robert A. Feuillet, *Introduction à la Bible. 2. Nouveau Testament*. Tournais, Belgium: Desclée, 1959. 2:337-74.

2266 L. B. Gangsei, "A Teaching Syllabus on the Book of Acts," master's thesis, Princeton Theological Seminary, Princeton NJ, 1959.

2267 Joseph M. Gettys, *How to Study Acts*. Richmond, Virginia: John Knox, 1959.

2268 E. M. B. Green, "Syria and Cilicia: A Note," *ET* 71/2 (1959): 52-53.

2269 Ernst Fuchs, "Meditationen zu Ernest Haenchens Kommentar über die lukanische Apostelgeschichte," *VerkF* 1 (1960): 67-70.

2270 J. W. Roberts, "The Study of the Acts of the Apostles Yesterday and Today," *RQ* 4 (1960): 173-88.

2271 W. C. van Unnik, "The 'Book of Acts'—the Confirmation of the Gospel," *NovT* 4/1 (1960): 26-59.

2272 Miguel Mascialino, "¿Como se está estudéando el libro de los Hechos de los Apóstoles en la actualidad?" *RBib* 24 (1962): 51.

2273 Donald Guthrie, "Recent Literature on the Acts of the Apostles," *VoxE* 2 (1963): 33-49.

2274 F. V. Filson, "Live Issues in the Acts," *BR* 9 (1964): 26-37.

2275 A. García del Moral, "Un posible aspecto de la tesis y unidad del libro de los Hechos," *EB* 23/1 (1964): 41-92.

2276 C. Ghidelli, "Studi sugli Atti degli Apostoli," *ScC* 93/Supp 3 (1965): 390-98.

2277 J.-C. Lebram, "Zwei Bemerkungen zu katechetischen Traditionen in der apostelgeschichte," *ZNW* 56/3-4 (1965): 203-13.

2278 William Barclay, *The Gospels and Acts*. 1: *The First Three Gospels*. London: SCM Press, 1966.

2279 W. W. Gasque, "The Historical Value of the Book of Acts: An Essay in the History of New Testament Cricitism," *EQ* 41/2 (1969): 68-88.

2280 I. Howard Marshall, "Recent Study of the Acts of the Apostles," *ET* 80/10 (1969): 292-96.

2281 L. Schenke, "Die Apostelgeschichte," *ZZ* 23 (1969): 458-63.

2282 George D. Kilpatrick, "Language and Text in the Gospels and Acts," *VC* 24/3 (1970): 161-71.

2283 G. M. Lee, "New Testament Gleanings," *Bib* 51/2 (1970): 235-40.

2284 E. M. Panosian, et al., "Focus on Acts," *BibView* 4/1 (1970): 11-58.

2285 H. Klein, "Zur Frage nach dem Abfassungsort der Lukaschriften," *EvT* 32 (1972): 467-77.

2286 H. Moxnes, "Fra jødisk sekt till verdensreligion. Adolf von Harnack og plaseringen av Lukas-Acta innenfor urkristendommens utvikling," *NTT* 73/3-4 (1972): 229-55.

2287 W. C. van Unnik, et al., "Essays on the Gospel of Luke and Acts: Proceedings of the Ninth Meeting of *Die Nuwe-Testamentiese Werkgemeenskap van Suid-Afrika*," *Neo* 7 (1973): 1-103.

2288 W. W. Gasque, "Did Luke Have Access to Traditions about the Apostles and the Early Churches?" *JETS* 17/1 (1974): 45-48.

2289 D. Gill, "The Structure of Acts 9," *Bib* 55/4 (1974): 546-48.

2290 John B. Polhill, "Introduction to the Study of Acts," *RevExp* 87 (1974): 385-401.

2291 Frank Stagg, "The Unhindered Gospel," *RevExp* 71/4 (1974): 451-62.

2292 Dwight E. Stevenson, "Preaching from the Book of Acts," *RevExp* 71/4 (1974): 511-19.

2293 C. H. Talbert, "An Introduction to Acts," *RevExp* 71/4 (1974): 437-49.

2294 C. H. Talbert, *Literary Patterns, Theological Themes and the Genre of Luke-Acts*. Missoula MT: Scholars Press, 1974.

2295 Malcolm O. Tolbert, "Contemporary Issues in the Book of Acts," *RevExp* 71/4 (1974): 521-31.

2296 Allison A. Trites, "The Importance of Legal Scenes and Language in the Book of Acts," *NovT* 16/4 (1974): 278-84.

2297 A. J. Mattill, "The Jesus-Paul Parallels and the Purpose of Luke-Acts: H. H. Evans Reconsidered," *NovT* 17 (1975): 15-46.

2298 R. Pummer, "The Samaritan Pentateuch and the New Testament," *NTS* 22/4 (1975-1976): 441-43.

2299 Nils A. Dahl, "The Purpose of Luke-Acts," in *Jesus in the Memory of the Early Church*. Minneapolis MN: Augsburg, 1976. Pp. 87-98.

2300 Erich Grässer, "Acta-Forschung seit 1960," *TRu* 41/2 (1976): 141-94; 41/3 (1976): 259-90; 42/1 (1977): 1-68.

2301 E. Haenchen, "Die Apostelgeschichte," *EQ* 50 (1977): 121.

2302 George D. Kilpatrick, "The Historic Present in the Gospels and Acts," *ZNW* 68/3 (1977): 258-62.

2303 E. Plümacher, "Wirklichkeitserfahrung und Geschichtesschreibung bei Lukas. Erwägungen zu den Wir-Stücken der Apostelgeschichte," *ZNW* 58/1-2 (1977): 2-22.

2304 G. Schneider, "Der Zweck des Lukanischen Doppelwerks," *BZ* 21/1 (1977): 45-66.

2305 J. Kremer, "Les Actes des Apôtres. Traditions, redaction, Theologie," *BETL* 48/1 (1977-1978): 611.

2306 C. Ghidelli, "Situazioni di peccato secondo il libro degli Atti," *ScC* 106/3-4 (1978): 253-65

2307 Niels Hyldahl, "Die Erforschung der Apostelgeschichte: Linien und Tendenzen," *SNTU-A* 3 (1978): 159-67.

2308 G. Mangatt, "The Acts of the Apostles: An Introduction," *BB* 4/2 (1978): 75-82.

2309 Benigno Papa, "Tensioni e unita della Chiesa. Ricerca storico-teologica negli Atti degli Apostoli," *ÉTR* 53 (1978): 136.

2310   Jerome D. Quinn, "The Last Volume of Luke: The Relation of Luke-Acts to the Pastoral Epistles," *PRS* 5 (1978): 62-75.

2311   P. J. Sena, "The Acts of the Apostles," *BibTo* 95 (1978): 1546-52.

2312   C. H. Talbert, ed., *Perspectives on Luke-Acts*. Macon GA: Mercer University Press, 1978.

2313   Johann C. Emmelius, "Tendenzkritik und Formengeschichte: Der Beitrag Franz Overbecks zur Auslegung der Apostelgeschichte im 19. jh," *TLZ* 104 (1979): 124-29.

2314   W. W. Gasque, "A History of the Criticism of the Acts," *TL* 104 (1979): 193-96.

2315   Edgar Haulette, "Actes des Apôtres. Un guide de lecture," *ÉTR* 54 (1979): 170.

2316   Robert J. Karris, "Missionary Communities: A New Paradigm for the Study of Luke-Acts," *CBQ* 41 (1979): 80-97.

2317   Robert J. Karris, *What Are They Saying about Luke and Acts? A Theology of the Faithful God*. New York: Paulist, 1979.

2318   R. B. Williams, "Reflections on the Transmission of Tradition in the Early Church," *Enc* 40 (1979): 273-85.

2319   É. Delebecque, "Les deux prologues des Actes des Apôtres," *RT* 80/4 (1980): 628-34.

2320   William S. Kurz, "Luke-Acts and Historiography in the Greek Bible," *SBLSP* 10 (1980): 283-300.

2321   D. L. Tiede, *Prophecy and History in Luke-Acts*. Philadelphia: Fortress Press, 1980.

2322   François Bovon, "Évangile de Luc et Actes des Apôtres," in J. Auneau, ed., *Évangiles synoptiques et Actes des apôtres* (Petite bibliothèque des sciences bibliques. Nouveau Testament #4). Paris: Desclée, 1981. Pp. 195-283.

2323   François Bovon, "Luc: portrait et projet," *LV* 30/153-54 (1981): 9-18.

2324   P. Gibert, "L'invention d'un genre littéraire," *LV* 30/153-54 (1981): 19-33.

2325   Susan Marie Praeder, "Luke-Acts and the Ancient Novel," *SBLSP* 11 (1981): 269-92.

2326   F. F. Bruce, "The Acts of the Apostles Today," *BJRL* 65/1 (1982): 36-56.

2327   Earl Richard, "The Creative Use of Amos by the Author of Acts," *NovT* 24/1 (1982): 37-53.

2328   N. Richardson, *The Panorama of Luke: An Introduction to the Gospel of Luke and the Acts of the Apostles*. London: Epworth, 1982.

2329   R. J. Cassidy and P. J. Scharper, eds., *Political Issues in Luke-Acts*. Maryknoll NY: Orbis, 1983.

2330   L. O'Reilly, "Chiastic Structures in Acts 1-7," *PIBA* 7 (1983): 87-103.

2331   E. Plümacher, "Acta-Forschung 1974-1982," *TR* 48/1 (1983): 1-56.

2332   David L. Barr and Judith L. Wentling, "The Conventions of Classical Biography and the Genre of Luke-Acts," in Charles H. Talbert, ed., *Luke-Acts: New Perspectives from the Society of Biblical Literature*. New York: Crossroad, 1984. Pp. 63-88.

2333   G. Betori, "L'Antico Testamento negli Atti. Stato della ricerca e spunti di riflessione," *RBib* 32 (1984): 211-36.

2334   Robert L. Brawley, "Paul in Acts: Lucan Apology and Conciliation," in Charles H. Talbert, ed., *Luke-Acts: New Perspectives from the Society of Biblical Literature*. New York: Crossroad, 1984. Pp. 129-47.

2335   Thomas L. Brodie, "Greco-Roman Imitation of Texts as a Partial Guide to Luke's Use of Sources," in Charles H. Talbert, ed., *Luke-Acts: New Perspectives from the Society of Biblical Literature*. New York: Crossroad, 1984. Pp. 17-46.

2336 Jacob Jervell, *The Unknown Paul: Essays on Luke-Acts and Early Christian History*. Minneapolis MN: Augsburg, 1984.

2337 Donald L. Jones, "The Title 'Servant' in Luke-Acts," in Charles H. Talbert, ed., *Luke-Acts: New Perspectives from the Society of Biblical Literature*. New York: Crossroad, 1984. Pp. 148-65.

2338 William S. Kurz, *Following Jesus: A Disciple's Guide to Luke and Acts*. Ann Arbor MI: Servant Books, 1984.

2339 R. F. O'Toole, *The Unity of Luke's Theology: An Analysis of Luke-Acts*. Good News Studies #9. Wilmington DE: Glazier, 1984.

2340 C. H. Talbert, ed., *Luke-Acts: New Perspectives from the Society of Biblical Literature Seminar*. New York: Crossroad, 1984.

2341 C. H. Talbert, "Promise and Fulfillment in Lucan Theology," in Charles H. Talbert, ed., *Luke-Acts: New Perspectives from the Society of Biblical Literature*. New York: Crossroad, 1984. Pp. 91-103.

2342 John T. Townsend, "The Date of Luke-Acts," in Charles H. Talbert, ed., *Luke-Acts: New Perspectives from the Society of Biblical Literature*. New York: Crossroad, 1984. Pp. 47-62.

2343 V. E. Vine, "The Purpose and Date of Acts," *ET* 96/2 (1984): 45-48.

2344 David Daube, "Neglected Nuances of Exposition in Luke-Acts," *ANRW* II.25.3 (1985): 2329-56.

2345 Judette M. Kolasny, "Pericopes of Confrontation and Rejection as a Plot Device in Luke-Acts," doctoral dissertation, Marquette University, Milwaukee WI, 1985.

2346 Arthur J. Dewey, "The Hymn in the Acts of John: Dance as Hermeneutic," *Semeia* 38 (1986): 67-88.

2347 Douglas R. Edwards, "Luke-Acts and the Ancient Romance Chaereas and Callirhoe: A Comparison of their Literary and Social Function," doctoral dissertation, Boston University, Boston MA, 1986.

2348 R. C. Tannehill, *The Narrative Unity of Luke-Acts: A Literary Interpretation.* 1: *The Gospel According to Luke.* Philadelphia: Fortress Press, 1986.

2349 P. van Linden, *The Gospel of Luke and Acts.* Wilmington DE: Glazier, 1986.

2350 F. Ó'Fearghail, "The Introduction to Luke-Acts: A Study of the Role of Lk 1,1-4,44 in the Composition of Luke's Two-Volume Work," doctoral dissertation, Pontifical Biblical Institute, Rome, 1987. 2 vols.

2351 P. F. Stuehrenberg, "The Study of Acts before the Reformation. A Bibliographic Introduction," *NovT* 29/2 (1987): 100-136.

2352 C. K. Barrett, "Luke/Acts," in D. A. Carson and H. G. M. Williamson, eds., *It Is Written: Scripture Citing Scripture* (festschrift for Barnabas Lindars). Cambridge: University Press, 1988. Pp. 231-44.

2353 W. W. Gasque, "A Fruitful Field: Recent Study of the Acts of the Apostles," *Int* 42/2 (1988): 117-31.

2354 Robert W. Wall, "The Acts of the Apostles in Canonical Context," *BTB* 18/1 (1988): 16-24.

2355 James M. Dawsey, "The Literary Unity of Luke-Acts: Questions of Style,"*NTS* 35 (1989): 48-66.

2356 W. W. Gasque, "The Historical Value of Acts," *TynB* 40 (1989): 136-57.

2357 Robert L. Brawley, *Centering on God: Method and Message in Luke-Acts.* Louisville KY: Knox, 1990.

2358 F. F. Bruce, "Chronological Questions in the Acts of the Apostles," in *A Mind for What Matters.* Grand Rapids MI: Eerdmans, 1990. Pp. 133-49.

2359 P. G. R. de Villiers, "The Medium is the Message: Luke and the Language of the New Testament against a Greco-Roman Background," *Neo* 24 (1990): 247-56.

2360 D. Gooding, *True to the Faith: A Fresh Approach to the Acts of the Appostles*. London: Hodder & Stoughton, 1990.

2361 S. E. Pattison, "A Study of the Apologetic Function of the Summaries of Acts," doctoral dissertation, Emory University, Atlanta GA, 1990.

2362 J. A. H. Reeves, "Apology, Threat, or a New 'Way': The Socio-Political Perspective of Luke-Acts," *EGLMBS* 10 (1990): 223-35.

2363 Earl Richard, ed., *New Views on Luke and Acts*. Collegeville MN: Luturgical Press, 1990.

2364 R. C. Tannehill, *The Narrative Unity of Luke-Acts: A Literary Interpretation*. 2. *The Acts of the Apostles*. Minneapolis MN: Fortress, 1990.

2365 G. Cowen, "Commenting on Commentaries on Acts," *CTR* 5 (1990-1991): 93-97.

2366 G. Betori, "Strutturazione degli Atti e storiografia antica," *CrNSt* 12 (1991): 251-63.

2367 Jacob Jervell, "Retrospect and Prospect in Luke-Acts Interpretation," *SBLSP* 30 (1991): 383-404.

2368 L. M. Maloney, *All that God had Done with Them: The Narration of the Works of God in the Early Christian Community as Described in the Acts of the Apostles*. American University Studies Series 7: Theology and Religion #91. Bern: Lang, 1991.

2369 David L. Mealand, "Hellenistic Historians and the Style of Acts," *ZNW* 82 (1991): 42-66.

2370 G. Mussies, "Variation in the Book of Acts," *FilN* 4 (1991): 165-82.

2371 J. H. Neyrey, ed., *The Social World of Luke-Acts: Models for Interpretation*. Peabody MA: Hendrickson, 1991.

2372 F. Ó'Fearghail, *The Introduction to Luke-Acts: A Study of the Role of Luke 1:1-4:44 in the Composition of Luke's Two-Volume Work.* Rome: Biblical Institute Press, 1991.

2373 M. A. Powell, *What Are They Saying About Acts?.* New York: Paulist, 1991.

2374 M. N. Ralph, *Discovering the First Century Church: The Acts of the Apostles, Letters of Paul and the Book of Revelation.* Mahwah NJ: Paulist, 1991.

2375 W. Übelacker, "Das Verhältnis von Lk/Apg zum Markusevangelium," in P. Luomanen, ed., *Luke-Acts: Scandinavian Perspectives.* Göttingen: Vandenhoeck & Ruprecht, 1991. Pp. 157-94.

2376 H. A. Brehm, "The Role of the Hellenists in Christian Origins: A Critique of Representative Models in Light of an Exegetical Study of Acts 6-8," doctoral dissertation, Southwestern Baptist Theological Seminary, Fort Worth TX, 1992.

2377 H. Mulder, *De Handelingen der Apostelen. Een bijbels reisboek.* Zoetermeer, Boekencentrum, 1992.

2378 D. W. Palmer, "Acts and the Historical Monograph," *Tyndale Bull* 43 (1992): 373-88.

2379 Mikeal C. Parsons and Joseph B. Tyson, eds., *Cadbury, Knox, and Talbert: American Contributions to the Study of Acts.* Atlanta GA: Scholars Press, 1992.

2380 J. P. White, "Lucan Composition of Acts 7:2-53 in Light of the Author's Use of Old Testament Texts," doctoral dissertation, Southwestern Baptist Theological Seminary, Fort Worth TX, 1992.

2381 S. Heid, "Das Heilige Land: Herkunft und Zukunft der Judenchristen," *K* 34-35 (1992-1993): 1-26.

2382 H. Botermann, "Der Heidenapostel und sein Historiker. Zaire historischen Kritik der Apostelgeschichte," *TBe* 24 (1993): 62-84.

2383 François Bovon, "Études lucaniennes. Rétrospective et prospective," *RTP* 125 (1993): 113-35.

2384 M. Harding, "On the Historicity of Acts: Comparing Acts 9:23-25 with 2 Corinthians 11:32-33," *NTS* 39 (1993): 518-38.

2385 William S. Kurz, *Reading Luke-Acts: Dynamics of Biblical Narrative.* Louisville KY: Westminster- John Knox, 1993.

2386 R. B. Moberly, "When Was Acts Planned and Shaped," *EQ* 65 (1993): 5-26.

2387 R. B. Moberly, "When Was Acts Planned and Shaped," *EQ* 65 (1993): 5-26.

2388 A. Moda, "Paolo prigioniero e martire. Storia e teologia," *BibO* 35 (1993): 235-61.

2389 T. Y. Mullins, "A Comparison between 2 Timothy and the Book of Acts," *AUSS* 31 (1993): 199-203.

2390 J. J. Murphy, "Early Christianity as a 'Persuasive Campaign': Evidence from the Acts of the Apostles and the Letters of Paul," in S. E. Porter and T. H. Olbricht, eds., *Rhetoric in the New Testament.* Sheffield: JSOT, 1993. Pp. 90-99.

2391 F. Siegert, "Mass Communication and Prose Rhythm in Luke-Acts," in S. E. Porter and T. H. Olbricht, eds., *Rhetoric in the New Testament.* Sheffield: JSOT, 1993. Pp. 42-58.

2392 J. H. Solbakk, "Lukas—legen," *NTT* 94 (1993): 219-33.

2393 F. Vouga and A. Riggert, "Die Geschichte des frühen Christentums als Evolution eines deterministischen Chaos," *WD* 22 (1993): 77-85.

2394 R. D. Witherup, "Cornelius Over and Over and Over Again: 'Functional Redundancy' in the Acts of the Apostles," *JSNT* 49 (1993): 45-66.

2395 G. Betori, "La strutturazione del libro degli Atti: una proposta," *RBib* 42 (1994): 3-34.

2396 David Gill and C. Gempf, *The Book of Acts in Its First Century Setting.* Volume II: *Graeco-Roman Setting.* Grand Rapids: Eerdmans, 1994.

2397   H. Merkel, "Israel im lukanischen Werk," *NTS* 40 (1994): 371-98.

2398   Bruce W. Winter and Andrew D. Clarke, *The Book of Acts in Its First Century Setting*. Volume I: *Ancient Literary Setting*. Grand Rapids: Eerdmans, 1994.

Jerusalem

2399   G. H. Summer, "The Administration of James in the Jerusalem Church," master's thesis, Southern Baptist Theological Seminary, Louisville KY, 1955.

2400   Georg Strecker, "Die sogenannte zweite Jerusalemreise des Paulus," *ZNW* 53 (1962): 67-77.

2401   Oscar Cullmann, "Dissensions within the Early Church," *USQR* 22/2 (1967): 83-92.

2402   D. R. de Lacey, "Paul in Jerusalem," *NTS* 20/1 (1973): 82-86.

2403   G. L. Bahnsen, "The Encounter of Jerusalem with Athens," *ATB* 13/1 (1980): 4-40.

2404   I. de la Potterie, "Les deux noms de Jérusalem dans Apôtres," *Bib* 63/2 (1982): 153-87.

2405   F. F. Bruce, "The Church of Jerusalem in the Acts of the Apostles," *BJRL* 67/2 (1985): 641-61.

2406   Randall C. Webber, "An Analysis of Power in the Jerusalem Church in Acts," doctoral dissertation, Southern Baptist Theological Seminary, Louisville KY, 1989.

2407   A. Moda, "Paolo prigioniero e martire. Gli avvenimenti gerosolimitiani," *BibO* 34 (1992): 193-252.

2408   J. M. Ross, "The Spelling of Jerusalem in Acts," *NTS* 38 (1992): 474-76.

2409   A. Campbell, "The Elders of the Jerusalem Church," *JTS* 44 (1993): 511-28.

2410   J. Morgado, "Paul in Jerusalem: A Comparison of His Visits in Acts and Galatians," *JETS* 37 (1994): 55-68.

Jerusalem conference

2411 F. Refoulé, "Le discours de Pierre à l'assemblée de Jérusalem," *RB* 64 (1957): 35-47.

2412 Veselin Kesich, "The Apostolic Council at Jerusalem," *SVTQ* 6/3 (1962): 108-17.

2413 T. Fahy, "The Council of Jerusalem," *ITQ* 30/3 (1963): 232-61.

2414 P. Gaechter, "Geschichtliches zum Apostelkonzil," *ZKT* 85/3 (1963): 339-54.

2415 F. C. Fensham, "The Convention of Jerusalem: A Turning Point in the History of the Church," *NGTT* 10 (1969): 32-38.

2416 M. Simon, "The Apostolic Decree and Its Setting in the Ancient Church," *BJRL* 52/2 (1970): 437-60.

2417 T. Holtz, "Die Bedeutung des Apostelkonzils für Paulus," *NovT* 16 (1974): 110-33.

2418 R. H. Stein, "The Relationship of Galatians 2:1-10 and Acts 15:1-35; Two Neglected Arguments," *JETS* 17/4 (1974): 239-42.

2419 R. G. Hoerber, "A Review of the Apostolic Council After 1925 Years," *CJ* 214 (1976): 155-59.

2420 David R. Catchpole, "Paul, James and the Apostolic Decree," *NTS* 23/4 (1976-1977): 428-44.

2421 M. A. Braun, "James' Use of Amos at the Jerusalem Council: Steps Toward a Possible Solution of the Textual and Theological Problems," *JETS* 20/2 (1977): 113-21.

2422 G. M. M. Pelser, "The Apostolic Synod—Luke and Paul: A Comparison (Afrikaans)" *HTS* 34 (1978): 81-90.

2423 C. K. Barrett, "Apostles in Council and in Conflict," *ABR* 31 (1983): 14-32.

2424 M.-É. Boismard, "Le 'Concile' de Jerusalem: Essai de critique littéraire," *ETL* 64 (1988): 433-40.

2425 T. Jergensen, "Acts 15:22-29. Historiske og eksegetiske problemer," *NTT* 90/1 (1989): 31-45.

2426 Royce Dickinson, "The Theology of the Jerusalem Conference: Acts 15:1-35," *RQ* 32/2 (1990): 65-83.

2427 A. Schmidt, "Das historische Datum des Apostelkonzils," *ZNW* 81 (1990): 122-31.

2428 Terrance Callan, "The Background of the Apostolic Decree," *CBQ* 55 (1993): 284-97.

2429 A. T. M. Cheung, "A Narrative Analysis of Acts 14:27-15:35: Literary Shaping in Luke's Account of the Jerusalem Council," *WTJ* 55/1 (1993): 137-54.

2430 A. J. M. Wedderburn, "The 'Apostolic Decree': Tradition and Redaction," *NovT* 35 (1993): 362-89.

2431 J. Rius-Camps, "La misión hacia el paganismo avalada por el Señor Jesús y el Espíritu Santo," *EB* 52 (1994): 341-60.

Jesus

2432 J. M. Stifler, *The Christ of Christianity. A Series of Studies Based on the Writings of Luke: "The Gospel of Luke" and "The Acts."* New York: Revell, 1915.

2433 George D. Kilpatrick, "The Spirit, God, and Jesus in Acts," *JTS* 15/1 (1964): 63.

2434 E. F. F. Bishop, "Guide to Those Who Arrested Jesus," *EQ* 40/1 (1968): 41-42.

2435 G. R. Greene, "The Portrayal of Jesus as Prophet in Luke-Acts," doctoral dissertation, Southern Baptist Theological Seminary, Louisville KY, 1975.

2436 J. A. Ziesler, "The Name of Jesus in the Acts of the Apostles," *JSNT* 4 (1979): 28-41.

2437 A. Sisti, "Il nome di Gesu negli Atti degli Apostoli," *Ant* 55/4 (1980): 675-94.

2438   Sharon H. Ringe, "The Jubilee Proclamation in the Ministry and Teaching of Jesus: A Tradition-Critical Study in the Synoptic Gospels and Acts," doctoral dissertation, Union Theological Seminary, New York, 1982.

2439   J. A. Fitzmyer, "Jesus in the Early Church through the Eyes of Luke-Acts," *ScrB* 17 (1987): 26-35.

2440   B. C. Frein, "The Literary Significance of the Jesus-as-Prophet Motif in the Gospel of Luke and the Acts of the Apostles," doctoral dissertation, St. Louis University, St. Louis MO, 1989.

2441   M. Korn, *Die Geschichte Jesu in veranderter Zeit. Studien zur bleibenden Bedeutung Jesu im lukanischen Doppelwerk.* WUNT #51. Tübingen: Mohr, 1993.

Jews in

2442   Emil Schürer, *A History of the Jewish People in the Time of Jesus Christ.* 5 vols. in 2. Edinburgh: T. & T. Clark, 1924.

2443   Gregory Dix, *Jew and Greek. A Study in the Primitive Church.* Westminster, England: Dacre Press, 1953.

2444   André Pelletier, "Valeur évocatrice d'un démarquage chrétien de la Septante," *Bib* 48/3 (1967): 388-94.

2445   L. C. Crockett, "Luke 4:25-27 and Jewish-Gentile Relations in Luke-Acts," *JBL* 88 (1969): 177-83.

2446   John G. Gager, "Jews, Gentiles, and Synagogues in the Book of Acts," *HTR* 79/1 (1986): 91-99.

2447   H. Dixon Slingerland, " 'The Jews' in the Pauline Portion of Acts," *JAAR* 54/2 (1986): 305-21.

2448   D. L. Tiede, " 'Glory to Thy People Israel!': Luke-Acts and the Jews," *SBLSP* 16 (1986): 142-51.

2449   Stephen G. Wilson, "The Jews and the Death of Jesus in Acts," in P. Richardson and D. Granskou, eds., *Anti-Judaism in Early Christianity. I. Paul and the Gospels.* Waterloo, Ontario: Wilfred Laurier Press, 1986. Pp. 155-64.

2450 Malcolm Lowe, "Real and Imagined Anti-Jewish Elements in the Synoptic Gospels and Acts," *JES* 24/2 (1987): 267-84.

2451 G. Betori, "Chiesa e Israele nel libro degli Atti," *RBib* 36 (1988): 81-97.

2452 H. Räisänen, "The Redemption of Israel: A Salvation-Historical Problem in Luke-Acts," in P. Luomanen, ed., *Luke-Acts: Scandinavian Perspectives*. Göttingen: Vandenhoeck & Ruprecht, 1991. Pp. 64-114.

2453 M. Rese, " 'Die Juden' im lukanischen Doppelwerk: Ein Bericht über eine längst nötige 'neuere' Diskussion," in C. Bussmann and W. Radl, eds., *Der Treue Gottes trauem: Beiträge zum Wekre des Lukas* (festschrift for Gerhard Schneider). Freiburg: Herder, 1991. Pp. 61-79.

2454 J. A. Sanders, "Who Is A Jew and Who Is A Gentile in the Book of Acts?" *NTS* 37 (1991): 434-55.

2455 L. M. Wills, "The Decpiction of the Jews in Acts," *JBL* 110 (1991): 631-54.

2456 B. W. W. Dombrowski, "Synagoge in Acts 6:9," in Zdzislaw Kapera, ed., *Intertestamental Essays* (festschrift for Józef Tadeusz Milik). Cracow: Enigma Press, 1992. Pp. 53-65.

2457 D. Gerber, "Luc et le Judaïsme," *FV* 92 (1993): 55-66.

2458 M. Harding, "On the Historicity of Acts: Comparing Acts 9:23-25 with 2 Corinthians 11:32-33," *NTS* 39 (1993): 518-38.

2459 R. F. O'Toole, "Reflections on Luke's Treatment of the Jews in Luke-Acts," *Bib* 74 (1993): 529-55.

Judaism

2460 E. Haenchen, "Judentum und Christentum in der Apostelgeschichte," *ZNW* 54 (1963): 155-87.

2461 H. W. Boers, "Psalm 16 and the Historical Origin of the Christian Faith," *ZNW* 60/1-2 (1969): 105-10.

2462   E. Earle Ellis, "Midraschartige Züge in den Reden der Apostelgeschichte," *ZNW* 62 (1971): 94-104.

2463   B. H. Charnov, "Shavout, 'Matan Torah,' and the Triennial Cycle," *Judaism* 28 (1974): 332-36.

2464   Robert P. Gordon, "Targumic Parallels to Acts XIII 18 and Didache XIV 3," *NovT* 16/4 (1974): 285-89.

2465   Robert L. Brawley, "The Pharisees in Luke-Acts: Luke's Address to Jews and his Irenic Purpose," doctoral dissertation, Princeton Theological Seminary, Princeton NJ, 1978.

2466   M. M. B. Turner, "The Sabbath, Sunday and the Law in Luke/Acts," in D. A. Carson, ed., *From Sabbath to Lord's Day*. Grand Rapids MI: Zondervan, 1982. Pp. 99-157.

2467   Donald L. Jones, "The Title Huios Theou (υἱὸς θεοῦ) in Acts," *SBLSP* 15 (1985): 451-63.

2468   E. P. Sanders, "Judaism and the Grand "Christian" Abstractions: Love, Mercy, and Grace," *Int* 39 (1985): 357-372.

2469   Jack T. Sanders, "The Pharisees in Luke-Acts," in D. E. Groh and Robert Jewett, eds., *The Living Text* (festschrift for E. W. Saunders). Lanham MD: University Press of America, 1985. Pp. 141-88.

2470   Jack T. Sanders, "The Jewish People in Luke-Acts," *SBLSP* 16 (1986): 110-29.

2471   Jack T. Sanders, *The Jews in Luke-Acts*. Philadelphia: Fortress Press, 1987.

2472   Joseph B. Tyson, "Scripture, Torah, and Sabbath in Luke-Acts," in E. P. Sanders, ed., *Jesus, the Gospels, and the Church* (festschrift for William R. Farmer). Macon GA: Mercer University Press, 1987. Pp. 89-104.

2473   Joseph B. Tyson, ed., *Luke-Acts and the Jewish People*. Minneapolis MN: Augsburg, 1988.

2474   J. A. Weatherly, "The Jews in Luke-Acts," *TynB* 40 (1989): 107-17.

2475   M. Collin and P. Lenhardt, *Évangile et tradition d'Israël*. Paris: Cerf, 1990.

2476   J. Bradley Chance, "The Jewish People and the Death of Jesus in Luke-Acts," *SBLSP* 21 (1991): 50-81.

2477   D. B. Gowler, *Host, Guest, Enemy and Friend: Portraits of the Pharisees in Luke and Acts*. New York: Peter Lang, 1991.

2478   Joseph B. Tyson, "Jews and Judaism in Luke-Acts: Reading as a Godfearer," *NTS* 41 (1995): 19-38.

Judas Iscariot
2479   Otto Betz, "The Dichotomized Servant and the End of Judas Iscariot," *RevQ* 5 (1964): 43-58.

2480   A. B. Gordon, "The Fate of Judas According to Acts 1:18," *EQ* 43/2 (1971): 97-100.

2481   Kim Paffenroth, "The Stories of the Fate of Judas and Differing Attitudes Towards Sources," *EGLMBS* 12 (1992): 67-81.

Kerygma
2482   Vernon D. Maxted, "The Kingdom in the Book of Acts," master's thesis, Midwestern Baptist Theological Seminary, Kansas City KN, 1955.

2483   R. F. Gates, "The Apostolic Message of Peter as Found in the Book of Acts," master's thesis, Southwestern Baptist Theological Seminary, Fort Worth TX, 1959.

2484   C. H. Talbert, "Redaction Critical Quest for Luke the Theologian," *Persp* 11/1-2 (1970): 171-222.

2485   J. Clitton, "Shaping the Kerygma: A Study of Acts," *LivL* 10/4 (1973): 522-30.

2486   S. S. Smalley, "Spirit, Kingdom, and Prayer in Luke-Acts," *NovT* 15 (1973): 59-71.

2487 C. Di Sante, "The Missionizing of the East and the Meaning of Mission in the New Testament," in Frank K. Flinn and Tyler Hendricks, eds., *Religion in the Pacific Era.* New York NY: Paragon House Publishers, 1985. Pp. 3-13.

2488 Erich Grässer, "Ta peri tès basileias," in Françios Refoulé, ed., *À cause de l'Évangile: Études sur les synoptiques et les Actes* (festschrift for Jacques Dupont). Paris: Cerf, 1985. Pp. 709-25.

2489 A. Buzard, "Acts 1:6 and the Eclipse of the Biblical Kingdom," *EQ* 66 (1994): 197-215.

2490 D. A. DeSilva, "Paul's Sermon in Antioch of Pisidia," *BSac* 151 (1994): 32-49.

eucharist

2491 S. Aalen, "Versuch einer Analyse des Diakonia-Begriffes im Neuen Testament," in William Weinrich, ed., *The New Testament Age* (festschrift for Bo Reicke). 2 vols. Macon GA: Mercer University Press, 1984. 1:1-13.

2492 Luis F. Landaria, "Eucaristía y escatología," *EE* 59/229 (1984): 211-16.

2493 John T. Pless, "Implications of Recent Exegetical Studies for the Doctrine of the Lord's Supper: A Survey of the Literature," *CTQ* 48/2-3 (1984): 203-220.

2494 J. Timothy Coyle, "The Agape—Eucharist Relationship in 1 Corinthians 11," *GTJ* 6/2 (1985): 411-24.

2495 Donald Farmer, "The Lord's Supper Until He Comes," *GTJ* 6/2 (1985): 391-401.

2496 E. A. LaVerdiere, "The Eucharist in the New Testament and the Early Church—VI: The Breaking of the Bread. The Eucharist in the Acts of the Apostles," *Emmanuel* 100 (1994): 324-35.

Love

2497 E. F. F. Bishop, "Faith Has Still Its Olivet and Love Its Galilee," *EQ* 44/1 (1972): 3-10.

2498   Joseph Allen, "Renewal of the Christian Community: A Challenge for the Pastoral Ministry," *SVTQ* 29/4 (1985): 305-323.

2499   Paul D. Fueter, "The Therapeutic Language of the Bible," *IRM* 75 (1986): 211-221.

Luke, the person

2500   A. T. Robertson, *Luke the Historian in the Light of Research*. New York: Scribner, 1920.

2501   F. C. Grant, "Luke the Historian," in *The Growth of the Gospels*. New York: Abingdon, 1933. Pp. 151-75.

2502   Franz Dornseiff, "Lukas der Schriftsteller," *ZNW* 35 (1936): 129-55.

2503   W. M. Ramsay, *Luke the Physician and Other Studies in the History of Religion*. Grand Rapids MI: Baker, 1956.

2504   C. J. Hemer, "Luke the Historian," *BJRL* 60/1 (1977): 28-51.

2505   J. A. Fitzmyer, *Luke the Theologian: Aspects of His Teaching*. New York: Paulist Press, 1987.

2506   I. Howard Marshall, *Luke: Historian and Theologian*. Enlarged ed., Grand Rapids MI: Eerdmans, 1989.

2507   N. M. van Ommeren, "Was Luke an Accurate Historian?" *BSac* 148 (1991): 57-71.

2508   E. Plümacher, "Die Missionsreden der Apostelgeschichte und Dionys von Halikarnass," *NTS* 39/2 (1993): 161-77.

2509   J. H. Solbakk, "Lukas—legen," *NTT* 94 (1993): 219-33.

2510   H. Merkel, "Israel im lukanischen Werk," *NTS* 40 (1994): 371-98.

LXX

2511   R. A. Martin, "Semitic Traditions in Some Synoptic Accounts," *SBLSP* 26 (1987): 295-335.

2512   H. van de Sandt, "An Implication of Acts 15:6-21 in the Light of Deuteronomy 4.29-35 (LXX)," *JSNT* 46 (1992): 73-97.

2513 Marion L. Soards, "The Speeches in Acts in Relation to Other Pertinent Ancient Literature," *ETL* 70 (1994): 65-90.

2514 H. van de Sandt, "The Quotations in Acts 13:32-52 as a Reflection of Luke's LXX: Interpretation," *Bib* 75 (1994): 26-58.

magic

2515 S. Agouridis, "Die Stellung der Apostelgeschichte zur Magie der hellenistischen Zeit," *DBM* 5/2-3 (1978): 119-35.

2516 Marc Lods, "Argent et magie dans le livre des Actes," *PL* 28/4 (1980): 287-93.

2517 Alberto Casalegno, "Evangelização e praticas mágicas nos Actos dos Apóstolos," *PerT* 24 (1992): 13-28.

Matthias

2518 A. Jaubert, "L'election de Mattheas et le tirage au sort," *TU* 112 (1973): 267-80.

2519 J. Capmany Casamitjana, "El perfil del obispo en la elección de Matías," *RCT* 14 (1989): 309-22

2520 J. Rius-Camps, "Las variantes de la recensión occidental de los Hechos de los Apóstoles," *FilN* 6 (1994): 53-64.

Miracles

2521 John Fenton, "The Order of the Mircales Performed by Peter and Paul in Acts," *ET* 77/1 (1966): 381-83.

2522 R. L. Hamblin, "Miracles in the Book of Acts," *SouJT* 17/1 (1974): 19-34.

2523 Robert Bever, "Restoring the Seven Punitive Miracles in Acts to the Prophetic Genre," doctoral dissertation, Lutheran School of Theology, Chicago IL, 1984.

2524 C. K. Barrett, "Faith and Eschatology in Acts 3," in E. Grässer and O. Merk, eds., *Glaube und Eschatologie* (festschrift for W. G. Kümmel). Tübingen: Mohr, 1985. Pp. 1-17.

2525 René Latourelle, "Originalité et fonctions des miracles de Jésus," *Greg* 66/4 (1985): 641-653.

2526   Timothy N. Boyd, "The Laying on of Hands," *BI* (1989): 9-10.

missiology

2527   Martin Schlunk, *Die Apostelgeschichte. Das Missionsbuch des Neuen Testaments. Eine Übersicht*. Berlin: Burckhardthaus Verlag, 1937.

2528   E. Kellerhals, *Das neue Gottesvolk. Ein Missions Bibelstudium über Gemeinde und Mission in der Apostel geschichte*. Stuttgart: Evang. Missionsverlag, 1938.

2529   A. W. Argyle, "St. Paul and the Mission of the Seventy," *JTS* N.S. 1 (1950): 63.

2530   Y. K. Chang, "The Evangelistic Emphases of the Acts of the Apostles," doctoral dissertation, Southwestern Baptist Theological Seminary, Fort Worth TX, 1951.

2531   V. Hasler. "Judenmission und Judenschuld," *TZ* 24 (1968): 173-90.

2532   A. J. Malherbe, "The Apologetic Theology of the Preaching Peter," *RQ* 13 (1970): 205-23.

2533   P. Ternant, "L'Esprit du Christ et L'intervention humaine dans l'envoi en mission en époque néotestamentaire," *NRT* 95 (1973): 367-92.

2534   Cal Guy, "The Missionary Message of Acts," *SWJT* 17/1 (1974): 49-64.

2535   Harold R. Cook, "Who Really Sent the First Missionaries?" *EMQ* 11/4 (1975): 233-39.

2536   J. Valiamangalam, "To the End of the Earth," *BB* 2/3 (1976): 220-27.

2537   R. F. Hock, "The Workshop as a Social Setting for Paul's Missionary Preaching," *CBQ* 41/3 (1979): 438-50.

2538   Ken Kilinski, "How Churches Can Follow Antioch's Model," *EMQ* 15/1 (1979): 19-23.

2539   F. Schnider, "Wie wird eine Gemeinde missionarisch: Überlegungen zu Apg 2,42-47," in Walter Friedberger and Franz Schnider, eds., *Theologie—Gemeinde—Seelsorger*. Munich: Kösel-Verlag, 1979. Pp. 118-25.

2540   J. Matthey, "La mission de l'église au temps des apôtres et au temps de Luc," *LV* 30/153-54 (1981): 61-71.

2541   Beverly R. Gaventa, " 'You Will Be My Witnesses': Aspects of Mission in the Acts of the Apostles," *Miss* 10/4 (1982): 413-25.

2542   Robert Culver, "Authority for a Going and Sending Ministry in the Christian Mission of World Evangelism," in Morris Inch and Ronald Youngblood, eds., *The Living and Active Word of God* (festschrift for Samuel J. Schultz). Winona Lake IN: Eisenbrauns, 1983. Pp. 157-70.

2543   Giuseppe Frizzi, "La 'missioné' in Luca-Atti: Semantica, critica e apologia lucana," *RBib* 32 (1984): 395-423.

2544   R. R. Recker, "The Lordship of Christ and Mission in the Book of Acts," *RR* 37/3 (1984): 177-86.

2545   C. H. H. Scobie, "Jesus or Paul: The Origin of the Universal Mission of the Christian Church," in Peter Richardson and John C. Hurd, eds., *From Jesus to Paul* (festschrift for Francis Wright Beare). Waterloo, Ontario: Wilfrid Laurier University Press, 1984. Pp. 47-60.

2546   Donald Senior, "The Mission Perspective of Luke-Acts," in Donald Senior and C. Stuhlmueller, eds., *The Biblical Foundations of Mission*. 2nd ed. London: SCM, 1984. Pp. 255-79.

2547   C. Di Sante, "The Missionizing of the East and the Meaning of Mission in the New Testament," in Frank K. Flinn and Tyler Hendricks, eds., *Religion in the Pacific Era*. New York NY: Paragon House Publishers, 1985. Pp. 3-13.

2548   Orlando E. Costas, "The Mission of Ministry," *Miss* 14/4 (1986): 463-72.

2549   Yoshiaki Hatori, "Evangelism: The Bible's Primary Message," *ERT* 12 (1988): 5-16.

2550   Justin S. Ukpong, "Mission in the Acts of the Apostles: From the
       Perspective of the Evangelized," *AfTJ* 17/1 (1988): 72-88.

2551   M. A. Seifrid, "Messiah and Mission in Acts: A Brief Response to
       J. B. Tyson," *JSNT* 36 (1989): 47-50.

2552   Justo L. González, "Pluralismo, justicia y misión: un estudio
       bíblico sobre Hechos 6:1-7," *Apuntes* 10 (1990): 3-8.

2553   T. S. Rainer, "Church Growth and Evangelism in the Book of
       Acts," *CTR* 5 (1990-1991): 57-68.

2554   L. Panier, "Portes ouvertes à la foi. La mission dans les Actes des
       Apôtres," *LV* 40/205 (1991): 103-21.

2555   M. Dumais, *Communauté et mission. Une lecture des Actes des
       Apôtres pour aujourd'hui*. Paris: Desclee, 1992.

2556   H. E. Dollar, *A Biblical-Missiological Exploration of the
       Cross-Cultural Dimensions in Luke-Acts*. San Francisco CA:
       Mellen Research University Press, 1993.

2557   E. Plümacher, "Die Missionsreden der Apostelgeschichte und
       Dionys von Halikarnass," *NTS* 39 (1993): 161-77.

2558   R. L. Loubser, "Wealth, House Churches and Rome: Luke's
       Ideological Perspective, *JTSA* 89 (1994): 59-69.

2559   M. Trotter, "Acts in Esther," *QR* 14/4 (1994-1995): 435-47.

passion

2560   R. J. Cassidy, "Luke's Audience, the Chief Priests, and the
       Motives for Jesus' Death," in R. J. Cassidy and P. J. Scharper,
       eds., *Political Issues in Luke-Acts*. Maryknoll NY: Orbis, 1983. Pp.
       146-67.

2561   E. J. Via, "According to Luke: Who Put Jesus to Death?" in R. J.
       Cassidy and P. J. Scharper, eds., *Political Issues in Luke-Acts*.
       Maryknoll NY: Orbis Books, 1983. Pp. 122-45.

2562   Donald W. McCullough, "If Jesus Is Lord, Why Does It Hurt?"
       RJ 35/7 (1985): 11-14.

2563 Lloyd Gaston, "Anti-Judaism and the Passion Narrative in Luke and Acts," in P. Richardson and D. Granskou, eds., *Anti-Judaism in Early Christianity: 1. Paul and the Gospels.* Waterloo: Wilfrid Laurier University Press, 1986. Pp. 127-53.

2564 Joseph B. Tyson, *The Death of Jesus in Luke-Acts.* Columbia: University of South Carolina Press, 1986.

2565 Earl Richard, "Jesus' Passion and Death in Acts," in D. D. Sylva, ed., *Reimaging the Death of the Lucan Jesus.* Frankfurt: Hain, 1990. Pp. 125-52.

2566 Marion L. Soards, "A Literary Analysis of the Origin and Purpose of Luke's Account of the Mockery of Jesus," in Earl Richard, ed., *New Views on Luke and Acts.* Collegeville MN: Liturgical Press, 1990. Pp. 86-93.

2567 J. Bradley Chance, "The Jewish People and the Death of Jesus in Luke-Acts," *SBLSP* 21 (1991): 50-81.

Paul, apostle and theologian

2568 W. M. Ramsay, *Pauline and Other Studies in Early Christian History.* New York: A. C. Armstrong & Son, 1906.

2569 Rudolf Bultmann, "Neueste Paulusforschung. 1. Zur Bekehrung und zum ausseren Lebensgang des Paulus," *TR* N.F. 6 (1934): 229-46.

2570 Anton Fridrichsen, *The Apostle and His Message.* Uppsala: Almquist & Wiksells, 1947.

2571 G. Graystone, "Catholic Bibliography of St Paul's Life and Writings," *Scr* 6 (1953-1954): 56-59.

2572 Jacques Dupont, "Pierre et Paul dans les Actes," *RB* 64 (1957): 35-47.

2573 Donald K. Campbell, "Paul's Ministry at Ephesus—A Devotional Study," *BSac* 118 (1961): 304-10.

2574 M. F. Unger, "Archaeology and Paul's Visit to Iconium, Lystra, and Derbe," *BSac* 118/470 (1961): 107-12.

2575   E. P. Blair, "Paul's Call to the Gentile Mission," *BR* 10 (1965): 19-33.

2576   Aleksy Klawek, "Św. Pawel Przybywa do Europy," *RB* 18/3 (1965): 175-801.

2577   Norbert Lohfink, "Eine alttestamentliche Darstellungsform für Gotteserscheinungen in den Damaskusberichten," *BZ* N.S. 9 (1965): 246-57.

2578   H. van Straelen, "Paulus und die anonymen Christen," *TPQ* 114/4 (1966): 332-39.

2579   Jacob Jervell, "Paulus: der Lehrer Israels. Zu den apologetischen Paulusreden in der Apostelgeschichte," *NovT* 10/2-3 (1968): 164-90.

2580   H. W. Mare, "Pauline Appeals to Historical Evidence," *BETS* 11/3 (1968): 121-30.

2581   D. R. de Lacey, "Paul in Jerusalem," *NTS* 20/1 (1973): 82-86.

2582   M. A. Robinson, "Spermologos: Did Paul Preach from Jesus' Parables?" *Bib* 56/2 (1975): 231-40.

2583   S. Dockx, "L'ordination de Barnabé et de Saul d'après Actes 13:1-3," *NRT* 98/3 (1976): 238-58.

2584   Angel Rodenas, "San Pablo sometido al psicoanalisis: ¿Un mundo paranoico?" *CuBí* 34 (1977): 167-77.

2585   J.-F. Collange, "De Jésus de Nazareth à Paul de Tarse," *LVie* 139 (1978): 87-95.

2586   R. F. Hock, "Paul's Tentmaking and the Problem of his Social Class," *JBL* 97 (1978): 555-64.

2587   Rick Hordern, "Paul as a Theological Authority," *USQR* 33/3-4 (1978): 133-49.

2588   J. Duncan M. Derrett, "Miscellanea: A Pauline Pun and Judas' Punishment," *ZNW* 72 (1981): 132-33.

2589 J. Schmitt, "Les discours missionnaires des Actes et l'histoire des traditions prépauliniennes," *RechSR* 69/2 (1981): 165-80.

2590 Robert Culver, "Authority for a Going and Sending Ministry in the Christian Mission of World Evangelism," in Morris Inch and Ronald Youngblood, eds., *The Living and Active Word of God* (festschrift for Samuel J. Schultz). Winona Lake IN: Eisenbrauns, 1983. Pp. 157-70.

2591 Jan P. Versteeg, "De doop volgens het Nieuwe Testament," in Willem van 't Spijker, et al., eds., *Rondom de doopvont: leer en gebruik van de heilige doop in het NT en in de geschiedenis van de westerse kerk.* Kampen: De Groot Goudriaan, 1983. Pp. 9-133.

2592 Karl H. Schelkle, "Im Leib oder Ausser des Leibes: Paulus als Mystiker," in William C. Weinrich, ed., *The New Testament Age* (festschrift for Bo Reicke). 2 vols. Macon GA: Mercer University Press, 1984. 2:455-65.

2593 C. H. H. Scobie, "Jesus or Paul: The Origin of the Universal Mission of the Christian Church," in Peter Richardson and John C. Hurd, eds., *From Jesus to Paul* (festschrift for Francis Wright Beare). Waterloo, Ontario: Wilfrid Laurier University Press, 1984. Pp. 47-60.

2594 Jouette M. Bassler, "Luke and Paul On Impartiality," *Bib* 66/4 (1985): 546-52.

2595 Kevin N. Giles, "Apostles before and after Paul," *Ch* 99/3 (1985): 241-56.

2596 Kakichi Kadowaki, "Mit dem Körper lesen: Paulus und Dogen," in Hans Waldenfels and Thomas Immoos, eds., *Fernöstliche Weisheit* (festschrift for Heinrich Dumoulin). Mainz: Matthias Grünewald Verlag, 1985. Pp. 68-78.

2597 Eduard Schweizer, "The Testimony to Jesus in the Early Christian Community," *HBT* 7/1 (1985): 77-98.

2598 C. K. Barrett, "Old Testament History according to Stephen and Paul," in Wolfgang Schrage, ed., *Studien zum Text und zur Ethik des Neuen Testaments* (festschrift for Heinrich Greeven). Berlin: de Gruyter, 1986. Pp. 57-69.

2599   Robert L. Reymond, "The Justification of Theology with a Special
Application to Contemporary Christology," *Pres* 12/1 (1986): 1-16.

2600   John T. Townsend, "Acts 9:1-29 and Early Church Tradition,"
SBLSP 27 (1988): 119-31.

2601   R. B. Hays, "The Righteous One as Eschatological Deliverer: A
Case Study in Paul's Apocalyptic Hermeneutics," in Joel Marcus
and Marion Soards, eds., *Apocalyptic and the New Testament*
(festschrift for J. Louis Martyn). Sheffield: JSOT Press, 1989. Pp
191-215.

2602   D. S. Dockery, "Acts 6-12: The Christian Mission beyond
Jerusalem," *RevExp* 87 (1990): 423-37.

2603   Darrell L. Bock, "Athenians Who Have Never Heard," in William
Crockett, et al., eds., *Through No Fault of Their Own: The Fate of
Those Who Never Heard*. Grand Rapids MI: Baker, 1991. Pp.
117-24.

2604   Clark H. Pinnock, "Acts 4:12: No Other Name Under Heaven,"
in William Crockett, et al., eds., *Through No Fault of Their Own:
The Fate of Those Who Never Heard*. Grand Rapids, MI: Baker,
1991. Pp. 107-15.

2605   T. J. Leary, "Paul's Improper Name," *NTS* 38 (1992): 467-69.

2606   J. Murphy-O'Connor, "Paul and Gallio," *JBL* 112 (1993): 315-17.

2607   H. Szesnat, "What Did the σκηνοποιός Paul Produce?" *Neo* 27
(1993): 391-402.

2608   Victor Furnish, "On Putting Paul in His Place," *JBL* 113 (1994):
3-17.

Paul, Areopagus
2609   George T. Montague, "Paul and Athens," *BibTo* 49 (1970): 14-23.

2610   W. G. Morrice, "Where Did Paul Speak in Athens—On Mars' Hill
or Before the Court of the Areopagus?" *ET* 83/12 (1972): 377-78.

2611   Hans Conzelmann, "Die Rede des Paulus auf dem Areopag,"
BEvT 65 (1974): 91-105.

2612 Rudolf Bultmann, "Sermon sur le descours de Paul à Áreopage," *VS* Suppl. 114 (1975): 303-13.

2613 R. F. O'Toole, "Paul at Athens and Luke's Notion of Worship," *RBib* 89/2 (1982): 185-97.

Paul in Acts

2614 Paul Delatte, *Les Épîtres de Saint Paul replacées dans le milieu historique des Actes des Apôtres.* 2 tomes. Nouvelle édition. Louvain: Saint-Alphonse; Paris: A. Giraudon, 1928-1929.

2615 L. P. Pherigo, "Paul's Life after the Close of Acts," *JBL* 70 (1951): 277-85.

2616 M. S. Enslin, "Once Again, Luke and Paul," *ZNW* 61/3-4 (1970): 253-71.

2617 L. K. Yang, "Enacting the Acts of God: One Important Aspect of the Life and Proclamation of Jesus and Paul," *SEAJT* 14/2 (1973): 21-33.

2618 C. Burchard, "Paulus in der Apostelgeschichte," *TLZ* 100/12 (1975): 881-95.

2619 Boyd Reese, "The Apostle Paul's Exercise of His Rights as a Roman Citizen as Recorded in the Book of Acts," *EQ* 47/3 (1975): 138-45.

2620 C. K. Barrett, "Acts and the Pauline Corpus," *ET* 88/1 (1976): 2-5.

2621 F. F. Bruce, "Is the Paul of Acts the Real Paul?" *BJRL* 58/2 (1976): 282-305.

2622 Robert J. Kepple, "The Hope of Israel: The Resurrection of the Dead, and Jesus: A Study of Their Relationship in Acts with Particular Regard to the Understanding of Paul's Trial Defense," *JETS* 20/3 (1977): 231-41.

2623 Marco Adinolfi, "San Paolo e le Auorità Romane negli Atti degli Apostoli," *Ant* 53/3-4 (1978): 452-70.

2624   A. J. Mattill, "The Value of Acts as a Source for the Study of
       Paul," *PRS* 5 (1978): 76-98.

2625   C. Chia-shih, "The Role of Paul in the Acts of the Apostles," *TJT*
       1 (1979): 109-24.

2626   P. Boyd Mather, "Paul in Acts as 'Servant' and 'Witness'," *BR* 30
       (1985): 23-44.

2627   W. O. Walker, "Acts and the Pauline Corpus Reconsidered," *JSNT*
       24 (1985): 3-23.

2628   David P. Moessner, "The Christ Must Suffer: New Light on the
       Jesus—Peter, Stephen, Paul Parallels in Luke-Acts," *NovT* 28/3
       (1986): 220-56.

2629   Robert L. Brawley, "Paul in Acts: Aspects of Structure and
       Characterization," *SBLSP* 27 (1988): 90-105.

2630   John T. Carroll, "Literary and Social Dimensions of Luke's
       Apology for Paul," *SBLSP* 27 (1988): 106-18.

2631   David P. Moessner, "Paul in Acts: Preacher of Eschatological
       Repentance to Israel," *NTS* 34/1 (1988): 96-104.

2632   R. I. Pervo, *Luke's Story of Paul*. Minneapolis MN: Fortress, 1990.

2633   Danile R. Schwartz, "The End of the Line: Paul in the Canonical
       Book of Acts," in W. S. Babcock, ed., *Paul and the Legacies of
       Paul*. Dallas TX: S.M.U. Press, 1990. Pp. 3-24.

2634   S. J. Kelley, "And Your Young Will See Visions: A Functionalist
       Literary Reading of the Visions to Saul and Peter in Acts,"
       doctoral dissertation, Vanderbilt University, Nashville TN, 1991.

2635   B. M. Rapske, "The Importance of Helpers to the Imprisoned Paul
       in the Book of Acts," *TynB* 42 (1991): 3-30.

2636   F. S. Spencer, *The Portrait of Philip in Acts: A Study of Roles and
       Relations*. JSNT Supplement Series #67. Sheffield: JSOT, 1992.

2637   J. C. Beker, "Luke's Paul as the Legacy of Paul," *SBLSP* 32
       (1993): 511-19.

2638 J. C. Lentz, *Luke's Portrait of Paul.* SNTSMS #77. Cambridge, University Press, 1993.

2639 T. B. Slater, "The Presentation of Paul in Acts," *BB* 19 (1993): 19-46.

Paul, chronology

2640 S. Dockx, "Chronologie de la vie de Saint Paul, depuis sa conversion jusqu'à son séjour à Rome," *NovT* 13/4 (1971): 261-304.

2641 S. Dockx, "Chronologie paulinienne de l'année de la grande collecte," *RB* 81 (1974): 183-95.

2642 S. Dockx, "Essai de chronologie pétrinienne," *RechSR* 62/2 (1974): 221-41.

2643 C. J. Hemer, "Acts and Galatians Reconsidered," *Themelios* 2/3 (1977): 81-88.

Paul, conversion of

2644 D. M. Stanley, "Paul's Conversion in Acts: Why the Three Accounts?" *CBQ*, 15 (1953): 315-38.

2645 A. Girlanda, "De Conversione Pauli in Actibus Apostolorum tripliciter narrata," *VD* 39/2 (1961): 66-81.

2646 Gerhard Lohfink, "Eine alttestamentliche Darstellungsform für Gotteserscheinungen in den Damaskusberichten," *BZ* N.S. 9/2 (1965): 246-57.

2647 S. Lundgren, "Ananias and the Calling of Paul in Acts," *ST* 25/2 (1971): 117-22.

2648 F. J. Leenhardt, "Abraham et la Conversion de Saul de Tarse, suivi d'unc Note sur 'Abraham Dans Jean 8'," *RHPR* 53 (1973): 331-51.

2649 S. Sabugal, "La conversion de S. Pablo en Damasco: ciudad de Siria o region de Qumran?" *Aug* 15/5 (1975): 213-24.

2650 O. F. A. Meinardus, "The Site of the Apostle Paul's Conversion at Kaukab," *BA* 44/1 (1981): 57-59.

2651 J. Kelly, "The Conversion of St. Paul," *Emmanuel* 88/10 (1982): 563-65, 576.

2652 R. F. Collins, "Paul's Damascus Experience: Reflections on the Lukan Account," *LouvS* 11/2 (1986): 99-118.

2653 David P. Moessner, "The Christ Must Suffer: New Light on the Jesus—Peter, Stephen, Paul Parallels in Luke-Acts," *NovT* 28/3 (1986): 220-56.

2654 P. Neri, "La visone di Gesù da parte di Paolo sulla via di Damasco," *BibO* 30 (1988): 121-22.

Paul, impriosnment & trial of

2655 B. Brinkmann, "Nun Sanctus Paulus Ephesi fuerit captivus," *VD* 19 (1939): 321-22.

2656 C. Spicq, "Saint Paul, prisonnier," *VS* 71 (1944): 20-24.

2657 C. O. Mashburn, "A Survey of the Possible Events, Problems and Dates Between the Two Roman Imprisonments of the Apostle Paul," doctoral dissertation, Golden Gate Baptist Theological Seminary, Mill Valley CA, 1950.

2658 G. S. Duncan, "Were Paul's Imprisonment Epistles Written from Ephesus?" *ET* 67 (1955-1956): 163-66.

2659 M. Miguens, "Pablo Prisionero," *SBFLA* 8 (1957-1958): 5-112.

2660 R. W. Orr, "Paul's Voyage and Shipwreck," *EQ* 35/2 (1963): 103-104.

2661 F. F. Bruce, "St. Paul in Rome," *BJRL* 46 (1963-1964): 326-45.

2662 J. M. Gilchrist, "On What Charge Was Paul Brought to Rome," *ET* 78 (1966-1967): 264-66.

2663 Timothy D. Barnes, "An Apostle on Trial," *JTS* 20/2 (1969): 407-19.

2664 A. Acworth, "Where Was St. Paul Shipwrecked? A Re-examination of the Evidence," *JTS* 24/1 (1973): 190-93.

2665 P. Pokorn , "Die Romfahrt des Paulus und der antike Roman,"
      ZNW 64/3-4 (1973): 233-44.

2666 W. R. Long, "The Trial of Paul in the Book of Acts: Historical,
      Literary, and Theological Considerations," doctoral dissertation,
      Brown University, Providence RI, 1982.

2667 C. K. Barrett, "Paul Shipwrecked," in Barry Thompson, ed.,
      Scripture: Meaning and Method (festschrift for A. T. Hanson).
      Hull: University Press, 1987. Pp. 51-64.

2668 B. M. Papske, "Pauline Imprisonment and the Lukan Defense of
      the Missionary Prisoner Paul in Light of Greco-Roman Sources,"
      doctoral dissertation, University of Aberdeen, Aberdeen UK, 1992.

2669 T. A. Hawthorne, "Discourse Analysis of Paul's Shipwreck: Acts
      27:1-44," JTT 6 (1993): 253-73.

Paul's travels in
2670 F. Brannigan, "Nautisches über die Romfahrt des heiligen Paulus,"
      TGl 25 (1933): 170-86.

2671 W. A. McDonald, "Archaeology and St. Paul's Journey in Greek
      Lands," BA 3 (1940): 18-24; 4 (1941): 1-10; 5 (1942): 36-48.

2672 M. M. Parvis, "Archaeology and St. Paul's Journeys in Greek
      Lands, Part IV—Ephesus," BA 8 (1945): 62-73.

2673 D. T. Rowlingson, "The Geographical Orientation of Paul's
      Missionary Interests," JBL 69 (1950): 341-44.

2674 S. Geit, "Le second voyage de saint Paul à Jérusalem," RevSR 25
      (1951): 265-69.

2675 S. Geit, "Les trois premiers voyages de saint Paul à Jérusalem,"
      RechSR 41 (1953): 321-48.

2676 T. H. Campbell, "Paul's Missionary Journeys as Reflected in His
      Letters," JBL 74 (1955): 80-87.

2677 J. Dupont, "Chronologie paulinienne," RB 62 (1955): 55-59.

2678 W. Rees, "St. Paul's First Visit to Philippi," *SCR* 6 (1955): 99-105.

2679 J. Dupont, "La mission de Paul à 'Jerusalem'," *NovT* 1 (1956): 275-303.

2680 H. Metzger, *Les Routes de Saint Paul dans l'Orient grec*. Paris: Delachaux & Niestlé, 1956.

2681 S. Giet, "Nouvelles remarques sur les voyages de Saint Paul à Jérusalem," *RevSR* 31 (1957): 329-42.

2682 G. Schille, "Die Fragwürdigkeit eines Itinerars der Paulusreisen," *TLZ* 84 (1959): 165-74.

2683 Marco Adinolfi, "San Paolo a Pozzuoli," *RivBib* 8 (1960): 206-24.

2684 J. Dauvillier, "À propos de la venue de saint Paul à Rome. Notes sur son procès et son voyage maritime," *BLE* 61 (1960): 3-26.

2685 A. Vitti, "San Paolo alla volta di Roma," *BibO* 3 (1961): 48-52.

2686 G. Ogg, "Derbe," *NTS* 9 (1962-1963): 367-70.

2687 P. E. Davies, "The Macedonian Scene of Paul's Journeys," *BA* 26 (1963): 91-106.

2688 F. F. Bruce, "St. Paul in Rome," *BJRL* 46 (1963-1964): 326-45.

2689 S. Zeitlin, "Paul's Journeys to Jerusalem," *JQR* 57 (1967): 171-78.

2690 R. P. C. Hanson, "The Journey of Paul and the Journey of Nikias: An Experiment in Comparative Historography," *StudE* 4 (1968): 315-18.

2691 J. L. Vesco, "Le troisième voyage de Paul en Asie Mineure," *BTS* 144 (1972): 6-20.

2692 V. K. Robbins, "By Land and by Sea: A Study in Acts 13-28," *SBLSP* 15 (1976): 381-96.

2693 Donald R. Miesner, "The Missionary Journeys Narrative: Patterns and Implications," *PRS* 5 (1978): 199-214.

2694 W. P. Bowers, "Paul's Route through Mysia. A Note on Acts xvi.8," *JTS* 30 (1979): 507-11.

2695 F. F. Bruce, "St. Paul in Macedonia," *BJRL* 61/2 (1979): 337-54.

2696 O. F. A. Meinardus, "Paul's Missionary Journey to Spain: Tradition and Folklore," *BA* 41 (1979): 61-63.

2697 É. Delebecque, "Les deux Versions du Voyage de Saint Paul de Corinthe à Troas," *Bib* 64/4 (1983): 556-64.

2698 J. A. Fitzmyer, "The Pauline Letters and the Lucan Account of Paul's Missionary Journeys," *SBLSP* 27 (1988): 82-89.

Pentecost
2699 R. J. Hardy, "Three Papers on the Text of Acts: 1. The Reconstruction of the Torn Leaf of Codex Bezae; 2. And When the Day of Pentecost Was Fully Come; 3. The Greek Text of Codex Laudianus," *HTR* 16 (1923): 163-86.

2700 M. W. Smith, *On Whom the Spirit Came. A Study of the Acts of the Apostles*. Philadelphia: Judson, 1948.

2701 E. Lohse, "Die Bedeutung des Pfingstberichtes im Rahme des lukanischen Geschichtswerkes," *EvT* 13 (1953): 426-36.

2702 C. C. Ryrie, "The Significance of Pentecost," *BSac* 112 (1955): 330-39.

2703 S. MacLean Gilmour, "Easter and Pentecost," *JBL* 81/1 (1962): 62-66.

2704 P.-H. Menoud, "La Pentecôte lucanienne et l'histoire," *RHPR* 42/2-3 (1962): 141-47.

2705 M. Pontet, "Pentecôte et charité fraternelle," *Chr* 9/35 (1962): 340-54.

2706 J. Abri, "The Theological Meaning of Pentecost, " *KS* 4/1 (1965): 133-51.

2707   Gerhard Voss, "Durch die Rechte Gottes erhöt, hat er den Geist ausgegossen (Apg 2,33). Pfingstgeschehen und Pfingstbotschaft nach Apostelgeschichte Kap. 2," *BK* 21/2 (1966): 45-47.

2708   Joseph D. Collins, "Discovering the Meaning of Pentecost," *Scr* 20 (1968): 73-79.

2709   M. Limbeck, "Pfingsten: Der Heilige Geist und die Kirche," *LS* 20 (1969): 232-45.

2710   Amédée Brunot, "La Pentecôte d'Ephèse," *BTS* 144 (1972): 4-5.

2711   Michel Gourgues, "Lecture christologique du Psaume CX et fête de la Pentecôte," *RB* 83/1 (1976): 5-24.

2712   F. Cocchini, "L'evoluzione storico-religiosa della festa de Pentecoste," *RBib* 25 (1977): 297-326.

2713   I. Howard Marshall, "The Significance of Pentecost," *SJT* 30/4 (1977): 347-69.

2714   P. Matta-El-Meskin, "La Pentecôte," *Irén* 50/1 (1977): 5-45.

2715   P. L. Maier, "The First Corinthians: Pentecost and the Spread of Christianity," *SB* 8 (1978): 47.

2716   D. Mínguez, "Pentecostes. Ensayo de semiotica narrativa en Hch," *CBQ* 40 (1978): 643.

2717   A. Étienne, "Étude du récit de l'événement de Pentecôte dans Actes 2," *FV* 80/1 (1981): 47-67.

2718   L. Panier, "La mort de Judas. Éléments d'analyse sémiotique du récit de la pentecôte," *LV* 30/153-54 (1981): 111-22.

2719   É. Delebecque, "Ascension et Pentecôte dans les Actes des Apôtres selon le codex Bezae," *RT* 82/2 (1982): 79-89.

2720   Daniel R. Mitchell, "Peter and the Power of Pentecost," *FundJ* 4/10 (1985): 32.

2721   P. W. van der Horst, "Hellenistic Parallels to the Acts of the Apostles 2:1-47," *JSNT* 25 (1985): 49-60.

2722   Timothy N. Boyd, "The Feast of Pentecost," *BI* 12/3 (1986): 70-73.

2723   R. E. Osborne, "The Power of Pentecost," *Impact* 16 (1986): 27-36.

2724   S. Hauerwas, "The Church as God's New Language," in Garrett Green, *Scriptural Authority and Narrative Interpretation.* (festschrift for Hans W. Frei). Philadelphia: Fortress Press, 1987. Pp. 179-98.

2725   Yoshiaki Hatori, "Evangelism: The Bible's Primary Message," *ERT* 12 (1988): 5-16.

2726   D. Cloete and D. J. Smit, "Its Name was Called Babel. . ..," *JTSA* 86 (1994): 81-87.

2727   J. Kremer, "Biblische Grundlagen zur Feier der Fünfzig Tage," *HD* 48 (1994): 3-15.

2728   A. J. M. Wedderburn, "Traditions and Redaction in Acts 2:1-13," *JSNT* 55 (1994): 27-54.

persecution
2729   F. Pereira, "Persecution in Acts," *Bhash* 4/2 (1978): 131-55.

2730   Maurice Carrez, "Notes sur les événements d'Ephèse et l'appel de Paul à sa citoyenneté romaine," in François Refoulé, ed., *À cause de l'Évangile: Études sur les synoptiques et les Actes* (festschrift for Jacques Dupont). Paris: Cerf, 1985. Pp. 769-77.

2731   John J. Kilgallen, "Persecution in the Acts of the Apostles," in Gerald O'Collins and G. Marconi, eds., *Luke and Acts* (festschrift for Emilio Rasco). Mahwah NJ: Paulist Press, 1993. Pp. 143-60.

Peter
2732   J. N. Sanders, "Peter and Paul in the Acts," *NTS* 2 (1955): 133-43.

2733   M. Miguens, "Pietro nel conciglio apostòlico," *RBib* 10/3 (1962): 240-51.

2734   R. E. Osborne, "Where Did Peter Go?" *CJT* 14/4 (1968): 274-77.

2735   A. J. Malherbe, "The Apologetic Theology of the Preaching Peter," *RQ* 13 (1970): 205-23.

2736   P. W. van der Horst, "Peter's Shadow: Thc Religio-Historical Background of Acts 5:15," *NTS* 23/2 (1977): 204-12.

2737   A. D'Souza, "The Sermons of Peter in the Acts of the Apostles," *BB* 4/2 (1978): 117-30.

2738   T. D. Lea, "How Peter Learned the Old Testament," *SouJT* 22 (1980): 99.

2739   David P. Moessner, "The Christ Must Suffer: New Light on the Jesus—Peter, Stephen, Paul Parallels in Luke-Acts," *NovT* 28/3 (1986): 220-56.

2740   F. J. Matera, "Acts 10:34-43," *Int* 41/1 (1987): 62-66.

Pharisees
2741   Robert L. Brawley, "The Pharisees in Luke-Acts: Luke's Address to Jews and his Irenic Purpose," doctoral dissertation, Princeton Theological Seminary, Princeton NJ, 1978.

2742   Jack T. Sanders, "The Pharisees in Luke-Acts," in D. E. Groh and Robert Jewett, eds., *The Living Text* (festschrift for E. W. Saunders). Lanham MD: University Press of America, 1985. Pp. 141-88.

2743   David R. Gowler, "A Socio-Narratological Character Anaylsis of the Pharisees in Luke-Acts," doctoral dissertation, Southern Baptist Theological Seminary, Louisville KY, 1989.

2744   David R. Gowler, *Host, Guest, Enemy and Friend: Portraits of the Pharisees in Luke and Acts*. New York: Lang, 1991.

2745   G. D. Schwartz, "The Pharisees and the Church," *BibTo* 31 (1993): 301-304.

Philip
2746   F. F. Bruce, "Philip and the Ethiopian," *JSS* 34 (1989): 377-86.

2747   D. S. Dockery, "Acts 6-12: The Christian Mission beyond Jerusalem," *RevExp* 87 (1990): 423-37.

2748   J. Rius-Camps, "Jesús y el Espíritu Santo conducen la misión
       hacia Europa," *EB* 52/4 (1994): 517-34.

2749   C. S. de Vos, "The Significance of the Change from οἶκος to
       οἰκία in Luke's Account of the Philippian Gaoler," *NTS* 41/2
       (1995): 292-96.

politics

2750   R. J. Cassidy and P. J. Scharper, eds., *Political Issues in Luke-Acts*.
       Maryknoll NY: Orbis, 1983.

2751   R. F. O'Toole, "Luke's Position on Politics and Society in
       Luke-Acts," in R. J. Cassidy and P. J. Scharper, eds., *Political
       Issues in Luke-Acts*. Maryknoll NY: Orbis Books, 1983. Pp. 1-17.

2752   P. F. Esler, *Community and Gospel in Luke-Acts: The Social and
       Political Motivations of Lukan Theology*. Cambridge: University
       Press, 1987.

2753   D. L. Balch, "Comments on the Genre and a Political Theme of
       Luke-Acts: A Preliminary Comparison of Two Hellenistic
       Historians," *SBLSP* 19 (1989): 343-61.

prayer

2754   P. T. O'Brien, "Prayer in Luke-Acts," *TynB* 24 (1973): 111-27.

2755   S. S. Smalley, "Spirit, Kingdom and Prayer in Luke-Acts," *NovT*
       15 (1973): 59-71.

2756   Allison A. Trites, "Some Aspects of Prayers in Luke-Acts,"
       SBLSP 7 (1977): 59-78.

2757   Jospeh Hug, "La prière dans le livre des Actes des Apôtres,"
       BCPE 30/5-6 (1978): 38-39.

2758   Steven F. Plymale, "The Prayer Texts of Luke-Acts," doctoral
       dissertation, Northwestern University, Evanston IL, 1986.

Prologue

2759   Schuyler Brown, "The Prologues of Luke-Acts in Their Relation
       to the Purpose of the Author," *SBLSP* 5 (1975): 1-14.

2760   L. C. A. Alexander, "Luke-Acts in its Contemporary Setting with Special Reference to the Prefaces," doctoral dissertation, Oxford University, Oxford UK, 1977.

2761   G. Menestrina, "L'incipit dell'espitola 'Ad Diognetum,' Luca 1:1-4 et Atti 1:1-2," *BibO* 19 (1977): 215-18.

2762   Schuyler Brown, "The Role of the Prologues in Determining the Purpose of Luke-Acts," in Charles H. Talbert, ed., *Perspectives on Luke-Acts.* Macon GA: Mercer University Press, 1978. Pp. 99-111.

2763   V. K. Robbins, "Prefaces in Greco-Roman Biography and Luke-Acts," *SBLSP* 8/2 (1978): 193-208.

2764   Terrance Callan, "The Preface of Luke-Acts and Historiography," *NTS* 31 (1985): 576-81.

2765   F. Ó'Fearghail, "The Introduction to Luke-Acts: A Study of the Role of Lk 1,1-4,44 in the Composition of Luke's Two-Volume Work," doctoral dissertation, Pontifical Biblical Institute, Rome, 1987. 2 vols.

property
2766   Ben Johnson, "The Question of Property in the New Testament," in Béla Harmati, ed., *Christian Ethics and the Question of Property.* Geneva: Lutheran World Federation, 1982. Pp. 50-58.

2767   P. W. van der Horst, "Hellenistic Parallels to the Acts of the Apostles 2:1-47," *JSNT* 25 (1985): 49-60.

2768   D. B. McGee, "Sharing Possessions: A Study in Biblical Ethics," in Naymond Keathley, ed., *With Steadfast Purpose* (festschrift for Jack Flanders). Waco TX: Baylor University Press, 1990. Pp. 163-78.

Qumran
2769   William A. Beardslee, "The Casting of Lots at Qumran and in the Book of Acts," *NovT* 4 (1960): 245-52.

2770   Jan de Waard, "Quotation from Deuteronomy in Acts 3:22-23 and the Palestinian Text: Additional Arguments," *Bib* 52/4 (1971): 537-40.

2771 Everett Ferguson, "Qumran and Codex D," *RevQ* 8/29 (1972): 75-80.

2772 David L. Mealand, "Community of Goods at Qumran," *TZ* 31 (1975): 129-39.

2773 B. E. Thiering, "Qumran Initiation and New Testament Baptism," *NTS* 27/5 (1981): 615-31.

2774 J. Murphy-O'Connor, "The Damascus Document Revisited," *RB* 92 (1985): 223-46.

2775 Chrys C. Caragounis, "Divine Revelation," *ERT* 12 (1988): 226-39.

2776 B. W. W. Dombrowski, "Synagoge in Acts 6:9," in Zdzislaw Kapera, ed., *Intertestamental Essays* (festschrift for Józef Tadeusz Milik). Cracow: Enigma Press, 1992. Pp. 53-65.

reader criticism
2777 Susan Marie Praeder, "Jesus-Paul, Peter-Paul, and Jesus-Peter Parallelisms in Luke-Acts: A History of Reader Response," *SBLSP* 14 (1984): 23-39.

2778 S. J. Kelley, "And Your Young Will See Visions: A Functionalist Literary Reading of the Visions to Saul and Peter in Acts," doctoral dissertation, Vanderbilt University, Nashville TN, 1991.

2779 V. Fusco, "Point of View and 'Implicit Reader' in Two Eschatological Texts in Frans van Sebroeck, et al., eds., *The Four Gospels 1992* (festschrift for Frans Neirynck). BETL #100. 2 vols. Louvain: Peeters, 1992. 2:1677-96.

2780 J. A. Darr, "Narrator as Character: Mapping a Reader Oriented Approach to Narration in Luke-Acts," *Semeia* 63 (1993): 43-60.

reader criticism
2781 Susan Marie Praeder, "Jesus-Paul, Peter-Paul, and Jesus-Peter Parallelisms in Luke-Acts: A History of Reader Response," *SBLSP* 14 (1984): 23-39.

2782 S. J. Kelley, "And Your Young Will See Visions: A Functionalist Literary Reading of the Visions to Saul and Peter in Acts," doctoral dissertation, Vanderbilt University, Nashville TN, 1991.

2783 V. Fusco, "Point of View and 'Implicit Reader' in Two Eschatological Texts in Frans van Sebroeck, et al., eds., *The Four Gospels 1992* (festschrift for Frans Neirynck). BETL #100. 2 vols. Louvain: Peeters, 1992. 2:1677-96.

2784 J. A. Darr, "Narrator as Character: Mapping a Reader Oriented Approach to Narration in Luke-Acts," *Semeia* 63 (1993): 43-60.

Relation to Paul
2785 C. C. Stone, "Points of Contact between the Acts and the Pauline Epistles," doctoral dissertation, Southern Baptist Theological Seminary, Louisville KY, 1928.

2786 Otto Bauernfeind, "Zur Erage nach der Entscheidung zwischen Paulus und Lukas," *ZST* 23 (1954): 59-88.

2787 D. R. Adams, "The Suffering of Paul and the Dynamics of Luke-Acts," doctoral dissertation, Yale University, New Haven CT, 1979.

2788 Don Jackson, "Luke and Paul: A Theology of One Spirit from Two Perspectives," *JETS* 32 (1989): 335-44.

relation to OT
2789 Norbert Lohfink, "Eine alttestamentliche Darstellungsform für Gotteserscheinungen in den Damaskusberichten," *BZ* N.S. 9 (1965): 246-57.

2790 J. Garralda and J. Casaretto, "Uso del Antiquo Testamento en los primeros capitulos de 'Hechos'," *RevB* 28/1 (1966): 35-39.

2791 W. R. Hanford, "Deutero-lsaiah and Luke-Acts: Straightforward Universalism?" *CQR* 168/367 (1967): 141-52.

2792 J. E. Wood, "Isaac Typology in the New Testament," *NTS* 14 (1968): 583-89.

2793 Roger Tomes, "Exodus 14: The Mighty Acts of God: An Essay in Theological Criticism," *SJT* 22/4 (1969): 455-78.

2794   T. R. Carruth, "The Jesus-as-Prophet Motif in Luke-Acts," doctoral dissertation, Baylor University, Waco TX, 1973.

2795   F. J. Leenhardt, "Abraham et la Conversion de Saul de Tarse, suivi d'unc Note sur 'Abraham Dans Jean 8'," *RHPR* 53 (1973): 331-51.

2796   T. C. G. Thornton, "Stephen's Use of Isaiah LXVI.1," *JTS* 25/2 (1974): 432-34.

2797   Nils A. Dahl, "The Story of Abraham in Luke-Acts," in *Jesus in the Memory of the Early Church.* Minneapolis MN: Augsburg, 1976. Pp. 66-86.

2798   P. B. Decock, "Isaiah in Luke-Acts," doctoral dissertation, Pontifical University Gregorium, Rome, 1977.

2799   E. Lucchesi, "Précédents non bibliques à l'expression néo-testamentaire: 'Les temps et les moments'," *JTS* 28 (1977): 537-40.

2800   F. F. Bruce, "The Davidic Messiah in Luke-Acts," in G. A. Tuttle, ed., *Biblical and Near Eastern Studies* (festschrift for W. S. LaSor). Grand Rapids MI: Eerdmans, 1978. Pp. 7-17.

2801   R. Heerspink, "The Use of Psalm Citations in the Gospel of Luke and the Book of Acts," doctoral dissertation, Calvin Theological Seminary, Grand Rapids MI, 1979.

2802   F. Manns, "Essais sur le Judeo-Christianisme," *RBib* 27 (1979): 433-37.

2803   W. C. Kaiser, "The Promise to David in Psalm 16 and its Application in Acts 2:25-33 and 13:32-37," *JETS* 23 (1980): 219-29.

2804   Earl Richard, "The Old Testament in Acts: Wilcox's Semitisms in Retrospect," *CBQ* 42/3 (1980): 330-41.

2805   S. T. Lachs, "Hebrew Elements in the Gospels and Acts," *JQR* 71 (1980-1981): 31-43.

2806   P. B. Decock, "The Understanding of Isaiah 53:7-8 in Acts 8:32-33," *Neo* 14 (1981): 111-33.

2807 Donald H. Juel, "Social Dimensions of Exegesis: The Use of Psalm 16 in Acts 2," *CBQ* 43/4 (1981): 543-56.

2808 Earl Richard, "The Creative Use of Amos by the Author of Acts," *NovT* 24/1 (1982): 37-53.

2809 G. Dautzenberg, "Psalm 110 im Neuen Testament," in Hans Becker and Reiner Kaczynski, eds., *Liturgie und Dichtung: Ein interdisziplinäres Kompendium.* 1. *Historische Präsentation.* Sankt Ottilien: EOS Verlag, 1983. Pp. 141-71.

2810 Walter Kaiser, "The Promise of God and the Outpouring of the Holy Spirit," in Morris Inch and Ronald Youngblood, eds., *The Living and Active Word of God* (festschrift for Samuel J. Schultz). Winona Lake, Ind: Eisenbrauns, 1983. Pp. 109-22.

2811 Agustín del Agua Perez, "El papel de la 'escuela midrásica' en la configuración del Nuevo Testamento," *EE* 60/234 (1985): 333-49.

2812 Mark W. Karlberg, "Legitimate Discontinuities between the Testaments," *JETS* 28 (1985): 9-20.

2813 Alfons Weiser, "Tradition und lukanische Komposition in Apg 10:36-43," in Françios Refoulé, ed., *À cause de l'Évangile: Études sur les synoptiques et les Actes* (festschrift for Jacques Dupont). Paris: Cerf, 1985. Pp. 757-67.

2814 C. K. Barrett, "Old Testament History according to Stephen and Paul," in Wolfgang Schrage, ed., *Studien zum Text und zur Ethik des Neuen Testaments* (festschrift for Heinrich Greeven). Berlin: de Gruyter, 1986. Pp. 57-69.

2815 Jouette M. Bassler, "A Man for All Seasons: David in Rabbinic and New Testament Literature," *Int* 40/2 (1986): 156-69.

2816 Paul D. Fueter, "The Therapeutic Language of the Bible," *IRM* 75 (1986): 211-221.

2817 Thomas L. Brodie, "Luke the Literary Interpreter: Luke-Acts as a Systematic Rewriting and Updating of the Elijah-Elisha Narrative in 1 and 2 Kings," doctoral dissertation, University of St. Thomas Aquinas, Rome, 1987.

2818   F. F. Bruce, "Paul's Use of the Old Testament in Acts," in Gerald F. Hawthorne and Otto Betz, eds., *Tradition & Interpretation in the New Testament* (festschrift for E. Earle Ellis). Grand Rapids MI: Eerdmans, 1987. Pp. 71-79.

2819   Jacques Dupont, "Le Seigneur de tous," in Gerald F. Hawthorne and Otto Betz, eds., *Tradition & Interpretation in the New Testament* (festschrift for E. Earle Ellis). Grand Rapids, MI: Eerdmans, 1987. Pp. 229-36.

2820   Jack T. Sanders, "The Prophetic Use of the Scriptures in Luke-Acts," in C. A. Evans and William F. Stinespring, eds., *Early Jewish and Christian Exegesis* (festschrift for W. H. Brownlee). Atlanta GA: Scholars Press, 1987. Pp. 191-98.

2821   F. Ó'Fearghail, "Israel in Luke-Acts," *PIBA* 11 (1988): 23-43.

2822   Darrell L. Bock, "The Use of the Old Testament in Luke-Acts: Christology and Mission," *SBLSP* 29 (1990): 494-511.

2823   John T. Carroll, "The Use of Scripture in Acts," *SBLSP* 29 (1990): 512-28.

2824   C. L. Stockhausen, "Luke's Stories of the Ascension: The Background and Function of a Dual Narrative," *EGLMBS* 10 (1990): 251-63.

2825   C. K. Barrett, "Attitudes to the Temple in the Acts of the Apostles," in W. Horbury, ed., *Templum Amicitiae: Essays on the Second Temple* (festschrift for Ernst Bammel. Sheffield: JSOT, 1991. Pp. 345-67.

2826   J. M. Schubert, "The Image of Jesus as the Prophet like Moses in Luke-Acts as Advanced by Luke's Reinterpretation of Deuteronomy 18:15-18 in Acts 3:22 and 7:37," doctoral dissertation, Fordham University, New York, 1992.

2827   H. van de Sandt, "An Implication of Acts 15:6-21 in the Light of Deuteronomy 4.29-35 (LXX)," *JSNT* 46 (1992): 73-97.

2828   J. P. White, "Lucan Composition of Acts 7:2-53 in Light of the Author's Use of Old Testament Texts," doctoral dissertation, Southwestern Baptist Theological Seminary, Fort Worth TX, 1992.

2829 Darrell L. Bock, "The Son of David and the Saint's Task: The Hermeneutics of Initial Fulfillment," *BSac* 150 (1993): 440-57.

2830 Daniel Marguerat, "La mort d'Ananias et Saphira dans la stratégie narrative de Luc," *NTS* 39 (1993): 209-26.

2831 G. L. Prato, "Idolatry Compelled to Search for Its Gods: A Peculiar Agreement between Textual Tradition and Exegesis," in Gerald O'Collins and G. Marconi, eds., *Luke and Acts* (festschrift for Emilio Rasco). Mahwah NJ: Paulist Press, 1993. Pp. 181-96.

2832 H. Merkel, "Israel im lukanischen Werk," *NTS* 40 (1994): 371-98.

2833 T. E. Brawley, "For Blessing All Families of the Earth: Covenant Traditions in Luke-Acts," *CThM* 22/1 (1995): 18-26.

resurrection

2834 F. J. Briggs, *The Acts of the Risen Lord*. London: Methodist Book Room, 1911.

2835 A. Schmitt, "Ps 16;8-11 als Zeugnis der Auferstehung in der Apg," *BZ* 17/2 (1973): 229-48.

2836 K. H. Crumbach, "Auferstehungszeugnis," *GeistL* 48/2 (1975): 81-84.

2837 Robert J. Kepple, "The Hope of Israel: The Resurrection of the Dead, and Jesus: A Study of Their Relationship in Acts with Particular Regard to the Understanding of Paul's Trial Defense," *JETS* 20/3 (1977): 231-41.

2838 R. F. O'Toole, "Christ's Resurrection in Acts 13:13-52," *Bib* 60/3 (1979): 361-72.

2839 Veselin Kesich, "Resurrection, Ascension, and the Giving of the Spirit," *GOTR* 25/3 (1980): 249-60.

2840 R. F. O'Toole, "Activity of the Risen Jesus in Luke-Acts," *Bib* 62/4 (1981): 471-98.

2841 Johannes M. Nützel, "Vom Hören zum Glauben: Der Weg zum Osterglauben in der Sicht des Lukas," in Lothar Lies, ed., *Praesentia Christi* (festschrift for Johannes Betz). Düsseldorf: Patmos, 1984. Pp. 37-49.

2842 Anthony Hoekema, "Heaven: Not Just an Eternal Day Off," *CT* 29 (1985): 18-19.

2843 Raymond E. Brown, *A Risen Christ in Eastertime: Essays on the Gospel Narratives of the Resurrection.* Collegeville MN: Liturgical Press, 1991.

salvation
2844 I. de la Potterie, "L'economia fede-sacramento nel nuovo testamento," in P.-R. Tragan, ed., *Fede e sacramenti negli scritti giovannei.* Rome: Edizioni Abbazia, 1972. Pp. 27-46.

2845 Kevin N. Giles, "Salvation in Lukan Theology: Salvation in the Book of Acts," *RTR* 42/2 (1983): 45-49.

2846 Harold L. Wilmington, "The Filling of the Spirit," *FundJ* 2/10 (1983): 52.

2847 Michael R. Austin, "Salvation and the Divinity of Jesus," *ET* 96 (1985): 271-75.

2848 Luis F. Ladaria, "Dispensatio en S. Hilario de Poitiers," *Greg* 66/3 (1985): 429-55.

2849 René Latourelle, "Originalité et fonctions des miracles de Jésus," *Greg* 66/4 (1985): 641-53.

2850 Malcolm J. McVeigh, "The Fate of Those Who've Never Heard: It Depends," *EMQ* 21/4 (1985): 370-79.

2851 Jaroslav B. Stanek, "Lukas: Theologie der Heilgeschichte," *CVia* 28/1-2 (1985): 9-31.

2852 W. Rakocy, "Trionfo del piano salvifico di Dio," doctoral dissertation, Pontifical University Gregorium, Rome, 1991.

2853 M. Dumais, "Le salut universal par le Christ selon les Actes des Apôtres," *SNTU-A* 18 (1993): 113-31.

2854   J. T. Squires, *The Plan of God in Luke-Acts*. SNTSMS #76.
       Cambridge: University Press, 1993.

Simon Magus
       2855   E. Haenchen, "Simon Magus in der Apostelgeschichte," *GNT* 3
              (1973): 267-79.

       2856   W. A. Meeks, "Simon Magus in Recent Research," *RSR* 3/3
              (1977): 137-42.

       2857   Roland Bergmeier, "Die Gestalt des Simon Magus in Apg 8 und
              in der Simonianischen Gnosis—Aporiae einer Gesamtdeutung,"
              ZNW 77/3 (1986): 267-75.

       2858   Susan R. Garrett, *The Demise of the Devil: Magic and the Demonic
              in Luke's Writings*. Minneapolis MN: Fortress Press, 1989.

sociology
       2859   Agustín del Agua Perez, "El papel de la 'escuela midrásica' en la
              configuración del Nuevo Testamento," *EE* 60/234 (1985): 333-49.

       2860   Burton L. Mack, "The Innocent Transgressor: Jesus in Early
              Christian Myth and History," *Semeia* 33 (1985): 135-65.

       2861   Richard I. Pervo, "Social and Religious Aspects of the Western
              Text," in Dennis E. Groh and Robert Jewett, eds., *The Living Text*
              (festschrift for Ernest W. Saunders). Lanham MD: University Press
              of America, 1985. Pp. 229-41.

       2862   B. C. P. Aymer, "A Socio-Religious Revolution: A Sociological
              Exegesis of the 'Poor' and 'Rich' in Luke-Acts," doctoral dissert-
              ation, Boston University, Boston MA, 1987.

       2863   Stanley J. Samartha, "Religion, Culture and Power—Three Bible
              Studies," *RS* 34 (1987): 66-79.

       2864   David R. Gowler, "A Socio-Narratological Character Anaylsis of
              the Pharisees in Luke-Acts," doctoral dissertation, Southern Baptist
              Theological Seminary, Louisville KY, 1989.

       2865   H. E. Dollar, *A Biblical-Missiological Exploration of the
              Cross-Cultural Dimensions in Luke-Acts*. San Francisco CA:
              Mellen Research University Press, 1993.

2866 L. T. Johnson, "The Social Dimensions of Soteria in Luke-Acts and Paul," *SBLSP* 32 (1993): 520-36.

source criticism

2867 George Horner, *The Coptic Version of the New Testament in the Southern Dialect. 6: The Acts of the Apostles.* Oxford: Clarendon, 1922.

2868 H. C. Hoskier, "Some Study of P^{45} with Special Reference to the Bezan Text," *BBC* 12 (1937): 51-57.

2869 R. A. Martin, "Syntactical Evidence of Aramaic Sources in Acts I-XV," *NTS* 11/1 (1964): 38-59.

2870 Norman Perrin, "The Evangelist as Author: Reflections on Method in the Study and Interpretation of the Synoptic Gospels and Acts," *BR* 17 (1972): 5-18.

2871 Joseph B. Tyson, "Source Criticism of the Gospel of Luke," in Charles H. Talbert, ed., *Perspectives on Luke-Acts.* Macon GA: Mercer University Press, 1978. Pp. 24-39.

2872 I. Z. Herman, "Un tentativo di analisi strutturale di *Atti* 2,41-4,35 secundo il metodo di A. J. Greimas," *Ant* 56/2-3 (1981): 467-74.

2873 F. Hahn, "Zum Problem der antiochenischen Quelle in der Apostelgeschichte," in B. Jaspert, ed., *Rudolf Bultmanns Werk und Wirkung.* Darmstadt: Wissenschaftliche Buchgesellschaft, 1984. Pp. 316-31.

2874 Thomas L. Brodie, "Towards Unraveling the Rhetorical Imitation of Sources in Acts: 2 Kgs 5 as One Component of Acts 8:9-40," *Bib* 67/1 (1986): 41-67.

2875 J. Taylor, "The Making of Acts: A New Account," *RB* 97 (1990): 504-24.

speeches

2876 C. Lattey, *The Acts of the Apostles.* "Westminster Version of the Sacred Scriptures: The New Testament," Vol. 2, Part 2. Edited by Cuthbert Lattey & Joseph Keating. London: Longmans, Green & Co., 1936.

2877 L. P. Leavell, "An Investigation of the Authenticity of Certain Pauline Speeches in Acts," doctoral dissertation, New Orleans Baptist Theological Seminary, New Orleans LA, 1954.

2878 John T. Townsend, "The Speeches in Acts," *ATR* 42 (1960): 150-59.

2879 R. B. Ward, "The Speeches of Acts in Recent Study," *RQ* 4 (1960): 189-98.

2880 J.-C. Lebram, "Der Aufbau der Areopagrede," *ZNW* 55/3-4 (1964): 221-43.

2881 T. Francis Glasson, "The Speeches in Acts and Thucydides," *ET* 76/5 (1965): 165.

2882 T. Jacobs, "De christologie van de redevoeringen der Handelingen," *Bij* 28/2 (1967): 177-96.

2883 J. W. Bowker, "Speeches in Acts: A Study in Proem and Yelammedenu Form," *NTS* 14/1 (1967-1968): 96-111.

2884 Paul Schubert, "The Final Cycle of Speeches in the Book of Acts," *JBL* 87/1 (1968): 1-16.

2885 E. Earle Ellis, "Midraschartige Züge in den Reden der Apostelgeschichte," *ZNW* 62 (1971): 94-104.

2886 J. Navone, "Speeches in Acts," *BibTo* 65 (1973): 1114-17.

2887 J. Julius Scott, "Stephen's Speech: A Possible Model for Luke's Historical Method?" *JETS* 17/2 (1974): 91-97.

2888 Max Wilcox, "A Foreword to the Study of the Speeches in Acts," *StJudLAnt* 12/1 (1975): 206-51.

2889 L. Legrand, "The Areopagus Speech, its Theological Kerygma and its Missionary Significance," *BETL* 41 (1976): 337-50.

2890 Rex A. Koivisto, "Stephen's Speech: A Case Study in Rhetoric and Biblical Inerrancy," *JETS* 20/4 (1977): 353-64.

2891 M. B. Dudley, "The Speeches in Acts," *EQ* 50/3 (1978): 147-55.

2892   A. D'Souza, "The Sermons of Peter in the Acts of the Apostles,"
BB 4/2 (1978): 117-30.

2893   Fred Veltman, "The Defense Speeches of Paul in Acts," *PRS* 5
(1978): 243-56.

2894   J. Kurichianil, "The Speeches in the Acts and the Old Testament,"
ITS 17/2 (1980): 181-86.

2895   F. G. Downing, "Ethical Pagan Theism and the Speeches in Acts'
NTS 27/4 (1981): 544-63.

2896   G. H. R. Horsley, "Speeches and Dialogue in Acts," *NTS* 32/4
(1986): 609-14.

2897   Evald Lovestam, "En gammaltestamentlig nyckel till Paulus-talet
I Miletos," *SEÅ* 51/52 (1986-1987): 137-47.

2898   Rex A. Koivisto, "Stephen's Speech: a Theology of Errors?" *GTJ*
8 (1987): 101-14.

2899   F. J. Matera, "Acts 10:34-43," *Int* 41/1 (1987): 62-66.

2900   C. J. Hemer, "The Speeches of Acts. 2. The Areopagus Address,"
TynB 40/2 (1989): 239-59.

2901   F. F. Bruce, "The Significance of the Speeches for Interpreting
Acts," *SouJT* 33/1 (1990): 20-28.

2902   S. E. Porter, "Thucydides 1.22.1 and Speeches in Acts: Is There
a Thucydidean View?" *NovT* 32 (1990): 121-42.

2903   S. J. Kistemaker, "The Speeches in Acts," *CTR* 5 (1990-1991):
31-41.

2904   C. A. Estridge, "Suffering in Contexts of the Speeches of Acts,"
doctoral dissertation, Baylor University, Waco TX, 1991.

2905   R. C. Tannehill, "The Functions of Peter's Mission Speeches in the
Narratives of Acts," *NTS* 37 (1991): 400-14.

2906   M. Me. Adam, "Philosophy and the Bible: The Areopagus
Speech," *Faith and Philos* 9 (1992): 135-50.

2907 P. Sciberras, "The Figure of Paul in the Acts of the Apostles: The Areopagus Speech," *MeliT* 43 (1992): 1-15.

2908 C. Cook, "Travelers Tales and After-Dinner Speeches: The Shape of Acts of the Apostles," *NBlack* 74 (1993): 442-57.

2909 K. O. Sandnes, "Paul and Socrates: The Aim of Paul's Areopagus Speech," *JSNT* 50 (1993): 13-26.

2910 J. A. Trumbower, "The Historical Jesus and the Speech of Gamaliel," *NTS* 39 (1993): 500-17.

2911 R. F. Wolfe, "Rhetorical Elements in the Speeches of Acts 7 and 17," *JTT* 6 (1993): 274-83.

2912 John J. Kilgallen, "Paul's Speech to the Ephesian Elders: Its Structure," *ETL* 70 (1994): 112-21.

2913 R. F. O'Toole, "What Role Does Jesus' Sayings in Acts 20:35 Play in Paul's Address to the Ephesian Elders?" *Bib* 75 (1994): 329-49.

2914 Marion L. Soards, "Agabus's Speech in Caesarea," in *The Speeches in Acts: Their Content, Context, and Concerns.* Louisville: John Knox/Westminster Press, 1994. Pp. 108-109.

2915 Marion L. Soards, "Demetrius's Speech," in *The Speeches in Acts: Their Content, Context, and Concerns.* Louisville: John Knox/Westminster Press, 1994. Pp. 102-103.

2916 Marion L. Soards, "Festus's Speech," in *The Speeches in Acts: Their Content, Context, and Concerns.* Louisville: John Knox/Westminster Press, 1994. Pp. 120-22.

2917 Marion L. Soards, "Gallio's Speech to the Corinthian Jews," in *The Speeches in Acts: Their Content, Context, and Concerns.* Louisville: John Knox/Westminster Press, 1994. Pp. 101-102.

2918 Marion L. Soards, "Gamaliel's Speech to the Council," in *The Speeches in Acts: Their Content, Context, and Concerns.* Louisville: John Knox/Westminster Press, 1994. Pp. 53-55.

2919 Marion L. Soards, "James's Speech at the Jerusalem Conference," in *The Speeches in Acts: Their Content, Context, and Concerns.* Louisville: John Knox/Westminster Press, 1994. Pp. 92-95.

2920 Marion L. Soards, "Paul's Speech at Antioch of Pisidia," in *The Speeches in Acts: Their Content, Context, and Concerns.* Louisville: John Knox/Westminster Press, 1994. Pp. 79-88.

2921 Marion L. Soards, "Paul's Speech before Felix," in *The Speeches in Acts: Their Content, Context, and Concerns.* Louisville: John Knox/Westminster Press, 1994. Pp. 118-19.

2922 Marion L. Soards, "Paul's Speech before Fetus," in *The Speeches in Acts: Their Content, Context, and Concerns.* Louisville: John Knox/Westminster Press, 1994. Pp. 119-20.

2923 Marion L. Soards, "Paul's Speech before King Agrippa," in *The Speeches in Acts: Their Content, Context, and Concerns.* Louisville: John Knox/Westminster Press, 1994. Pp. 122-27.

2924 Marion L. Soards, "Paul's Speech before the Council," in *The Speeches in Acts: Their Content, Context, and Concerns.* Louisville: John Knox/Westminster Press, 1994. Pp. 114-16.

2925 Marion L. Soards, "Paul's Speech(es) during the Sea Voyage to Rome," in *The Speeches in Acts: Their Content, Context, and Concerns.* Louisville: John Knox/Westminster Press, 1994. Pp. 122-27.

2926 Marion L. Soards, "Paul's Speech in the Middle of the Areopagus," in *The Speeches in Acts: Their Content, Context, and Concerns.* Louisville: John Knox/Westminster Press, 1994. Pp. 95-100.

2927 Marion L. Soards, "Paul's Speech to the Corinthian Jews," in *The Speeches in Acts: Their Content, Context, and Concerns.* Louisville: John Knox/Westminster Press, 1994. Pp. 100-101.

2928 Marion L. Soards, "Paul's Speech to the Ephesian Elders," in *The Speeches in Acts: Their Content, Context, and Concerns.* Louisville: John Knox/Westminster Press, 1994. Pp. 104-108.

2929   Marion L. Soards, "Paul's Speech to the Jerusalem Jews," in *The Speeches in Acts: Their Content, Context, and Concerns.* Louisville: John Knox/Westminster Press, 1994. Pp. 111-14.

2930   Marion L. Soards, "Paul's Speech to the Roman Jewish Leaders," in *The Speeches in Acts: Their Content, Context, and Concerns.* Louisville: John Knox/Westminster Press, 1994. Pp. 130-33.

2931   Marion L. Soards, "Peter's Speech and the Disciples' Prayer Prior to the Enrollment of Matthias," in *The Speeches in Acts: Their Content, Context, and Concerns.* Louisville: John Knox/Westminster Press, 1994. Pp. 26-31.

2932   Marion L. Soards, "Peter's Speech at Cornelius's House," in *The Speeches in Acts: Their Content, Context, and Concerns.* Louisville: John Knox/Westminster Press, 1994. Pp. 70-77.

2933   Marion L. Soards, "Peter's Speech at the Jerusalem Conference," in *The Speeches in Acts: Their Content, Context, and Concerns.* Louisville: John Knox/Westminster Press, 1994. Pp. 90-92.

2934   Marion L. Soards, "Peter's Speech at Pentecost," in *The Speeches in Acts: Their Content, Context, and Concerns.* Louisville: John Knox/Westminster Press, 1994. Pp. 31-38.

2935   Marion L. Soards, "Peter's Speech in Solomon's Portico of the Temple," in *The Speeches in Acts: Their Content, Context, and Concerns.* Louisville: John Knox/Westminster Press, 1994. Pp. 38-44.

2936   Marion L. Soards, "Peter's Speech to the Circumcision Party," in *The Speeches in Acts: Their Content, Context, and Concerns.* Louisville: John Knox/Westminster Press, 1994. Pp. 77-79.

2937   Marion L. Soards, "Peter's Speech to the Jewish Authorities after His and John's Arrest," in *The Speeches in Acts: Their Content, Context, and Concerns.* Louisville: John Knox/Westminster Press, 1994. Pp. 44-47.

2938   Marion L. Soards, "The Pharisees' Speech in the Council," in *The Speeches in Acts: Their Content, Context, and Concerns.* Louisville: John Knox/Westminster Press, 1994. Pp. 116-17.

2939 Marion L. Soards, "The Prayer of the Apostles and Their Friends," in *The Speeches in Acts: Their Content, Context, and Concerns*. Louisville: John Knox/Westminster Press, 1994. Pp. 47-50.

2940 Marion L. Soards, "The Speech by the Twelve Prior to the Appointment of the Seven," in *The Speeches in Acts: Their Content, Context, and Concerns*. Louisville: John Knox/Westminster Press, 1994. Pp. 55-57.

2941 Marion L. Soards, "The Speech of Barnabas and Paul at Lystra" in *The Speeches in Acts: Their Content, Context, and Concerns*. Louisville: John Knox/Westminster Press, 1994. Pp. 88-90.

2942 Marion L. Soards, "The Speech of James and the Jerusalem Elders," in *The Speeches in Acts: Their Content, Context, and Concerns*. Louisville: John Knox/Westminster Press, 1994. Pp. 109-110.

2943 Marion L. Soards, "The Speech of Peter and the Apostles to the Council," in *The Speeches in Acts: Their Content, Context, and Concerns*. Louisville: John Knox/Westminster Press, 1994. Pp. 50-53.

2944 Marion L. Soards, "The Speech of the Ephesian Town Clerk," in *The Speeches in Acts: Their Content, Context, and Concerns*. Louisville: John Knox/Westminster Press, 1994. Pp. 103-104.

2945 Marion L. Soards, "The Speech to the Jews from Asia," in *The Speeches in Acts: Their Content, Context, and Concerns*. Louisville: John Knox/Westminster Press, 1994. Pp. 110-11.

2946 Marion L. Soards, "The Speeches in Acts in Relation to Other Pertinent Ancient Literature," in *ETL* 70 (1994): 65-90.

2947 Marion L. Soards, "Stephen's Speech," in *The Speeches in Acts: Their Content, Context, and Concerns*. Louisville: John Knox/Westminster Press, 1994. Pp. 57-70.

2948 Marion L. Soards, "Tertullus's Speech," in *The Speeches in Acts: Their Content, Context, and Concerns*. Louisville: John Knox/Westminster Press, 1994. Pp. 117-18.

2949 Marion L. Soards, "The Words of the Risen Jesus and the Angels to the Apostles," in *The Speeches in Acts: Their Content, Context, and Concerns*. Louisville: John Knox/Westminster Press, 1994. Pp. 22-26.

2950 K.-K. Yeo, "A Rhetorical Study of Acts 17:22-31," *JianD* 1 (1994): 75-107.

spirit

2951 C. E. Blakeway, *The Gospel of the Holy Ghost. An Outline of Bible Study Based upon the Acts of the Apostles*. London: S.P.C.K., 1913.

2952 James T. Gillespie, "The Work of the Holy Spirit as Shown in the Book of Acts," doctoral dissertation, Southern Baptist Theological Seminary, Louisville KY, 1930.

2953 M. W. Smith, *On Whom the Spirit Came. A Study of the Acts of the Apostles*. Philadelphia: Judson, 1948.

2954 J. S. Ramsey, *In the Spirit. Separate Studies of Acts and the Revelation*. Jacksonville, Florida: Convention Press, 1960.

2955 W. Tom, "Vervuld met de Heilige Geest. Norm of uitzondering?" *GTT* 61 (1961): 74-76.

2956 O. Knoch, "Erfüllt vom Heiligen Geiste. Die Einheit der Kirche nach der Apostelgeschichte," *BK* 18/2 (1963): 34-38.

2957 C. Journet, "La mission visible de l'Esprit-Saint," *RT* 65 (1965): 357-97.

2958 J. R. Fowler, "Holiness, the Spirit's Infilling, and Speaking with Tongues," *Para* 2 (1968): 7-9.

2959 W. Kern, "Das Fortgehen Jesu und das Kommen des Geistes oder Christi Himmelfahrt," *GeistL* 41/2 (1968): 85-90.

2960 M. Limbeck, "Pfingsten: Der Heilige Geist und die Kirche," *LS* 20 (1969): 232-45.

2961 Troy Organ, "A Cosmomogical Christology," *CC* 88/44 (1971): 1293-95.

2962 J. K. Parratt, "The Holy Spirit and Baptism. Part 1. The Gospels and the Acts of the Apostles," *ET* 82/8 (1971): 231-35.

2963 J. Riedl, "Der Heilige Geist wird euch in alle Wahrheit einführen," *BL* 44 (1971): 89-94.

2964 R. Massó, "La promesa del Espíritu," *CuBí* 29 (1972): 342-48.

2965 F. F. Bruce, "The Holy Spirit in the Acts of the Apostles," *Int* 27/2 (1973): 166-83.

2966 S. S. Smalley, "Spirit, Kingdom and Prayer in Luke-Acts," *NovT* 15 (1973): 59-71.

2967 H. L. Drumwright, "The Holy Spirit in the Book of Acts," *SouJT* 17/1 (1974): 3-17.

2968 D. Mínguez, "Hechos de los Apóstoles. Comunidad de creyentes Impulsados por el Espíritu," *SalT* 65/1-2 (1975): 106-13.

2969 G. Mangatt, "The Pentecostal Gift of the Spirit," *BiBe* 2 (1976): 227-39, 300-14.

2970 J. Berchmans, "Anointed with Holy Spirit and Power," *Je* 8/45 (1978): 201-17.

2971 F. Bourassa, "L'Esprit Saint 'communion' du Pére et du Fils," *SE* 30/1 (1978): 5-37.

2972 M. Dumais, "Ministères, charismes et Esprit dans l'œuvre de Luc," *EgT* 9/3 (1978): 413-53.

2973 A. G. Fuente, "El Espiritu Santo y los sacramentos: el dato Biblico," *Ang* 55 (1978): 366-414.

2974 Thomas Marsh, "Holy Spirit in Early Christian Teaching," *ITQ* 45/2 (1978): 101-16.

2975 Bruce Terry, "Baptized in One Spirit," *RQ* 21/4 (1978): 193-299.

2976 Veselin Kesich, "Resurrection, Ascension, and the Giving of the Spirit," *GOTR* 25/3 (1980): 249-60.

2977 P. M. J. Stravinskas, "The Role of the Spirit in Acts 1 and 2," *BibTo* 18/4 (1980): 263-68.

2978 M. M. B. Turner, "Luke and the Spirit: Studies in the Significance of Receiving the Spirit in Luke-Acts," doctoral dissertation, Trinity Hall, Cambridge MA, 1980.

2979 J. R. W. Stott, "Setting the Spirit Free," *CT* 25/11 (1981): 786-90.

2980 M. M. B. Turner, "The Significance of Receiving the Spirit in Luke-Acts: A Survey of Modern Scholarship," *TJ* 2/2 (1981): 131-58.

2981 M. M. B. Turner, "Spirit Endowment in Luke-Acts: Some Linguistic Considerations," *VoxE* 12 (1981): 45-63.

2982 H. Geisen, "Der Heilige Geist als Ursprung und treibende Kraft des christlichen Lebens. Zu den Geistaussagen der Apostelgeschichte," *BK* 37/4 (1982): 126-32.

2983 Walter Kaiser, "The Promise of God and the Outpouring of the Holy Spirit," in Morris Inch and Ronald Youngblood, eds., *The Living and Active Word of God* (festschrift for Samuel J. Schultz). Winona Lake, Ind: Eisenbrauns, 1983. Pp. 109-22.

2984 Harold L. Wilmington, "The Filling of the Spirit," *FundJ* 2/10 (1983): 52.

2985 Elmar Salmann, "Trinität und Kirche: eine dogmatische Studie," *Cath* 38/4 (1984): 352-74.

2986 C. H. Talbert, "Discipleship in Luke-Acts," in Fernando F. Segovia, ed., *Displeship in the New Testament*. Philadelphia: Fortress Press, 1985. Pp. 62-75.

2987 Walt Russell, "The Anointing With the Holy Spirit in Luke-Acts," *TriJ* 7/1 (1986): 47-63.

2988 M.-E. Rosenblatt, "Under Interrogation: Paul as Witness in Juridical Contexts in Acts and the Implied Spirituality for Luke's Community," doctoral dissertation, Graduate Theological Union, Berkeley, 1987.

2989 Michael Wolter, "Apollos und die Ephesinischen Johannesjünger," *ZNW* 78/1-2 (1987): 49-73.

2990 A. Godin, "Geschichte einer Trauer und eines neuen Pneumas (eines neuen Atems): Gedanken eines Psychoanalytikers über drei Texte der Apostelgeschichte; tr by Kurt Gins," in Kurt Krenn, et al., eds., *Archiv für Religionspsychologie*, Bd. 18. Göttingen: Vandenhoeck & Ruprecht, 1988. Pp. 19-37.

2991 F. R. Harm, "Structural Elements Related to the Gift of the Holy Spirit in Acts," *CJ* 14/1 (1988): 28-41.

2992 F. F. Bruce, "Luke's Presentation of the Spirit in Acts," *CTR* 5 (1990-1991): 15-29.

2993 Odette Mainville, *L'Esprit dan l'œuvre de Luc*. Héritage et projet 45. Saint-Laurent, Fides, 1991.

2994 R. P. Menzies, *The Development of Early Christian Pneumatology with Special Reference to Luke-Acts*. Sheffield: JSOT Press, 1991.

2995 G. Segalla, *Charisma e istituzione a servizio della carità nelle Atti degli Apostoli*. Padova: Libreria Gregoriana Editrice, 1991.

2996 John N. Suggit, "The Holy Spirit and We Resolved. . .," *JTSA* 79 (1992): 38-48.

2997 M. Dumais, "Le salut universal par le Christ selon les Actes des Apôtres," *SNTU-A* 18 (1993): 113-31.

2998 J. D. G. Dunn, "Baptism in the Spirit: A Response to Pentecostal Scholarship on Luke-Acts," *JPTh* 3 (1993): 3-27.

2999 David A. Handy, "Acts 8:14-25," *Int* 47 (1993): 289-94.

3000 R. P. Menzies, "Spirit and Power in Luke-Acts: A Response to Max Turner," *JSNT* 49 (1993): 11-20.

3001 J. Driver, "The Trouble with Inclusiveness: A Perspective on the Acts of the Apostles," *SMR* 157 (1994): 24-31.

3002 M. Trotter, "Acts in Esther," *QR* 14/4 (1994-1995): 435-47.

spirit, gifts of
3003 John Koenig, "From Ministry to Ministry: Paul as Interpreter of Charismatic Gifts," *USQR* 33/3-4 (1978): 167-74.

3004 Veselin Kesich, "Resurrection, Ascension, and the Giving of the Spirit," *GOTR* 25/3 (1980): 249-60.

3005 S. A. Panimolle, "Il battesimo e la Pentecoste dei samaritani," in Giustino Farnedi, ed., *Traditio et progressio: studi liturgici.* Rome: Benedictina-Edizioni, 1988. Pp. 413-36.

Stephen
3006 C. K. Harrop, "The Influence of the Thought of Stephen upon the Epistle to the Hebrews," doctoral dissertation, Southern Baptist Theological Seminary, Louisville KY, 1955.

3007 L. W. Barnard, "Saint Stephen and Early Alexandrian Christianity," *NTS* 7/1 (1960-1961): 31-45.

3008 O. Sottritti, "Stefano, testimone del Signore," *RBib* 10/2 (1962): 182-88.

3009 Giovanni Rinaldi, "Stefano," *BibO* 6/4-5 (1964): 153-62.

3010 U. Borse, "Der Rahmentext im Umkreis der Stephanusgeschichte," *BibL* 14/3 (1973): 187-204.

3011 B. Bagatti, "Nuove testimonianze sul luogo della lapidazione di S. Stefano," *Ant* 49/4 (1974): 527-32.

3012 V. Ravanelli, "La testimonianza di Stefano su Gesù Cristo," *SBFLA* 24 (1974): 121-41.

3013 J. Julius Scott, "Stephen's Speech: A Possible Model for Luke's Historical Method?" *JETS* 17/2 (1974): 91-97.

3014 G. Stemberger, "Die Stephanusrede (Apg 7) und die judische Tradition," *SNTU-A* 1 (1976): 154-74.

3015 M. H. Scharlemann, "Stephen's Speech: A Lucan Creation?" *CJ* 4/2 (1978): 52-57.

3016 J. Julius Scott, "Stephen's Defense and the World Mission of the People of God," *JETS* 21/2 (1978): 131-41.

3017 G. Schneider, "Stephanus, die Hellenisten und Samaria," *BETL* 48 (1979): 215-40.

3018 Thomas L. Brodie, "The Accusing and Stoning of Naboth (1 Kgs 2:18-13) as One Component of the Stephen Text," *CBQ* 45/3 (1983): 417-32.

3019 P. Trudinger, "Stephen and the Life of the Primitive Church," *BTB* 14/1 (1984): 18-22.

3020 C. K. Barrett, "Old Testament History according to Stephen and Paul," in Wolfgang Schrage, ed., *Studien zum Text und zur Ethik des Neuen Testaments* (festschrift for Heinrich Greeven). Berlin: de Gruyter, 1986. Pp. 57-69.

3021 David P. Moessner, "The Christ Must Suffer: New Light on the Jesus—Peter, Stephen, Paul Parallels in Luke-Acts," *NovT* 28/3 (1986): 220-56.

3022 F. F. Bruce, "Stephen's Apologia," in Barry Thompson, ed., *Scripture: Meaning and Method* (festschrift for A. T. Hanson). Hull: University Press, 1987. Pp. 37-50.

3023 P. Dschulniggg, "Die Rede des Stephanus im Rahmen des Berichtes über sein Martyrium," *Jud* 44 (1988): 195-213.

3024 D. A. DeSilva, "The Stoning of Stephen: Purging and Consolidating an Endangered Institution," *SBT* 17/2 (1989): 165-85.

3025 D. S. Dockery, "Acts 6-12: The Christian Mission beyond Jerusalem," *RevExp* 87 (1990): 423-37.

3026 G. Jankowski, "Stephanos: Eine Auslegung von Apostelgeschichte 6-8,3," *TexteK* 15 (1992): 2-38.

3027 S. Légasse, *Stephanos. Histoire et discours d'Étienne dans les Actes des Apôtres.* Paris: Cerf, 1992.

3028 Edvin Larsson, "Temple-Criticism and the Jewish Heritage: Some Reflexions on Acts 6-7," *NTS* 39 (1993): 379-95.

3029 C. Amos, "Renewed in the Likeness of Christ: Stephen the Servant Martyr," *IrBibStud* 16 (1994): 31-37.

textual criticism

3030 August Pott, *Der abendländische Text der Apostelgeschichte und die Wir-Quelle* Leipzig: Hinrichs, 1900.

3031 Honoratus Coppieters, *De historia textus Actorum Apostolorum.* Lovanni: J. Van Linthout, 1902.

3032 George Horner, *The Coptic Version of the New Testament in the Northern Dialect. 4: The Catholic Epistles and the Acts of the Apostles. Edited from MS Oriental 424.* Oxford: Clarendon, 1905.

3033 E. Nestle, "Zur Einteilung der Apostelgeschichte im Codex B," *ZNW* 7 (1906): 259-60.

3034 E. S. Buchanan, "More Pages from the Fleury Palimpsest," *JTS* 8 (1906-1907): 96-100.

3035 E. S. Buchanan, *The Four Gospels from the Codex Corbeiensis.* Old-Latin Biblical Texts #5. Oxford: Clarendon, 1907.

3036 E. S. Buchanan, "Some Noteworthy Readings of the Fleury Palimpsest," *JTS* 9 (1907-1908): 98-100.

3037 G. Morin, "Un lectionnaire mérovingien avec fragments du texte occidental des Actes des Apôtres," *RBén* 25 (1908): 161-66.

3038 E. S. Buchanan, "The Codex Veronensis," *JTS* 10 (1908-1909): 120-26.

3039 Alfred Valentine-Richards, "The History and Present State of New Testament Textual Criticism," *Essays on Some Biblical Questions of the Day.* Edited by Henry Barclay Swete. "Cambridge Biblical Essays." London: Macmillan, 1909. Pp. 507-39.

3040 Stephen Gaselee, "Two Fayoumic Fragments of the Acts," *JTS* 11 (1909-1910): 514-17.

3041 E. S. Buchanan, "Further Notes on the Fleury Palimpsest," *JTS* 12 (1910-1911): 277-80.

3042 J. E. Belser, "Zur Geschichte des Textes der Akta," *TQ* 93 (1911): 23-34.

3043 F. C. Conybeare, "The Old Georgian Version of Acts," *ZNW* 12 (1911): 131-40.

3044 E. A. Hutton, *An Atlas of Textual Criticism. Being an Attempt to Show the Mutual Relationship of the Authorities for the Text of the New Testament up to about 1000 A.D.* Cambridge: University Press, 1911.

3045 John Chapman, "The Diatessaron and the Western Text of the Gospels," *RBén* 29 (1912): 233-52.

3046 E. A. Loew, "The Codex Bezae," *JTS* 14 (1912-1913): 385-88.

3047 G. Mercati, "On the Non-Greek Origin of the Codex Bezae," *JTS* 15 (1913-1914): 448-51.

3048 A. C. Clark, *The Primitive Text of the Gospels and Acts*. Oxford: Clarendon, 1914.

3049 F. Prat, "Le texte occidental des Actes des apôtres," *RecSR* 5 (1914): 472.

3050 A. C. Clark, "The Primitive Text of the Gospels and Acts: A Rejoinder," *JTS* 16 (1914-1915): 225-40.

3051 Henri Munier, "Recueil de manuscrits coptes de l'Ancien et du Nouveau Testament," *BIFAO* 12 (1916): 245-57.

3052 F. C. Conybeare, "A New Vulgate MS of Acts," *JTS* 20 (1918-1919): 44-54.

3053 Victor Martin, "Les papyrus du Nouveau Testament et l'histoire du texte," *RTP* N.S. 7 (1919): 43-72.

3054 August Pott, *Der Text des Neuen Testaments nach seiner geschichtlichen Entwickelung.* "Aus Natur und Geisteswelt. Sammlung wissenschaftlich-gemeinverstandlicher Darstellungen," 134. Bandchen. 2. Aufl. Leipzig; Berlin: Teubner, 1919.

3055 A. Hebbelynck and H. Thompson, "L'unité et l'âge du papyrus copte biblique or. 7594 du British Museum," *Mus* 34 (1921): 71

3056 R. J. Hardy, "Three Papers on the Text of Acts: 1. The Reconstruction of the Torn Leaf of Codex Bezae; 2. And When the Day of Pentecost Was Fully Come; 3. The Greek Text of Codex Laudianus," *HTR* 16 (1923): 163-86.

3057 J. Leipoldt, "The Coptic Version of the Acts of the Apostles," *CQR* 96 (1923): 351-56.

3058 W. N. Stearns, "Recently Published Fragmentary Texts of the New Testament: A Summary," *JBL* 42 (1923): 135-36.

3059 E. A. Lowe, "The Codex Bezae and Lyons," *JTS* 25 (1923-1924): 270-74.

3060 John Chapman, "The Codex Amiatinus and Cassiodorus," *RBén* 38 (1926): 139-50; 39 (1927): 12-32.

3061 A. M. Coleman, *The Biblical Text of Lucifer of Cagliari.* Welwyn: Herts, 1927.

3062 Rendel Harris, "The Western Greek Text of Acts: A Surprising Discovery," *BBC* 4 (1927): 15-16.

3063 M.-J. Lagrange, "Un nouveau papyrus contenant un fragment des Actes," *RB* 36 (1927): 549-60.

3064 A. H. Salonius, "Die griechischen Handschriftenfragmente des Neuen Testaments in den Staatlichen Museen zu Berlin," *ZNW* 26 (1927): 97-119.

3065 H. A. Sanders, "A Papyrus Fragment of Acts in the Michigan Collection," *HTR* 20 (1927): 1-20.

3066 A. C. Clark, "The Michigan Fragment of the Acts," *JTS* 29 (1927-1928): 18-28.

3067   R. L. Poole, "A Stage in the History of the Laudian MS of Acts,"
       JTS 29 (1927-1928): 399-400.

3068   B. W. Bacon, "Some 'Western' Variants in the Text of Acts,"
       HTR 21 (1928): 113-45.

3069   John Chapman, "The Codex Amiatinus Once More," *RBén* 40
       (1928): 130-34.

3070   R. J. Hardy and W. H. P. Hatch, "The Vulgate, Peshitto, Sahidic,
       and Bohairic Versions of Acts and the Greek Manuscripts," *HTR*
       21 (1928): 69-95.

3071   Donald W. Riddle, "The Rockefeller-McCormick Manuscript,"
       JBL 48 (1929): 248-56.

3072   J. A. Findlay, "On Variations in the Text of d and D," *BBC* 9
       (1931): 10-11.

3073   D. Plooij, "The Bezan Problem," *BBC* 9 (1931): 12-17.

3074   J. Lindblom, "Nya handskriftsfynd till gamla och nya
       testamentet," *STK* 8 (1932): 154-61.

3075   Silva New, "The New Chester Beatty Papyrus," *JBL* 51 (1932):
       73-74.

3076   F. C. Burkitt, "The Chester Beatty Papyri," *JTS* 34 (1933):
       363-68.

3077   Edgar J. Goodspeed, "The Letter of Jesus Christ and the Western
       Text," *ATR* 15 (1933): 105-14.

3078   W. H. P. Hatch, "Six Coptic Fragments of the New Testament
       from Nitria," *HTR* 26 (1933): 99-108.

3079   Frederic G. Kenyon, *Recent Developments in the Textual Criticism
       of the Greek Bible*. London: Oxford University Press, 1933.

3080   Silva New, "Note 23. The Michigan Papyrus Fragment 1571," *BC*
       5 (1933): 262-68.

3081   H. A. Sanders, "The Egyptian Text of the Four Gospels and Acts," *HTR* 26 (1933): 77-98.

3082   B. H. Streeter, "The Primitive Text of the Acts," *JTS* 34 (1933): 232-41.

3083   Frederic G. Kenyon, *The Chester Beatty Biblical Papyri.* Fasc. 1: *General Introduction.* Fasc. 2: *The Gospels and Acts, Text, Plates.* London: Walker, 1933-1934.

3084   P. Collomp, "Les Papyri Chester Beatty," *RHPR* 14 (1934): 130-43.

3085   P. L. Hedley, "The Egyptian Texts of the Gospels and Acts," *CQR* 118 (1934): 23-39, 188-230.

3086   Jean Héring, "Observations critiques sur le texte des Évangiles et des Actes de P⁴⁵," *RHPR* 14 (1934): 144-54.

3087   M.-J. Lagrange, "Le papyrus Beatty des Actes des Apôtres, *RB* 43 (1934): 161-71.

3088   Augustinus Merk, "Codex Evangeliorum et Actuum ex collectione Chester Beatty," in *Miscellanea Biblica.* 2: *Scripta pontificii instituti biblici.* Romae: Schola typographica Pio X, 1934. 2:375-406.

3089   James A. Montgomery, "The Ethiopic Text of Acts of the Apostles," *HTR* 27 (1934): 169-205.

3090   H. A. Sanders, "Recent Text Studies in the New Testament," *ATR* 16 (1934): 266-82.

3091   E. R. Smothers, "Les Papyrus Beatty de la Bible grecque," *RechSR* 24 (1934): 12-34.

3092   H. A. Sanders, "Manuscript No. 16 of the Michigan Collection," in Rodney Potter Robinson, ed., *Philological Studies in Honor of Walter Miller.* The University of Missouri Studies. Columbia MO: University of Missouri, 1936. Pp. 141-89.

3093   J. M. Creed, "Two Collations of the Text of Acts in Codex 876: A Vindication of Mr. Valentine-Richards," *JTS* 38 (1937): 395-99.

3094 Frederic G. Kenyon, "Some Notes on the Chester Beatty Gospels and Acts," in Robert P. Casey, Silva Lake, and Agnes K. Lake, eds., *Quantulacumque: Studies Presented to Kirsopp Lake*. London: Christophers, 1937. Pp. 145-48.

3095 J. L. Koole, "Die koptischen übersetzungen der Apostelgeschichte," *BBC* 12 (1937): 65-73.

3096 M. L. W. Laistner, "The Latin Versions of Acts Known to the Venerable Bede," *HTR* 30 (1937): 37-50.

3097 G. Lindeskog, "De senaste textfynden tiu Nya Testamentet," *SEÅ* 2 (1937): 169-73.

3098 H. A. Sanders, "A Third Century Papyrus of Matthew and Acts," in R. P. Casey, et aL., eds., *Quantulacumque: Studies Presented to Kirsopp Lake*. London: Christophers, 1937. Pp. 151-61.

3099 R. V. G. Tasker, "The Nature of the Text of the Chester Beatty Papyrus in Acts," *JTS* 38 (1937): 383-94.

3100 H. Duensing, "Zwei christlich-palästinisch-aramäische Fragmente aus der Apostelgeschichte," *ZNW* 37 (1938): 42-46.

3101 H. A. Sanders and J. M. Creed, "Two Collations of the Text of Acts in Codex 876," *JTS* 39 (1938): 260.

3102 C. C. Tarelli, "Omissions, Additions, and Conflations in the Chester Beatty Papyrus," *JTS* 40 (1939): 382-87.

3103 J. L. Boyer, "The Text of Acts," master's thesis, Oberlin Graduate School of Theology, Oberlin OH, 1940.

3104 Martin Dibelius, "The Text of Acts: An Urgent Critical Task, *JR* 21 (1941): 421-31.

3105 William D. McHardy, "James of Edessa's Citations from the Philoxenian Text of the Book of Acts," *JTS* 43 (1942): 168-73.

3106 George D. Kilpatrick, "Western Text and Original Text in the Gospels and Acts," *JTS* 44 (1943): 24-36.

3107   William D. McHardy, "The Philoxenian Text of the Acts in the
Cambridge Syriac MS Add. 2053," *JTS* 45 (1944): 175.

3108   R. C. Stone, *The Language of the Latin Text of Codex Bezae; With
an Index Verborum.* "Illinois Studies in Language and Literature,"
Vol. 30, Nos. 2-3. Urbana, IL: University of Illinois Press, 1946.

3109   Bruce M. Metzger, "Recently Published Greek Papyri of the New
Testament," *BA* 10 (1947): 25-44.

3110   Gunnar Rudberg, "Kring Codex Cantabrigiensis," *SEÅ* 12 (1947):
287-92.

3111   W. B. Sedgwick, "St. Luke and the π-text," *ET* 59 (1947-1948):
222-23.

3112   William D. McHardy, "The Text of Acts in James of Edessa's
Citations and in the Cambridge Add. MS. 1700," *JTS* 50 (1949):
186-87.

3113   C. Lattey, "The Antiochene Text," *Scr* 4 (1949-1951): 273-77.

3114   F. Amiot, *Gestes et textes des Apôtres. Actes, Epîtres, Apocalypse.
Trad. et notes.* Textes pour l'histoire sacrée choisis et présentes par
Daniel-Rops. Paris: A. Fayard, 1950.

3115   Martin Dibelius, "Der Text der Apostelgeschichte ('Die nachste
Aufgabe')," in *Aufsätze zur Apostelgeschichte* (her ausgegeben von
Heinrich Greeven): *FRLANT* N.F. 42. Heft, 1951. Pp. 76-83.
English translation 1956.

3116   Frederic G. Kenyon, *Handbook to the Textual Criticism of the New
Testament.* Grand Rapids: Eerdmans, 1951.

3117   P.-H. Menoud, "The Western Text and the Theology of Acts,"
NTS 2 (1951): 19-32.

3118   A. W. Argyle, "The Elements of New Testament Textual
Criticism," *BT* 4 (1953): 118-25.

3119   Lucien Cerfaux, "Citations scripturaires et tradition textuelle dans le Livre des Actes," in Lucien Cerfaux, *Études d'Exégèse et d'Histoire Religieuse*. 2 vols. BETL #6-7. Gembloux: J. Duculot, 1954. 2:93-103.

3120   Paul Glaue, "Der älteste Text der geschichtlichen Bücher des Neuen Testaments," *ZNW* 45 (1954): 90-108.

3121   A. F. J. Klijn, "A Medieval Dutch Text of Acts," *NTS* 1 (1954-1955): 51-56.

3122   Gerard Garitte, *L'ancienne version géorgienne des Actes des Apôtres d'après deux manuscrits du Sinaï.* "Bibliothèque du Muséon," Vol. 38. Louvain: Publications Universitaires, 1955.

3123   George D. Kilpatrick, "Codex Bezae and Mill," *JTS* N S. 6 (1955): 235-38.

3124   Manfred Karnetzki, "Textgeschichte als überlieferungsgeschichte," *ZNW* 47 (1956): 170-80.

3125   Michel Tarchnišvilli, "à propos de la plus ancienne version géorgienne des Actes des Apôtres," *Mus* 69 (1956): 347-68.

3126   E. Haenchen, "Zum Text der Apostelgeschichte," *ZTK* 54 (1957): 22-55.

3127   J. N. Birdsall, "The Text of the Acts and the Epistles in Photius," *JTS* N.S. (1958): 278-91.

3128   Jean Duplacy, "Où en est la critique textuelle du Nouveau Testament?" *RechSR* 46 (1958): 270-313.

3129   Hans Lietzmann, "Die Chester-Beatty-Papyri des Neuen Testaments," in *Kleine Schriften. 2: Studien zum Neuen Testament.* "Texte und Untersuchungen zur Geschichte der altchristlichen Literatur," 68. Bd. = 5. Reihe, Bd. 13. Herausgegeben von Kurt Aland. Berlin: Akademie-Verlag, 1958. Pp. 160-69.

3130   A. F. J. Klijn, "A Survey of the Researches into the Western Text of the Gospels and Acts (1949-1959)," *NovT* 3 (1959): 1-27, 161-73.

3131 Frank Pack, "The 'Western' Text of Acts," *RQ* 4 (1960): 220-34.

3132 R. Kasser, ed., *Papyrus Bodmer XVII. Actes des Apôtres, Epîtres de Jacques, Pierre, Jean et Jude.* Cologny-Genève: Bibliotheca Bodmeriana, 1961.

3133 Eldon J. Epp, "The 'Ignorance Motif' in Acts and Anti-Judaic Tendencies in Codex Bezae," *HTR* 55 (1962): 51-61.

3134 P. Prigent, "Un nouveau texte des Actes: Le Papyrus Bodmer XVII, p 74," *RHPR* 42/2-3 (1962): 169-74.

3135 Charles Perrot, "Un Fragment Christo-palestinien Découvert à Khirbet Mird: Actes des Aptres," *RB* 70 (1963): 506-55.

3136 Thorleif Boman, "Das textkritische Problem des sogenannten Aposteldekrets," *NovT* 7/1 (1964): 26-36.

3137 Richard Glover, " 'Luke the Antiochene' and Acts," *NTS* 11/1 (1964): 97-106.

3138 J. Kerschensteiner, "Beobachtungen zum altsyrischen Actatext," *Bib* 45/1 (1964): 63-74.

3139 Pierson Parker, "Three Variant Readings in Luke-Acts," *JBL* 83 (1964): 165-70.

3140 Walter Thiele, "Ausgewählte Biespiele zur Charakterisierung des 'westlichen' Texte der Apostelgeschichte," *ZNW* 56/1-2 (1965): 51-63.

3141 R. P. C. Hanson, "The Provenance of the Interpolator in the 'Western' Text of Acts and of Acts Itself," *NTS* 12/3 (1965-1966): 211-30.

3142 Eldon J. Epp, "Coptic Manuscript G67 and the Role of Codex Bezae as a Western Witness in Acts," *JBL* 85/2 (1966): 197-212.

3143 R. P. C. Hanson, "The Ideology of Codex Bezae in Acts," *NTS* 14 (1967-1968): 282-86.

3144 E. Haenchen and P. Weigandt. "The Original Text of Acts?" *NTS* 14/4 (1968): 469-81.

3145 Y. Tissot, "Les prescriptions des presbytres (Actes 15,41,D). Exégèse et origine du décret dans le texte syro-occidental des *Actes*," *RB* 77/3 (1970): 321-46.

3146 Jan de Waard, "Quotation from Deuteronomy in Acts 3:22-23 and the Palestinian Text: Additional Arguments," *Bib* 52/4 (1971): 537-540.

3147 Everett Ferguson, "Qumran and Codex D," *RevQ* 8/29 (1972): 75-80.

3148 Robert A. Kraft, "A Sahidic Parchment Fragment of Acts 27:4-13 at the University Museum, Philadelphia (E 16690 Coptic 1)," *JBL* 94/2 (1975): 256-65.

3149 James M. Robinson and Robert A. Kraft, "A Sahidic Parchment Fragment of Acts 27:4-13 at the University Museum, Philadelphia (E 16690 Coptic 1)," *JBL* 94/2 (1975): 256-65.

3150 E. G. Edwards, "On Using the Textual Apparatus of the UBS Greek New Testament," *BT* 28/1 (1977): 121-42.

3151 J. Fernández y Fernández, "El manuscrito de Pedro de Valencia que ileva por título en su portada: 'Una gran parte de la Estoria Apostoaalica en los Actos y en la Epístola ad Gálatas'," *CuBí* 34 (1977): 155.

3152 Frank Stagg, "Establishing a Text for Luke-Acts," *SBLSP* 7 (1977): 45-58.

3153 Frank Stagg, "Textual Criticism for Luke-Acts," *PRS* 5 (1978): 152-65.

3154 George D. Kilpatrick, "Three Problems of New Testament Text," *NovT* 21/4 (1979): 289-92.

3155 I. M. Ellis, "Codex Bezae at Acts 15," *IBS* 2 (1980): 134-40.

3156 R. S. MacKenzie, "The Latin Column in Codex Bezae," *JSNT* 6 (1980): 58-76.

3157 J. R. Royse, "The Ethiopic Support for Codex Vaticanus in Acts," *ZNW* 71/3-4 (1980): 258-62.

3158 Eldon J. Epp, "The Ascension in the Textual Tradition of Luke-Acts," in Elton J. Epps and Gordon D. Fee, eds., *New Testament Textual Criticism* (festschrift for Bruce M. Metzger). Oxford: Clarendon Press, 1981. Pp. 131-45.

3159 É. Delebecque, "De Lystres a Philippes (Ac 16) avec le Codex Bezae," *Bib* 63/3 (1982): 395-405.

3160 F. Neirynck, "Note sur le texte occidental des Actes," *ETL* 58/1 (1982): 105.

3161 D. Parker, "A 'Dictation Theory' of Codex Bezae," *JSNT* 15 (1982): 97-112.

3162 H. W. Bartsch, "Traditionsgeschichtliches zur 'Goldenen Regel' und zum Aposteldekret," *ZNW* 75/1 (1984): 128-32.

3163 Ben Witherington, "The Anti-Feminist Tendencies of the 'Western' Text in Acts," *JBL* 103/1 (1984): 82-84.

3164 R. S. MacKenzie, "The Western Text of Acts: Some Lucanisms in Selected Sermons," *JBL* 104/4 (1985): 637-50.

3165 Richard I. Pervo, "Social and Religious Aspects of the Western Text," in Dennis Groh and Robert Jewett, eds., *The Living Text* (festschrift for Ernest Saunders). Lanham MD: University Press of America, 1985. Pp. 229-41.

3166 Gijs Bouwman, "Der Anfang der Apostelgeschichte und der 'westliche' Text," in Tjitze J. Baarda, ed., *Text and Testimony: Essays on New Testament and Apocryphal Literatue* (festschrift for A. F. J. Klijn). Kampen: Hok, 1988. Pp. 46-55.

3167 J. K. Elliott, "The Text of Acts in the Light of Two Recent Studies," *NTS* 34/2 (1988): 250-58.

3168 T. C. Geer, "Codex 1739 in Acts and Its Relationship to Manuscripts 945 and 1891," *Bib* 69/1 (1988): 27-46.

3169 S. H. Levinsohn, *Textual Connections in Acts.* SBLMS #31. Atlanta GA: Scholars Press, 1988.

3170 J. Smit Sibinga, "Acts 9,37 and Other Cases of Ellipsis Obiecti," in Tjitze J. Baarda, ed., *Text and Testimony: Essays on New Testament and Apocryphal Literatue* (festschrift for A. F. J. Klijn). Kampen: Hok, 1988. Pp. 242-46.

3171 S. P. Brock, "The Lost Old Syriac at Luke 1:35 and the Earliest Syriac Terms for the Incarnation," in William L. Petersen, *Gospel Traditions in the Second Century: Origins, Recensions, Text, and Transmission.* Notre Dame IN: University of Notre Dame Press, 1989. Pp 117-31.

3172 S. Peter Cowe, "The Armeno-Georgian Acts of Ephesus: A Reconsideration," *JTS* 40/1 (1989): 125-29.

3173 T. C. Geer, "The Two Faces of Codex 33 in Acts," *NovT* 31/1 (1989): 39-47.

3174 W. A. Strange, "The Problem of the Text of Acts," doctoral dissertation, Oxford University, Oxford UK, 1989.

3175 E. Cothenet, "Les deux Actes de apôtres ou les Actes des deux apôtres," *EV* 100/29 (1990): 425-30.

3176 T. C. Geer, "The Presence and Significance of Lucanisms in the 'Western' Text of Acts," *JSNT* 39 (1990): 59-76.

3177 C. D. Osburn, "The Search for the Original Text of Acts—The International Project on the Text of Acts," *JSNT* 44 (1991): 39-55.

3178 J. H. Petzer, "St. Augustine and the Latin Version of Acts," *Neo* 26 (1991): 33-50.

3179 H.-M. Schenke, ed., *Apostelgeschichte 1:1-15:3 im mittelägyptischen Dialekt des Koptischen.* Texte und Untersuchungen zur Geschichte der altchristlichen Literatur #137. Berlin: Akademie Verlag, 1991.

3180 J. W. Childers, "Corrigenda to Gérard Garitte's Edition of the Old Georgian Acts," *OrChr* 77 (1993): 227-32.

3181 W. A. Meeks, "Who Went Where and How? A Consideration of Acts 17:14," *BT* 44/2 (1993): 201-206.

3182   J. H. Petzer, "The Textual Relationships of the Vulgate and Acts,"
NTS 39/2 (1993): 227-45.

3183   J. H. Petzer, "Variation in Citations from the Old Testament in the
Latin Version of Acts," *JNSL* 19 (1993): 143-57.

3184   G. Betori, "La strutturazione del libro degli Atti: una proposta,"
RBib 42 (1994): 3-34.

3185   A. D. Bulley, "Hanging in the Balance: A Semiotic Study of Acts
20:7-12," *EgT* 25 (1994): 171-88.

3186   C. Niccum, "A Note on Acts 1:14," *NovT* 36 (1994): 196-99.

3187   J. Rius-Camps, "Las variantes de la recensión occidental de los
Hechos de los Apóstoles," *FilN* 6 (1994): 53-64.

3188   Gert Steyn, *Septuagint Quotations in the Context of the Petrine and
Pauline Speeches in the Acta Apostolorum.* Kampen: Hok Pharos,
1995.

theology, various themes

3189   Ernst von Dobschütz, *Christian Life in the Primitive Church.*
Translated by George Bremner, and edited by W. Morrison.
"Theological Translation Library," Vol. 18. New G. P. Putnam;
London: Williams & Norgate, 1904.

3190   C. H. Dodd, "The History and Doctrine of the Apostolic Age," in
T. W. Manson, ed., *A Companion to the Bible.* New York:
Scribner, 1939. Pp. 390-417.

3191   Jacques Dupont, "Repentir et Conversion d'après les Actes des
Apôtres," *SE* 12 (1960): 137-73.

3192   Bo Reicke, "Apostlagarningarnas teologi," *SEÅ* 36 (1960): 1-12.

3193   B. J. Bamberger, "The Sadducees and the Belief in Angels,"in
JBL 82/4 (1963): 433-35.

3194   Gerhard Delling, "Zur Taufe von 'Hausern' im(1984): 53-80.
Urchristentum," *NovT* 7 (1965): 285-311.

3195 F. X. Hezel, " 'Conversion' and 'Repentance' in Lucan Theology," *BibTo* 37 (1968): 2596-2602.

3196 J. S. Hazelton, "El problema de la revelación en el Libro de los Hechos," *CuT* 2 (1972): 213-29.

3197 Johannes Panagopoulos, "Zur Theologie der Apostelgeschichte," *NovT* 14/2 (1972): 137-59.

3198 T. R. Carruth, "The Jesus-as-Prophet Motif in Luke-Acts," doctoral dissertation, Baylor University, Waco TX, 1973.

3199 Stephen G. Wilson, *The Gentiles and the Gentile Mission in Luke-Acts.* SNTS Monograph Series #23. Cambridge: University Press, 1973.

3200 S. Stowers, "The Synagogue in the Theology of Acts," *RQ* 17/3 (1974): 129-43.

3201 J. K. Elliott, "Jerusalem in Acts and the Gospels," *NTS* 23 (1976-1977): 462-69.

3202 Benjamin J. Hubbard, "Commissioning Stories in Luke-Acts: A Study of Their Antecedents, Form and Content," *Semeia* 8 (1977): 103-26.

3203 J. S. Croatto, "El Demonio: La Muerte de un Simbolo," *RevB* 40/169 (1978): 147-52.

3204 George D. Kilpatrick, "Again Acts 7:56: Son of Man?" *TZ* 34/4 (1978): 232.

3205 Dieter Luhrumann, "Glaude im frühen Christentum," *TLZ* 103 (1978): 188-91.

3206 N. M. Flanagan, "The What and How of Salvation in Luke-Acts," in D. Durken, ed., *Sin, Salvation, and the Spirit.* Collegeville MN: Liturgical Press, 1979. Pp. 203-13.

3207 M. Sabbe, "The Son of Man Saying in Acts 7,56," in J. Kremer, ed., *Les Actes des Apôtres.* BETL #48. Louvain: University Press, 1979. Pp. 241-79.

3208 R. I. Garrett, "The Inaugural Addresses of Luke-Acts," doctoral dissertation, Southern Baptist Theological Seminary, Louisville KY, 1980.

3209 D. L. Balas, "The Meaning of the 'Cross'," in Andreas Spira and Christoph Klock, eds., *The Easter Sermons of Gregory of Nyssa.* Cambridge, Massachusetts: Philadelphia Patristic Foundation, 1981. Pp. 305-18.

3210 S. Lyonnet, "La voie' dans les Actes des Apôtres," *RechSR* 69/1 (1981): 149-64.

3211 F. D. Weinert, "The Meaning of the Temple in Luke-Acts," *BTB* 11 (1981): 85-89.

3212 Jack T. Sanders, "The Salvation of the Jews in Luke-Acts," *SBLSP* 12 (1982): 467-83.

3213 Jay E. Adams, "The Church and Her Rights," *FundJ* 2/7 (1983): 16-19.

3214 J. M. Ford, "Reconciliation and Forgiveness in Luke's Gospel," in R. J. Cassidy and P. J. Scharper, eds., *Political Issues in Luke-Acts.* Maryknoll NY: Orbis Books, 1983. Pp. 80-98.

3215 Donald H. Juel, *Luke-Acts: The Promise of History.* Atlanta GA: John Knox Press, 1983.

3216 Joseph Pathrapankal, "Creative Crises of Leadership in the Acts of the Apostles," *IJT* 32/1 (1983): 52-60.

3217 L. Doohan, "Images of God in Luke-Acts," *MillSt* 13 (1984): 17-35.

3218 Joseph G. Kelly, "Lucan Christology and the Jewish-Christian Dialogue," *JES* 21 (1984): 688-708.

3219 Bernard P. Robinson, "The Place of the Emmaus Story in Luke-Acts," *NTS* 30/4 (1984): 481-97.

3220 Joseph Allen, "Renewal of the Christian Community: A Challenge for the Pastoral Ministry," *SVTQ* 29/4 (1985): 305-23.

3221 J. Timothy Coyle, "The Agape—Eucharist Relationship in Corinthians 11," *GTJ* 6/2 (1985): 411-24.

3222 Donald L. Jones, "The Title huios theou in Acts," *SBLSP* 24 (1985): 451-63.

3223 M. P. W. Lewela, "Mary's Faith—Model of Our Own: A Reflection," *AFER* 27 (1985): 92-98.

3224 Erich Lubahn, "Wer ist schuld am Kreuzestode Jesu: Eine Auslegung von Apg 4,27f; 3,18," in Heinz Kremers and Erich Lubahn, eds., *Mission an Israel in heilsgeschichtlicher Sicht* Neukirchen-Vluyn: Neukirchener Verlag, 1985. Pp. 12-23.

3225 Burton L. Mack, "The Innocent Transgressor: Jesus in Early Christian Myth and History," *Semeia* 33 (1985): 135-65.

3226 Antonio Orbe, "Cristo, sacrificio y manjar," *Greg* 66/2 (1985): 185-239.

3227 C. H. Talbert, "Discipleship in Luke-Acts," in F. F. Segovia, ed., *Discipleship in the New Testament.* Philadelphia: Fortress Press, 1985. Pp. 62-75.

3228 R. Fowler White, "The Last Adam and His Seed: An in Theological Preemption," *TriJ* 6 (1985): 60-73.

3229 G. E. Witte, "Salvation and the Law in Luke-Acts," doctoral dissertation, Union Theological Seminary in Virginia, Richmond VA, 1985.

3230 E. Asante, "The Theological Jerusalem of Luke-Acts," *AfTJ* 15 (1986): 172-82.

3231 James A. Berquist, "Good News to the Poor: Why Does This Lucan Motif Appear to Run Dry in the Book of Acts?" *BTF* 18/1 (1986): 1-16.

3232 John R. Donahue, "The 'Parable' of the Sheep and the Goats: A Challenge to Christian Ethics," *JTS* 47/1 (1986): 3-31.

3233 D. L. Tiede, " 'Glory to Thy People Israel!': Luke-Acts and the Jews," *SBLSP* 16 (1986): 142-51.

3234 Robert L. Brawley, *Luke-Acts and the Jews: Conflict, Apology, and Conciliation.* SBL Monograph Series #33. Atlanta GA: Scholars Press, 1987.

3235 Jeff Cranford, "The Synagogue of the Libertines," *BI* 13/3 (1987): 40-41.

3236 Euan Fry, "The Temple in the Gospels and Acts," *BT* 38/2 (1987): 213-21.

3237 J. Kenneth Grider, "Predestination as Temporal Only," *WesTJ* 22 (1987): 56-64.

3238 F. J. Matera, "Acts 10:34-43," *Int* 41/1 (1987): 62-66.

3239 F. D. Weinert, "Luke, Stephen and the Temple in Luke-Acts," *BTB* 17 (1987): 88-90.

3240 A. P. Athyal, "Towards a Soteriology for the Indian Society: Guidelines from Luke-Acts," *BB* 14 (1988): 132-48.

3241 J. Bradley Chance, *Jerusalem, the Temple, and the New Age in Luke-Acts.* Macon GA: Mercer University Press, 1988.

3242 Beverly R. Gaventa, "Toward a Theology of Acts: Reading and Rereading," *Int* 42/2 (1988): 146-57.

3243 S. P. Brock, "The Lost Old Syriac at Luke 1:35 and the Earliest Syriac Terms for the Incarnation," in William L. *Gospel Traditions in the Second Century: Recensions, Text, and Transmission.* Notre Dame University of Notre Dame Press, 1989. Pp 117-31.

3244 Charles L. Cohen, "Two Biblical Models of Conversion: An Example of Puritan Hermeneutics," *ChH* 58 (1989): 182-96.

3245 Brigid C. Frein, "The Literary Significance of the Jesus-as-Prophet Motif in the Gospel of Luke and the Acts of the Apostles," doctoral dissertation, St. Louis University, St. Louis MO, 1989.

3246 Susan R. Garrett, *The Demise of the Devil: Magic and the Demonic in Luke's Writings.* Minneapolis MN: Fortress Press, 1989.

3247   R. B. Hays, "The Righteous One as Eschatological Deliverer: A Case Study in Paul's Apocalyptic Hermeneutics," in Joel Marcus and Marion Soards, eds., *Apocalyptic and the New Testament* (festschrift for J. Louis Martyn). Sheffield: JSOT Press, 1989. Pp 191-215.

3248   John J. Kilgallen, " 'Peace' in the Gospel of Luke and Acts of the Apostles," *SM* 38 (1989): 55-79.

3249   J. L. Stotts, "By What Authority...? (Matthew 21:23): Unscholarly Foray into Acts 2:44-45; 4:32-35," in Robert L. ed., *Reformed Faith and Economics*. Lanham University Press of America, 1989. Pp 3-13.

3250   H. C. Kee, *Good News to the Ends of the Earth: The Theology of Acts*. London: SCM, 1990.

3251   F. J. Matera, "Responsibility for the Death of Jesus according to the Acts of the Apostles," *JSNT* 39 (1990): 77-93.

3252   C. L. Stockhausen, "Luke's Stories of the Ascension: The Background and Function of a Dual Narrative," *EGLMBS* 10 (1990): 251-63.

3253   D. S. Dockery, "The Theology of Acts," *CTR* 5 (1990-1991): 43-55.

3254   Jacob Jervell, "Retrospect and Prospect in Luke-Acts Interpretation," *SBLSP* 21 (1991): 383-404.

3255   Dennis Sweetland, *Our Journey with Jesus: Discipleship in Luke and Acts*. Collegeville: Luturgical Press, 1991.

3256   D. E. Aune, "Christian Prophecy and the Messianic Status of Jesus," in James H. Charlesworth, ed., *The Messiah: Developments in Earliest Judaism and Christianity*. Minneapolis: Fortress Pr, 1992. Pp. 404-22.

3257   S. K. Park, "The Influence of 2 and 4 Maccabees for the Concept of Piety in Luke-Acts," doctoral dissertation, Southwestern Baptist Theological Seminary, Fort Worth TX, 1992.

3258   J. D. G. Dunn, "Baptism in the Spirit: A Response to Pentecostal
       Scholarship on Luke-Acts," *JPTh* 3 (1993): 3-27.

3259   R. L. Loubser, "Wealth, House Churches and Rome: Luke's
       Ideological Perspective, *JTSA* 89 (1994): 59-69.

3260   R. L. Mowery. "The Disappearance of the Father: The References
       to God the Father in Luke-Acts," *Enc* 55/4 (1994): 353-58.

wealth
3261   John P. Allison, "The Concept of Wealth in Luke-Acts," doctoral
       dissertation, New Orleans Baptist Theological Seminary, New
       Orleans LA, 1960.

3262   Ben Johnson, "The Question of Property in the New Testament,"
       in Béla Harmati, ed., *Christian Ethics and the Question of
       Property*. Geneva: Lutheran World Federation, 1982. Pp. 50-58.

3263   D. W. Hager, "Wealth and the Jerusalem Community: The Old
       Testament Influence on Luke's Portrayal in Acts," doctoral
       dissertation, Southern Baptist Theological Seminary, Louisville,
       KY, 1987.

We-passages
3264   Richard Glover, " 'Luke the Antiochene' and Acts," *NTS* 11/1
       (1964): 97-106.

3265   V. K. Robbins, "The We-Passages in Acts and Ancient Sea
       Voyages," *BR* 20 (1975): 5-18.

3266   V. K. Robbins, "By Land and by Sea: The We-Passages and
       Ancient Sea Voyages," *PRS* 5 (1978): 215-42.

3267   Walther Bindemann, "Verkundigter Verkundiger. Das Paulusbild
       der Wir-Stucke in der Apostelgeschichte: seine Aufnahme und
       Bearbeitung durc h Lukas," *TLZ* 114/10 (1989): 705-20.

Women in
3268   Horace E. Coker, "Women and the Gospel in Luke-Acts," doctoral
       dissertation, Southern Baptist Theological Seminary, Louisville KY,
       1954.

3269 Q. Quesnell, "The Women at Luke's Supper," in R. J. Cassidy and P. J. Scharper, eds., *Political Issues in Luke-Acts*. Maryknoll NY: Orbis, 1983. Pp. 59-79.

3270 B. Buby, "Mary, a Model of Ecclesia Orans, in Acts 1:14," Theodore A. Koehler, ed., *Marian Studies*. Vol. 35. Dayton OH: Mariological Society of America, 1984. Pp. 87-99.

3271 Jos Janssens, "Il cristiano di fronte al martirio imminente: testimonianze e dottrina nella chiesa antica," *Greg* 66/3 (1985): 405-427.

3272 Virginia Burrus, "Chastity as Autonomy: Women in the Stories of the Apocryphal Acts," *Semeia* 38 (1986): 101-35.

3273 Richter Reimer, *Women in the Acts of the Apostles: A Feminist Liberation Perspective*. Trans. Linda M. Maloney. Minneapolis: Fortress Press, 1995.

word studies
3274 Jacques Dupont, "Ἀνελήμφθη (Acts 1:2)," *NTS* 8 (1962): 154-57.

3275 Frederic P. Cheetham, "Acts 2:47: ἔχοντες χάριν πρὸς ὅλον τὸν λαόν," *ET* 74 (1963-1964): 214-15.

3276 George D. Kilpatrick, "*Laoi* at Luke ii.31 and Acts iv.25, 27," *JTS* 16 (1965): 127.

3277 W. S. Udick, "Metanoia as Found in the Acts of the Apostles," *BibTo* 28 (1967): 1943-46.

3278 Everett Ferguson, "The Hellenists in the Book of Acts," *RQ* 12/4 (1969): 159-80.

03279 Leslie C. Allen, "The Old Testament Background of (προ)ὡρισμένη in the New Testament," *NTS* 17/1 (1970-1971): 104-108.

3280 Gerhard Delling, "Das Letzte Wort der Apostelgeschichte," *NovT* 15/3 (1973): 193-204.

3281 I. Howard Marshall, "New Wine in Old Wineskins: V. The Biblical Use of the Word 'Ekklesia'," *ET* 84/12 (1973): 359-64.

3282   J. H. Roberts, "Ekklēsia in Acts—Linguistic and Theology: A Venture in Methodology," *Neo* 7 (1973): 73-93.

3283   B. H. Throckmorton, "Σοζειν, σοτερια in Luke-Acts," *StudE* 6 (1973): 515-26.

3284   Donald L. Jones, "The Title κυριος in Luke-Acts," *SBLSP* 4/2 (1974): 85-101.

3285   Frank Stagg, "The Unhindered Gospel," *RevExp* 71/4 (1974): 451-62.

3286   C. J. Hemer, "The Adjective 'Phrygia'," *JTS* 27/1 (1976): 122-26.

3287   S. A. Panimolle, "La charis negli Atti e nel quarto vangelo," *RBib* 25/2 (1977): 143-58.

3288   Joseph Plevik, " 'The Eleven and Those with Them' According to Luke," *CBQ* 40/2 (1978): 205-11.

3289   Max Wilcox, "The 'God-Fearers' in Acts: A Reconsideration," *JSNT* 13 (1981): 102-22.

3290   Donald L. Jones "The Title Παις in Luke-Acts," *SBLSP* 12 (1982): 217-26.

3291   George D. Kilpatrick, "Epithuein and Epikrinein in the Greek Bible," *ZNW* 74/1 (1983): 151-53.

3292   Dennis D. Sylva, "*Ierousalèm* and *Hierosoluma* in Luke-Acts," *ZNW* 74 (1983): 207-21.

3293   Charles H. Cosgrove, "The Divine δει in Luke-Acts: Investigations into the Lukan Understanding of God's Providence," *NovT* 26 (1984): 168-90.

3294   C. Burchard, "A Note on Ῥῆμα in JosAs 17:1F; Luke 2:15, 17; Acts 10:37," *NovT* 27/4 (1985): 281-95.

3295   Kevin N. Giles, "Luke's Use of the Term 'Ekklesia' with Special Reference to Acts 20.28 and 9.31," *NTS* 31/1 (1985): 135-42.

03296 Wayne Grudem, "Does κεφαλη ('Head') Mean 'Source' or 'Authority Over' in Greek Literature: A Survey of 2,336 Examples," *TriJ* 6 (1985): 38-59.

3297 Peter R. Rodgers, "Acts 2:18: καὶ προφητεύσουσιν," *JTS* 38 (1987): 95-97.

3298 T. David Anderson, "The Meaning of ἔχοντες χάριν πρὸς in Acts 2:47," *NTS* 34/4 (1988): 604-10.

3299 Gert Steuernagel, "'Ακούοντες μὲν τῆς φωνῆς: Ein Genitiv in der Apostelgeschichte," *NTS* 35/4 (1988-1989): 619-24.

3300 J. Carrón Pérez, "El significado de ἀποκαταστάσεως en Hch 3,21," *EB* 50/1-4 (1992): 375-94.

3301 C. Munier, "Le témoignage du livre des Actes sur l'initiation chrétienne," in *Memoriam sanctorum venerantes* (festschrift for Victor Saxer). Rome: Pontifical Press, 1992. Pp. 587-97.

3302 J. M. Ross, "The Spelling of Jerusalem in Acts," *NTS* 38 (1992): 474-76.

3303 A. Suhl, "Zum Titel πρώτῳ τῆς νήσου," *BZ* 36 (1992): 220-26.

3304 A. Barbi, "The Use and Meaning of (Hoi) Ioudaioi in Acts," in Gerald O'Collins and G. Marconi, eds., *Luke and Acts* (festschrift for Emilio Rasco). Mahwah NJ: Paulist Press, 1993. Pp. 123-42.

3305 S. Haar, "Lens or Mirror: The Image of Simon and Magic in Early Christian Literature," *LTJ* 27 (1993): 113-21.

3306 R. E. Oster, "Supposed Anachronism in Luke-Acts' Use of συναγωγή," *NTS* 39/2 (1993): 178-208.

3307 B. Prete, "Il contenuto ecclesiologico del termine 'eredità' (κλῆρος) in Atti 26,18," *SacD* 38 (1993): 625-53.

3308 H. Szesnat, "What Did the σκηνοποιός Paul Produce?" *Neo* 27 (1993): 391-402.

3309 P. Ellingworth, "Acts 13:38—A Query," *BT* 45 (1994): 242-43.

3310 J. Everts, "Tongues or Languages? Contextual Consistency in the Translation of Acts 2," *JPT* 4 (1994): 71-80.

3311 C. S. de Vos, "The Significance of the Change from οἶκος to οἰκία in Luke's Account of the Philippian Gaoler," *NTS* 41/2 (1995): 292-96.

worship

3312 ｜E. Glenn Hinson, "Worship in the First Century Church," *BI* 1/2 (1975): 34-41.

3313 R. F. O'Toole, "Paul at Athens and Luke's Notion of Worship," *RBib* 89/2 (1982): 185-97.

PART THREE

Commentaries

3314 H. Cornish, *Acts of the Apostles*. London: Evans, 1900.

3315 R. J. Knowling, *The Acts of the Apostles*. "The Expositor's Greek Testament." Edited by W. Robertson Nicoll. New York: Dodd, Meade & Co., 1900.

3316 J. Vernon Bartlet, *The Acts*. The New-Century Bible. New York/Edinburgh: Oxford/T. C. & E. C. Jack, 1901.

3317 F. N. Peloubet, *The Teacher's Commentary on the Acts of the Apostles*. New York; London: Oxford University Press, 1901.

3318 W. G. Moorehead, *Outline Studies in Acts, Romans, First and Second Corinthians, Galatians and Ephesians*. Chicago; New York; Toronto; London; Edinburgh: Fleming H. Revell, 1902.

3319 F. C. Ceulemans, *Commentarius in Actus Apostolorum*. Malines: H. Dessain, 1903.

3320 E. H. Plumptre, *The Acts of the Apostles*. "The New Testament Commentary," Vol. 5. Edited by Charles John Ellicott. London; Paris; New York; Melbourne: Cassell, 1903.

3321 J. E. Belser, *Die Apostelgeschichte. übersetzt und erklärt.* Kurzgefasster wissenschaftlicher Kommentar zu den heiligen Schriften des Neuen Testamentes, 3. Band I. Hälfte. Herausgegeben von Bernhard Schäfer und P. Erasmus Nagl. Wien: Mayer, 1905.

3322 A. E. Hillard, *The Acts of the Apostles with Introduction, Notes, and Maps*. "Rivingtons' Books of the Bible." London: Rivingtons, 1905.

3323 Otto Pfleiderer, *Die Entstehung des Christentums*. München: J. F. Lehmann, 1905.

3324 V. Rose, *Les Actes des Apôtres*. "La Pensée chrétienne. Textes et Études." Paris: Bloud, 1905.

3325 Émile Le Camus, *L œuvre des Apôtres. Fondation de l'Église chrétienne*. 3 tomes. Paris: H. Ouden, 1906.

3326 G. H. Gilbert, *A Short History of Christianity in the Apostolic Age.* "Constructive Bible Studies." Edited by Ernest DeWitt Burton. Chicago: Univ. of Chicago Press, 1906.

3327 Rudolf Knopf, *Die Apostelgeschichte.* "Die Schriften des Neuen Testaments." Herausgegeben von Johannes Weiss. 2 Bde. Bd. 1: *Die drei älteren Evangelien. Die Apostelgeschichte.* Göttingen: Vandenhoeck & Ruprecht, 1906. 2. Aufl., 1907. 3. Aufl., 1917 (Herausgegeben von Wilhelm Bousset und Wilhelm Heitmüller. 4 Bde. Bd. 3).

3328 Thomas Morrison, *The Acts of the Apostles and the Epistles of Paul Arranged in the Form of a Continuous History.* 3d ed. Edinburgh; London: Oliphant, Anderson & Ferrier, 1906.

3329 Bernhard Weiss, *A Commentary on the New Testament.* 4 vols. Vol. 2: *Luke-The Acts.* Translated by George H. Schodde and Epiphanius Wilson. New York; London: Funk & Wagnalls, 1906.

3330 Marcus Dods, et al., "The Acts of the Apostles," *An Exposition of the Bible. A Series of Expositions Covering All the Books of the Old and the New Testament.* Vol. 5: *St. Luke-Galatians.* Hartford, Connecticut: S. S. Scranton, 1907. Pp. 289-512.

3331 H. P. Forbes, *The Johannine Literature and the Acts of the Apostles.* International Handbooks to the New Testament. New York; London: G. P. Putnam, 1907.

3332 Alexander Maclaren, *The Acts.* 2 vols. "Expositions of Holy Scripture." London; New York; Toronto: Hodder & Stoughton, 1907.

3333 B. Reynolds and G. H. S. Walpole, *Handbook to the Acts of the Apostles. For the Use of Teachers and Students.* Part 1: *Chapters 1-15.* Part 2: *Chapters* 16-28. "Rivingtons Handbooks to the Bible and Prayer-Book." London: Rivingtons, 1907.

3334 J. Stadler, *Djela Apostolska od sv. Luka.* Sarajevo, 1907.

3335 H. Andrews, *The Acts of the Apostles.* The Westminster New Testament. New York/London: Revell/Andrew Melrose, 1908.

3336   G. H. Gilbert, *Acts. The Second Volume of Luke's Work on the Beginnings of Christianity with Interpretative Comment.* "The Bible for Home and School." Edited by Shailer Mathews. New York: Macmillan, 1908.

3337   E. Jacquier, "Les Actes des Apôtres," in *Histoire des livres du Nouveau Testament.* Tome 3. 3ᵉ éd. Paris: J. Gabalda, 1908. Pp. 1-188.

3338   E. M. Knox, *The Acts of the Apostles.* London: Macmillan, 1908.

3339   F. Niebergall, *Lukas. Die Apostelgeschichte.* "Handbuch zum Neuen Testament," Bd. 5. Herausgegeben von H. Lietzmann. Tübingen: J. C. B. Mohr, 1908.

3340   John Brown, *The Students' Comprehensive Topical Bible Commentary.* Toledo OH: O. A. Browning, 1909.

3341   Eugène de Faye, *Étude sur les origines des églises de l'âge apostolique.* "Bibliotheque de l'École des hautes Études. Sciences religieuses," Tome 23. Paris: Ernest Leroux, 1909.

3342   Adolf Harnack, *New Testament Studies.* 3: *The Acts of the Apostles.* Translated by J. R. Wilkinson. "Crown Theological Library," Vol. 27. New York: G. P. Putnam; London: Williams & Norgate, 1909.

3343   L. Ragg, *The Church of the Apostles. Being an Outline of the History of the Church of the Apostolic Age.* "The Church Universal," Vol. 1. Edited by W. H. Hutton. New York: Macmillan, 1909.

3344   E. W. Rice, *Peoples Commentary on the Acts.* "Green Fund Book," No. 2. 4th ed. Philadelphia: American Sunday School Union, 1909.

3345   W. S. Hooton, *Turning-Points in the Primitive Church.* "Thynnes Theological Library." London: Chas. J. Thynne, 1910.

3346   H. C. O. Lanchester, *The Acts of the Apostles.* "Smaller Cambridge Bible for School." Cambridge: University Press, 1910.

3347   P. V. Girard, *Les quatre Évangiles et les Actes des Apôtres.* Tours: A. Cattier, 1911.

3348   J. Mader, *Die heiligen vier Evangelien und die Apostelgeschichte*. Einsiedeln: Benziger, 1911.

3349   H. Pfeifer, *Die Geschichte der Apostel und des Urchristentums*. Leipzig: Hahn, 1911.

3350   W. R. Shook, *A Brief Explanatory Commentary and Lexicon on the New Testament*. Chicago: Hammond, 1911.

3351   E. Dentler, *Die Apostelgeschichte. übersetzt und erklärt*. Mergentheim: Karl Ohlinger, 1912.

3352   W. H. Flecker, *The Acts of the Apostles*. 2 parts. London: W. B. Clive, 1912.

3353   W. M. Furneaux, *The Acts of tlte Apostles. A Commentary for English Readers*. Oxford: Clarendon Press, 1912.

3354   A. C. Gaebelein, *The Acts of the Apostles: An Exposition*. London: Pickering & Inglis, 1912.

3355   Erwin Preuschen, *Die Apostelgeschichte*. "Handbuch zum Neuen Testament," Bd. 4, Teil 1. Tübingen: J. C. B. Mohr (Paul Siebeck), 1912.

3356   A. C. Gaebelein, *The Annotated Bible*. Vol. I: *The Gospels and the Book of Acts*. New York: "Our Hope"; Glasgow: Pickering & Inglis; Winnipeg: Northwestern Bible & Tract Depot, 1913.

3357   Gustav Hoennicke, *Die Apostelgeschichte erklärt*. "Evangtheol. Bibliothek. Kommentar zum N.T." Leipzig: Quelle & Meyer, 1913.

3358   E. Jacquier, *Le Nouveau Testament dans l'Église chrétienne*. Tome 2: *Le Texte du Nouveau Testament*. Paris: Gabalda, 1913.

3359   R. Staude, *Neues Testament: Apostelgeschichte*. Dresden: Bieyl & Kammerer, 1913.

3360   H. H. Wendt, *Die Apostelgeschichte*. "Kritischexegetischer Kommentar über das Neue Testament," 3. Abtheilung, 8. Aufl. Begrundet von Heinr. Aug. Wilh. Meyer. Göttingen: Vandenhoeck & Ruprecht, 9. Aufl., 1913.

3361 Karl Aner, *Die Apostelgeschichte*. Praktische Bibelerklärung, 7. Tübingen: Mohr, 1915.

3362 G. A. McLaughlin, *Commentary on the Acts of the Apostles*. Chicago: Christian Witness Co., 1915.

3363 C. F. Sitterly, *Jerusalem to Rome. The Acts of the Apostles. A New Translation and Commentary, with Introduction, Maps, Reconstructions and Illustrations from Christian Art*. New York; Cincinnati: Abingdon, 1915.

3364 E. S. Young, *Acts of the Apostles*. Elgin, Illinois. Bible Student Co., 1915.

3365 T. A. Burge, *Acts of the Apostles*. 2 vols. New York: Benziger, 1916.

3366 W. F. Burnside, *The Acts of the Apostles*. The Greek Text Edited with Introduction and Notes for the Use of Schools. Cambridge Greek Testament for Schools and Colleges. Cambridge: University Press, 1916.

3367 W. O. Carver, *The Acts of the Apostles*. Nashville: Broadman, 1916.

3368 William Evans, *The Gospels and the Acts of the Apostles*. "Through the Bible Book by Book." New York; Chicago; Toronto; London; Edinburgh: Fleming H. Revell, 1917.

3369 R. Hutchings and M. C. Synge, *Studies in the Acts of the Apostles. Chapters 1-12*. Edited by S. C. Carpenter. London: S.P.C.K., 1917.

3370 C. E. Stansfield, *The Acts of the Apostles*. London: Teachers and Taught Officers, 1917.

3371 Charles J. Callan, *The Acts of the Apostles, with a Practical Critical Commentary for Priests and Students*. New York: Joseph F. Wagner, 1919.

3372 Charles R. Erdman, *The Acts. An Exposition*. Philadelphia: Westminster, 1919.

3373 F. Ogara, *Hechos Apostólicos en Lecciones Sacras*. Tomo 1: *San Pedro (c. 1-12)*. Tomo 2: *Sait Pablo (c. 13-28)*. Bilbao: Editorial Viscaina, 1919.

3374 Allan Menzies, "The Acts of the Apostles," *A Commentary on the Bible*. Edited by Arthur S. Peake. New York: Thomas Nelson; London: T. C. & E. C. Jack, 1920. Pp. 776-884.

3375 A. Omodeo, *Prolegomeni alla storia dell' età apostolica. 1: Gli Atti degli Apostoli*. "Studi Filosofici," 5. Diretti da Giovanni Gentile. Messina: Casa editrice Giuseppe Principato, 1920.

3376 I.-C. Fillion, "Les Actes des Apôtres," in *La Sainte Bible. Commentée d'après la Vulgate et les textes originaux à l'usage des séminaires et du clergé*. Tome 7. 4ᵉ éd. Paris: Letouzey & Ané, 1921. Pp. 610-817.

3377 Eduard Meyer, *Ursprung und Anfänge des Christentums*. 3 Bde. Stuttgart; Berlin: J. G. Cotta, 1921-1923.

3378 Maurice Goguel, *Introduction au Nouveau Testament*. Tome 3: *Le livre des Actes*. "Bibliothèque historique des religions." Paris: Ernest Leroux, 1922.

3379 E. L. Hawkins, *The Student's Guide to the Gospels and the Acts.*. Ofxord: A. T. Shrimpton, 1897. New and enlarged edition. London: Giles, 1922.

3380 F. Marshall, *The Acts of the Apostles—Revised Version. With Introduction and Notes*. "The School and College Edition." London: George Gill & Sons, 1922.

3381 A. Reukauf and H. Winzer, *Geschichte der Apostel*. "Evangelischer Religionsunterricht," Bd. 9. Herausgegeben von A. Reukauf und E. Heyn. 2. Aufl. Leipzig: Ernst Wunderlich, 1907. 3. Aufl., 1911. 4. Aufl., 1922.

3382 Alexander Souter, "Acts," in his *Pelagius's Expositions of Thirteen Epistles of St Paul. 1: Introduction*. "Texts and Studies," Vol. 9, No. 1. Edited by J. Armitage Robinson. Cambridge: University Press, 1922. Pp. 169-71.

3383 Theodor Zahn, *Die Apostelgeschichte des Lucas.* 1: Kap. 1-12. "Kommentar zum Neuen Testament," Bd. 5, H. 1. Herausgegeben von Theodor Zahn. 3. Aufl., Leipzig; Erlangen: A. Deichert (Werner Scholl): 1922.

3384 A. W. F. Blunt, *The Acts of the Apostles. In the Revised Version. With Introduction and Commentary.* The Clarendon Bible. Edited by Herbert Wild and G. H. Box. Oxford: Clarendon Press, 1923.

3385 A. Camerlynck, *Commentarius in Actus Apostolorum.* Ed. 6. "Commentarii Brugenses in S. Scripturam a J. A. Van Steenkiste primum editi." 7th ed., A. Camerlynck and A. Vander Heeren. Bruges: Carolus Beyaert, 1923.

3386 F. J. Knecht, *A Practical Commentary on Holy Scripture for the Use of Those Who Teach Bible History.* Translated and Adapted from the 16th German ed. 4th English ed. London, St. Louis MO: Herder, 1923.

3387 H. F. Rall, *New Testament History: A Study of the Beginnings of Christianity.* "Bible Study Textbook Series." New York, Abingdon, 1923.

3388 W. Nawijn, *Aanteekeningen en Woordenlijstje bij de Handelingen der Apostelen.* Kampen: J. H. Kok, 1924.

3389 Jakob Schäfer, *Die Apostelgeschichte. übersetzt und erklärt.* Steyl; Kaldenkirchen (Rhl.): Missionsdruckerei, 1924.

3390 Charles Brown, *The Acts of the Apostles.* 2 vols. London: R.T.S., 1924-1925.

3391 Ferdinand Brockes, *Die Apostelgeschichte des Lukas. Umschrieben und erlaut.* Halle: Heimat-Verlag, 1925.

3392 L. E. Browne, *The Acts of the Apostles: With Introduction and Notes.* The Indian Church Commentaries. London: S.P.C.K., 1925.

3393 M. Cecilia, *The Acts of the Apostles: With Introduction and Annotations.* London: Burns, Oates & Washbourne, 1925.

3394   Charles Knapp, *The Acts of the Apostles. With Introduction, Map and Notes. Revised Version.* "Commentary for Schools." London: T. Murby, 1925.

3395   A. Loisy, *Les Actes des Apôtres.* Paris: F. Rieder, 1925.

3396   Jakob Schäfer, *Das heilige Evangelium Jesu Christi und die Apostelgeschichte. übersetzt und erklärt.* Steyl: Missionsdruckerei, 1925.

3397   Emilio Cristofoletti, *Gli Atti degli apostoli: Traduzione e note.* Letture bibliche. Torino: Società Ed. Internazionale, 1926.

3398   E. Jacquier, *Les Actes des Apôtres.* 2ᵉ éd. "Études bibliques." Paris: Victor Lecoffre, 1926.

3399   Evelyn Parker, *Introduction to the Acts of the Apostles and the Epistles of St. Paul.* London; New York; Toronto; Bombay; Calcutta; Madras: Longmans, Green & Co., 1927.

3400   P. Simon, *Praelectiones biblicae ad usum scholarum. N. T.* Tomus 2: *Introductio et commentarius in Actus Apostolorum, Epistolas et Apocalypsim.* Roma; Torino: Marietti, 1927.

3401   C. J. Södergren, *The Acts with Commentaries.* Rock Island, Illinois: Augustana Book Concern, 1927.

3402   Theodor Zahn, *Die Apostelgeschichte des Lucas.* 2: Kap. 13-28. "Kommentar zum Neuen Testament," Bd. 5, H. 2. Herausgegeben von Theodor Zahn. 4. Aufl., Leipzig: A. Deichert (Werner Scholl): 1927.

3403   "The Acts of the Apostles," in C. H. Irwin, ed., *The Universal Bible Commentary.* London, Manchester, Toronto, Madrid, Lisbon, Budapest: Religious Tract Society, 1928. Pp. 442-72.

3404   E. J. Bucknell, "The Acts of the Apostles," in Charles Gore, et al., eds., *A New Commentary on Holy Scripture.* III: *The New Testament.* London: S.P.C.K., 1928. 3:320-78.

3405   Eugène de Faye, *Les Actes des Apôtres.* "La Bible du Centenaire," Tome 2. Paris, 1928.

3406   Charles Gore, et al., eds., *A New Commentary on Holy Scripture.*
       III: *The New Testament.* London: S.P.C.K., 1928.

3407   C. H. Irwin, ed., *The Universal Bible Commentary.* London,
       Manchester, Toronto, Madrid, Lisbon, Budapest: Religious Tract
       Society, 1928.

3408   W. F. Moulton, *The Old World and the New Faith. Notes upon the
       Historical Narrative Contained in the Acts of the Apostles.* "Books
       for Bible Students." Edited by A. E. Gregory. London: C. H.
       Kelly, 1896. 2d ed. London: Epworth Press, 1928.

3409   Alex Pallis, *Notes on St. Luke and the Acts.* London; Edinburgh;
       Glasgow; Copenhagen; New York; Toronto; Melbourne; Capetown;
       Bombay; Calcutta; Madras; Shanghai: Oxford University Press,
       1928.

3410   E. W. Burch, "Acts of the Apostles," in F. C. Eisèlen, et al., eds.,
       The Abingdon Bible Commentary. Nashville: Abingdon-Cokesbury,
       1929. Pp. 1904-34.

3411   Carles Cardó and Antoni Maria de Barcelona, "Actes dels
       Apòstols," in *La Sagrada Biblia. Nou Testament.* Barcelona:
       Editorial Alpha, 1929. 13:1-80.

3412   F. C. Eiselen, et al., eds., *The Abingdon Bible Commentary.*
       Nashville: Abingdon-Cokesbury, 1929.

3413   J. E. Niederhuber, *Das NeueTestament für religiöse Gebildete nach
       dem Griechischen übersetzt und erklärt.* Teil 2. *Die
       Apostelgeschichte und die vier grossen Paulusbriefe.* Regensburg:
       Josef Habbel, 1930.

3414   Arthur Quiller-Couch, *The Acts of the Apostles. With an
       Introduction.* London: J. M. Dent & Sons, 1930.

3415   Frank E. Allen, *The Acts of the Apostles.* Boston: Christopher
       Publishing House, 1931.

3416   F. W. A. Bosch, *Through the Book of Acts With a Guide.*
       RichmondVA: Onward Press, 1931.

3417 F. J. Foakes-Jackson, *The Acts of the Apostles.* Moffatt New Testament Commentary. New York: Richard R. Smith, 1931.

3418 W. G. Scroggie, *The Acts of the Apostles.* "The Study Hour Series." London; Edinburgh: Marshall, Morgan & Scott, 1931.

3419 Lyder Brun, *Segen und Fluch im Urchristentum.* "Skrifter utgitt av Det Norske Videnskaps-Akademi i Oslo," 2. Hist. Filos. Klasse. 1932. Nr. I. Oslo: Dybwad, 1932.

3420 E. J. Bucknell, *The Acts of the Apostles.* London: S.P.C.K., 1932.

3421 W. M. Miller, *Tafseer kitabi A'mali rasoolan.* Leipzig: August Preis, 1932.

3422 David Smith, "The Acts of the Apostles," *The Disciples' Commentary on the New Testament. Vol.* 4. London: Hodder & Stoughton, 1932. Pp. 1-284.

3423 J. de Zwaan, *De Handelingen der Apostelen.* "Tekst en Uitleg. Praktische Bijbelverklaring," 2: *Het Nieuwe Testament.* 2nd. ed. Door F. M. Th. Böhl en A. van Veldhuizen. Groningen: J. B. Wolters, 1932.

3424 Adrien Boudou, *Actes des Apôtres. Traduits et commentés.* Verbum Salutis #7. Paris: Gabriel Beauchesne, 1933.

3425 A. C. Clark, *The Acts of the Apostles. A Critical Edition with Introduction and Notes on Selected Passages.* Oxford: Clarendon, 1933.

3426 I. Snoek, *De Handelingen der apostelen.* Rotterdam: Nijgh & Van Ditmar, 1933.

3427 P. Boggio, *Gli Atti degli Apostoli e la prima Epistola ai Corinzi.* Edizioni Favero #10. Vicenza: Favero, 1934.

3428 Karl Bornhauser, *Studien zur Apostelgeschichte.* Gütersloh: C. Bertelsmann, 1934.

3429 R. C. H. Lenski, *The Interpretation of the Acts of the Apostles.* Columbus, Ohio: Lutheran Book Concern, 1934.

3430 F. Mahr, *Eine Einführung in die Apostelgeschichte*. Meitlingen: Christkönigsverlag, 1935.

3431 Wilhelm Michaelis, *Das Neue Testament verdeutscllt und erläutert*. Bd. 2: *Taten der Apostel, Briefe, Offenbarung* (=Kröners Taschenausgabe, Bd. 121). Leipzig, 1935.

3432 Andrew Sledd, *His Witnesses. A Study of the Book of Acts*. Nashville: Cokesbury, 1935.

3433 J. Aberly, "The Acts," in Herbert C. Alleman, ed., *New Testament Commentary. A General Introduction to and a Commentary on the Books of the New Testament*. Philadelphia: The Board of Publication of the United Lutheran Church in America, 1936. Pp. 399-442. Rev. ed., 1944.

3434 Herbert C. Alleman, ed., *New Testament Commentary. A General Introduction to and a Commentary on the Books of the New Testament*. Philadelphia: The Board of Publication of the United Lutheran Church in America, 1936. Rev. ed., 1944.

3435 Otto Cohausz, "Die Apostelgeschichte," in *Herders Bibelkommentar*. Bd. 12. Freiburg: Herder, 1936. Pp. 241-488.

3436 Sigurd Odland, *Fortolkning av Apostlenes gjerninger. For troende og tenkende bibellesere*. Oslo: Lutherstift, 1936.

3437 H. E. Dana, *Jewish Christianity. An Expository Survey of Acts 1-12, James, 1 and 2 Peter, Jude and Hebrews*. New Orleans: Bible Institute Memorial Press, 1937.

3438 J. Keulers, *De Handelingen der Apostel*. "De Boeken van het N.T.," 4. Roermond-Maaseik: J. J. Romen & Zonen, 1937. 2. uitgave, 1952.

3439 Hugh Pope, *The Catholic Students' "Aids" for the Study of the Bible. Vol. 5: The New Testament. Acts, Epistles and Apocalypse*. 2d ed. London: Burns, Oates & Washbourne, 1937.

3440 R. Eaton, *Acts of the Apostles*. 2 vols. London: C.T.S., 1938.

3441 Holger Mosbech, *Apostlenes Gerninger, indledet og forklaret*. Kopenhavn: Gyldendal, 1929. 2. Udg., 1938.

3442 Sigurd Odland, *Kommentar till Apostlagärningarna.* övers. från norskan av M. Berglid och D. Hedegard. Stockholm: Fosterl.-stift, 1938.

3443 Silvio Rosadini, *Actus Apostolorum et epistolae Paulinae.* "Institutiones introductoriae in libros N.T.," Tomus 2. Romae: Apud Aedes Universitatis gregorianae, 1938.

3444 Otto Bauernfeind, *Die Apostelgeschichte.* Theologischer Handkommentar zum Neuen Testament, Band 5. Bearbeitet von P. Althaus und Andere. Leipzig: A. Deichert, 1939.

3445 A. Crampon, *Les Actes des Apôtres, traduction faite sur le texte original par le Chanoine A. Crampon. Traduction, introduction et notes revues par A. Tricot.* Paris, Tournai, Rome: Desclée, 1939.

3446 Peter Ketter, *Die Apostelgeschichte.* Stuttgart: Kepplerhaus, 1939.

3447 H. Leo Boles, *A Commentary on Acts of the Apostles.* Nashville TN: Gospel Advocate, 1941.

3448 Ernest Gordon, *Notes From A Layman's Greek Testament.* Boston: W. A. Wilde, 1941.

3449 J. Renié, *Manuel d'Écriture sainte.* Tome 5: *Les Actes des Apôtres. Les Épitres catholiques. L'Apocalypse.* Lyon; Paris: E. Vitte, 1936. 2ᵉ éd., 1941.

3450 W. A. Dowd, "Acts of the Apostles," in *A Commentary on the New Testament.* Prepared by the Catholic Biblical Association: The Catholic Biblical Association, 1942. Pp. 365-405.

3451 C. T. Craig, *The Beginning of Christianity.* New York; Nashville: Abingdon-Cokesbury, 1943.

3452 G. T. Stokes, *The Acts of the Apostles.* 2 vols. in "The Expositor's Bible," Vol. 5. Grand Rapids MI: Wm. B. Eerdmans, 1943. Pp. 289-512.

3453 D. A. Frøvig, *Kommentar til Apostlenes Gjerninger. Med innledning.* Oslo: Aschehoug, 1944.

3454 Juan Straubinger, *Los Hechos de los Apóstoles. Traducción directa del original griego, notas y comentario.* Montevideo: Ediciones Aldu, 1945.

3455 G. C. Morgan, *The Acts of the Apostles.* New York; Chicago; London; Edinburgh: Fleming H. Revell, 1924. London: Pickering & Inglis, 1946.

3456 D. W. Martin, *Witnesses to the World. A Popular Commnentary on the Acts of the Apostles.* "Jackson Series." Huntington, Indiana: Our Sunday Visitor Press, 1947.

3457 R. Rackham, *The Acts of the Apostles. An Exposition.* "Westminster Commentaries." Edited by Walter Lock and D. C. Simpson. 13th ed. London: Methuen, 1947.

3458 Rupert Storr, *Die Apostelgeschichte.* Stuttgart: Schwabenverlag, 1947.

3459 B. H. Carroll, *The Acts.* 8: *An Interpretation of the English Bible,* J. B. Cranfill, ed. New York; Chicago; Toronto; London; Edinburgh: Fleming H. Revell, 1916. Nashville: Broadman, 1943. 1948 (Vol. 12).

3460 Wilfred L. Knox, *The Acts of the Apostles.* Cambridge: University Press, 1948.

3461 M. Lepin, *Actes des Apôtres, Epîtres, Apocalypse.* St.-Étienne: Dumas, 1948.

3462 John Calvin, *Commentary Upon the Acts of the Apostles.* Edited from the Original English Translation of Christopher Fetherstone, by Henry Beveridge. 2 vols. Edinburgh: Calvin Translation Society, 1844; Grand Rapids MI: Eerdmans, 1949.

3463 F. Amiot, *Gestes et textes des Apôtres. Actes, Epîtres, Apocalypse. Trad. et notes.* Textes pour l'histoire sacrée choisis et présentes par Daniel-Rops. Paris: A. Fayard, 1950.

3464 F. W. Grosheide, *De Handelingen der Apostelen (Korte Verklaring).* Kampen: J. H. Kok, 1950.

3465   A. Makrakis, *Interpretation of the Entire Neu Testament*. Vol. 2: *The Acts of the Apostles*. Translated by Albert George Alexander. Chicago: Orthodox Christian Education Society, 1950.

3466   J. Kürzinger, *Die Apostelgeschichte*. "Die Heilige Schrift in deutscher übersetzung. Echter-Bibel. Das Neue Testament." Herausgegeben von Karl Staab. Würzburg: Echter, 1951.

3467   J. A. Findlay, *The Acts of the Apostles: A Commentary*. London: S.C.M., 1952.

3468   William Kelly, *An Exposition of the Acts of the Apostles. With a New Version of a Corrected Text*. 3d ed. London: C. A. Hammond, 1952.

3469   I. Saint-Arnaud, *Les Actes des Apôtres. Traduction sur le texte grec et annoté pour le compte de l'Association catholique des études bibliques au Canada*. Montreal: Éditions Fides, 1952.

3470   E. M. Zerr, *Bible Commentary*. Vol. 5: *Matthew-Romans*. St. Louis: Mission Messenger, 1952.

3471   C. S. Dessain, "The Acts of the Apostles," in Bernard Orchard, et al., eds., *A Catholic Commentary on Holy Scripture*. London, Edinburgh, Paris, Melbourne, Toronto, New York: Nelson, 1953. Pp. 1018-44.

3472   H. A. Guy, *The Acts of the Apostles*. London: Macmillan, 1953.

3473   Willibald Michaux, "De la Communaute de Jérusalem aux Églises pauliniennes," *BVC* 3 (1953): 72-82.

3474   R. R. Williams, *The Acts of the Apostles*. Torch Bible Commentaries. Edited by John Marsh, Alan Richardson, and R. Gregor Smith. London: S.C.M., 1953.

3475   F. F. Bruce, "The Acts of the Apostles," in F. Davidson, et al., eds., *The New Bible Commentary*. 2nd ed. London: InterVarsity Fellowship, 1954.

3476   F. Davidson, et al., eds., *The New Bible Commentary*. 2nd ed. London: InterVarsity Fellowship, 1954.

3477 Maurice Goguel, *The Birth of Christianity.* "Jesus and the Origins of Christianity," 2. Translated by H. C. Snape. London: George Allen & Unwin, 1953. New York: Macmillan, 1954.

3478 P. J. Perk, *Die Apostelgeschichte. Werden und Wachsen der jungen Kirche.* Stuttgart: Kepplerhaus, 1954.

3479 J. Renié, *Actes des Apôtres.* "La Sainte Bible. Texte Latin et traduction française d'après les textes originaux avec un commentaire exégétique et theologique," Tome 2, Ire partie. Sous la direction de Louis Pirot et Albert Clamer. Paris: Letouzey & Ané, 1951. 4e éd., 1954.

3480 A. Schlatter, *Die Apostelgeschichte ausgelegt für Bibelleser.* "Schlatters Erläuterungen zum Neuen Testament," 4. Teil. Stuttgart: Calwer, 1913. 1948. z. Aufl. Berlin: Evangelische Verlagsanstalt, 1954.

3481 Lucien Cerfaux, *La communità degli Apostoli,* A. M. Martinelli, trans. Milano: Vita e Pensiero, 1955.

3482 Lilian E. Cox, "The Acts of the Apostles," in G. H. Davies, et al., eds., *The Twentieth Century Bible Commentary.* Rev. ed. New York: Harper, 1955. Pp. 450-74.

3483 G. H. Davies, et al., eds., *The Twentieth Century Bible Commentary.* Rev. ed. New York: Harper, 1955.

3484 J. A. Alexander, *The Acts of the Apostles.* 2 vols. New York/London: Scribner/Nisbet, 1857. Frequently reprinted, including: *The Acts of the Apostles. Two Volumes Complete in One.* Classic Commentary Library. Grand Rapids MI: Zondervan, 1956.

3485 "The Acts of the Apostles," in Francis D. Nichol, ed., *The Seventh-day Adventist Bible Commentary.* Washington DC: Review and Herald Publishing Association, 1957. 6:113-464.

3486 H. K. Moulton, *The Acts of the Apostles. Introduction and Commentary.* "The Christian Students' Library," No. 12. Published for the Senate of Serampore by the Christian Literature Society, 1957.

3487 Francis D. Nichol, ed., *The Seventh-day Adventist Bible Commentary*. Washington DC: Review and Herald Publishing Association, 1957.

3488 C. H. Rieu, *The Acts of the Apostles by Saint Luke*. Translated with an Introduction and Notes. "Penguin Books." Edinburgh: R. & R. Clark, 1957.

3489 John Wesley, Adam Clarke, Matthew Henry, et al., *One Volume New Testament Commentary*. Grand Rapids MI: Baker, 1957.

3490 C. S. C. Williams, *The Acts of the Apostles*. "Harper's New Testament Commentaries." New York: Harper, 1957.

3491 Henry Alford, *The Greek Testament. With a Critically Revised Text, a Digest of Various Readings, Marginal References to Verbal and Idiomatic Usage, Prolegomena, and a Critical and Exegetical Commentary. With revisions by Everett F. Harrison*. 2: *Acts, Romans, Corinthians*. Chicago: Moody Press, 1958.

3492 Lucien Cerfaux and Jacques Dupont, *Les Actes des Apôtres*. Introduction de L. Cerfaux. Traduction et notes de J. Dupont. La Sainte Bible traduite en français sous la direction de l'École Biblique de Jérusalem #7. 2nd ed. Paris: Les Éditions du Cerf, 1958.

3493 Ronald A. Knox, *A New Testament Commentary for English Readers*. Vol. 2: *The Acts of the Apostles; St. Paul's Letters to the Churches*. New York: Sheed & Ward, 1954. London: Burns, Oates & Washbourne, 1958.

3494 C. C. Martindale, *The Acts of the Apostles*. "Stonyhurst Scripture Manuals." Westminster, Maryland: Newman; London: Longmans, Green & Co., 1958.

3495 Giuseppe Ricciotti, *The Acts of the Apostles. Text and Commentary*. Translated by Laurence E. Byrne. Milwaukee: Bruce, 1958.

3496 Charles W. Carter and Ralph Earle, *The Acts of the Apostles*. The Evangelical Commentary. Grand Rapids MI: Zondervan, 1959.

3497 Donald E. Demaray, *The Acts of the Apostles*. Grand Rapids MI: Baker, 1959.

3498 Maurice Farelly, *Les Actes des Apôtres*. "La Bible ouverte." Neuchâtel: Delachaux & Niestlé, 1959.

3499 Walter Luthi, *Les Actes des Apôtres*. Geneve: Labor et Fides, 1959.

3500 N. M. Flanagan, *The Acts of the Apostles*. "New Testament Reading Guide." Edited by B. M. Ahern, K. Sullivan, and W. G. Heidt. Collegeville MN: Liturgical Press, 1960.

3501 John H. Gerstner, "Acts," *The Biblical Expositor*. Vol. 3. Consulting Editor, Carl F. H. Henry. Philadelphia: A. J. Holman, 1960. Pp. 183-224.

3502 E. R. Lewis, *The Acts of the Apostles and the Letters of St. Paul*. "The London Divinity Series," Vol. 5. London: James Clarke, 1960.

3503 Frank Stagg, *The Book of Acts*. Nashville: Broadman Press, 1960.

3504 Albert C. Winn, *The Acts of the Apostles*. "The Layman's Bible Commentary," Vol. 20. Balmer H. Kelly, Editor. Richmond VA: John Knox Press, 1960.

3505 Matthew Henry, "An Exposition, with Practical Observations, on the Acts of the Apostles," in *Commentary on the Whole Bible*. New One Volume Edition. Edited by Leslie F. Church. Grand Rapids MI: Zondervan, 1961. Pp. 434-550.

3506 A. Van Pyn, *Acts of the Apostles*. London: Pickering & Inglis, 1961.

3507 John B. Polhill, *Acts*. New American Commentary #26. Nashville: Broadman Press, 1972.

3508 E. Haenchen. *The Acts of the Apostles*. 1971

3509 K. Kliesch, *Apostelgeschichte* . Stuggarter Kleiner Kommentar. Stuttgart: Verlag Katholisches Bibelwerk, 1986.

3510 Edvin Larsson, *Apostla-Gärningarna 13-20*. Kommentar till Nya Testamentet #5B. Uppsala: EFS-förlaget, 1987.

3511   F. L. Arrington, *The Acts of the Apostles: An Introduction and Commentary*. Peabody MA: Hendrickson, 1988.

3512   W. H. Willimon, *Acts*. Interpretation: A Bible Commentary for Teaching and Preaching. Atlanta: John Knox, 1988

3513   F. Pastor, *Henchos de los Apóstolos*. Madrid: Sociedad de Educación Atenas, 1989.

3514   F. F. Bruce, *The Acts of the Apostles: The Greek Text with Introduction and Commentary*. 3rd rev. ed. Grand Rapids MI: Eerdmans, 1990.

3515   S. J. Kistemaker, *Exposition of the Acts of the Apostles*. New Testament Commentary. Grand Rapids MI: Baker, 1990.

3516   J. R. W. Stott, *The Message of Acts: To the Ends of the Earth*. Downer Grove IL: InterVarsity Press. 1990.

3517   D. J. Williams, *Acts*. New International Biblical Commentary #5. Peabody MA: Hendrickson, 1990.

3518   L. T. Johnson, *The Acts of the Apostles* Sacra Pagina Series #5. Collegeville MN: Liturgical Press, 1992.

3519   I. Howard Marshall, *The Acts of the Apostles* New Testament Guides. Sheffield: JSOT, 1992.

3520   C. E. Faw, *Acts*. Believers Church Bible Commentary. Scottsdale PA: Herald, 1993.

3521   J. Rius-Camps, *Commentari als Fets dels Apòstols*. Barcelonia: Facultat de Teologia de Catalunya, 1993.

3522   C. K. Barrett, *A Critical and Exegetical Commentary on the Acts of the Apostles*. Vol 1. *Preliminary Introduction and Commentary on Acts I-XIV*. ICC. Edinburgh: T. & T. Clark, 1994.

3523   Mikeal C. Parsons, "Acts of the Apostles," in *Mercer Commentary on the Bible*, ed. Watson E. Mills and Richard F. Wilson. Macon GA: Mercer University Press, 1994. Pp. 1083-1122.

Author Index

310 BIBLIOGRAPHIES FOR BIBLICAL RESEARCH

Perrot, Charles, 0879, 1131, 3135
Pervo, R. I., 2632
Pervo, Richard I., 0126, 0151, 0244, 0254,
    0295, 0531, 0757, 0761, 0871,
    0880, 0921, 0928
1282, 1289, 1360, 1419, 1937, 2861, 3165
Pesch, R., 0583, 0614, 0672, 0827
Petofi, J. S., 1487
Petzer, J. H., 0013, 0251, 0273, 3178, 3182,
    3183
Pfeifer, H., 3349
Pfleiderer, Otto, 1970, 1978, 3323
Pherigo, L. P., 2615
Pickard, W. M., 1101
Pierce, F. M., 0176, 2201
Pierce, J. A., 1744
Pierce, Rice A., 0750
Pilgrim, W. E., 2149
Pinnock, Clark H., 0446, 2604
Pistelli, E., 0592
Plassart, A., 1378, 2162
Pless, John T., 0343, 2493
Plevik, Joseph, 0281, 0386, 1037, 3288, 496
Plooij, D., 1398, 3073
Plötz, K., 1759
Plümacher, E., 0883, 0888, 1034, 1847,
    2303, 2331, 2508, 2557
Plumptre, E. H., 3320
Plunkett, Mark A., 0845
Plymale, Steven F., 2758
Pokorn, P., 1658, 2665
Polhill, John B., 0552, 0892, 2290, 3507
Ponguta, H. S., 0025
Pontet, M., 2705
Poole, R. L., 3067
Pope, Hugh, 3439
Poque, Suzanne, 0949
Porter, R. J., 0759
Porter, S. E., 2902
Pott, August, 3030, 3054
Poulton, Gary M., 1351
Powell, M. A., 2373
Praeder, Susan Marie, 1235, 1647, 1654,
    1927, 2325, 2777, 2781
Prat, F., 3049
Prato, G. L., 0656, 2831
Prete, B., 0117, 0504, 1637, 1697, 3307
Preuschen, Erwin, 3355
Prigent, P., 3134
Puig, R. Cunill, 1741
Pummer, R., 2298

Purves, George T., 2033
Quesnell, Q., 3269
Quiller-Couch, Arthur, 3414
Quinn, Jerome D., 0975, 2310
Rackham, R., 1971, 3457
Radermakers, J., 1308
Radl, W., 0965, 1138, 1826
Ragg, L., 3343
Rainer, T. S., 2553
Räisänen, H., 2452
Rakocy, W., 0969, 2852
Rall, H. F., 3387
Ralph, M. N., 2374
Ramsay, W. M., 1979, 2037, 2220, 2503
Ramsey, J. S., 2954
Rapske, B. M., 2635
Rapuano, Yehudah, 0735
Rasco, E., 0243, 0264, 0379, 0389, 0529,
    0547
Ravanelli, V., 3012
Ravarotto, E., 1118
Rayan, A., 2068, 2113
Read, David H. C., 1474
Recker, R. R., 1872, 2544
Redalie, Y., 1237
Rees, W., 2678
Reese, Boyd, 1546, 1587, 1613, 2619
Reeves, J. A. H., 2362
Refoulé, F., 1169, 2411
Refoulé, P., 1156
Reicke, Bo, 0742, 3192
Reimer, Richter, 3273
Rengstorf, K. H., 0131
Renié, J., 3449, 3479
Rese, M., 2453
Reukauf, A., 3381
Reyero, S., 1633
Reymond, Robert L., 0814, 1279, 1400,
    1440, 1494, 2599
Reynolds, B., 3333
Ricciotti, Giuseppe, 3495
Rice, E. W., 3344
Richard, Earl, 0619, 0646, 1136, 2327,
    2363, 2565, 2804, 2808
Richardson, N., 2328
Richter-Reimer, I., 1217
Riddle, Donald W., 3071
Riedl, J., 1709, 2963
Rieu, C. H., 3488
Riggert, A., 2393
Riggs, Jack R., 0642